Jonathan

JONATHAN PHILBIN BOWMAN:
MEMORIES, REFLECTIONS, TRIBUTES

Cartoon by Jim Cogan

Jonathan

JONATHAN PHILBIN BOWMAN:
MEMORIES, REFLECTIONS, TRIBUTES

John Bowman
with **Eimer Philbin Bowman**

HOW TATT PRESS

First published in 2002 by
HOWTATT PRESS
P.O. BOX 8584
DUBLIN • IRELAND

British Library Cataloguing in Publication Data.
A catalogue record for this book is available from the British Library.

ISBN: 0 9541488 1 9 Hardback
0 9541488 0 0 Paperback

This book is set in 11.5 on 13.5 point Adobe Garamond

Layout by Susan Waine
Printed in Ireland by ßetaprint Limited, Dublin

Contents

	Preface	VII
	Introduction – EIMER PHILBIN BOWMAN	XI
1	'I like the feeling of being famous'	1
2	'Jonathan, are you still talking?'	30
3	'An expert, not a trainspotter'	60
4	'Under the laughter…'	79
5	'And what was Jonathan like?'	129
6	'They were like this pair of loveable vagabonds…'	162
7	'…they're probably going to die at thirty-five'	193
8	'If anything, it was like a country funeral'	211
9	'… the guy made you wince and think'	243
	Afterword – ABIE PHILBIN BOWMAN	260
	'Farewell', caricature – JIM COGAN	264
	'who else but Jonathan?' – poem, CONOR FERGUSON	265
	Index of Contributors	266
	Acknowledgements	268

For Saul and in memory of Jonathan

Preface

The idea for this book came to me when I read John S. Doyle's appreciation of Jonathan in the *Sunday Independent* and Eoghan Harris's column about him in the *Sunday Times*. Other writers too caught aspects of Jonathan's character and personality, sometimes with insights that were revelatory to his own family. I was prompted by a number of his friends and by many of those who wrote letters of condolence to publish some of the newspaper coverage when he died, along with some excerpts from broadcast programmes. And when I read letters such as those from his boyhood friend Ruan O'Donnell or from Ann Marie Hourihane or Charles Brady, I appreciated the insights they contained. Another such letter was that from Adele King, the singer and comedienne, 'Twink', including her memories from her 'first encounter with the boy wonder' when Jonathan was nine to her last meeting with him twenty-two years later – just weeks before his death. It was clear that some of the memories of Jonathan reflected in these private letters should also be considered for inclusion.

It was true – as Drapier put in *The Irish Times* after his death – that Jonathan could be 'something of an acquired taste and took some getting to know'. He had a tendency to divide the jury. He could still elicit the begrudger's dismissal: but there were fewer and fewer of them. And many of them, especially if they encountered him personally – as scores of letters attest – became fans. I thought he deserved that to be recorded. I suppose I always had a nagging doubt about how well Jonathan could answer in the parable of the talents. It was through reading the mailbag when he died that I regretted ever doubting him in that regard. His temperament was suited to journalism and broadcasting. He enjoyed it. As one letter-writer put it: 'There was a sense that he couldn't quite believe his luck, that he was being sent to try out something which was so much fun. There was an apparent zest and exuberance in so much of what he wrote.'

In its first phase this book took on a shape akin to a scrapbook:

cuttings, excerpts from letters, photographs, cartoons and caricatures, some poems, and some other mementos. The readership I had in mind was the community to whom I felt closest in the aftermath of his death: family, friends, his colleagues and the huge number of acquaintances and strangers who wrote to us to express their condolence. It was for them that this book was initially compiled. Whether it would be privately printed for this immediate circle only or whether it should be more widely available was a question that I thought should be best left until later. I should add that I was charmed and impressed by many of the comments and felt obliged to include some of them. Jonathan had endured enough brickbats in his time – some of them hard-earned – and if the tide had turned, I thought that this should be reflected in these pages.

As I collated the early material, I realized that there were some omissions. Many individuals had expressed their condolence in person and talked to us about the Jonathan they remembered. In some such cases I requested that they write a brief account of their memories of him for this book. And at a late stage, where I thought an important dimension to his career was not covered, I invited some contributions. Finally, Eimer has kept a diary and journal since Jonathan was aged two and that has been quoted throughout the book.

Although I have included some discursive asides to help contextualize these letters, no attempt has been made to offer a comprehensive biographical portrait. At first I was apprehensive that readers who were expecting such an approach might feel disappointed. I suggest that they approach the book as an anthology – or as they would the edited diaries or collected letters of an individual. The comparison with an edited diary may come closest, but with one key difference. Published diaries offer glimpses of the subject's life through the writer's own lens and include gossip and commentary on friends, colleagues and acquaintances. In this case it is the latter who do the writing and we see Jonathan and his world through their many and varied lenses.

Note that the original order of the letters and contributions has usually been determined by the age of Jonathan when the correspondent first comments on him. Inevitably, this results in some coverage of his adult years in the early part of the portrait. But I think this disadvantage is off-set by access to the full tone of the letter. However where a contributor writes about quite separate episodes, these are broken up and included where appropriate in the overall chronology. Inevitably when editing such diverse material some of these decisions have had to be arbitrary. This results in a narrative which can be uneven – but then this is inevitably the case in books based on edited letters or diaries. I have silently standardized spellings, punctuation, and use of capitals; and I have made minor corrections – especially in the broadcast transcripts – in the interests of clarity. Although most expressions of condolence have been excluded, in some few cases where they formed an integral part of the writer's comments on Jonathan they may have been retained.

For those readers unfamiliar with his biographical details we include here his obituary from *The Irish Times*: 'Jonathan Philbin Bowman: Journalist who was "daring and principled"'.

> Jonathan Philbin Bowman was born in Dublin on 6 January, 1969. He first attended Sunnyside playgroup where one morning, on hearing his teacher thank God for a fine day, he patiently explained to her that it had nothing to do with God and everything to do with cloud formations.
>
> He subsequently attended Sandford Parish School and Sandford Park School in Ranelagh. To the understandable concern of his parents, he chose not to complete his formal education and left his final school, Newpark Comprehensive, in Blackrock, Co. Dublin at the age of sixteen. Aided by a word processor that finally enabled his fingers to keep up with his fierce speed of thought, he immediately embarked on what became, due both to his youth and precocious intellect, a very public career in journalism and broadcasting.
>
> His first professional credit was as photographer for *Image* magazine. In the early 1990s he wrote for *In Dublin*, the *Sunday Tribune* and the *Sunday Times*. He joined Carr Communications in September 1992 to work as a communications trainer where, thanks to his particular affinity with high technology (it could barely keep up with him), he was especially effective in training groups of electronic engineers to clarify and simplify their presentations.
>
> Extraordinarily articulate, and a gifted mimic, with the ability to speak spontaneously without deviation, hesitation or repetition, he appeared to have found his natural medium when for two years (1993-1994) he co-presented *The Rude Awakening* on FM104. Using a variety of personae he entertained the country with prankster phone calls live on air to such august bodies as Hibernian Insurance and the IDA regarding the demise of uninsured goldfish and a

scheme to make fuel from the excess potato crop. In what must be unique in the annals of broadcasting, he also charmed the then serving Taoiseach, Mr Reynolds, into reviewing a Whitney Houston concert at the Point.

Impatient and mischievous, his was not an easy talent to manage. A former colleague recalls trying to persuade the station to renew his contract: 'I told them they were off their heads to let him go but they couldn't see it.' In the autumn of 1994 he joined the *Sunday Independent* on contract. Appreciated and encouraged, he found a home there. In September 1998 he began a weekly log that suited his talent for life admirably. He never missed a deadline. He treated those within his orbit sans fear or favour, treading blithely on all sorts of powerful toes regardless of the consequences to his own advancement. He thrived on constant intellectual stimulation and many of those he interviewed in depth became firm friends.

The editor of the *American Spectator* remembers him as 'daring and principled – an unusual combination in a journalist.' Unusual too in that his intellect never seemed to threaten his compassion. At the age of twenty he fathered a son and took on the role of single parent with great gusto and good humour. Friends, old or new, humble or exalted, found in him an inexhaustible well of empathy and laughter. He was energetic, high-spirited and enthusiastic about everything except sport, in which he had no interest whatsoever.

For an individual to live with such intensity places untold demands on the psyche. It too needs replenishing from time to time in order to achieve a balanced if perhaps a slightly duller life. Jonathan Philbin Bowman's interest in Buddhism was more than a passing flirtation. His soul was growing apace and asking for the time to do it. Sadly it was not to be but he added immeasurably during his short life to the society in which we live and for that we must be grateful. The password to access his hi-tech powerbook was 'Love' and it is with love he will always be remembered by everyone who knew him.

The Irish Times, 11 March 2000

Introduction

by EIMER PHILBIN BOWMAN

Half a year, then a year and a half, then
ten and a half – the pathos of a child's fractions, turn-
ing up each summer.
– ROBERT LOWELL, 'Summer' from *For Lizzie and Harriet*

Towards the end of my pregnancy with Jonathan, I went to visit Mother Rita Philbin, my father's first cousin, then mistress of novices at the Convent of the Sacred Heart, Mount Anville. She had a gentle manner. As we walked in the grounds she turned and said to me: 'I'm sure you will teach this child all the right things.' I did not know how to answer. When I had been at a Sacred Heart school myself, I had studied Latin and remembered the moment when I learned that the translation of the verb *educare*, to educate, was 'to lead out from within'. I had always thought it meant to impose from without. I made a clumsy attempt to communicate how I hoped to 'teach' my child and registered what I sensed was her disappointment.

Jonathan shortly after his first birthday. A portrait by Jim Gowan

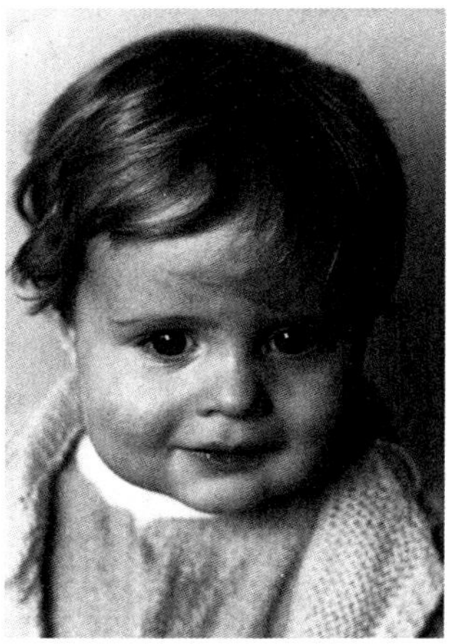

Jonathan was born on 6 January 1969. I was in my final year of medicine and later it pleased him to think that he had managed to attend medical lectures in UCD during the months before his birth. Soon we could not imagine our lives without him. He radiated happiness and seemed alert to everything around him. When he was able to support his body, we rigged up a baby bouncer in his bedroom and he danced with delight at the freedom it gave him. So effortlessly did he fit into our lives that by the time he was about three months old, John, who, in addition to his work in RTE, was still studying history and politics at Trinity, began to wonder out loud about having another baby. In June I sat my final medical exams and on 31 December, just a few hours before the year ended, Jonathan's sister, Emma, was born. She arrived home in time to celebrate his first birthday six days later.

Now a junior doctor, I struggled with the competing demands of two babies and an internship post with night duty. It quickly became clear that something had to give. I had always thought that, like my mother, I could combine a career and family, but this family and this career had coincided at their most demanding. With reluctance I made the decision to postpone my internship and become a full-time mother. It was not until 1977, when Jonathan was eight, that I was to return to medicine. The time and energy that would have gone into my work was now directed towards the children. Each new step they took seemed to erase the memory of the one that preceded it: in January 1971, I began to keep diary notes and, sometime later, a journal. Written up at intervals over the next eighteen years, it recorded conversations, incidents and milestones which otherwise might have been forgotten.

As a baby, Jonathan had wonderful cadences in his voice. He could get three or four tones into the single syllable 'Hi'; a couple of weeks after his second birthday he started to put three words together. During that year his vocabulary grew rapidly. At some point I had come across Glenn Doman's 'Teach your baby to read' kit. It used a flash-card method, with first words like Mummy and Daddy in three-inch high print, and the instructions stressed that it should be fun to do and treated as a game. Over that summer a few times every week we would 'play' the flash-card game; by the time Jonathan started playschool in September he was able to read ten words. That December the number had risen to twenty-six and now – bored with the bigger print – he would no longer review all

Jonathan and Emma, aged seven and six, on their first French holiday, Britanny, June 1976

Jonathan and Eimer, Val Andre, June 1976

the words he knew at a sitting. Any worries I had that I was exposing him too early to reading were dispelled when Emma, not yet two, who had been observing these sessions over my shoulder, asked if I would teach her and I discovered that she could already read the first three words. She wanted to join him in everything but he was beginning to want to concentrate by himself and would say: 'Emma too mall' She, perhaps in retaliation, was going through a phase of saying 'I'm a boy; Don Don is a dirl.'

We had started to build up a small library of children's books, among them the Ladybird collection of all the classic children's stories in their Well-Loved Tales series. There was an expanding non-fiction section on every topic imaginable. But it was the volume entitled *Tricks and Magic* which made the greatest impact on Jonathan and triggered his fascination with this subject. He first mastered simple tricks, practised on us, and watched professional magicians on television and at parties – intently. Soon, with the help of an old Hallowe'en costume designed by my mother, he was giving his first professional performances at children's parties. I was apprehensive at first, but reports back were enthusiastic.

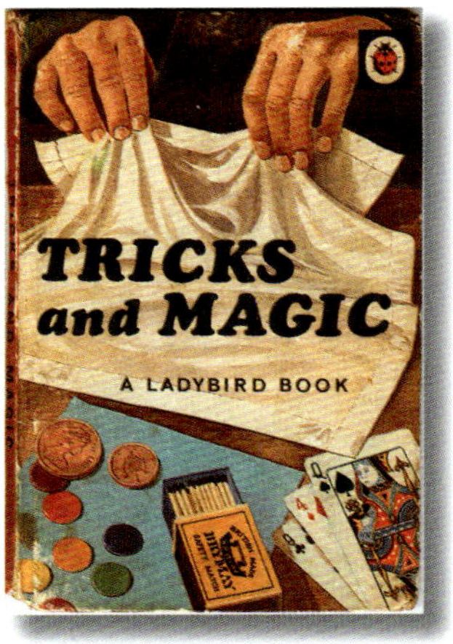

The book which prompted Jonathan's early fascination with magic

Jonathan and Emma shared a bedroom and most nights for a half an hour or so before bedtime we spent reading. We tried to keep a balance between fiction and non-fiction and usually ended every night with a poem. At first these were nursery rhymes. But then we came across A.A. Milne's *When We Were Very Young* and read it over and over until we knew nearly every poem by heart before graduating to *Now We Are Six*. In both these books Winnie the Pooh, Christopher Robin's Teddy Bear, is a central figure, and at some point Jonathan decided to call his Teddy 'Winnie'. The closing lines from the poem 'Us Two' were, in Jonathan's case, prophetic.

So wherever I am, there's always Pooh,
There's always Pooh and Me.
'What would I do?' I said to Pooh
'If it wasn't for you,' And Pooh said: 'True,
It isn't much fun for One, but Two
Can stick together,' says Pooh, says he
'That's how it is,' says Pooh.

They did stick together – Winnie was the only possession he held onto throughout his life, carrying it via a book launch on the day he left home. Whenever the stitching came undone, I or my mother were called on to mend it. On one occasion I found Winnie left on my floor with a note pinned to his chest: 'Sew me now.' By the time Jonathan and Winnie were aged ten, stitching was not enough. Winnie was threadbare and I spent an entire journey to Cork knitting a new suit on which, after Saul's birth, my mother embroidered the initials J and S.

We were also indebted to her for a present of *The Oxford Book of Children's Verse*, edited by Iona and Peter Opie, published in 1973. Now out of print, it brought together the notable poems written for children over a period of five hundred years from Chaucer in the fourteenth century via A.A. Milne to Ogden Nash in the twentieth. Every Christmas Eve since 1973, in anticipation of Santa – we have read 'A Visit from St Nicholas' by Clement Clarke Moore. My diary tells me that on the eve of Emma's eighth birthday we read two poems with what must have seemed appropriate titles at the time: 'Against Quarrelling and Fighting' and 'Against Idleness and Mischief' – both written by Isaac Watts in the eighteenth century.

In books, or work, or helpful play,
Let my first years be passed,
That I may give for every day
Some good account at last.

Television did not play a big part in our lives during those years. We had a small portable black-and-white Sony with a nine-inch screen. It took up the space of about half a dozen books. We had only one rule about watching it, but it was effective – that the

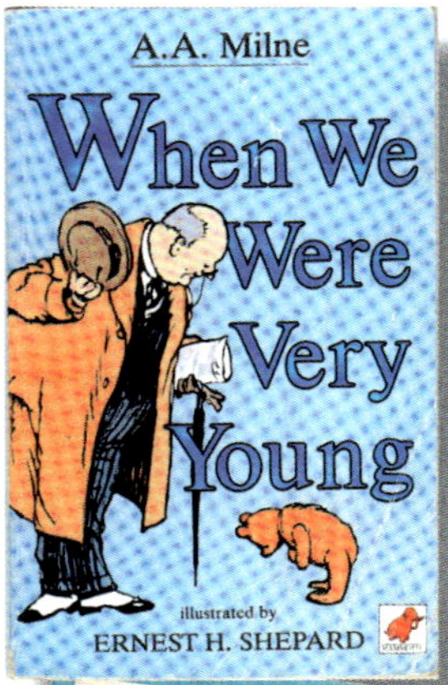

A.A. Milne's classics were first published in the 1920s

children couldn't put it on at random but must know the particular programme they wanted to see. *Sesame Street*, with its clever blend of humour and education, was never missed and they liked to pronounce the letter Z as zee.

In 1972 a friend asked me to come along to the first Women's Liberation meeting which was being held in Gaj's restaurant in Baggot Street. The discussions on that first night and on subsequent meetings were informed, lively and stimulating. Betty Friedan's book, *The Feminine Mystique*, just published in the United States, had played a key role in the growth of the women's movement there; reading it motivated me to return to some career path. I felt my life could still not accommodate the demands of a medical post and decided instead to approach the Department of Psychology in Trinity, where, over the next three years, I did a postgraduate degree. This exposure to psychology added a new dimension to my relationship with 'the babies' as we continued to call them, although Jonathan had, by now, started primary school. When they were in the bath, I would fill odd-shaped containers with similar amounts of water to test Piaget's theories on a child's concept of volume. But the greatest influence was a course I took on behaviour modification. B.F. Skinner's theory that a child learns almost entirely through conditioning and that reward rather than punishment is the most successful way of bringing about a desired behaviour change made a lot of sense. We put it to the test, it worked and was built into our lives – the children even began using it on us.

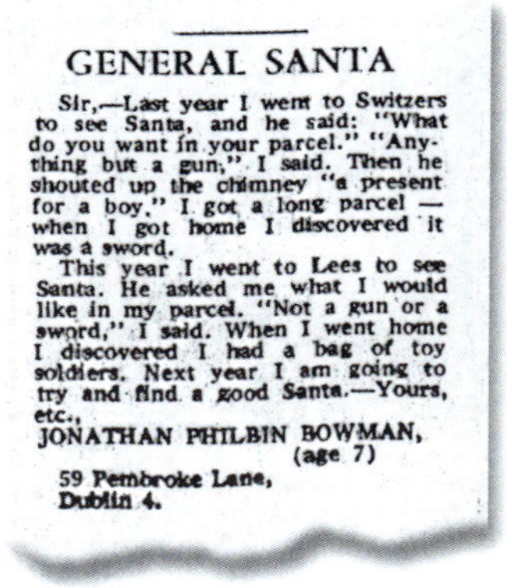
GENERAL SANTA

Sir,—Last year I went to Switzers to see Santa, and he said: "What do you want in your parcel." "Anything but a gun," I said. Then he shouted up the chimney "a present for a boy." I got a long parcel — when I got home I discovered it was a sword.

This year I went to Lees to see Santa. He asked me what I would like in my parcel. "Not a gun or a sword," I said. When I went home I discovered I had a bag of toy soldiers. Next year I am going to try and find a good Santa.—Yours, etc.,

JONATHAN PHILBIN BOWMAN, (age 7)
59 Pembroke Lane,
Dublin 4.

'When Santa failed him in two successive years he was dismayed.' Jonathan's first venture into print, *The Irish Times* letters page, December 1976

I'm not sure of the extent to which Jonathan's pacifism was influenced by a strict rule in his primary school not to allow toy guns – or, indeed, any war toys – in the classroom. But by the time he visited Santa aged six it was a fully formed concept. When Santa failed him in two successive years he was dismayed. Trying to avert his loss of faith, I told him that when adults were cross about such things, they sometimes wrote a letter to the newspapers. He liked the idea, we drafted it together, and sent it to *The Irish Times.* On the day his letter was published, I overheard him say to Emma: 'I like the feeling of being famous'. Maybe it should have sounded a warning bell.

In the long summer holidays before they were old enough to go to summer camps, we devised what we called 'at home school'. Despite its name, all activities qualified. Emma, who says they were 'hot-housed', recalls us doing a scientific experiment where I

Angela Magennis recalled meeting Jonathan at a press reception in Waterstone's bookshop in spring 1988. He was leaving home that day and moving into a new flat, 'hence the reason that he was carrying some personal belongings including his tattered Teddy Bear around with him'.

blindfolded them with underpants over their heads and put, amongst other things, Colman's mustard powder on their tongues to see if they could identify the taste! In retrospect, perhaps, I should have been focussing more on self-care skills. My journal tells me that one morning around this time, Jonathan, thinking he had dressed himself, came in asking for help just to put on a T-shirt. However he had forgotten to put on underpants, his trousers were back to front and his socks askew.

Jonathan and Emma continued to share a room throughout primary school. They seemed content in one another's company and did not seek outside friendships until about aged eight or nine when their paths began to diverge and they were able to come and go freely to a few neighbours' houses. Most evenings, we continued to read together. As they got older, I found suitable short stories by authors such as Frank O'Connor, Mary Lavin and William Trevor. One evening when Jonathan was nine, I read them a Michael McLaverty story and when I came to the end Jonathan asked: 'Is that all?' Whereas Emma seemed to understand that an apparently ordinary event was significant in the life of the character, Jonathan was always impressed by the extraordinary.

His own reading was eclectic. All his life he loved 'How to...'

books; at this stage it was how to be a secret agent or a detective. If something caught his eye, he read it and was not put off by the fact that it was an adult publication. At age seven I found him tucked up with my *Teach Yourself Italian.* By nine he had scoured all volumes of the *Encyclopaedia Britannica* for references to magic. Once he was interested in a topic, he pursued it until he had mastered it. As he got older, I noticed how he could pick up any book that caught his attention and, it seemed, get to the essence of it very quickly. He had enormous powers of concentration – if he was interested in something it did not matter what was going on around him, he was not distracted. At thirteen, on a children's television programme, he felt confident enough to review George Orwell's *Nineteen Eighty-four.*

Our time together as a family of four ended in 1981 when Abie was born. By then Jonathan had started secondary school, I was nearly a psychiatrist and John was finishing a book on de Valera. We were ready to start all over again. But this time Abie had four of us to contend with. By 1988 when our fourth child Daniel was born, he was already an uncle. Jonathan, now something of an expert on parenting, arrived in to visit us with Saul, aged three months, asleep in his arms.

Looking back on his life, I see his decision to leave school as the moment when he ceased to follow the path laid out and took off on an uncharted journey. We never knew what to expect next or what – when he became a more public figure – people who stopped us in the street might say. Being his parent was sometimes like holding on tight to the string of a kite as it careered and danced across the sky, sometimes relaxing when it floated gently to land. In the end we had to let go of the string.

I

'I like the feeling of being famous'

– comment by Jonathan aged seven to his sister Emma in December 1976 after his Santa letter was published in *The Irish Times*

Perhaps because Eimer and I had both lived as children in the Dublin neighbourhood of Ballsbridge, we have always thought of it as more of a suburb than it had become by the time our first two children, Jonathan and Emma, were growing up there in the 1970s. By then, so many offices, government agencies and embassies had moved their headquarters to Ballsbridge that there were fewer families in the neighbourhood than had been the case when we were young. Its greater cosmopolitanism can be measured by the fact that the small stretch of Pembroke Lane where we lived included the headquarters of both the Russian Church of Our Lady in Exile and that of the Communist Party of Ireland. Which had more followers I cannot say.

It remained a child-friendly neighbourhood, especially because the amenities of Herbert Park were close by. Among our neighbours then were psychologist and writer PAULINE HALL and her husband, architect Frank Hall. Their children shared the same early education as our children. Pauline wrote that Jonathan's death had prompted the family into reminiscing about him as a small boy.

> We were both charmed and a little surprised at his aplomb and chattiness, especially to myself – quite beyond his years. I remember when Jonathan was in our place in Raglan Road that I thought that I could fob him off by explaining that I was studying psychology: it only further whetted his lively mind. We had great conversations. Later again, he was the star turn as a boy magician at Tom's birthday party.* Really he was close in spirit if not in years

* Tom Hall, the film producer.

Emma at Sunnyside playgroup, autumn 1973

to the small guests, but his black outfit, tall hat and stage props made him mysterious also. After the magic show, I remember trying to decide what was the best explanation to give to parents who arrived before we had the chance to wash the soot marks off the faces of the audience.

Both Jonathan and Emma attended the Sunnyside playgroup in Morehampton Road in Donnybrook.* ALYNA HEALY was a teacher there.

I had the pleasure of having Jonathan in my care with Elizabeth Moloney all those years ago. I loved him so much that I was always talking about him and people thought he must be one of my own children! With most children in the playgroup we had a role in introducing the concept of numbers and colours, but not with Jonathan; he excelled beyond his years in all things academic. But I will see forever the amazement in those blue eyes under a haystack of blond curls when I would play my imagination games. One of his favourites was 'The house is on fire' game. He threw himself into the game with his usual enthusiasm – phoning fire brigades and so on in a high state of excitement. Years later Elizabeth used to tell me he would be reminiscing about Alyna's games.

Jonathan spent two happy years at Sunnyside. Its founder, ELIZABETH MOLONEY, was a leading pioneer in the Irish Pre-School Playgroups Association. She wrote:

When Jonathan arrived in the playgroup he was a bright, cheerful, serious, talkative, sunshine child. I fell immediately for his charm, his charisma and, of course, when I think of Jonathan I also think of his sister, Emma. She was so together and focussed on learning all she could about the three R's: Jonathan on the other hand was a 'Why?', 'What if?', 'When?', 'Says who?' child. Jonathan was not so interested in how to overcome a challenge but rather in asking why the challenge needed to be overcome. What will we gain? How did Ireland become that shape? There were many times, while he was with us, that I had to go off and research his question. When he would ask me a question to which I did not know the answer, I would say: 'I have to go and look that up' and he would look puzzled and say: 'But why don't you know that?' And I always felt that he was perfectly right: 'Why didn't I know that?' I

* Jonathan first attended the playgroup in September 1971 when he was two years and nine months old. A month later Eimer noted that 'he has come out of himself and grown up. He has more confidence, is more curious, and knows things I don't know he knows.'

Jonathan with Elizabeth Moloney, a still from RTE *Learning for Life: the first five years,* a documentary on pre-school education, recorded autumn 1973, transmitted 6 March 1974

remember so well the time he was interested in elephants. By the time he had asked me all his questions I could have written a thesis on elephants; and to this day people wonder why I know so much about elephants. Jonathan is the answer. He had long conversations with us. He was very interested in the world and all its wonders and he would look intently at you and you would feel that every bit of information you could muster up was going to be squeezed out of you. All this was done without aggression. I never saw Jonathan lose his temper, be annoyed, even look slightly cross; but neither did I see Emma even look slightly cross. I put it down to the fact they were so loved by everyone they came in contact with that they did not know what being unkind, bad-tempered, cross was about; it was not part of their lives. They never joined in if some of the children tried to introduce wargames; even at that age Jonathan was anti-war, anti-guns.

Jonathan loved a joke, loved to have his leg pulled, loved to listen to you singing songs; and the song that always reminds me of him is 'Granddad, granddad, we love you'. I don't know the name of it. He had a great capacity to love. He just loved it when I told my silly stories about the mouse that lived under the floorboards. He knew well that it was all made up but that was what amused him: the very thought of this imaginary mouse doing all these things. Most of the other children half-believed that it actually existed.

And then he discovered magic. I am not sure whether all this came from the visit of our magician; or, before that, from doing the actions for three little dickie birds. He was intrigued by magic and his why, when, how, what questions came hot and heavy.

And so started the second stage of our relationship, after he had left the playgroup and came back as a 'graduate' to entertain the children. They loved him. When he came back to do his magic show, he was so professional, so together; and I, in his mind, had to be instructed carefully and then watched and prompted as I acted as his assistant. He would type out my instructions, get me to read them before the performance and constantly ask me did I remember what I was to do. There was one particular part of the performance when I was to bring in the empty jug for orange at breaktime and I was to say, as instructed: 'We have no orange juice for break.' And he would take the jug and say his magic words and pour orange out of, I think, a paper bag, and save the day. But he had me on tenterhooks in case I got my part of the act wrong.

Later on he came back, sometimes to collect his little brothers, sometimes because he was passing, and again he had long conversations about life; he was so interested in his brothers, in the other children, in what I was doing, in discussing everything. He was so determined to make things better, to try to get people to understand what life was about and how it should be. He had such high standards; he believed in the goodness of people, but that some people needed guidance. He was very young still and full of energy and joy; he would never have grown old. He dashed in one day with a microphone – he was doing some roving microphone programme – and would I speak there and then about my ideas on education? His total belief in my ability to do such a thing meant that I said something; he seemed pleased and he ran off again.

Saul was a joy to him; he so much enjoyed being a father; and his own parents had been such good role models that he instinctively knew how to love his son.

Jonathan was one of those people whom you cannot and do not want to forget. I miss his energy, the excitement of knowing him, the way he turned an ordinary day into turmoil. All those ordinary things you were about to do had to be forgotten as he enticed you down the road of making the world a better place to live in.

The poet EAVAN BOLAND, a friend of both Eimer and myself, recalled Jonathan from babyhood.

My first memory of Jonathan is vivid. It was winter. He was barely a fortnight old. He was lying on a blanket, with a shock of hair. And yet already, in that room, he was a presence. My next memories are not at all as clear or separate. For a long time he was a sparkling, small character with yellow curls, almost always beside his sister. But in the foreground for all that; never the background.

Already he'd begun to pick words out with decision, and sometimes with an interest in their future rather than their past. I was doing interviews for a piece I wrote for *The Irish Times* – several pieces in fact – and Jonathan was the subject of one of them. He was a very small boy. I explained something about a poem – maybe its rhyme scheme. He looked at me intently and said – putting his words together very definitely – 'I'm quite aware of that'.

And that awareness is what seemed – at least at first – to define Jonathan for me. His quick attention was a feature of everything. He loved words. He paid attention to conversation. He answered questions with unusual speed and decision. He read and understood what he was reading. He seemed, even at the very young age he was then, to be starting up a conversation with the world to which he felt entirely equal.

In the summer of 1974, at Eavan's request, the Ulster poet John Hewitt* stayed with us for a weekend during a writers' conference in Dublin. On Sunday we took him to Glenasmole in the Dublin mountains where he went for a walk with Jonathan, then aged five. On his return Jonathan whispered quietly to Eimer: 'He kept saying: "I, I...," but didn't finish the sentence.' This Eimer explained was 'Aye, Aye,' in response to Jonathan's conversation.

In her series of articles in *The Irish Times* earlier that year EAVAN BOLAND** regretted that in society, and especially in Irish schools at the time, poetry had 'become the casualty of unimaginative teaching and forced appeals to the memory.' She found it

> ...interesting to see that many mothers in the pre-school years are going back like Eimer Bowman with Jonathan, to the best way of communicating poetry – not as a test for memory or a rehearsal for academic success, but as a method of self-discovery, a way in which a child can learn about himself and his world, through his own method of reasoning, without having to borrow the alien and often inferior reasoning of the adult.

*John Hewitt (1907-1987), Belfast-born poet. He described himself as 'an Irishman of planter stock, by profession an art gallery man, politically a man of the left.'

**Eavan's frequent visits to our house throughout these years also contributed to Jonathan and Emma's sense of poetry as part of everyday life. In August 1979, just before leaving to be writer in residence in the University of Iowa, she read 'Night Feed' for them before it was published in the following Saturday's *Irish Times*.

Jonathan aged five

In this article Eavan wrote that she had found Jonathan

> …especially winning, independent and enquiring. The most magic moment of seeing Jonathan read poetry came, in fact, without prompting him in the least. That it occurred at all is, perhaps, due to the fact that a child of five is finding his own individuality, sensing his own uniqueness, and that in this process poetry is a particular ally. Many of the poems he has learned from babyhood are by A. A. Milne, who has captured the defiance and discovery of childhood with particular assurance. Jonathan said that he knew a poem and then, unassisted, with obvious delight recited this:
>
> *When I was one*
> *I had just begun.*
> *When I was two*
> *I was nearly new.*
> *When I was three*
> *I was hardly me.*
> *When I was four*
> *I was not much more.*
> *When I was five*
> *I was just alive.*'

The Irish Times, 17 January 1974

Eavan's daughter SARAH CASEY – some years Jonathan's junior – recalled him performing an impromptu magic show in our house:

> It was a big, bright room. Jonathan was at one end of it doing magic tricks. At one point he said something like: 'I'd pay you to let me come and do magic tricks on your birthday.' And that really stayed with me afterwards. Also my Mum reminded me of it, because she was very touched and amused by it.

Writing after he died, EAVAN BOLAND recalled that her real sense of Jonathan 'came into focus' when he became interested in magic.

> Children never have casual interests. Their stamps, books, paints, garden tools and doll collections always stand for something. And Jonathan's magic stood for something as well. I remember him one summer afternoon doing magic tricks for my daughters. They were far too small to be anything but awed and delighted and confused. Some of the magic tricks worked; some were too difficult. We were in a long room looking out on the garden and for a while I watched this small, flushed boy manoeuvering his way through ropes and cards and metal. There was a generosity and intentness about his performance that touched me deeply. Especially considering that at least half of his audience were not at all sure what the Ace of Hearts should be doing anyway. Somehow, from that afternoon, I took

An impromptu magic show. 'I'd pay you to let me come and do magic tricks on your birthday', he told Sarah Casey.

away my true and unchanging impression of Jonathan. Inasmuch as this bright, fierce and impatient son of my close friends had been a puzzle to me until then, that afternoon solved it. I realized that magic and Jonathan were made for one another. In many ways, he had already had a magical childhood. Extraordinarily loved and deeply understood, magic gave him a way of continuing the promise of that childhood as he turned towards adulthood. And besides, it had a particular delight for him because it bypassed the oppressions of logic, the rules of ordinary routine, the restrictions for which he had so little tolerance. It promised – and for a moment seemed to deliver – a world where his own quicksilver sense of things could be confirmed.

Jonathan did manage to 'turn professional' as a boy magician and performed at the children's parties of some of our friends. COLM Ó'BRIAIN – a contemporary of mine at Belvedere – and his wife Muireann, who was a classmate of Eimer's at the Sacred Heart in Leeson Street, were among those who engaged his services. Colm has had a varied career: he has been an actor, theatre director, broadcaster and television producer, director of the Arts Council, general secretary of the Labour Party, and special advisor to Michael D. Higgins, as Arts minister. He credits his family with giving Jonathan some of his earliest paid employment.

Jonathan, the magician, drawn by Beth O'Halloran

The thought of entertaining any greater number of children than three always terrified my wife, Muireann, so she decided to hire Jonathan as an 'act' for the birthday party of one of our daughters. She probably had in mind that she would be able to handle his price and his size, and they both came to what she considered a suitable financial arrangement. I am not sure whether Jonathan was more interested in fame than fortune, but he came to our house and performed his magic tricks, to the delight of a number of children in the age range of six to eight.

It was intriguing to see the professionalism that Jonathan brought to his task. He was skilful in his performance, and accompanied himself with a patter that captivated his young audience, and, I have to admit, the few adults present as well. What was astonishing to me, as one well used to 'stage nerves', was the confidence and assuredness that he exuded, with the verbal skills and vocabulary of a much older person. The magic of the day was compounded by the presence of a young French woman – the friend of our then current *au pair* – who had suffered from restricted growth as a child and was no taller than the party-goers. Our children by that time were used to the size and presence of this lovely young woman, but their friends were agog at the sight of a

LAMBERT PUPPET THEATRE & MUSEUM 30 Est. 1972

> person who in looks and voice was an adult, but who in stature was no bigger than themselves. She invented and played games with them after Jonathan had finished his performance, and when the time came to go home that day, the young party-goers really believed they had been in a magic kingdom. Jonathan probably progressed swiftly to other interests in his life, but for years his reputation as a magician lived on in our household, and for the duration of our daughters' childhood he was referred to as 'The Magic Boy'.

The celebrated puppeteer EUGENE LAMBERT could remember the first time he had met Jonathan as a young child after a performance at the Lambert Puppet Theatre.

> At the time we were playing Oscar Wilde's story *The Selfish Giant.* I think that Jonathan would not have been more than seven years old at the time. After the show I spoke to you, but Jonathan, with his exuberance and enthusiasm, broke into the conversation. He wanted to talk about the show. I was amazed to hear his comments and his observations. He had a grasp of the story and an understanding of the deeper meaning of the work. Even then we could see he was a very special child. Jonathan's many visits to the puppet theatre as a child were always an event for us as he was so articulate and outgoing. *Alice in Wonderland* was one of his favourite stories. He once said that he would like to follow Alice down the rabbit hole and meet some of the characters. I can imagine his encounter with the Mad Hatter and the March Hare. There would have been dialogue between them that even Lewis Carroll could not have imagined.
>
> I met him several times at Dublin Theatre Festival functions. He was always very complimentary about our puppet theatre. On one occasion we were discussing different types of puppetry and different shows we were bringing in for our puppet festival. I happened to say that I would love to do some adult shows. He said that it would be a pity if I were not to continue to produce and present children's theatre as it had such a great influence on him as a child.*

Jonathan's favourite hotel was Ballymaloe House Hotel in Shanagarry, Co. Cork. He knew it well, having been brought there

*Just before his fifth birthday Jonathan had been brought for his first visit to the Lambert Puppet Theatre to see *Hansel and Gretel.* Eimer's journal records that later that evening he called to her from his bed 'saying he was "afraid of witches". I told him there were no witches, that it was not a good story for children and to tell me whenever he was frightened since there was no point in worrying about imagined things. I said: "They are only thought up – like your designs." And he replied: "They are not thought up – they are learned. What you learn is what someone else thought up."'

from the age of two. Eimer's journal records his response to his first visit, how he 'loved the farm, found an egg, rode a pony and made two friends.' At that time there were a few inexpensive rooms in The Loft – a stableyard building simply converted for staff and some guests, such as ourselves, whose modest budgets needed protection. I can remember the room charge: it was five shillings each, 30 cent in today's money, for Jonathan's and Emma's bunk beds and ten shillings each for Eimer and myself. Jonathan was among the first generation of children – led by Ivan and Myrtle Allen's grandchildren – who experienced the tradition of Children's Tea at 5 p.m.

This was an important event in the day and more of a children's dinner party than a high tea. It also provided for Jonathan a cosmopolitan audience – with an ever-changing cast of children of all nationalities, ranging from three to fourteen, to be found there each evening. Some would be ultrapolite, perhaps astonished at the potential anarchy which might erupt at any moment; and wondering who the scruffy and perhaps muddy children were who strolled in late and seemed to presume that it was *their* dinner table. It was. These were the Allen grandchildren, who grew in number every year. New recruits to the staff were assigned to be in charge of Children's Tea. Perhaps Myrtle Allen believed that if they could survive this challenge, no crisis in the dining room would ever trouble them. Children's Tea was a *table d'hôte* affair in theory. But since no reasonable – or unreasonable – request was ever turned down at Ballymaloe, Jonathan had a mission to broaden the menu choice. He had a fair notion of the evening dinner menu and had a tendency to encourage *à la carte* ordering by some of the other young guests. There was, perhaps, an ulterior motive here too: he wanted to be an early graduate to join his parents at their evening dinner.

MYRTLE ALLEN wrote that Wendy – her eldest child – had the best Jonathan story. It concerned a row which Wendy's eldest son, Sasha, had had with him.

> She found him, as a small boy, being beaten up by Sasha after some row. The tears were streaming down his face as he shouted 'I'm not going to hit you. I'm a pacifist.' When it was all over, he demanded to have a letter of apology from Sasha – I don't think he probably got it, but that is the proper way to conduct pacifism, I think.

When Timmy and Darina Allen refurbished some farmyard buildings and cottages at their farm nearby for renting during the summer, we spent many summer holidays there when Jonathan and Emma were still young. This was before Darina established the now famous Ballymaloe Cookery School in Kinoith. The publisher MICHAEL GILL recalled Jonathan there one summer.

> He was at the peak of his magic period. The Bowmans were in the White Cottage. The Gills were in the Gate Lodge. Jonathan seemed to materialize at all hours to demonstrate his latest trick or discovery. There was always a single-minded urgency about his appearance. Our girls, Fionnuala and Marianne, were not always impressed – after all this was boring, boy's behaviour – but Jonathan was not to be dissuaded. However, the girls' lack of interest eventually seemed to sting and the day we left for home he took his revenge by turning a powerful hose on Fionnuala, thereby lowering even further the – happily temporary! – reputation of boys in our house.

DARINA ALLEN had known Jonathan from childhood and recalled especially these summer holidays when we stayed in Kinoith.

> Jonathan, with his mop of blond curly hair, spent hours in my kitchen. He would run through the door, always bursting to share some new excitement. During his magician phase – which seemed to last for ages – he'd be desperate to show me the latest trick he had learned. He was terrifically precocious and maddeningly bright and exasperatingly logical. Even as young as seven or eight, he relished a debate and would run rings around me, insisting on arguing for ages on some minute point while I tried to cook. He'd watch me making bread, help to pack picnics and fill the bottle of meths, so we could cook sausages on my ancient little camp stove in Glenbower Wood. Jonathan loved an adventure, chasing the hens, collecting the eggs from the hen house, or playing with the kittens and Wowie, our wiry little terrier. Life for Jonathan was a voyage of discovery, never dull – he was unique – we loved him dearly.

The artist PAUL MOSSE was living and painting in a loft in Kinoith during these years. Jonathan befriended him from that time. Paul wrote:

> I remember Jonathan coming up to my studio in Kinoith from quite a young age. He was about eight or nine, a slight, fair, curly-haired kid. He had his father's mouth, yet, at the same time, had a strong look of both his parents. He was then, as he was all his life, uninhibited in diving headlong into any topic that interested him. He seemed interested in everything and ready to talk about it all;

> and had no tiresome deference to age. Any subject that was worth probing was probed with gusto. He lived life to the full then, and as he did later in the more public eye.

In the summer of 1980 I can especially remember one episode at Kinoith when Darina Allen was complaining about 'today's children' and how unproductive they could be. They seemed somewhat idle that day and the raspberry bushes were laden with ripe fruit. Overhearing this complaint, I hatched a plot with Jonathan. We volunteered to round up the children and attempt a record blitz at picking raspberries; we sold it to the children as an opportunity to play a trick on Darina. So as we picked the fruit, we isolated some unripe and rotting raspberries – along with leaves and stems to one bowl while secretly collecting kilos of wonderful fruit in another large container. There were about eight children and in double-quick time we had completed our task. We then presented Darina with the small bowl of unripe and indifferent fruit, suggesting that some 'visitors' must have been helping themselves overnight and that this was the best we could manage. Darina – clearly crestfallen but remaining, as always, the optimistic diplomat – congratulated the group of children on their efforts. They had some difficulty in suppressing their giggles until it was announced that there was another batch. The children then separated to reveal a bountiful container of many kilos of superb fruit. Timmy promptly took the team picture, which was entitled The Great Kinoith Raspberry-Picking Machine.

TIMMY ALLEN's hobby was photography. He printed all his own work and loved to share his enthusiasm with any children who showed an interest.

> One of the earliest memories I have of Jonathan is his interest in photography and cameras. At that stage I had my own darkroom and was amazed at how quickly he understood the fundamentals of a camera. I have always loved teaching people how to develop and print photographs and I think Jonathan was my most receptive – and irreverent – student. I often wonder whether our sessions in the darkroom did not sow the seeds for his own interest in photography.

Artist and musician BETH O'HALLORAN knew Jonathan from childhood and was pleased that 'he wasn't one to hold a grudge and that we were able to be kind adults who openly cared for each other.' She recalled Jonathan as something of an outsider in the gang of children of his age who were growing up in our Dublin

neighbourhood in the 1970s. The O'Halloran's house at No. 1 Raglan Road was across the lane from our mews. Beth recalled coming on a holiday with us to Kinoith and recalled Jonathan

> ...listening to the *Hitchhiker's Guide to the Galaxy* on his Walkman. He had a huge pair of headphones and was trying to spark a similar interest for me by stretching the headphones so we could both listen. I'd never heard of the *Guide* before and found it difficult to concentrate, but I do remember his contagious enthusiasm and desire to share the source of his excitement with me. And that's a very consistent memory I have of him. It seems to me he was often very ahead of us neighbourhood children. I feel like I was one of a cluster of children who didn't quite understand Jonathan and his extroverted expressions of his intelligence.
>
> I remember very clearly a day when Jonathan had devised a plan to feel more included – a treasure hunt. It was really well planned – he had written elaborate sets of clues and marked the neighbourhood with little white chalk arrows to help us know we were on the right track to get to the prize. He had taped a fifty

Timmy Allen's photograph of The Great Kinoith Raspberry-Picking Machine *Back row*: Sasha Whelan, Jonathan and Emma, Ivan Whelan, Isaac Allen; *In front*: Phelim Harty, Toby and Lydia Allen. With the exception of Jonathan and Emma, all are grandchildren of Ivan and Myrtle Allen.

A typical outdoor scene at the Pine Forest Art Centre.

pence piece to a paper plate in an abandoned lot on Clyde Road. I remember tearing it off without much gratitude for all the thought that had gone into the plan. I feel that growing up I often missed all he was trying to offer as my sources of stimulation were somehow more needy of immediacy than his. He had a joy of process that I missed until much later in life. I remember a video cassette with his collection of Channel 4 station identification segments. He'd rush to record whenever the 4 would appear. And I found myself seeing there was something there to be appreciated that I hadn't noticed.

When Jonathan was seven and Emma six, they began attending the Pine Forest Art School in the Dublin mountains for some weeks each summer. The school was founded by Mary Carroll and her husband, the late Ray Carroll. Their daughter Sarah, a contemporary of Jonathan, was a pupil and helper, later a teacher, and now runs it with her mother. Jonathan and Emma were enthusiastic pupils there for many summers. SARAH CARROLL wrote:

> My memories of him go back twenty-five years – and I wouldn't have missed knowing him for the world. Mary and I talked of just how much he entertained, infuriated, charmed and provoked: from pictures of him with his Rubik's cube driving every adult to tears while unable to keep up with him; to the lecture he gave Ray (a fairly similar temperament), a lecture on the difference between atheism and agnosticism; to the Jonathan we knew so well being roasted on the *Late Late Show*; to his emergence as a journalist, with the benefit of photographer and puppeteer behind him; to seeing him with Saul. He was a truly, truly remarkable person. I will miss him – with the memory making me a better person.

Occasionally, when Jonathan was young, he would pester me to bring him on a tour of the RTE studios. Sometimes at the end of a rehearsal, I would bring him. On the night of the announcement of his death, DEREK WALSH, a sound engineer in RTE television wrote:

> About twenty-five years ago, I was on the sound control desk on TV when you brought in your very young son and asked me to tell him what I did. I have never forgotten the impression he made on me that day. He was fascinatingly vital and questioning, and had you told me he was fourteen years old instead of about seven, I could well have believed it. I have observed his career in the intervening years but have never forgotten that little boy. I doubt I ever will.

Parents are not necessarily the best judges of the abilities of their own children – and especially of their first child. Often, of course, they reckon their own child is exceptional. Eimer and I certainly thought this to be probable in Jonathan's case, but we were aware that parents might not be the best judges on such matters. Teachers, on the other hand, and especially form teachers who experience some hundreds of children of the same age in the course of a few years work, are well placed to make comparisons. NOELLE CARSON was a student teacher in Sandford National School in Ranelagh in Dublin when she briefly taught Jonathan. When he died, she wrote:

> I was a student teacher on teacher practice with Ms. Hodges when I met Jonathan. He was sitting in the front row and Ms. Hodges surreptitiously and proudly said: 'That's Jonathan Bowman, John Bowman's son.' He was unforgettable, effervescent, perky and one of the most articulate and intelligent seven-year-olds I ever met. I remember him so well with his shock of hair and impish laughter. I knew then, even as a student teacher, that he had an originality and freshness that was rare and that he would go far.

ROBERT DOWDS was assistant principal and an influential teacher at Sandford National School. I remember his complaint in the school report he gave Jonathan at aged ten: it was to the effect that he had a tendency to turn the class into a debating society, preferably to discuss his latest preoccupations. At that time I was preparing to visit Britain to interview Malcolm MacDonald, who had been Dominions Secretary in the 1930s, and whose constructive relationship with Eamon de Valera had transformed Anglo-Irish relations. Clearly Jonathan had picked up on my enthusiasm and absorption and thought the topic suitable for classroom discussion. Some years ago when I was researching MacDonald's political papers in the University of Durham archives, I came across a file, marked 'Correspondence with John Bowman, Dublin concerning MM's relationship with Eamon de Valera.' In the file I found a letter from myself in which I had reported to MacDonald that he would be pleased to learn that he was once again a household name in Ireland since my ten-year-old son Jonathan's latest school report stated that he was inclined to be a chatterbox, '...with interesting stories to tell about famous people such as Malcolm MacDonald.'

Robert Dowds reckoned that being able to remember so much of Jonathan twenty years after teaching him was 'an indication of the huge impact he must have had on you all and on his son, Saul.'

BEST SUMMER SCHOOL

The Pine Forest Art Centre

Some of our best friends spent many happy and creative summer fortnights here as they grew up. You get collected from Stillorgan, or Dundrum, or wherever, and that's you gone for the day, high up into the mountains where you learn about oil-painting, and clay-modelling and batik. Contact Mary Carroll at 955598.

Jonathan acknowledged his indebtedness to the Pine Forest Art Centre in *In Dublin*'s listing of the 300 best things about Dublin. This was to mark Dublin's millennium.
In Dublin, 14 April 1988

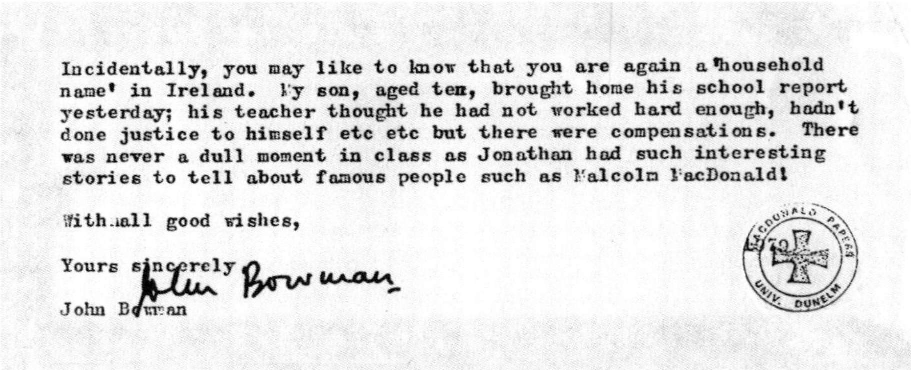
Incidentally, you may like to know that you are again a 'household name' in Ireland. My son, aged ten, brought home his school report yesterday; his teacher thought he had not worked hard enough, hadn't done justice to himself etc etc but there were compensations. There was never a dull moment in class as Jonathan had such interesting stories to tell about famous people such as Malcolm MacDonald!

With all good wishes,

Yours sincerely

John Bowman

Extract from my letter to Malcolm MacDonald, 29 June 1979, University of Durham Archives.

While teaching Jonathan, Robert Dowds remembered him writing 'a brilliant modern parody of Shakespeare's "Seven Ages of Man". I was so impressed, I kept a copy of it.' Jonathan entitled it: 'The seven ages of man: revised edition; this is what we hope dear (but dead) Willy would have wanted.' It reads:

At first the baby still muling and puking – but in the incubator;
Then the schoolboy with wit at peak trying placidly to dodge lines;
Then the lover with Coke in hand skidding across the roller disco rink or perhaps punk with safety-pin through nose;
Next ungrateful school-leavers complaining to Charlie's angels about P.A.Y.E.
Soon the astronaut from head to toe in shiny aluminium, ray-gun in hand ready for anything;
Then the High Court judge kicking fruit and nut papers down the corridor on television;
Then the O.A.P. who is A.L.O.N.E. (comforted by Jim McCann)
And finally, the money-lender, cigar in mouth, strolling through Brown Thomas. *

This was a homework exercise, and Jonathan added a suggestion concerning its deserved mark: 'This is written to be appreciated by people of culture and most of all good taste'. And he impertinently predicted the comment which would be Mr Dowds's adjudication

* Some notes may be useful. Charlie's Angels was the title of a television detective series. When Charles Haughey became Taoiseach in 1979, his female supporters were sometimes referred to as Charlie's angels. Another reference is to a contemporary television commercial showing a judge emerging from his chambers, enjoying a Cadbury's Fruit and Nut chocolate bar. He skips down the corridor kicking the wrapping paper before him. A.L.O.N.E. is a Dublin-based charity set up by Willie Bermingham for old people who live alone. Jim McCann is a singer. Brown Thomas is Dublin's most exclusive department store.

on his efforts: 'furthermore all the reader's reactions have been anticipated, leading to an average of "not a supersonic masterpiece".'

Robert Dowds recalled that Jonathan was a member of the second sixth class he had taught in his career and he reckoned them as 'perhaps the most interested and, to me, intellectually challenging group of children I've taught. Every decision had to be explained. Fortunately, they also had a strong sense of fair play and justice too. This included Jonathan.' But Jonathan was 'always a challenge to teach. In some respects this was beneficial to me as it forced me to be on my toes. However, it could lead to problems with subjects such as Irish in which he was not interested at that stage. Also, his absolute determination to argue his case meant it was sometimes difficult for others to get a look in.'

The historian RUAN O'DONNELL was among Jonathan's closest friends during his years in primary school. I can remember the special regard which Jonathan had for him from an early age, finding in him a soulmate with whom he could conspire to test the adult world's tolerances as they were growing up. Ruan recalled that 'within a short period we became friends, soon afterwards best friends' and he reckoned it 'no exaggeration' to state that his personality and outlook on life had been affected by this early bond, perhaps more than he could now evaluate.

> I recall Jonathan's unshakable conviction and enthusiasm for anything he found interesting. These phases, as you know, happened frequently. There were no half-measures with him once a subject attracted his attention, and one was relentlessly challenged to concur. Eclecticism hardly conveys the breadth of themes which fired his insatiable curiosity; stand out ones for me include the technique and performance of magic (at a preposterously early age), computers (encouraged by your commissioning him to type drafts of your de Valera book), collectable playing cards, board games, chess and numerology.
>
> Jonathan taught me to play chess in school one time and bombarded me with games until I became quite proficient for my age. I recall the day when Mr Dowds noticed our inattention and unexpectedly came down to the back of the class, centre aisle, where we sat. When Mr Dowds discovered that Jonathan and I had drawn a chessboard in a copybook and were using hand-drawn, torn out paper pieces, he was simultaneously aghast and bemused. That was probably the worst of our class-time offences. Another unusual school experience was our devising a rhyme in order to

learn the names of the 32 counties – Mr Dowds was very impressed and had us perform it for the class.

I also recall the day Jonathan decided that he would insist on being acknowledged as Philbin Bowman. There was no room for equivocation on this issue. Every roll call Jonathan would either fail to answer when his name was read out without the 'Philbin' or would demand an immediate correction, much to the astonishment of Mr Dowds. His persistence and vehemence on this matter were typical of his tenacity on matters of principle, of which he had many. A key lifelong issue for him, of course, was pacifism – a very brave position to adopt and declare in a schoolyard and one not calculated to endear him to certain elements. He and I disagreed about this matter and often debated it, with no ill-will arising. Constructive arguments between Jonathan and me were very common and sharpened my powers of analysis. This undoubtedly contributed to my later involvement in debating and history and I hope that his positive influence was in some way reciprocated. In our early teens we once claimed affiliation to an international war-gaming and role-playing association in order to gate-crash the Trinity College Games Club on Sunday afternoons. Needless to say, this was not my idea!

As a father myself, with a son just a little younger than Saul, I am even more impressed at this remove with Jonathan's handling of his parental obligations. I am aware that this was a difficult time for him and that it took supreme confidence and vision to take the hardest route of all. The often hilarious modifications to his social life arising from this responsibility were probably unique and indicative of his irrepressible dynamism.

At the risk of sounding maudlin, I must tell you that I was jolted into a most unwelcome revelation on learning of Jonathan's death, namely, that a large part of my childhood has now disappeared. It is not simply that my companion of so many days and events is gone, but the fact that no one but he is capable of contextualising or understanding the experience that shaped my formative years.

In preparing this book, I had sent Robert Dowds part of the sequence on Sandford National School, including that letter from Ruan. He replied that he felt Ruan's comments about Jonathan gave 'a real flavour of what he was like in school'. He added that 'Ruan O'Donnell was an incredibly loyal and supportive friend' to Jonathan at this time. As indicated, 'Jonathan in fifth and sixth classes, when I taught him, was most uncompromising and brave in expressing his views. This sometimes got him into sticky situations where he might get physically threatened. Never once, to my knowledge, did Ruan fail to stand by him at such times.' He added that

> ...one of Jonathan's great hobbyhorses was pacifism which he preached to anyone who'd listen. At breaktime I never recall him playing football. He always seemed to be standing in the corner preaching pacifism, arguing a philosophical point or showing someone an interesting trick. I recall him talking to me about the philosopher A.J.Ayer's views about religion. At the time I was having quite a few doubts about my own Christian faith and I didn't entirely appreciate what he said. I think his intellectual honesty had an unsettling impact on others as well. I think this was why not every pupil appreciated him as much as Ruan did.

ROBERT DOWDS also recalled that when he was ill his father Alex, a retired teacher, had occasionally stood in for him. Alex Dowds was

> ...quite gifted mathematically and spent some of the time doing mathematical puzzles with the children. Jonathan clearly loved the challenge of these from what both he and my father said. Indeed, my father, who'd had forty-six years' teaching experience at that stage, marvelled at how well Jonathan worked them out.

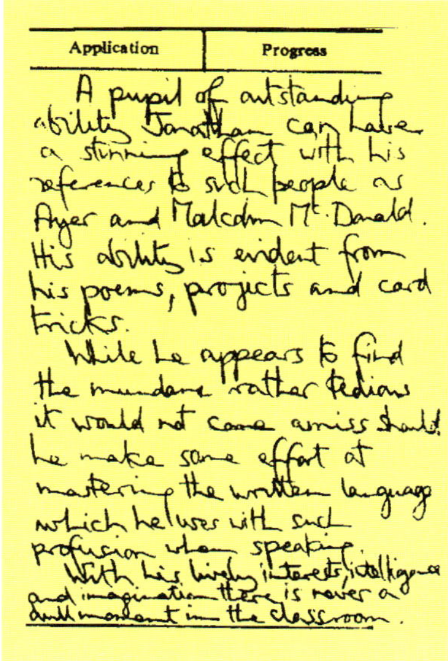

Application	Progress

A pupil of outstanding ability Jonathan can have a stunning effect with his references to such people as Ayer and Malcolm McDonald. His ability is evident from his poems, projects and card tricks.
While he appears to find the mundane rather tedious it would not come amiss should he make some effort at mastering the written language which he uses with such profusion when speaking.
With his lively interests, intelligence and imagination there is never a dull moment in the classroom.

When Jonathan completed fifth class, aged ten, Robert Dowds praised his wide range of interests and his 'poems, projects and card tricks'. However, he complained that Jonathan found the 'mundane rather tedious' and needed to master the written language. 'With his lively interests, intelligence and imagination, there is never a dull moment in the classroom.'

When they were seven, the boys in Jonathan's class all joined the cub scout section of the Sandford Group of the Scout Association of Ireland. What we did not anticipate was the problem which arose concerning the Scout Promise – the oath. DERMOT JAMES, historian of the Sandford Scouts, suggests that scruples about 'the duty to God' section of the Promise had become apparent 'in various European countries long before it became an issue here in Ireland, and attempts to resolve the situation almost split some of the national associations concerned.' The issue was further complicated in Ireland by the existence of a rival scouting organization, the Catholic Boy Scouts of Ireland. And, in his opinion, since the latter was

> ...unlikely to countenance any move to remove God from the Promise, this put the Scout Association of Ireland in a difficult position in that if it went along with such a move, it risked being regarded as being even worse than the usual 'Protestant' perception – it risked being labelled atheistic; and there was even a danger of it being accused of being anti-religious! This was serious stuff two or three decades ago, and that was the situation

when Jonathan wanted to join; so the rule requiring new members to take the Promise as it stood continued to be enforced.

There was the further complication that the Sandford Scout Group was attached not to the school but to the Church of Ireland parish. The leaders of such a scout group 'were unlikely to be in the vanguard of a campaign to remove the Duty to God clause of the Promise; but even if they felt such a change was desirable, this would be decided at the highest level, so the hands of the local leaders would have been "tied" in any case.'

ROBERT KERR was more directly involved in Jonathan's challenge to the system:

> I was Jonathan's Cub Scout Leader when he joined the Pack in 1976. I remember it very well indeed as he caused quite a problem! In many respects he was very like any other seven year old who had just been thrust into the turmoil of 36 boys for ninety minutes of fun and games. Like each of them when they arrived first, he clearly had fun but was also a little overawed by the whole spectacle of everyone in uniform and the rituals that went with that. None of this would mark him out as being any different from the others, but it was my privilege as leader to take the new boys for their first few sessions of badgework, when we tried to explain what cub scouting was all about. During these I saw a boy who was clearly not the norm. Far from the wide-eyed child who swallowed anything fed to him, here was a boy who told me – without the slightest trace of nervousness or uncertainty – that he didn't believe in God, so he wouldn't say that bit of the Scout Promise.
>
> Of the many hundred boys who made their Promise to me as their cub leader, only two stand out, one who asked to make the Promise in Irish – which was fine with me, as I spoke Irish pretty well – and Jonathan. Here was a real problem and one which ultimately remained unresolved. It must be remembered that scouting was founded as a Christian organization based on rather Victorian values which don't translate well to the modern world, however comfortably they fitted in the 1970s. Around about the time of Jonathan's request to take the Promise without affirming his duty to God there was a heavy debate going on in scouting headquarters about just this point. Jonathan's case was never raised with them, as far as I know, but we as leaders had all been let know very forcefully that no changes to the Scout Promise could be accepted. I was a young leader and followed that party line conscientiously, believing in it myself. My recollection is that I told Jonathan that no such derogation could be made. I do know that his mother, Eimer, was very displeased at his not being allowed join

the Pack without taking the Promise! I had referred the matter to Canon Carter [the then Rector], as sponsor for the whole group, and he was very strongly of the opinion that without swearing a duty to God, no boy could join the Pack. So that was Jonathan's goose cooked, both from the organization as a whole and from the sponsor of the group. I had no options left, but to be honest I don't think I was really looking for any. He was probably in and out of the Cub Pack in about ten weeks.

RACHEL FEHILY, now a barrister, is an exact contemporary of Jonathan and was in his class at both playschool and primary school.

Sandford National was a fantastic school. Our class arrived during the 1970s just as the old-fashioned regime of the strict chalk-throwing, ear-twisting Mr Davis was coming to an end.

Sally Sheils, his daughter, was our teacher in first class and eventually went on to be the head of the school. She had a strong influence on its ethos. It was a very liberal, open, mixed denomination school. There was a good mix of pupils from all backgrounds but there were quite a few parents who were artists, architects, journalists, therapists and actors. so I suppose it was quite fashionable at the time. Jonathan was in my class from senior infants to sixth class. Jonathan was an incredibly loquacious, kind, gentle, blond, curly-haired, little boy.

Our creative side was definitely encouraged in Sandford. I particularly remember Jonathan loving art classes. There was a gang of us who hung out together – Stephen Hall, Cliona Carney, Jonathan and me. We all went through a phase of refusing to paint anything representational. Jonathan loved anything subversive that didn't entail outright disobedience. Our efforts in art were appalling and more paint went on us than on the paper. Jonathan loved arguing the point with our beleaguered art teacher: 'Can you not understand – it's abstract art?'

We did our best to undermine every class, and Jonathan had a real knack for getting teachers off the subject and into a row. Literally hours of boring Irish, Maths and English would disappear as Jonathan and Mr Dowds would argue hysterically about whether Ireland should go to the Soviet Union for the Moscow Olympics or not. Anything with any political content was fascinating to Jonathan. From a very early age he was wonderful at figuring out what other people felt passionately about and challenging them about it. He had great practice for his future career on many of our teachers. I remember him infuriating many adults as a child and he did it in such a way that he didn't actually do anything wrong – he just managed to get under their skin.

One person he particularly managed to irritate was our housekeeper, Mrs Butterfield. She looked after my family – we were seven children and all lived together on Clyde Road. [*From another source I can report that Mrs Butterfield was akin to a Victorian grandmother; and that 'nobody ever crossed her', not even her employers, Rachel's parents*] Jonathan and Emma and my brother Morgan and I were in and out of each other's houses frequently as he lived around the corner on Pembroke Lane, in the mews which my parents as young architects had converted when they were first married.

We were all quite in awe of Mrs Butterfield and a little bit afraid to show her any of the disrespect reserved for our parents and teachers. Jonathan had no such qualms. I remember one afternoon for no apparent reason Jonathan – about eight at the time – quizzed Mrs Butterfield about her voting preferences. Mrs B condescended to tell Jonathan that she was a great supporter of Charles J. Haughey and had always voted Fianna Fáil. A massive row ensued. At that time Charlie was a highly controversial figure and Jonathan decided to wind up Mrs B. How could she vote for such a man and his party? Why did she do it? Mrs B replied that her family had always voted for Fianna Fáil in an effort to end the discussion. This was a red rag to Jonathan. Could she not think for herself? Why did she follow her family voting pattern? At this stage Mrs B had had enough of the 'young pup' as she called him. She promptly showed him the door and told him to come back when he had manners. For anyone else that would have been enough. We all were subdued at this stage and relieved that the row was over. Two minutes later, to our amazement, Jonathan stormed back into our house wagging his finger to make his final point. We were all speechless at his audacity and I think at that stage forcible ejectment was the end of the argument.

At the end of the school year in fifth and sixth class things got quite relaxed and we were allowed to perform our little plays. Jonathan was mad about magic and had developed a huge interest in Houdini. He told us that he had been studying escapolgy and was going to perform a great escape for the class. He insisted that we tie him to a chair and watch while he set himself free. I remember the other kids being absolutely amazed by this and we all had to wait while Jonathan struggled unsuccessfully to free himself. I think a teacher eventually untied him. Jonathan was a very determined child and was not put off by this early failure. He was going to be as good as Houdini. He insisted that we tie him up with our skipping ropes and belts during every break-time – and as small children we were delighted to do this. I have very vivid memories of Jonathan tied to chairs and gates during lunch hour, struggling to get free while we all watched.

Jonathan loved anything new or faddish. He always was the first one in class with the Rubik's cube and then the first one to solve it. He had a calculator before anyone else. He knew all the lyrics to 'Hit me with your rhythm stick' by Ian Dury and the Blockheads. We would howl laughing to the lyrics 'Two fat persons – click, click, click – Hit me!' He had every gadget known to man. We all watched *Top of the Pops*, *Fawlty Towers*, *Not the Nine O'Clock News*, *Kenny Everett's Video Show* and *Monty Python's Flying Circus* religiously. Jonathan knew all the words and could mimic for Ireland. I can't think of a time in my life when we all laughed so much over so little.

We were horribly precocious children and knew far too much about everything – especially sex. I remember we had all separately managed to get our hands on books or information at home on the topic. There was a series on nudists at the time called 'Let's go naked.' It was about nudists in Europe who did everything without clothing. We used to get hysterical about the idea of going shopping or having barbeques without clothes on. Jonathan's favourite joke was the concept of people becoming pregnant by strangers because they bumped into each other by mistake in nudist camps.

At another end of term play, Jonathan and the gang decided we would do an existential play about the meaning of life. We were all about ten at the time. Instead of the play being on the stage, we had nothing on the stage and Stephen arrived from the back of class in a hooded cloak delivering the meaningful line 'By the pricking of my thumbs, something wicked this way comes' and ran out of the classroom, banging the door. All the other kids were a bit puzzled. Then Jonathan crawled out from under a table and stated to the underage audience – 'I am the thing. The thing is what I am.' Cliona and I wailed and looked suitably distressed. I don't think Beckett could have done any better!

He was a very generous child and would share everything he had with his friends. He loved to give and receive little presents and I remember he was the first boy who ever gave me a present. He brought me back a coral necklace from a family holiday. I in turn used to give him little gifts too of candles and books. His generous spirit extended to the younger kids in the school and he would beg to be allowed go to the other classes and show them his magic tricks. Jonathan to me was exactly the same as an adult as he was as a child. He was a determined, argumentative child, fascinated by popular culture and music. He was old beyond his years when he was young and paradoxically he seemed to be able to retain many positive childlike qualities when he became an adult.

SALLY SHIELS was the youngest recruit to the teaching staff at Sandford National School during Jonathan's time there. She was the daughter of the previous headmaster and was a very popular and innovative teacher. And she became school principal – for some, a controversial choice because of her youth. But she quickly proved to be an outstanding principal – successful with both parents and pupils.

Whenever I think of Jonathan, an absolute zest for life and learning and fun without fail accompanies that thought. He was always so vivacious with such an innocent sense of fun – such as when he came up to tell me the secret of my nickname. With some trepidation I asked what it was, only to be told with great delight that it was 'Sallio'. He then wanted to know could he call me that and we made a deal that he could, except when an inspector was in the room.

My first memory of Jonathan always has Emma as an integral part of it. They complemented each other so perfectly: he defending her with his quick wit; and she – on one occasion that I shall never forget – flooring someone for saying something she didn't like either to, or about, Jonathan. I came upon her sitting astride the poor boy who had been so foolish and who was now flat on his back! I remember Jonathan telling his latest joke – no matter how long to the punchline – and also being able to hold a class silent with his stories. He was enjoying the joke or story so much himself that it was infectious: even when the joke was truly not funny, he seemed to still make it appear funny.

Jonathan and Emma were my ideal of how a brother and sister should be – each delighting in the other and their closeness was extraordinary. They were so bright, happy and confident and particularly so with adults. Emma found her peers more interesting than Jonathan did. He regularly engaged adults in conversation – his knowledge at such a young age was remarkable and he always enlivened any class discussions, during which he was always in his element. He particularly enjoyed when I gave them the homework of finding out three pieces of information that I wouldn't know! I often felt he probably knew how easy that exercise was but chose to flatter me by finding out something unusual! He always told these stories with such energy and fun. All his classmates really enjoyed Jonathan and when one of them was feeling upset he often chimed in with something – which if not always appropriate – always cheered them up.

Sally Shiels recalled Jonathan defending Emma 'with his quick wit' and Emma flooring a boy who had been so foolish as to say something 'she didn't like either to, or about, Jonathan.'

He was so obviously adored at home and by his extended family that he had enormous security facing the world and I believe that this stood to him in so many ways. He absolutely adored parents and grandparents alike and I often felt a certain sadness that so few children get to experience that level of love and security in loving, as well as in being loved. I always have this sense of devilment around Jonathan whenever I think of him but I can never think of specific examples – maybe because such an innocence was inherent in anything he did do. He was really enchanted by whatever his latest passion happened to be.

I do know that when I heard that Jonathan was having a hard time when he went on to second level I was devastated. On the one hand I felt guilty for having failed to prepare him properly for life beyond primary school – where I do believe he was happy. On the other hand I felt bitterly angry that in order to prepare him it would have been necessary to suppress the essence of what made him so special and so greatly loved. And I felt terrific relief when he moved past second level to find so many areas in which to excel. It was always in his nature that he desired to embrace every aspect of life. He would move from one arena to another, one learning experience to another. And he was always going to get more out of life in a week – and give more to it – than many people do in many, many years of life. Perhaps what sums up Jonathan most for me is that whenever I think of him the child, I automatically smile. He and Emma were significant in making me know for certain that teaching was definitely what I wanted to do for the rest of my life.

AL O'DONNELL – a colleague in RTE – and father of Ruan, Jonathan's friend in Sandford National School, remembers Jonathan as someone who enjoyed the company of adults and who

> ...loved to raise the hare and really enjoyed fueling a good debate. He asked if I smoked. I said: 'Yes'. He was delighted, as he had a battery-powered fan in his pocket which he produced, and followed me about warning me of the dangers of smoking. I said: 'You are right of course, but that's it!' He made me promise to try to give up. To soften the lecture, he explained that I was not the only one, and that he had 'lots of other customers' for the fan! I found him very bright and intelligent, brave, funny, outspoken and unafraid; yet could easily be hurt, as he had a soft centre.

The broadcaster MIKE MURPHY gave this account of his first meeting with Jonathan, on Noelle O'Reilly's radio documentary about him which was broadcast on RTE Radio 1 the Saturday after he died.

> He would have had the most interesting future. But simply as a person he was a delight. I think Jonathan was nine or ten years of age when I met him. I recall it very, very well. I had never met him before. I used to drag my daughters around the art galleries on a Saturday morning whether they liked it or not; eventually they decided they did not and stopped going with me. But we went into Trinity College on this Saturday morning and there was some kind of a chess competition on, and a little boy came over to me and said: 'Wouldn't have expected to see you here.' I said: 'I beg your pardon.' He said: 'Wouldn't have thought you'd have been interested in chess.' 'Why not?' 'Wouldn't have thought with the sort of thing you do on television and radio that chess would have interested you.' 'Well it does actually; why would you be wondering whether or not ...'. 'It's just that you're not the type who'd be interested in chess.' I said: 'do you mind if I ask you your name?' 'He said Jonathan Philbin Bowman.' So I said: 'Very nice to meet you. I'm sure I'll meet you again.' I turned around to the girls as we were leaving and I said: 'Remember that name; you will be hearing that name in the future.'

And in a letter of condolence, MIKE MURPHY reminded us that he had known Jonathan for as long as twenty years 'of his short life'.

> I liked and admired him from the start. I believe he was as fond of me as I was of him. We both derived a deal of pleasure from our, sadly, too infrequent meetings. I loved his sheer curiosity, his interest in others, his inexhaustible energy and the generosity of his

> nature. Collectivism is all very well, but individualism – for me at any rate – is paramount. Jonathan had the courage to chart his own life as an expression of his beliefs and interests. His was a life led in glorious technicolour, while most of his contemporaries never got past grey. It's tragic, it's unfair, it's deeply shocking, but if the quality of a man or woman can be quantified or defined by the mark they made during their existence, then Jonathan's short, positive, illuminated life would gain him the best seat, at the best table in the Pantheon. And he'd like that.

The broadcaster and comedienne ADELE KING, better known under her stage name TWINK, worked with Jonathan on RTE television's game of charades, *Play the Game.* She was the regular captain of the women's team, so was always playing against Jonathan; he was an occasional player on the men's team. He entered into the spirit of the game and hugely enjoyed it. I was unaware until I received this letter that Twink's first encounter with him had been many years earlier. Jonathan had been fascinated by the first wave of electronic gadgets, and puzzles of all sorts – forerunners of the Rubik's cube – and he quickly mastered them. He persuaded his parents that he should accept an offer – a professional offer, I need hardly add – from the proprietor of a shop in Dublin to spend two hours on Saturday afternoons demonstrating them. Adele King wrote when Jonathan died:

> It is almost twenty-two years this week, since I visited a shop in the Powerscourt Town Centre to buy a techno gift of some sort for a friend of mine. As I walked into the small shop on the ground floor, I was drawn to a large crowd of customers standing watching someone or something with rapt attention. As I approached them curiously, I was fascinated to see that it was a small tousled-haired little boy, who was the epicentre of the crowd. Within seconds of approaching the crowd, I was aware of the gasps of sheer astonishment and audible comments such as 'My God, isn't he a little genius: wouldn't it make you ashamed of your life?'
>
> To my amazement the said little boy was giving all and sundry a breathtaking display of manual and mental dexterity, with an entire array of digital games, pocket Psions of the day. The manager, whom I knew from my college days, approached me, and on seeing my astonished look, promptly told me that the boy's name was Jonathan Philbin Bowman and he was all of nine years old.
>
> That was to be my first encounter with the boy wonder, and I, just like the punters in the shop, was hooked. It was to be a further ten years before we actually met on a professional basis at a book

With Twink on *Play the Game*, RTE, 23 October 1993.

launch we both had a part to play in. Shortly after that, he appeared for the first of what was to be a regular stint in the ten-year lifespan of *Play the Game* on RTE. The energy and enthusiasm he generated to all around him on that show was breathtaking, not to mention his inexhaustible knowledge of literature, films and theatre. He put all his efforts into what was always a scintillating performance.

Off the screen, I became one of his ardent admirers. I was, like most others, particularly women, drawn like a moth to the flame of this ebullient, effervescent young guy. He was like a battery cell, a force field; he had an extraordinary sense of the power of his own presence to all around him, and it was to that most generous, witty, vivacious and energetic of people that we were all drawn willingly, for what were sometimes hours and hours on end.

I bumped into only him a couple of weeks ago in Fitzers on Dawson Street. I had my two young daughters with me, and within seconds of meeting them he had them laughing hysterically at some old schoolyard prank he re-enacted for them. I could clearly see that although, they are only aged ten and six, they too were immediately sucked into that web of charm and good old-fashioned 'niceness' that poured so effortlessly and unassumingly from him.

So it was with the greatest distress and utter grief that I have tried to get my head around the events of the last few days. I have gone through all the stages, the shock, the disbelief, the endless tears and now the numbness, and the eternal question faced with the sudden loss of one so young and gifted.

Why?

Concerning his passing, I can only say that few will ever make such an impression in their life and death as did Jonathan; he is now an immortal part of Irish, and, in particular, of Dublin culture. I, for one, cannot imagine the thought of driving into the city at some stage in the foreseeable future on a dull Dublin day, without the prospects of the possibility of bumping into Jonathan somewhere: 'To put the sun in the sky and a smile on your face.'

2

'Jonathan, are you still talking?'

– TOBY ALLEN aged six to Jonathan aged twelve walking out of Funderland, Christmas 1981

In June 1980 Jonathan was aged eleven and a half when he finished sixth class at Sandford National School. He and Emma had been enrolled for their secondary education at Newpark Comprehensive shortly after it had evolved from Avoca Kingstown School in 1973. Newpark had established a reputation as a somewhat avant-garde, egalitarian, co-educational school, with the noted educationist Dr John Harris as headmaster. But although Jonathan had completed his primary education in the summer of 1980, he was not yet eligible for Newpark because he was too young by some days. So we decided to keep his place in Newpark while sending him to Sandford Park – the independent, non-denominational, boys' school in Ranelagh. We were then open-minded about which of these quite different schools might best suit him and had decided to review his options at the conclusion of that first year at Sandford Park. It was already clear that his intellectual ability was not being reflected in his academic results. He didn't dally over his homework and he preferred to talk than write. SALLY SHIELS, principal at his primary school, forwarded an assessment of Jonathan to his secondary school, Sandford Park. She listed his interests as 'magic, reading, chess, electric models and codes'. And in her general comments wrote:

> Jonathan needs to make more effort in most areas. He assumes that because he has the ability to do something he need not exert himself to do it. He contributes particularly well in debate and when experiments are being done.

On the night before his last day at primary school Eimer recorded a conversation she had with a sleepy Jonathan, saying to him that she hoped 'those teachers in Sandford Park take no nonsense from you so that you'll leave from there in greater glory.' She described his response: 'With a little smile he said: "I'd prefer to get high marks in magic than in English."' And she noted: 'So far he does.'

That September he took great enjoyment from the prospect of a school uniform with fashion parades and so on. He was up every morning, dressed like a soldier on parade, coming home full of news. There was some bullying also in the early weeks, mainly related to his being a pacifist. He was amused that one of those teasing him didn't wish it to be known that he himself was a Quaker lest the boys taunt him with 'Shiver! Shiver!'

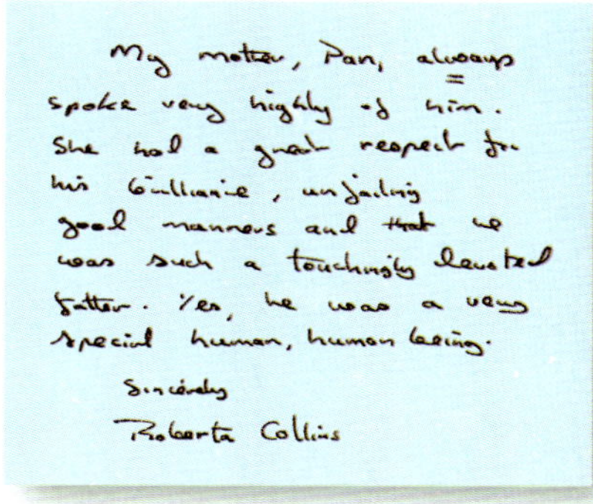
My mother, Pan, always spoke very highly of him. She had a great respect for his brilliance, unfailing good manners and that he was such a touchingly devoted father. Yes, he was a very special human, human being.

Sincerely

Roberta Collins

Extract from letter from Roberta Collins, daughter of Pan

In December he appeared on RTE 's *Late Late Show*. It was the annual Toy Show, which was – and still is – one of the highlights of the television year for children in Ireland. It had become something of a national institution since it dedicated an entire edition in early December each year to a comprehensive review of the toys which were especially popular or being promoted that Christmas. The toys, gadgets and games being shown were demonstrated by children. At that time Pan Collins was the programme's researcher and she also starred in the Toy Show by steering Gay Byrne through the minefield of children and technical gadgets that didn't always behave as they should. That year Pan invited Jonathan and Emma on the show, Emma to demonstrate the wonders of a spirograph and Jonathan to review a Paul Daniel's magic kit – Daniels being then the leading magician on British television. Emma did an impressive drawing of the planets orbiting around the sun – for which, to her dismay, she was given a doll's pram. Gay generously played second fiddle to Jonathan as performing magician and toy reviewer and appreciated how the audience took special enjoyment when he relieved Gay of all the spare money he had in his pocket. GAY BYRNE recalled that night.

> He did a magic trick and even then he made a tremendous impression on everybody because, of course, you have to have great self-confidence to make a magic trick come off. Not only did he do that but it wasn't a silent magic trick; he was full of the patter, full of the gags and the jokes while he bamboozled everybody. And his sheer verve and panache and self-confidence carried the evening.

The following is an excerpt from that first appearance by Jonathan on the *Late Late Show*.

Jonathan liked to persuade his adult audiences to gamble on his magic tricks. The outcome – as Gay Byrne is discovering here – was predictable. *Late Late Show*, RTE, 13 December 1980

JPB: [*holding a piece of string which has been threaded through a holed dice*] Do you have another pound? Right? Now you see what happens is that [*holds the string upright*] I can tell the dice to stop. And it stops.

GB: You can stop that dice anywhere on the string?

JPB: Anywhere on the string.

GB: So what's the bet?

JPB: The bet is that you can't. Now this is a very old trick. Houdini invented it originally, using a ball. He could stop the ball anywhere on the string by pulling it tight [*as Jonathan talks, he is demonstrating the trick*]. You pull it tight and that's how it's done. All you have to do is pull it tight. Now you will place a pound there that you can do it.

GB: Where's your pound? Put it down on the table.

JPB: I'll give you two-to-one.

GB : You'll give me two-to-one...

JPB: No I won't. I'll give you one, two, three to one!

GB : ...that I can stop it anywhere. [*Gay attempts the trick*] Stop! Stop! Stop! [*Gay fails*] Do it again, Jonathan.

JPB: Thank you [*beginning to pocket the money*]. And I win...

GB : ...you haven't done it again yet. Do it again. I want to see you doing it again.

JPB: Why do you want to see me doing it again?

GB : Because I want to make sure that you can do it. I couldn't do it.

JPB: I showed you I could do it.

GB : Do it again just to make me feel good about my three quid.

JPB: Okay, okay. There you are: [*demonstrates it three times in rapid succession*] Stop! Stop! Stop! [*Applause*]

GB : And you got these in the Paul Daniel's magic kit, did you?

JPB: Yes the Paul Daniel's money-making kit. [*Laughter*]

GB : Now I know you're into magic, Jonathan, what do you think of Paul Daniels? And he's going up in your estimation every minute.

JPB: Well now, he sells this one. Reasonably good, as you have, eh, witnessed.

GB: Yes indeed, I have witnessed. Jonathan Philbin Bowman, ladies and gentlemen. [*Applause*] I don't know why I'm applauding...

Late Late Show, RTE, 13 December 1980

GREG COLLINS was Jonathan's English teacher for his last term at Sandford Park School and Jonathan always expressed a great indebtedness to him. His contemporary assessment can be found in Jonathan's summer term report in 1981:

> Jonathan recently joined my class and shows great enthusiasm for the subject. He has produced a lot of written work in that short time and already shows a certain awareness of writers' styles and techniques. I hope he maintains his great interest in reading. Jonathan should have little difficulty in dealing with this subject in the years ahead.

When Jonathan died, Greg Collins wrote that the tributes paid to him testified 'to his great capacity for friendship' and he counted himself among those 'lucky ones' to have shared that friendship.

When Jonathan came to Sandford my first impression of the boy was the deep wistfulness of his eyes and the sensitivity of his expression. I remember a lively, amusing, zestful youth full of prankish merriment who came to me one day and asked if I knew any 'magic'; and then proceeded to demonstrate his 'tricks'. As one with, I hope, a good sense of humour I was delighted with this twelve year old with similar traits. His flippancy always fell short of insolence; he seemed to possess an in-built meter which prevented him from overstepping the mark and causing hurt or offence. It was impossible to dislike such a boy because you realise that he is simply out to amuse – there was never any guile or malice in his make-up. We had an instant rapport which was maintained for the rest of his life.

In my English class I soon discovered that Jonathan was way ahead of the others with his reading; in fact, I decided early on to let him bring in his own choice of books for the once-a-week reading class. How refreshing to see a first year reading and obviously enjoying Thomas Mann's *The Magic Mountain.* He said once that I encouraged his reading. I take no credit for this; Jonathan was a bookworm long before he met me! Unfortunately, bright teenage boys can sometimes, especially to their fellow students, appear tiresomely irritating and opinionated. Inevitably he became the victim of 'bullying' by his peer group. I imagine this was because of his precociousness and mental and verbal dexterity. At Sandford in those days, and doubtless in many other schools, any signs or suspicion of heightened sensibility caused a boy to be condemned as a 'swot'. Among teenagers, this attitude is slow to change. Youngsters are often jealous of intellectual curiosity in their class, and teachers can also think it leads to autodidactism. Unfortunately also for Jonathan, a preference for books to games may have affected relations with the 'sporting' set.

Waiting for Godot, Sandford Park production, November 1980.

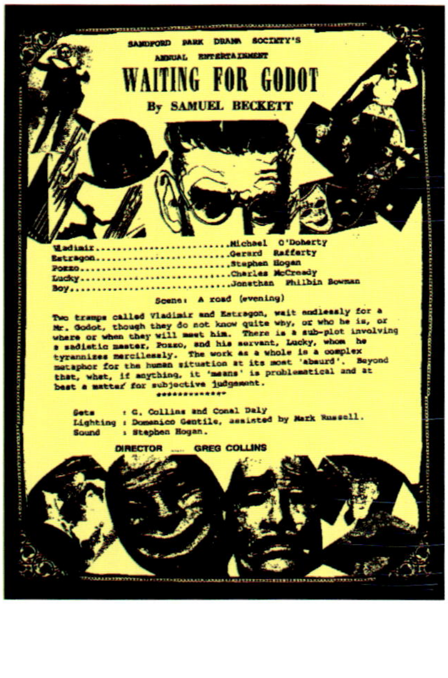

During that one year at Sandford I also detected in Jonathan a gift for mimicry and impersonation – actorial qualities which he often used to good effect later in life – especially during his time with Radio FM104. He once told me that if he ran short of material for his radio programme he would phone in questions with an assumed voice and answer his own queries! On a number of occasions I enjoyed his mimicry of certain well-known personalities in the political world. Getting back to Sandford, that year I directed *Waiting for Godot* and naturally I cast Jonathan as the 'Boy'. Four senior boys played the leads and it was a very happy and amusing series of rehearsals. Jonathan, whenever we met, always alluded to Godot and that it was the one experience he genuinely enjoyed while at Sandford. I was very sorry to see him leave the school at the end of his first year.

In general Jonathan's reports continued to admit his potential while emphasizing that he was not realizing it in his written work. One master credited him with 'excellent qualities of originality and imagination' and with having 'a very sophisticated approach for his age.' But, he added, Jonathan had 'adopted numerous devices to avoid doing written work.'

When it came to making a decision about whether Jonathan should stay on at Sandford Park or take up the place which we had reserved for him at Newpark, we had discussions with some of the teachers at Sandford Park. I can recall one in particular after we had made the decision that he would leave. This was with Bill Tector, deputy headmaster and, incidentally, a former Ireland rugby international. He was disappointed but still supportive. He accepted that Jonathan had been unhappy at Sandford Park and believed that in all the circumstances he could not criticize our decision. He reckoned that Jonathan was a challenging pupil to teach but thought any school which had lost a pupil of his ability should not find fault with him but should question why the system was failing to accommodate him. I always remembered this conversation and paid special tribute to Bill Tector at Jonathan's funeral.

His closing months in Sandford Park had been happier. Eimer wrote to the headmaster, Ian Steepe, in May: 'On the positive side he has greatly enjoyed some aspects of Sandford Park many of them associated with Mr Collins' teaching and the special interest he has taken in Jonathan's reading; he was also delighted to be included in the school play.' And again in June she acknowledged that, Jonathan had gained a great deal from Sandford Park – possibly even benefiting from 'the need to cope' with some of the difficulties he had experienced.*

Another glimpse of Jonathan at that stage is provided by an exact contemporary, EMILE DALY. Now a barrister, she recalled sharing a French language course with him at the Alliance Française in Dublin.

> He was more assertive and talkative – in English, much to the annoyance of the teacher – than any of the rest of us were. He was utterly happy to interrupt the class with little comments and various observations – something that I, as an inhibited eleven year

*EPB to Ian Steepe, 16 May and 18 June 1981.

> old, found much too confident and bold. What I would like to say is that looking back on that class with an adult perspective, one thing about Jonathan becomes completely obvious to me – although it didn't occur to me at the time. It is this: that such confidence can only emanate from the rare Irish family experience where children are loved and listened to; and are treated as being people who feel invested in because they are worth being listened to. I suppose this explains how he could be as self-possessed as he was at age twelve.

That summer Jonathan was becoming more of an adolescent. ANNA ROWAN, who works as cabin crew with Aer Lingus, met him during that summer. She was to have further encounters with him when he flew with Aer Lingus. And she last met him in January 2000 in Jurys Hotel in Ballsbridge in Dublin: 'we'd a quick two-minute chat, very naturally in the nicest, warmest way. He was holding my hand as he was talking to me and it was not in a flirtatious way. It seemed to me that he just had a huge love for people.' She recalled their first meeting in Herbert Park when she was fifteen and Jonathan was twelve when he persuaded her and her friend to play a doubles game with himself and Emma, two strangers three years their junior.

> He was playing tennis with his sister; and my friend and I were waiting for a court to become free to play. Jonathan invited us to play tennis, which I was amazed at because it was very unusual for a boy at the age of twelve to confidently ask two strange girls of fifteen to join in a tennis game. We did play tennis.

Our third child, Abie, was born that summer on 28 July; this was also my birthday. Eimer recorded in her journal:

> I had made a cake before leaving at short notice for the hospital and Jonathan who had been looking forward immensely to the new baby became a little petulant and asked: 'Is there no cream for the cake?' He rallied, kissed my tummy and made a wish. He was hoping his new brother would be someone to play games with. John wished for someone interested in history. The next day at lunchtime he walked from home to Holles Street Maternity Hospital, negotiating his way past the porter carrying flowers and a book. When I congratulated him on managing to gain entry at a time when children were excluded he replied – clearly believing it possible – that some people may well have thought he was a father. I laughed so much that Abie fell off my breast.

In September 1981 Jonathan and Emma both started in their new school, Newpark Comprehensive in Blackrock, Co. Dublin. Jonathan started in second year, Emma in first. His parents listed his ambitions – presumably in consultation with him – as 'to design a game; to write and debate.' His hobbies were listed as magic, board games, and writing computer programmes. He was delighted to discover that the leader of a games club which he had regularly gate-crashed at Trinity College would be teaching French and German. The novelist JAMES RYAN teaches English and history at Newpark. He recalled the time when he first noted Jonathan's presence in the school. It was during the lunchtime break.

> Bouncing along, conspicuously alert, smiling, a second year student passes by. Following closely are four or five other second years, chanting.
>
> 'Jona-than-Phil-bin-Bow-man.'
>
> Over and over again, tauntingly, 'Jona-than-Phil-bin-Bow-man.'
>
> Thinking that this fast-striding, cherub-faced individual is being bullied, I, the teacher on 'patrol' duty, intervene.
>
> 'What's going on?'
>
> His eyes close momentarily, his chin tilts upwards.
>
> 'Oh, them. I wouldn't worry.'
>
> He reflects briefly on what he has said, then adds, 'It's just the price of notoriety.'
>
> Suddenly, his expression of bemused contempt gives way to laughter. Loud, hearty laughter. He strides on, the taunting posse in pursuit. Still chanting.
>
> 'Jona-than-Phil-bin-Bow-man.'

JILL BELL LACEY was a few years Jonathan's senior at Newpark. She recalls that he 'stood out' from the moment he entered Newpark. Everybody knew him.

> They may not have known him personally, but he was there, loud and clear. His strong voice was the main thing that struck me, intelligent and very precise for a young lad of his age – he was streets ahead of me and many of his schoolmates: always his own man with firm opinions. I personally remember one instance when he got into a little bit of trouble. I was a prefect on tuck shop duty, arm up against the doorframe, letting four or five pupils into the shop at a time. When along came Jonathan, running down the corridor, head down, and straight under my arm he went into the shop, much to the dismay of the other pupils who were patiently waiting their turn to enter. I caught hold of him and brought him,

his feet barely touching the floor, to the Vice-Principal's office. The poor chap, I laugh now when I think of it and I am sure he would too.

JOHN HARRIS was headmaster when Jonathan became a pupil. He recalled that while many pupils could easily go unnoticed in a school of some 800 pupils, there was 'no possibility' of this in Jonathan's case because of his 'highly exuberant nature'. He had proved a challenge to many teachers because he ignored many of the conventions which would normally be expected of pupils, 'even in a relatively liberal school' like Newpark.

> This posed problems for those who had to try to persuade him to conform. For example, he saw no need to join the end of the lunch queue and insisted on marching straight up to the top, despite the best efforts of prefects to outwit this manoeuvre. I myself was not at the school during the whole of Jonathan's time there as it coincided with a period when I was seconded to the Department of Education. Nonetheless, this did not prevent news of Jonathan reaching me. I think of the time when one class that he was attending became so frustrated by his inability to stop talking that someone put a wastepaper basket over his head which Jonathan made no attempt to remove. It will be clear that Jonathan was not the easiest of pupils to cope with. I suppose that this is hardly surprising given the kinds of opinions he was to express later about schools and schooling during his *Late Late* appearances. Nevertheless, no one could fail to be struck by his extraordinary intelligence and frenetic mind – not to mention his unavoidable charm.

Jonathan's early school reports echoed some, by now, familiar themes: whereas many teachers commented on the fact that he made 'his presence felt in a very positive way', they were also critical of his presentation which tended to be 'haphazard and untidy.' At the end of third year his form master concluded: 'Jonathan bubbles over in various enthusiasms – so much so his feet sometimes leave the ground. However gravity is still to be reckoned with and it is at this level that care and attention to duties must be made. We all have no doubt that he will improve.' JAMES RYAN recalled how Jonathan – if bored – could make his presence felt in the classroom. He described an episode which took place in English class.

> Sitting in the front desk, one moment intensely engaged, the next dramatically bored, Jonathan is by far the most predominant

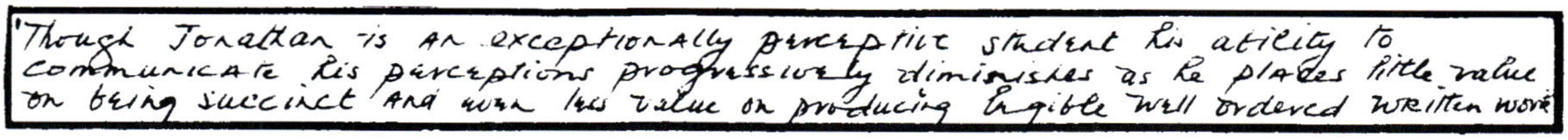
'Though Jonathan is an exceptionally perceptive student his ability to communicate his perceptions progressively diminishes as he places little value on being succinct and even less value on producing legible well ordered written work'.

James Ryan's contemporary assessment, end of Transition Year, summer 1984. Jonathan was fifteen.

presence in the room. Outside, it's drizzling. The neon light is flickering. Someone has written 'fuck' on the blackboard.

'One of the most interesting characters in *The Catcher in the Rye*', I begin, 'is Stradlater.'

Head resting on the palm of his splayed hand, Jonathan has his 'this-better-be-worth-listening-to' expression on.

'In many respects Stradlater is typical of his age group,' I continue, 'Let's look at some of his character traits. Anyone like to try identifying some of those traits?' I look around expectantly. No response.

Niamh takes pity. Raises her hand.

'Well, Niamh?'

Jonathan sighs.

'Stradlater wants to give the impression that he is tough.' Niamh speaks tentatively, casting around for reassurance.

Jonathan sighs again. This time very loudly.

'Jonathan, maybe you have something to say about Stradlater.'

'This is all so irrelevant. I mean, for God's sake. Look, here you are, here we are, going on about Stradlater. Why be so abstract? We have lots of Stradlaters here in this room. People who spend all their time in search of peer group approval.'

He swings around, points to a large, sleepy student in the back desk.

'Take Damien for example. This would all be much more relevant if Damien explained to the class why he wrote 'fuck' on the board. I mean, it's pure Stradlater.'

Damien, surfacing like a seal, tries to work out what's going on.

'That's really mean, picking on someone like that.' Niamh is indignant. Visibly angry.

'I'm not picking on someone like that…' Jonathan mimics her indignation. 'I'm just trying to make this relevant.'

'Bender,' Damien calls out, prompting a chorus of guffaws.

'Brilliant.' Jonathan stands up, triumphant. 'Brilliant, choice Stradlater behaviour.' He laughs uproariously.

'Sit down, Jonathan.' I speak quietly, turn to the class, very keen to move on. 'Open your books on page…let me see…page…'

Jonathan is smirking, waiting for me to get less flustered, waiting until he is sure I will not blow my top when he says 'It got a bit too relevant for you.'

I spend the rest of the class making sure that moment will not come.

Jonathan was, by now, becoming very interested in politics. He was a considerable help to me in carrying out research for the election results programmes in the three general elections of 1981-82. This was also the period when I was revising my thesis on de Valera's Ulster policy for publication as a book. Jonathan and Emma were both recruited to help with the challenge of preparing the index. Eimer recorded how one night I fell asleep downstairs after dinner.

> Jonathan referred to it as 'a severe case of indexitis'. Both he and Emma did take-offs of John's foibles until finally we woke him and made him laugh. When I said to Jonathan, 'Poor Dada; we're mocking him a lot.' He replied: 'Yes but he needs it; we need to keep him in touch with fantasy and protect him from over-exposure to reality.' And as I was thinking what a good comment this was, he added: 'Actually that's it in a nutshell, isn't it? I'll have to take him aside for a son to father talk!'

ROD ELEY recalled Jonathan as a very talkative young boy at this time when he was beginning to venture into the city alone to pursue some of his own interests.

> Jonathan several times called in to talk to me at the office I had in Liffey Street when he was making regular visits to Amnesty International, which had their office just down the hall; this was about 1981-82. Aged twelve/thirteen, Jonathan was typical of all young people of that age in any generation – full of curiosity about life and feelings for others, hopeful and open-minded and unprejudiced, eager to get to grips with the world and its problems.

GERRY GREGG, the television producer, who invited Jonathan as a schoolboy to participate in some children's programmes, wrote:

> As a young teenager I noticed he was brave as well as clever, deep as well as sharp, committed in his own inimitable way to making the world a better place.

During Transition Year Jonathan took two job placements, both chosen with care to reflect his interests: in a computer shop and in the offices of the Campaign for Nuclear Disarmament. He completed the first assignment with a sale or two to his credit, a presentation box of chocolates and a congratulatory letter to his form master. MAEVE WATSON recalled the impression he made during his second work experience project when he worked at the Irish branch of CND.

> To be perfectly honest he drove me mad in the beginning, then I got to know and really like him. He was so clever, witty, honest,

charming. He came to visit my boyfriend and me several times in our flat in Leeson Park where we had long discussions into the night.

Maeve Watson's boyfriend at that time, BRUCE CLARK, remembered Jonathan 'with great fondness' as, he thought, many did.

> I think we gave him some ghastly filing job that week he spent doing work experience in CND and, after a few days, he had the sense to tell us how boring and pointless the job was and where to stick it! He had this amazing mix of unworldly innocence and brilliant insight – and cutting humour of course.

Jonathan somehow managed to gain access to the earliest 'trade only' computer shows, despite their policy of considering school pupils as pests – all questions and no money. This was one of his trophies, a self-portrait with an early digital camera.

In arranging the CND job, Jonathan had sought the help of PATRICK COMERFORD who had given a talk at Newpark School on the political lobbying by the group. Patrick could recall an occasion when he was walking up the stairs to the CND offices in Liffey Street when he heard 'what I thought was my own voice'. It was Jonathan 'doing a complete mimic of the talk I had given in his school, accent finely tuned and talk word for word as if he had learned it off by heart – although I never had a script before me.' Patrick Comerford added:

> I know his father will think JPB followed his footsteps to become a journalist. But I also take some of the blame. He told me at Newpark, again in the CND offices in Liffey Street, and on many occasions later, that he wanted to leave school early and work as a journalist; and he held me up as an example because I was able to work and campaign at the same time. I found this embarrassing because I tried and failed to persuade him to stay on at school. I could see he was bright, and thought he would benefit by finishing school and going on to college. Anytime we would cross paths in the lobby or lift of *The Irish Times* or in Grafton Street, he would give a smirking smile and remind me that he blamed me for his decision to pursue a career in journalism.

Jonathan's school reports still reflected the same themes: promising, intelligent, but failing to do justice to his ability in his presentation of written work. Where a subject interested him there was engagement. One teacher noted a special project on twentieth century architecture: 'An active participant. He did not do a complete analysis of the work of Le Corbusier or Mies van der Rohe – but nearly. I hope Jonathan gained something from the course.' OWEN METCALFE, his form teacher, concluded at Christmas 1984:

> In the form group I have rarely seen anybody antagonize the rest of the group to the extent he did and survive; not only survive but continue fighting. I admire his courage and also his perception but I would like to see him become more sensitive towards others in group situations. I feel sure he will claim he has improved in this respect but I see room for further improvement. A very interesting student.

And at the end of Transition Year, Owen Metcalfe complained that Jonathan had 'a tendency to irritate others towards deafness', noting his ability to quickly antagonize other class members.

> His views are shrewd, often exceptionally well-thought out, and oral presentation of these ideas is fascinating for those who can keep up with him. He shows great courage in continuing to speak forth, despite at times enormous resistance. I think he is trying to listen more to others, slow down and be at least tolerant of other views. There is a long way to go before there is a tolerable acceptance of him by others, or others by him. He is a most interesting and stimulating member of this form and year group.

The curriculum at Newpark was somewhat experimental. The school had substituted the Group Certificate for the Intermediate Certificate and, being co-educational, encouraged all pupils to take cookery and home economics. ETHNA KENNY, at that time an examiner with the Department of Education, recalled Jonathan when he did his Group Certificate practicals at Newpark. She was the departmental examiner for sixty students there.

> On that particular sunny morning my exam students entered in single file, among them Jonathan, six to eight students for practicals. In the cookery room he worked at his table directly in front of me. I watched with much interest – he was so capable, confident in his work method and at the end of two-and-a-half hours he presented his menu, beautifully cooked, garnished to the last. Every utensil he used was washed, scrubbed and presented for inspection. In the needlework room he drew the most difficult test of the day. Nothing daunted, he sat at his Bernina sewing machine – the new ultra up-market machine to replace the old Singer machine of my youth. He pedalled away like a veteran and at the end of two hours handed up a most perfect specimen. Two incidents come to mind; and hopefully you will smile when you read that Jonathan put this examiner in her box and rightly so – no offence given and none taken. All students had been asked well in advance to bring in their exam requirements from their homes: Jonathan's was an already washed tablecloth which he had to iron.

He duly set about his cloth, damping down, rolling up, heating iron and so on. In passing on my walk around, I said: 'Jonathan, be very careful with that cloth, it is valuable and hand-embroidered.' His answer was: 'Oh we use these all the time at home for supper!' [*This was far-fetched. Jonathan knew enough to bring what looked to him like the best tablecloth: but could not differentiate it from those in daily use.*] Finally on my last day of twelve at Newpark, Jonathan was waiting for me all alone in the corridor, sad-looking. He said: 'May I speak to you? If you thought I was rude or unruly in the classroom I did not mean to be. I apologise. Students who worked with me felt I was "showing off" and that you did not like it.' We parted good friends and I wished him well in his future career.

'Jonathan was an important part of my education and growing up. He introduced me to ideas, films and music.'– Laura Mays

LAURA MAYS, an architecture graduate and furniture designer, was a contemporary of Jonathan at Newpark. She wrote that even before she met him, as a new girl arriving at the school in fourth year she had heard about him. He was 'famous, notorious even' and known by all from first to sixth years.

I had started in the fourth year in Newpark, adolescent, shy, unsure of myself; and there was Jonathan, a fully formed individual, confident, able to talk with adults as equals, and complete with rapid-fire wit, a mop of curly hair and idiosyncratic handwriting. I had never encountered anyone like him and at first was daunted. His ability to engage in a rollercoaster debate with anyone about anything was frankly intimidating, but I soon discovered the warmth and engagement with people and ideas that lay behind the repartee.

Jonathan was an important part of my education and growing up. He was the first feminist, pacifist and unashamedly anti-sports boy I'd ever met. He introduced me to ideas and films and music – Dud and Pete, Dory Previn, Louden Wainwright III and early Bob Dylan. The first time I ever heard Louden Wainwright was Jonathan playing 'The Swimming Song' down the phone from his cassette player. And I remember sitting in St Stephen's Green, and Jonathan had a hand-held, battery-operated record player (this was in pre-Walkman days) with a pair of big old-fashioned headphones, and he played a Dory Previn record – the song: 'Did Jesus have a sister?' – and we took it in turns with the headphones.

I was only dimly aware of Jonathan's courageous attempts to leave school. It seemed to me he was already better informed and educated than anyone else and school was severely cramping his style. He left during fifth year and his absorption and rapid success in the wide world of journalism and the public arena meant that

> we lost touch. I was partly ashamed of my cowardly attachment to conventional education. I deeply regret not having maintained contact with Jonathan over the years but look back on our period of friendship with profound gratitude, affection and warmth. He was one of the most brilliant and unusual people I've ever met. He burnt brighter, and perhaps, sadly, that meant quicker.

Jonathan's interest in debating was enhanced by a chance opportunity to participate in a record-breaking attempt by the UCD Law Society for the longest continuous debate in the *Guinness Book of Records*. He was fifteen at the time and it was organized during Rag Week at UCD in 1984. The aim was to beat a 100-hour record then held by St Andrew's University in Scotland. The motion was: 'That this house would adjourn' and speakers were free to comment on anything from 'the state of the nation to the price of the pint to the morality of nuclear weapons or the lifestyle of Tibetan monks.'

I can recall how Jonathan's participation came about. I received a telephone call as one of a number of celebrity debaters invited to filibuster on any topic since it was necessary to debate around the clock for almost five days to surpass the existing record. Wishing them well, I declined, citing pressure of work, when Jonathan, who was in the room with me and who had picked up the general gist of what it was about, whispered to me: 'Tell them I'd love to do it.' Following this prompt, I said that I had a fifteen-year-old son who was a school debater and would like to participate. The society's secretary welcomed this offer with a promise that because of his age she would ensure that a special 'no heckling' rule would apply during his contribution. To this Jonathan protested: 'No. It's because I want the challenge of the hecklers that I'm volunteering. The more the better.' And that was how it was. I remember distinctly thinking that participating in such an event might kindle Jonathan's flagging enthusiasm for the education system. His parents always thought he would prosper under the more challenging and informal atmosphere of university. In the event, Jonathan hugely enjoyed the Law Society debate. Having said I was too busy to participate, I was in no position to drop in to hear him but, from all accounts, he performed well. The *Irish Independent* reported that the

> ...star debater of the week turned out to be 15-year-old Jonathan Philbin Bowman, a student of Newpark Comprehensive School, Blackrock, who took the debate by storm last Wednesday. Young

> Jonathan was present again last night [as the new record was established] to entertain the audience with regular witty comments on the speakers.

While Jonathan was still at school, he was keen to avail of any opportunities to work in journalism or broadcasting. He sometimes reviewed books for children and occasionally participated in radio or television programmes aimed at younger viewers. When he was keen to interview some individual, he might approach the editor of a school or student publication to promise them the interview. The art collector PATRICK J. MURPHY, chairman of the Arts Council, was chair of the ROSC exhibition in 1984.

> I first met Jonathan when he came to interview me about the conversion of the Guinness Hop Store and the holding of the ROSC international art exhibition there in 1984. He had telephoned my home to make an appointment. He was still a schoolboy of fifteen years and I will never forget his enthusiasm and his precociousness. He brought with him a little tape-recorder and he asked the most incisive and relevant questions about the building, the selection of the artists and the artistic concerns at that time. He was still relatively small of stature, with a striking head of curly hair and eyes that were full of animation. I felt sure that he would become a major broadcasting figure in a short time.

Jonathan was interested in the changes then transforming information technology. When reprographic colour copying was still in its infancy, he was keen to make use of it for a school project. This was why he called in on GREG MILLER, who ran the Colour Copy Centre in Dublin.

> I was sitting in my office in Fitzwilliam Square in 1985, when I first met the young man with scruffy hair who wanted a colour copy for a school project. What would normally take five minutes did in fact take five hours. I will never forget that Friday afternoon. It was one of the most memorable days I can recall, talking to a complete stranger, who was funny, friendly, and very intelligent.

As he was departing from Newpark School one day, JAMES RYAN was asked by Jonathan if he would oblige him by giving him a lift home. Jonathan – as the following account testifies – wanted more than the lift. In the context of his family's ongoing discussions with the school about his expressed desire to abandon secondary education, all parties had agreed that it might be helpful to have an assessment by Dr Helen Haughton, the educational psychologist. James Ryan recalled the car journey.

My route home from school involved passing quite close to where Jonathan lived. Very occasionally he asked for a lift.

'OK. Hop in. Just as far as the end of Appian Way.'

'It's not exactly what you would call an emergency', he begins. He was in fifth year at the time, frantic to take on the world. Determined to make his career at school unworkable.

'You', he continues emphatically, 'may not regard it as an emergency. In fact you may share my parents' view: you may see this as a necessity.'

'See what as necessity?'

Jonathan adjusts the seat belt, readjusts it, examines it.

He then checks the ashtray. Opens the glove compartment, takes out a tape, puts it back in.

'Aren't you finding my behaviour obsessive?' he asks, his inimitable humour percolating just below the surface.

'Very obsessive.'

'Good.' He takes out the tape. Reads the title. Nursery Rhymes. Puts it back in. Opens the ashtray. Adjusts his seat belt yet again.

'Jonathan, what's going on?' I ask, voice heavy with fatigue.

'I'm practising.' He twists his head maniacally. Rolls his eyes.

'Practising for what?'

'I have an appointment. In approximately twenty minutes I will be stretched out on a couch, telling my problems to a psychologist. My parents are insisting.' He wrings his hands. Inhales loudly through his nostrils. Exhales, equally loudly. Throws his head back.

'Why do you need to practise?' I ask, after a moment or two.

'Because I have no problems.' He laughs uproariously.

I laugh too.

Laugh whenever I think about his animated, iconoclastic response to things, his warmth.

Jonathan managed to leave school halfway through the Leaving Cert cycle, ruling out a further five or six years of study which might well have led to high-powered academic qualifications, but which would – more significantly – have delayed his entry into the world at large. A world about which he cared passionately. As it turned out, he could ill afford such delays. Time was not on his side.

I lamented his decision to leave school, but since his death I have come to admire the intuition which led him to do so.

DR HELEN HAUGHTON was the educational psychologist with whom Jonathan had the appointment when he travelled home from school with James Ryan. She wrote:

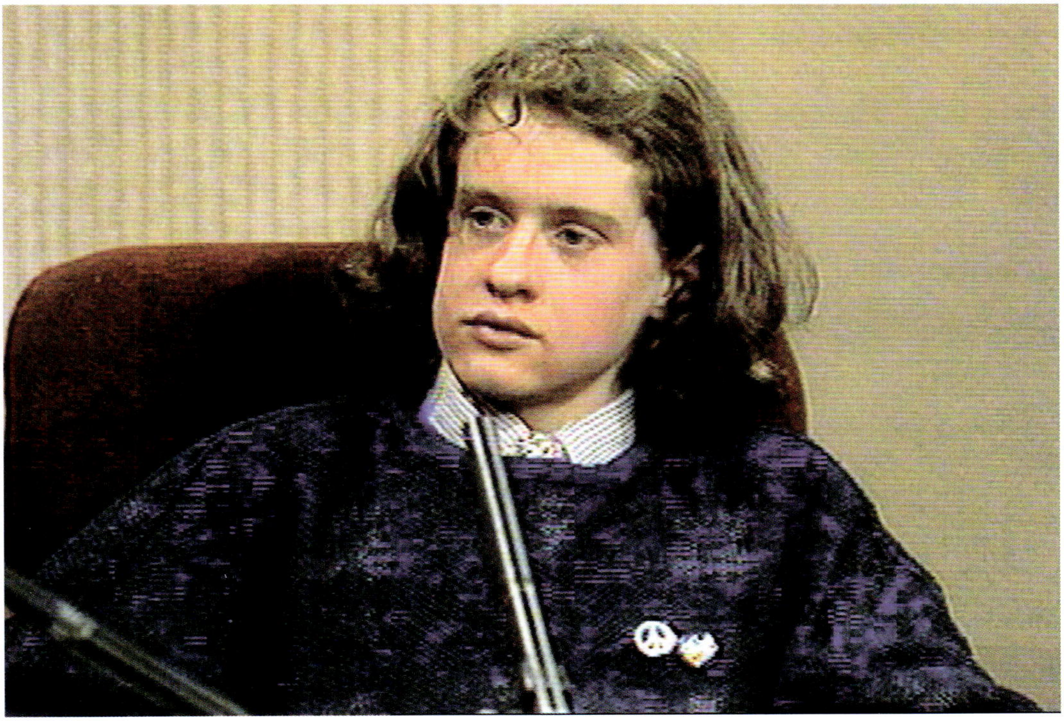

Jonathan shortly after he left school. Note the CND badge.

I knew Jonathan for a while when he was going through his mid-teen crisis – 'to school' or 'not to school'. He talked earnestly about this, and in the end, 'not to school' won, in spite of parental misgivings. Jonathan was a bright boy, and found standard school teaching the lowest common denominator, and certainly not for him. He was sure he could manage without Leaving Certificate, and his later life proved it. Like many of that age-group, Jonathan was in a hurry, felt he was adult, and could challenge the big world using initiative, inspiration and family support. Who can deny he was right? It takes a rare teenager to cut through the conventions of education, and see and grasp the wider scene – which is what Jonathan did.

DEREK WEST was one of Jonathan's teachers at Newpark and is now headmaster there. From the time he had heard of Jonathan's 'senseless, tragic death' he had 'felt drawn to his life', like so many others.

It would be phony of Newpark to lay claim to Jonathan. He left school and grasped the life beyond the classroom. I believe him when he said he learned far more beyond the school walls. We

(FOLLOWING PAGE)
Breton holiday, 1983. Jonathan sometimes complained of 'another boring adventure – window-shopping in Quimper'.

failed him. The system failed him – it just could not accommodate his mercurial thinking or his intolerance of the humdrum. This capacity to challenge us, even though he is no longer here, is extraordinary. His capacity to exasperate was also prodigious – I must confess he was the last pupil I ever struck (in sheer frustration and anger – my only defence). But, in the printed and spoken tributes, it's his vitality, the exuberance of his expression, his rampant iconoclasm which are singled out. I deeply regret that we were not able to tap adequately into that free spirit, that school was not able to either enhance or give structure to his soaring, speeding thought processes.

Today in education, we have learned to label all kinds of syndromes and to talk of special needs and educational disability. We have names for everything but we still rarely find the imagination to address the true individual, the free spirit, the lateral thinker, and the revolutionary. Jonathan had the potential to be all those things. I watched his progress from afar, not assiduously, and I gathered that he had become a competent print man, able to fill the columns with provocative ease. I am sure there was more to come.

MICHAEL CLASSON was headmaster at Newpark in Jonathan's final years there. It was with him that Eimer and I – and sometimes Jonathan – had the discussions about his desire to leave school.

> I remember so well the many meetings we had in that small office in Newpark and indeed the conflicting emotions which we experienced. I want to let you know how much I admired Jonathan as a pupil. He knew – I think – that despite all the nonsense that I had to appear to believe in, I felt that he was right to try to do his own thing, even if conflict were provoked. More and more I had been enjoying his work – particularly in the way he could empathize with those whose thoughts and perhaps lifestyles were not considered to be usual or conventional. I shall always remember Jonathan and I am glad that I had the chance to share in his most positive beliefs – it seems indeed a sad reality that 'those whom the gods love' do die young.

The summer before his decision to abandon formal education, Jonathan was in protest mode on our family holiday in Benodet in Brittany. Staying in an apartment overlooking the sea, which he had known and loved from childhood, he refused to go out of doors, proclaiming himself 'bored with the beach'. Eimer recorded the holiday in her journal.

> When the opportunity arose for us to stay on an extra week he

Sunday Independent
Sunday, September 6, 1998

sunday life

Breton beach memoirs

French Log

Jonathan Philbin Bowman

It was 1998, fourteen years later, before Jonathan returned to Benodet to experience it through Saul's ten-year-old eyes. He had obligations that week to write for the *Sunday Independent* (6 September 1998) and decided to contribute a diary of life at a French seaside resort. This was his first diary log. It became such a popular feature that he continued writing it until his death.

> revolted leaving us all miserable. A compromise was reached when John phoned a friend, Paul Brennan in Paris, who had a son of the same age and who agreed that Jonathan could stay a couple of days; we put him on the overnight train and he returned exhausted but content – just sixty hours later – a new person.

When we returned from this holiday he was in very good form and seemed to settle down to work in fifth year. However his Christmas report was not encouraging and his reaction to it was quite subdued. The following term was difficult and he was increasingly reluctant to get up for school each morning. At Easter 1985, he declined to join us for a week in Chamonix, preferring to go on the CND peace march in Aldermaston. Eimer's journal records:

> When we came back from a week away at Easter Jonathan announced to us that he had made the decision to leave school. He was adamant about this and refused our offer of support for whatever he would like to do over the following summer. He

> wanted to be self-supporting and even offered to pay us rent from the start of July! We thought he might take off and see a bit of the world for the summer but instead he burrowed in and took soundings, gradually extending his photographic entrepreneurship to *Image, Social and Personal* and individual commissions. He was immediately happier; there was a gradual decline of incidents and an increase in calm.

When Jonathan left school, he set about earning his living as a photographer, journalist, broadcaster and communications consultant. Initially he won some commissions as a photographer. The painter PATRICK SCOTT wrote:

> I recall the first time I met Jonathan. It was at the opening of Stephen Pearce's shop in Naas. He was disguised as a very young press photographer. I asked him what magazine he was working for, and he said he was 'freelance'. I didn't have to ask him his name. He had enough Bowman genes to make that superfluous. We got talking and I said I admired people who were in a hurry to get out into the grown-up world. He said: 'Would you ever mention that to my parents?'

The art critic DOROTHY WALKER, married to the architect, the late Robin Walker, also met Jonathan at this time.

> I first met Jonathan when he was sixteen and had decided that life could teach him more than school could; so he had left and taken up photography. He started off by taking photographs of people at art openings. It so happened that I needed a photograph for some publication, so I commissioned him to take my portrait. The photographs were a disaster but that was nothing new: I am a photogenic disaster. The company, however, was great, and I became devoted to the Great Bratsby, as we called him. No matter how drab the occasion, the irrepressible Jonathan was always good for a malicious giggle, and so one was always glad to see him. I miss him.

Jonathan always delighted in Abie's company and made him the subject of many photographic sessions. He had one of these photographs made into a lapel badge similar to the campaign buttons used in American elections. ANNE O'DONNELL, the feminist and political activist, wrote:

> I first got to know him when he was sixteen and I was working at the Rape Crisis Centre. He used to follow me around and tell me his views on the world and how useless was schooling and formal education. I was always very fond of him – at that time he used to

wear a little badge with a photo of his younger brother Abie on it: the 'only pure person in the world' is how he described Abie. It is as if he was destined to be a young father himself.

Anne O'Donnell recalled Jonathan's button badge featuring his photograph of Abie – 'the only pure person in the world'

The broadcaster and writer MYLES DUNGAN first came across Jonathan when he had gate-crashed the Dublin Film Festival by managing to buy a membership card although he was two years below the eighteen year age-limit. The age limit was especially important as it was a condition of the Festival's privileged status vis-à-vis the film censor. They were exempt from his scrutiny provided all those attending the cinema were adults and had paid an extra pound to become members of the Dublin Film Festival Society. Myles was one of the small committee which ran the festival.

One afternoon, towards the middle of the Festival, I was approached in the lobby of the Screen by one of the legion of volunteers whom we were shamelessly exploiting at the time. He had a problem: a complaint from a gentleman who had given his name as Jonathan Philbin Bowman. I assumed as pompous an air as I could manage and approached the source of the difficulty. I don't remember what the nature of the complaint was but it was articulated in ringing tones and with the sort of acerbic wit which you don't appreciate when you are hassled – and probably in the wrong. I argued back. He argued forward. We clearly differed. We didn't agree to differ. Then, inspired by a vague idea of what age my RTE colleague John Bowman's eldest son might be I asked: 'What age are you?' 'Sixteen' came the proud reply ('and well able for you at any age, matey' – was the subtext). 'Oh really,' I replied. 'Well in that case you are not entitled to a membership card, so therefore your complaint is irrelevant. Furthermore, I shall have to ask you to return your membership card forthwith!'

Jonathan, being Jonathan, absolutely refused to hand over his card and railed against any society which would not permit sixteen year olds in its ranks. He may even have pointed out that, though he was old enough to die for his country, he wasn't old enough to attend movies at the Dublin Film Festival. Pshaw!

I clucked. I sympathised. But I was firm. He'd have to hand it over and leave. But he wasn't going to do either, was he? He was going to sit-in in protest until something was done. So he sat. And sat. At around this time I started to sweat. We'd already been visited by uniformed detectives from Pearse Street on foot of a complaint about showing uncensored films and had explained to them that as an over-eighteen's Cclub we were not obliged to submit films for censorship. They had been very polite and said they would check it out and come back later. They were due back now and I had a bolshie, recalcitrant sixteen year old in the lobby who had been issued with a membership card and whose fertile young mind had already been exposed to who knew what depravity! I tried appealing to Jonathan's sense of fair play but he felt unable to help me.

The dock of the Central Criminal Court beckoned. Then, in a stroke of rare genius, I decided to anticipate the return of the Gardaí. I contacted them and told them about my little 'situation'. They arrived and spoke to the one-man protest – who was beginning to draw a crowd at this point. The result was much shrugging and sympathetic clucking. They acknowledged that I had a problem, but the bottom line was that it was my problem, not theirs.

Eventually I resorted to the last refuge of the scoundrel and phoned his Dad. Reluctantly Jonathan agreed to talk to him. He made a very good fist of arguing with his father and insisting on standing on his rights. When the conversation ended he was still *in situ* but clearly that incisive Bowmanesque logic (or perhaps just the brow-beating tactics of the habitual interviewer) had had their effect. He saved face by announcing that, in order not to jeopardise the future of the Dublin Film Festival or to give aid and succour to the Moral Mullahs, he was calling off his protest. Head aloft and dignity intact, he left the building.

Bank manager PAT MORGAN, who worked in the local branch of the Bank of Ireland in Ballsbridge, had been our family bank manager for some years. Shortly after he had left school I recall advising Jonathan to make an appointment to see him. Jonathan was still living at home and was being supported to that extent; but he was determined in all other respects to be financially independent. PAT MORGAN wrote:

Sometime in 1985 you called to the bank and told me that your eldest son had left school and that you felt little doubt that he was ready to make his way in the world and would do so. Having five children of my own, the eldest then in fourth year, I admired your certainty and courage in allowing him forge his own way. You mentioned that he would likely call for a loan to get his career started, that he had a number of tentative contracts and that a personal computer would be a necessary facility for his work. If I recall rightly you said you would go guarantor and may even have signed a letter of guarantee, but that Jonathan was not to know of this support.

I have tried to recall my first meeting with him. A slight,

> somewhat awkward, curly-haired young man, determined and sharp, sat in that small office on the ground floor of the old bank office which overlooked Pembroke Road. He sat with his legs crossed, at first lightly bent forward, probably slightly nervous but also I suspect wondering why the dickens he had to go through this rigmarole to get a few bob to which he felt absolutely entitled. I liked, at personal lending interviews, to find out about the individual, as experience had taught me that often the amount of money required and payback had more to do with personality than with the viability of the proposition. I was amazed at the breadth and depth of his reading and I recall that more time was taken up with a conversation on the style and clarity of the *Economist* than any other single item! That one so young would be aware of the magazine, its contents and editorial views I found surprising and that he might emulate the said style and clarity in his work I found agreeable and I immediately liked him. The couple of years that followed were either a feast or a famine, the largest beneficiary of his chequebook in those early days was Waterstone's, and sometimes when the cheques were presented to the bank the well was empty and the tide far out. I would have had a number of telephone conversations with him – all cordial and friendly. I resisted talking to you about his account though because you were guarantor I suppose I could have done so.

Business card, aged sixteen

Jonathan was eighteen when he made the broadcast which brought him to national attention in Ireland. For any readers of this book who are unfamiliar with Irish society in the 1980s, it should be emphasized that the popularity of RTE's *Late Late Show* at that period was phenomenal. It enjoyed an audience of close to one million, and often set the agenda for what the nation would be discussing in the weeks that followed. Jonathan was already two years out of school and had been busy working first as a freelance photographer, then as a journalist and broadcaster. I recall that he had various business cards printed at the time, in one of which he described himself as a communications consultant. He had become something of a figure around Dublin and this may have been the genesis of the invitation to appear on the programme. He told his parents about it only some hours before the broadcast. At that stage we were still hoping that he might reconsider his decision to drop out of formal education and reckoned that his decision to defend it so publicly probably meant that it was irrevocable.

What follows is RICHARD OAKLEY's account of this broadcast, as published in the *Sunday Tribune* in March 2000.

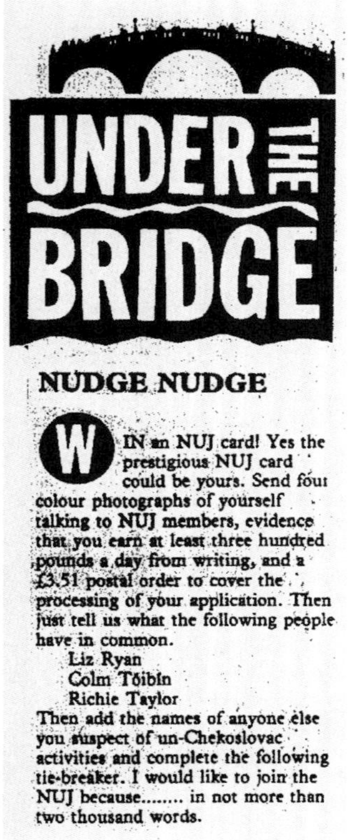
UNDER THE BRIDGE

NUDGE NUDGE

WIN an NUJ card! Yes the prestigious NUJ card could be yours. Send four colour photographs of yourself talking to NUJ members, evidence that you earn at least three hundred pounds a day from writing, and a £3.51 postal order to cover the processing of your application. Then just tell us what the following people have in common.

Liz Ryan
Colm Tóibín
Richie Taylor

Then add the names of anyone else you suspect of un-Chekoslovac activities and complete the following tie-breaker. I would like to join the NUJ because........ in not more than two thousand words.

Jonathan's mocking revenge in *In Dublin* to what he called the NUJ's 'Catch 22': you can't join the union unless you're earning a living as a journalist; and you can't do that without an NUJ card. *In Dublin*, 17 March 1988.

When Jonathan Philbin Bowman appeared in front of the nation on the *Late Late Show* in October 1987, aged eighteen, he started nearly every sentence with the words 'I think' and spoke at length on any subject he was asked about. He wore a navy suit, a blue and white striped shirt and a multi-coloured dickie bow. His hair was shoulder length and he was fresh-faced. Gay Byrne said he looked like Oscar Wilde. When introducing him, Byrne mentioned the fact that he had left formal education at the age of sixteen. He explained he was just eighteen now but said he had already developed the gift of the gab. He quoted Jonathan as saying that 'the government should pay him to just sit around and entertain people' and he told the audience and viewers that this 'young man' was making a name for himself as a social commentator.

As a tribute to the extraordinary character Jonathan Philbin Bowman was, the *Sunday Tribune* has decided, in the week following his death at just thirty-one, to print some of the interview that followed. It was for most people the first exposure they had to Bowman and probably is now the one they most remember.

GB: Now the first question which occurs is why did you leave school at sixteen?

JPB: I gave up school at sixteen because I was getting bored with it. For some people it can be good fun and for some it can be very boring. It can get to be a great limitation. In school, you have over 800 people there at any one time. It has to be very organized and has to be a certain way. I don't know if that works for individuals. I didn't like it. I don't like being told what to do very much.

GB : Surely though, Jonathan, you learn something in school?

JPB: Yes you do, but I think a lot of the things you learn in school are maybe things we shouldn't be teaching people. You learn to automatically respect people who are older than you: to respect authority; to get in on time; to fill in forms if you're not; not to break rules; and to do exactly what you are told to do. I don't think these are necessarily a good thing for people to be learning.

GB : Would you not have liked to go on to university?

JPB: I think university would be fun but I don't know that it has anything to offer that I don't sort of have already. I could get a degree, maybe, if I finished.

GB : The magic piece of paper.

JPB: Yes, but I don't think it is very magic. I don't think it is necessary and I think you meet a lot of people with degrees who are complete idiots.

10 NEWS FEATURES

The first flowering of JPB

Richard Oakley on when we first saw Jonathan, on the *Late, Late Show*

Sunday Tribune, 12 March 2000.

GB : I suppose you are experiencing that in a small society like Dublin, Ireland, anybody unusual is going to be picked on for jesting and joking and so on.

JPB: Of course. You get picked on and there is jesting and jostling but I think that is fun and I don't mind a bit of that. If people shout at me and find that funny, then that is fine. I like to make people laugh.

At this stage in the interview four phone calls from viewers were taken. Just one of them was in support of Jonathan. It was from a woman who hung up immediately after saying that she thought he was a breath of fresh air.

The following are just snippets from two of the other calls he received and the replies he gave.

The first caller complained that Jonathan was a bad example for her son who was repeating the Leaving Certificate. She said that if her son took Jonathan's advice, he would end up a bum.

CALLER: I think he is off-putting and very arrogant. I mean there is self-confidence and there is self-confidence, but I think there are some people who shove it down people's necks and he'd give me a pain to be quite honest.

GB : Could I just say with no disrespect that some of what you have said is complete nonsense? Your son doesn't have to complete his Leaving Certificate; there is a terrible assumption that he has to and there is a lot of pressure on him to do it, but if he does, it does not necessarily mean he will get a job.

Another caller asked Jonathan if he considered himself a yuppie.

JPB : I'm not a yuppie. I think the word yuppie was coined by marketeers in America to describe a certain market. They voted Reagan, they care only about themselves and money. If I was a yuppie, I would be in London now selling pieces of paper for other pieces of paper and making piles of money. I'm not interested in that, though. I am interested in writing and having fun and being active. I may be young, upwardly mobile and vaguely professional, but I am not a yuppie.

Gay Byrne, in response to the tone of some of the calls he took, told listeners and viewers that Bowman was just a guest like any other and was entitled to his opinion. He then told Jonathan, whom he was obviously impressed with, that he was doing great: 'Hang in there, kid.'

Defending his decision to leave formal education, *Late Late Show*, RTE, 2 October 1987.

Then just before the end of the interview Gay Byrne asked a question that, for the first time that night, made Jonathan Philbin Bowman really stop and think.

GB: How do you see yourself as a grand old man? Do you see yourself in journalism then or how do you picture yourself in forty years?

JPB: Wow – forty years is amazing. God I'll be old. I don't know what I'll be doing really.

GB: At eighteen who thinks of being fifty-eight?

Sunday Tribune, 12 March 2000

This broadcast on the *Late Late Show* proved controversial. Not surprisingly, RTE received many complaints from parents of students who were not as motivated concerning their career preferences as was Jonathan. The line this criticism took was: 'It's alright for him with his advantages but my child will need to respect the examination system.' I can recall arguments with Jonathan in which I sympathized with such parents. Jonathan – to me – often seemed unaware that whereas he, with his motivation and abilities, could brook the system, this was not necessarily true for others.

When Jonathan died we received a number of letters from individuals who were his exact contemporaries and who recalled this *Late Late* broadcast which they had seen when preparing for their own examinations. JOHN DARCY recalled Jonathan's 'cheeky and provocative' performance. 'He made a big impact that day on his peers – my entourage begrudged him his self-confidence, his "arrogance". Few people warm to Icarus.'

COLIN FOX had the same response and wrote to the *Sunday Independent*:*

> Arrogant little upstart, I thought. How sobering to hear that interview replayed in tribute on the radio last week. I sat in my car and listened intently to his every word and thought 'Bang on the money.' It was a lesson in life to realize that some thirteen years after it was first broadcast, I had developed my horizons broadly enough to hear what Jonathan was saying and not to colour my thinking by hearing with my eyes as before. I hope to learn from that.

SR. ELIZABETH MAXWELL, secretary general of the Conference of Religious of Ireland, was working in education when Jonathan made his criticism of the system.

> As a former teacher, I remember the heroic defiance of the examination system which is such a source of stress to teenagers and wondered how you, his parents, would cope with his stance. I followed his career and, in more recent times, I enjoyed his column in the *Sunday Independent* each week – such was his wit and verve and self-deprecating tone.

Another letter received was from Major General [retired] J.J.BARRY who had met me in the *Today Tonight* studios at RTE some weeks after Jonathan's controversial broadcast.

> Some begrudgers looked upon him as being precocious and arrogant. I congratulated you on being the father of such a brilliant young son, charismatic, manly and highly intelligent, and I was certain he would go places. I think you were astonished that I, an old soldier from another age, should speak so highly of one so

* *Sunday Independent*, 19 March 2000

Independent
WEEKENDER

What I was about to say before I was interrupted

Jonathan Philbin Bowman interviews Jonathan Philbin Bowman on those important questions in life, few of which were asked on the Late, Late

People don't need to go to school to get themselves a job

This country is pretty intolerant on whole ranges of sexuality . . .

We should tell the World Bank to get lost

I don't blame people who have emigrated

After the *Late Late Show* controversy, Jim Farrelly invited him to contribute this article to the *Irish Independent*, 10 October 1987

This portrait was taken on O'Connell Bridge to accompany the *Irish Independent* article

> young. I am glad I did but alas he is gone now and I'm shocked and saddened, even though I never met him. The vision of his sparkling eyes and lovely mischievous smile will always be with you.

Many of those who were to be friends and colleagues of Jonathan in later years first noticed him on this *Late Late Show* broadcast. FRANK CALLANAN, barrister and historian, recalled the impact which Jonathan had made on the *Late Late Show*:

> He commended to the nation his own example of not staying at school. The audience exploded in fury. Parents and school students alike howled abuse at Jonathan for daring to write down the value of their educational assets. Gay Byrne was taken aback, unprepared for the gale of rage that pinned Jonathan to the back of his seat. Fred Murphy – the Baggot Street newsagent and a member of the

audience that night – strove gamely to come to Jonathan's rescue. It was a baptism in fireworks, a spectacular and frightening initiation of a career as a controversialist. If one was to devise a crest of arms for Jonathan, the motto might be: even when wrong don't admit defeat but expedite escape by devising next attack.

Wine and food writer TOM DOORLY had noticed Jonathan in journalistic circles in Dublin before his appearance on the *Late Late Show*: 'long-haired, flamboyant, loud and always, without fail, accompanied by a different girl. The girl would always be very attractive and the venue, with equal regularity, would be one of the handful of cafés with pretensions to cappuccino production that Dublin could boast in those days.' Tom was then a features writer in the *Irish Independent* and Jonathan 'would occasionally float in and treat my then editor, Jim Farrelly, with a lack of deference' which Tom Doorly envied.

But when the *Late Late* appearance came around, I found myself rather irritated by this terrifying teenager with excess confidence. There he was, sitting beside Gaybo, getting all this attention ... and then the audience rounded on him. In their small-minded, unimaginative, parochial, patronising way. After a few minutes, I was converted. I was cheering for Jonathan.

3

'An expert, not a trainspotter'

– LOUDEN WAINWRIGHT III on Jonathan after being interviewed by him aged seventeen

In his early years as a freelance, Jonathan was fortunate to work for John S. Doyle, publisher and sometime editor of *In Dublin* magazine. This was Dublin's first listings magazine and made a considerable contribution to the artistic and social life of Dublin in the 1970s and 80s. Very many successful young journalists were first published in its pages. With Doyle as publisher, John Waters was editor when Jonathan first wrote for the magazine. Jonathan was soon sub-editing, writing, commissioning and being a willing worker in what was an ambitious but precarious undertaking.

During this period I have a clear recollection of phoning John S. Doyle when Jonathan, having gone to London on some assignment, failed to contact home for some days. He was seventeen and we had not yet learned to think of him as the adult he presumed he was. Concerned about his whereabouts, we enlisted John's help in tracing him. John was wise enough to honour our concern while not betraying Jonathan's independence. Jonathan, after all, had persuaded him to support a London trip with promises of exclusive interviews. No doubt what we saw as a case of a missing child, Jonathan – had he known of our anxiety – would have seen as a case of a foreign correspondent who hadn't phoned the office for a few days. When Jonathan died, JOHN S. DOYLE wrote the following memoir for the *Sunday Independent*, recalling 'a voice that demanded to be heard and was worth listening to'. The headline was 'A command performance, with a nod and that wink'.

living 91

A command performance, with a nod and that wink

John S Doyle, Jonathan's first editor, recalls a voice that demanded to be heard and was worth listening to

Sunday Independent, 19 March 2000

Jonathan, with the looks of young Dylan Thomas, the charm of Shelley, the curly locks of a cavalier and the wit of Oscar, would have found a home at the court of Louis XVI, where careers rose or foundered on the strength of a single bon mot: if not in line for the throne, he would surely have become prime minister.

He was famous for his TV and radio appearances, and could display a more considered version of that quick-witted brilliance in his writing. In person, in conversation, though, he was best of all. But conversation is not the right word: it was more a performance at which, if you were lucky, you could interject straight-man lines of the right flavour or tone, and at the right points, to keep the flow going. It was what Dermot Morgan – who wrongly thought it wasn't enough, that he should be making something permanent out of it – called a riff, like what a saxophone player does in any improvisation.

The thing about Jonathan was that he did not save himself; he was not careful. There are writers who are dull in company, keeping their pearls for the word-processor. Professional comedians do not waste their best material while talking to one or two; they either hoard it or try it out on you before polishing it later.

Jonathan, while he was talking to you, gave you the full performance; this was it, between where he had been and where he was heading; here were the jokes and the strange connections, the impersonations, the scandalous innuendo, which were not going to be repeated later; you got them now or you never got them. He was the opposite of a VCR: if you don't catch it on the night, you didn't catch it at all. All time was real time.

From a contact print of a photographic session in Conor Horgan's studio.

Okay, he might be of necessity sharing the performance with the immediate vicinity, because as he got more spirited, his voice got louder. Okay, if he was talking to you on his mobile phone, he might be winking at someone while talking to you, just as you had seen him wink at you when he was talking to someone else on the mobile. He was particularly good at the wink.

In his case, the wink meant: never mind that stuff, this is the real thing. This guy on the phone yah yah yah, but you and I know it doesn't matter. It was a mixture of flirtatiousness and flattery; he would try it on anyone, and it worked most of the time.

He would wink at Albert Reynolds just as easily as at one of his neighbours in Harold's Cross. He would wink at Tony O'Reilly. If he met Bill Clinton, it is likely that he winked. The sheer cheek was extraordinary; on reflection, it came not from a sense of superiority, a supercilious precociousness, but from the revolutionary idea that all men are equal. Like his fellow Baggot Streeter Patrick Kavanagh,

IN DUBLIN

40 Lr Ormond Quay
Dublin 1
Telephone: (01) 726622

Publisher & Editor John Doyle
Assistant Editor Maureen Gillespie
Art Director Syd Bluett
Contributing Editor J. Philbin Bowman
Advertising Roger Cole, Michelle Morris
Circulation Manager Tom Doyle
Accountant Jeanne Heery
Reception/Classifieds Jackie Reid
Photographer Tony O'Shea
Production Alwyn Gillespie, Barbara Nolan
Tallboy Pete Short

Jonathan was appointed contributing editor of *In Dublin* in March 1988. The new masthead in the issue of 3 March listed the roles of those running the magazine. See masthead for following issue, opposite page.

Caricature by Scratch to illustrate Jonathan's interview with the American novelist William Wharton, who declined to be drawn or photographed, 'Watch the Bird', *In Dublin*, 12 May 1988

He had the knack of making men feel
As small as they really were
Which meant as great as God had made them....

I first encountered this cheek when I was running *In Dublin* magazine. There was a commotion in the reception area and I went downstairs to see what was happening. The reception was where all kinds of strange people turned up: people with grievances, people with articles they wanted us to print, mad people, street-sellers, lonely hearts advertisers, and the various eccentrics who wandered the streets of Dublin at the time.

The receptionist was young but well able to handle the traffic. But this time there was a more than usual racket. There stood a youth with long blonde curls, wearing a bow tie and plimsolls. He was demanding to see the editor. He was, as I recall, making a video about something to do with the *Late Late Show*, and he had photographs that he felt we should use. He was about sixteen and was ordering people about the place. 'You!', he commanded, when I appeared, 'What do you do?' Though *In Dublin* at the time was a generally egalitarian kind of place, I was taken aback at being addressed in this manner. But I quickly realized there was nothing to be gained in getting into a huff; he would only, like Groucho, up the ante by getting into a minute-and-a-huff. And besides, he showed no signs of leaving if his wishes were not granted.

So he stayed, and over the next three years he wrote for the magazine. At times he seemed to write the whole thing single-handedly and spilled out a stream of ideas for articles, directions and people we should be pursuing. He became a kind of mascot for the magazine, intent on dragging it out of the tired seventies (this was the late eighties) and into the world of computers and mobile phones.

But my enduring memory of Jonathan is of his kindness. In August 1988, I called a meeting of staff and contributors to tell them that *In Dublin* was no more. It was a large meeting and there was not much to be said. It broke up in gloom. Then Jonathan took me aside and led me into my office, where he produced a bottle of wine, a corkscrew and glasses. We drank a glass of wine together. It meant more than I could say, or did say. The sky had fallen, but life could go on. He chose to stand beside me when to do otherwise would be perfectly understandable.

The enormous crowds at his funeral service were a fitting tribute to the love inspired by a gentleman whom John Bowman in his oration called 'my lovely boy'.

Sunday Independent, 19 March 2000

IN DUBLIN

40 Lr Ormond Quay
Dublin 1
Telephone: (01) 726622

Daddy Publisher & Editor John Doyle
Mummy Editor Maureen Gillespie
Window Cleaner Bluett
M.W.C.A.I (Ass.)
Baby Editor Jonathan Philbin Bowman
Corruption and Extortion Roger Cole, Michelle Morris
Beauty Editor Tom Doyle
Lion Tamer Jeanne Heery
Manicurist Jackie Reid
Image Maker Tony O'Shea
Production Alwyn Gillespie, Barbara Nolan
Fergus Cassidy
Complaints Pete Short

In the issue of 17 March 1988, Jonathan 'got at' the masthead with all management assigned new titles. That the 'Accountant' was renamed a 'Lion Tamer' was a joke intended for those who could remember the *Monty Python* sketch which was based on the assumption that all accountants wanted to be lion tamers. Pete Short was a street vendor of *In Dublin* outside Bewleys. He was interviewed by Jonathan, *In Dublin*, 31 March 1988.

PADDY KEHOE, now a feature writer with the *RTE Guide*, first met Jonathan when they were both young freelancers on *In Dublin*.

Jonathan was the new kid on the block, going around hoovering up everyone for interview. I remember him in particular at the Writers' Conference in Dun Laoghaire that year, gathering all-and-sundry manner of writers towards his tape recorder. I felt not a little envious, being something of a novice. Already he was more experienced.

One of the writers he interviewed for *In Dublin** was the playwright FRANK MCGUINNESS whose play 'Innocence' had been written for the 1986 Dublin Theatre Festival.

I'm just dropping you a line because I think I was one of the first people Jonathan interviewed back in 1986 for *In Dublin*. He looked about twelve years old and I didn't know what I was in for, but he quizzed me fiercely about the play; he had seriously read the text and I really liked his gentle intelligence. He was also

* 'Renaissance man', *In Dublin*, 2 October 1986.

Cartoon by Aongus Collins, to accompany an article by Jonathan on a Patrick Kavanagh literary weekend in Monaghan 'Talking along the Border', *In Dublin, 1987-1988 Annual*

determined to convince me I was famous and wanted to know how I handled fame, but was happy enough to accept my answer, which was a roar of laughter. There was an innocence about him I respected and from brief meetings with him since then, usually in the company of mutual friends, I believe he retained his good innocence.

The singer-songwriter Louden Wainwright III was among Jonathan's favourite singers when he was growing up. Like others, he likened Wainwright to Bob Dylan and had always been interested in the fact that he wrote his own material. It was no surprise to me when he announced that he was travelling to London especially to interview him for *In Dublin.** LOUDEN WAINWRIGHT recalled:

> One day way back in 1986 when I was living in London the publicist for my record company of the moment rang me at my flat in West Hampstead. He wondered if I would be willing to speak with a young Irish journalist about my music. I was told the writer would travel all the way from Dublin if I would meet with him face

* 'Lowdown on Loudon', *In Dublin*, 13 November 1986.

to face. I was promoting a new record at the time so I agreed and suggested that the meeting take place at my flat. Then I was warned that the young man coming to see me was *quite* young. When I asked how young that would be the reply was 'fifteen or sixteen'.* Suddenly I wasn't so sure. There must be some gimmick to this, I thought. How and/or why would a sixteen year old be interested in my music. Sixteen year olds like 'Spandau Ballet' – they did back then – not forty-year-old American confessional singer-songwriters. I decided it was probably a prank or perhaps a bizarre school assignment. Maybe the boy had a teacher at school who was an LW3 obsessive.

City Desk

LOWDOWN ON
LOUDON

● Jonathan Philbin Bowman talks to Loudon Wainwright, singer, songwriter and sometime actor who recently performed for an evening at the Olympia.

'Fame and wealth is what I'm after,
Bucks and praise are what I crave,
How I get them hardly matters,
for these things I'll be your slave.'
– Loudon Wainwright, Fame and Wealth

'WELL, I can get very bored by interviews, particularly if I have to do a bunch of them in a row, which is what inspired me to write that song. I'd just done six phone interviews in a row with Australian journalists and because of the time difference I had to get up at five o'clock in the morning to do it, so I was in kind of a bad mood.'

So says Loudon Wainwright III when I ask him if he really does hate interviews as much as he gives the impression he does in 'How old are you?' 'Since this record came out, all the journalists I've spoken to have been very defensive about that song. It's true that the song was inspired by doing interviews and being asked the same questions over and over again, but they're also questions that I pose to myself all the time. "Can I still do it?", "Am I good?", "Am I all washed up?", "How come I'm not as big as Bruce Springsteen?" I mean they're questions I ask myself all the time.'

The last time the completely wonderful, witty, cynical 'I like to think of it as being realistic', divorced genius Loudon Wainwright III was in Ireland was at Slattas Cois Laoi, in 1985. Unfortunately the audience booed and vegetabled him off the stage which we won't talk about except to say that it tells you something about the sort of people who go to Slattas Cois Laoi. 'I was vegetabled and also beer-canned off the stage. I didn't mind the fruit and vegetables, but I took umbrage to the beer tins and the cider bottles – which were plastic, but still. But, I was well paid, and so, these things happen.'

When we met in London ('It doesn't really matter where I live, I spend a lot of time in New York, and a lot of time here.') Loudon was travelling the next day to Holland, followed by Germany, and then Australia and Japan. Japan? How would he be received (or even understood) in Japan? 'A language problem? Well, I've never been to Japan so we're going to find out about that. That'll be my first trip, when I get there. I've played in places like Finland where the English is pretty minimal. It's a bit of a problem, but I choose to sing songs – in countries where English is not the main language – that are quite simple and I explain them slowly, and I actually sing them slowly. Of course I'm sure in a place like Japan that all of that might not help. But I'm told that they actually give the audience people translations of the songs that they read, or actually get it over headphones. We'll see if they get it. In Japan they like American things so maybe it'll work, maybe it won't. I've always wanted to go there anyway.'

Does Wainwright consider himself 'All-American'? 'Well, I'm certainly not All-American, but I am an American and I think that is reflected in, certainly, the way I dress. I don't know, that's for other people to say. I feel very American. I don't know, I'm confused and scared like everyone else and sceptical like a lot of people – I don't know if everybody else is sceptical. But, I'm

IN DUBLIN 18

In Dublin, 13 November 1986

However I was assured this was not the case. There was no gimmick. The young fellow was knowledgeable on the subject of my music and was a great fan to boot. I still wasn't completely convinced. Was this a case of some twisted potential, some indoctrination – an eight-track cassette piping not Mozart but Wainwright into the nursery while innocence slumbered? Then I remembered the last time something like this had happened. Ten years earlier a teenage music writer had accompanied me to and from Birmingham covering my gig for the *New Musical Express*. She was their wonderful prodigy at the time. Her name was Julie Burchill. I reflected on that. A time was set for the interview.

Jonathan Philbin Bowman arrived at my flat in Englewood Road right on time. He was sartorially turned out, dressed in a sharply cut suit with a monogrammed handkerchief poking out of the breast pocket of the jacket. In addition he was sporting a big bright silk necktie. Somehow, although resplendent in those duds, he seemed even younger than if he had showed up in dirty jeans and a torn T-shirt. His big eyes, thick curly hair, cherubic cheeks, and full lips suggested a young pre-dissipated Dylan Thomas. I offered him some tea and we sat down to do the interview.

Jonathan's natural determination to be taken seriously was quickly rewarded once we began. His questions were concise, funny, thought-provoking, and not at all precocious. Indeed he knew all of my records and all of the songs on them. He even knew the characters in the songs themselves, i.e. who was the mother of which kid. It wasn't just a case of having done his homework. A lot of the songs, songs with titles like 'Your mother and I', 'Unhappy anniversary', 'Glad to see you've got religion', and 'School days' had clearly affected him. I was amused, impressed, touched, and, naturally, flattered and charmed. 'This kid's got it', I thought. 'He's seen what all the other have missed!'

* In fact Jonathan was seventeen, but he looked much younger, as Frank McGuinness has already emphasised.

(FOLLOWING PAGE) One of Jonathan's most controversial reports was for *PC Report*, 1988. 'The real truth about PC dealers', *Computerscope*'s obituary tribute, recalled the impact which this article had made: 'Ever the extrovert with a taste for drama, his piece was written in the style of a detective novel, illustrated with several Chandleresque wry observations and pithy asides. Sadly, many of the dealers who were the butt of his comments failed to see the funny side...'

After the allotted time for the interview had passed, Jonathan turned off his tape-recorder and rose to leave. He didn't ask if we could go out for a drink nor did he suggest we spend a few hours together at Madame Tussaud's. That's what made him an expert and not a trainspotter; at the age of sixteen he was already a consummate professional. But before he left for Heathrow and his flight back to Dublin we exchanged numbers. I wanted to stay in touch with Jonathan. Happily for the next fifteen years I did.

Advertising executive CONOR FERGUSON wrote that Jonathan and he had 'got on well, bumped into each other frequently, but sadly never quite capitalised on what we had in common.' He wrote:

> The first thing you have to say about Jonathan was that you could generally – unless you were listening to The Prodigy or Motorhead on a turbo-charged Walkman – hear him before you'd spot him. Hand glued to mobile phone. Mobile phone glued to ear. Thick lips babbling in a language that was quite like English – only much faster. Where did he get it all? All that guff and bluster. Where did he find the time to think it all up, let alone get it all said. One occasionally got the impression that such was the quantity of *talk* queued up waiting to be uttered that he didn't always get the chance to think it through beforehand. This may sound a little bitchy, perhaps, but I'm sure Jonathan would be happy to concur. Because, if he had a 'role' as such, it wasn't to dictate to us the right way to think, or the correct manner to go about something, but to put an idea on our agenda and let us think about it ourselves.
>
> The downside to this requirement to Always Be Talking was that it made it difficult to get to know him. And alas I can't claim to have made much headway in that area myself. Our paths would collide at various events. Repartee would be exchanged. Wine would be consumed. Plans would be made. When, in the late 1980s, my father had the dubious honour of owning the Hendricks Gallery on St. Stephen's Green, Jonathan could always be relied on to show up and represent jumped-up middle-class young fellas in a way that filial obligation on my part disallowed. And it was always a great relief to see him. My parents welcomed his appearance too. My mother was particularly fond of him, his lippy demeanour notwithstanding. Indeed, I couldn't help feeling he was in some way being cited as an example of how I too could get ahead without necessarily getting a haircut. I particularly remember meeting him one night at what was then known as The Waterfront on Sir John Rogerson's Quay. The Ferguson family were gathered to hear my brother's band do criminal things to

some country classics. But on the quiet night that was in it he was only too happy to ensconce himself between my parents and make interesting noise, paying them the attention which they no doubt felt was lacking from their own brood of young adults. And he was quite the hit. And that seemed to be his thing in general: always leave an impression. It didn't necessarily have to be a good one – although, often as not, it was – just singular, characteristic, memorable. And that he did in no minor fashion.

Information technology was at this time in its infancy and Jonathan was fascinated by it. He was interested in it – as he had been from boyhood – for its own sake; but he was also keen to exploit it in terms of his own professional work. He adopted what I might call a periscopic outlook, keen to know what innovation or invention was imminent. And he was also delighted to proclaim the virtues of the new technology to those who had not yet discovered it.

Computerscope was a magazine for which Jonathan occasionally wrote. And when he died their tribute emphasised his extrovert personality even when very young. SIMON DUNNE, a former editor of *Network User*, recalled his first encounter 'with a precocious sixteen year old' who turned up on a stand he was managing at a computer exhibition in the RDS.

> 'A businessman came on the stand with Jonathan in tow, or rather Jonathan showed up with a businessman in tow. He asked about our computers with a fixed expression of derision. All his questions were insightful and to the point. He wandered off the stand, with the businessman still pleading to be allowed to buy any computer that matched the exacting standards of his teenage consultant. We all fell about laughing! Who was this kid?'

Another editor of the time remembers Bowman as being 'full of ideas but his copy was always late and he couldn't spell.' The current incumbent remembers meeting him for the first time as the assembled press waited for the beginning of a conference to be addressed by the then Microsoft chief executive Bill Gates. Bowman entered and went through the room regally introducing himself to each of the bemused hacks in the manner of a head of

It was the kind of day you couldn't see coming. I was sitting in my office chewing over a plate so the crumbs wouldn't fall on the floor when quicker than you could say *desktop publishing* the phone rang.

I picked it up.

"Hello" I said.

"Hello" said a voice on the other end of the line and I knew its owner meant business. He said his name was Quinn. Frank Quinn, and and he told me what he wanted done. It wasn't your ordinary, run of the mill case by any means, and I had my reservations — and no, before you ask. I don't mean I was going on holiday.

Quinn's game was publishing, and he wanted me to get the facts on some friends of his. They were in the computer business — selling, and he needed the lowdown on their modus operandi, *Operating System* as they call it these days. "Just one other thing Frank . . ." I said, before he hung up, "Your fees?" he inquired "Yeah," I said, "Ninety dollars a day. Plus expenses."

Frank said it didn't sound cheap. I told him my kind of operation wasn't, and he said he figured his backroom boys could come up with the cash. He'd only pay me after the job though, which was a drawback, but in my game you don't mess with guys like Quinn, not if you don't want to part with your Waterstone's charge card in a hurry, you don't.

Before he rang off, Frank told me not to use his name, or the name of his rag, *ComputerScope*, and he promised he'd stay in touch.

Jonathan was an early enthusiast for portable computing. He staged this photograph in Bewley's to illustrate an article in *Computerscope*, June 1988. He compared how writing away from home had changed over the centuries. In the eighteenth century the quill had some advantages: 'it was light, relatively cheap and portable' which, he added was the sales pitch for the then innovative laptop. But, he added, the quill had 'no RAM, it wasn't PC compatible, it often blew away. It broke. It leaked, and sometimes it tickled.'

> state meeting the teams before an important football match.

Some of Jonathan's early journalism chronicled this rapidly changing field. FRANK QUINN, publisher and editor of *Computerscope* and *PC Live,* commissioned a number of articles from him. He recalled that Jonathan 'was a familiar figure at our exhibitions, floating around our magazine stand and doing duty behind the desk just "for the crack"'.

> Jonathan was something of a gadget head, and he loved Apple Macs. In fact, he personified in many ways the cultish nature of Mac users, who seem to take a pride in being different – as if he wasn't different enough to start with. As publishers of computer magazines, we commissioned the occasional article from Jonathan. Product reviews were written in a style unlike any other – usually in English which owed more to satirical writing than bland old

'techie' content. His best example was when we published a 'plain man's guide to buying a PC' in a style tailor-made for Jonathan. We photographed him in classic detective garb, skulking around PC dealers. His interviews – with hapless salesmen who spoke jargon right over his head – were priceless. He backed these up with scathing assessments: 'I ran all the way up Camden Street. I had escaped.'

There was total fury of course when we published these incognito assessments of how badly PC dealers served their clients. Along with the threats of dealer's associations withdrawing advertising money, there were notes from ordinary people saying how well Jonathan poured scorn on the jargon-loving approach of most PC salesmen.

DEIRDRE PURCELL, the novelist and journalist, wrote that Jonathan's 'sense of life crackled so strongly' that his absence was 'hardly credible'. And she recalled their first meeting when he came to interview her for a computer magazine about her recent purchase of an Apple Mac computer.

We met in the Gresham Hotel. He must have been still in his teens and I was almost into middle-age but he made me feel alive and young and as though the notion of a generation gap was a complete myth. I have never seen such challenging eyes in a young man. The interview became a joyous teasing match I have never forgotten.

DR DEREK FREEDMAN, a specialist in sexually transmitted diseases and a campaigner on the need to more openly discuss the issue, had been interviewed for *In Dublin* magazine by Jonathan shortly after he had begun writing for the magazine.*

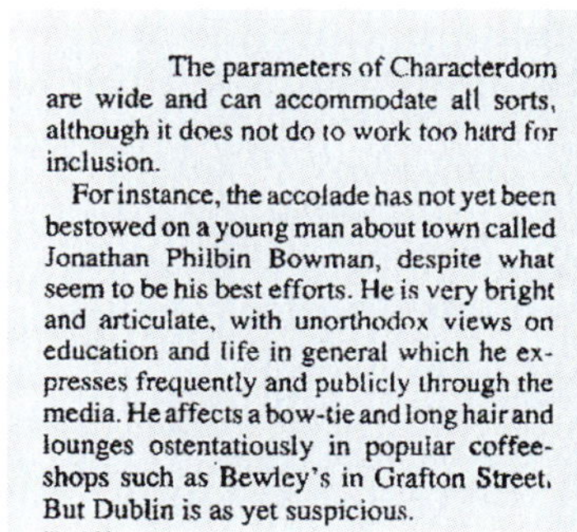
The parameters of Characterdom are wide and can accommodate all sorts, although it does not do to work too hard for inclusion.

For instance, the accolade has not yet been bestowed on a young man about town called Jonathan Philbin Bowman, despite what seem to be his best efforts. He is very bright and articulate, with unorthodox views on education and life in general which he expresses frequently and publicly through the media. He affects a bow-tie and long hair and lounges ostentatiously in popular coffee-shops such as Bewley's in Grafton Street. But Dublin is as yet suspicious.

Deirdre Purcell's contemporary comments on Jonathan in an Insight cityguide, *Dublin*, 1988.

When young Jonathan wanted to interview me on AIDS in the late 1980s, I was happy to help him but unsure as what to expect from the sixteen year old. He arrived, he took control, he entertained us, he was utterly relaxed on our couch. He explained that he had left school early as it had little more to teach him, and he did not see the point of going to university, when he could attend the university of life! This ran against the grain of our Dublin 6 fixation with education, but I could not be other than utterly impressed with his professionalism when it came to the nub of the interview. He had done the background research; he asked the pertinent questions; he adjusted his perception with the information given and wrote an accurate

* 'Safe sex and the banana republic', *In Dublin*, 2 April 1987.

and timely piece that brought information about HIV/AIDS risks and safe sex practices to an audience most in need of it. When he eventually departed, we felt stimulated and entranced by the interview and his company. We understood that he was no ordinary person, and perhaps he had made the right decision in eschewing the path of traditional education.

JOHN WATERS was editor of *In Dublin* when Jonathan first worked for it. In a letter to me he wrote the following account of his impression of the young Jonathan as a fledgling journalist.

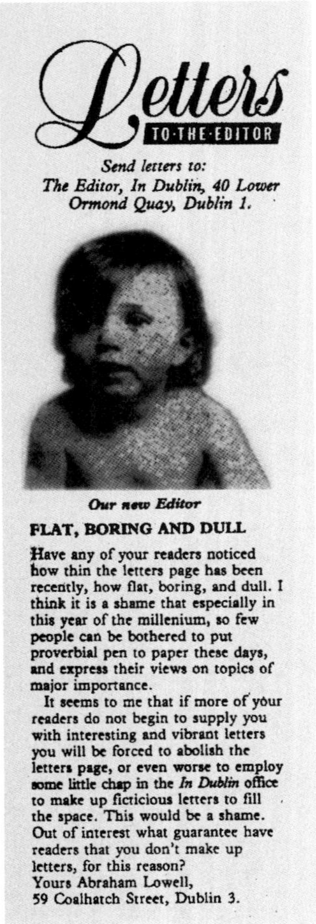

Letters TO THE EDITOR

Send letters to:
The Editor, In Dublin, 40 Lower Ormond Quay, Dublin 1.

Our new Editor

FLAT, BORING AND DULL

Have any of your readers noticed how thin the letters page has been recently, how flat, boring, and dull. I think it is a shame that especially in this year of the millenium, so few people can be bothered to put proverbial pen to paper these days, and express their views on topics of major importance.

It seems to me that if more of your readers do not begin to supply you with interesting and vibrant letters you will be forced to abolish the letters page, or even worse to employ some little chap in the *In Dublin* office to make up ficticious letters to fill the space. This would be a shame. Out of interest what guarantee have readers that you don't make up letters, for this reason?
Yours Abraham Lowell,
59 Coalhatch Street, Dublin 3.

Spoof letter to the editor, clearly an in-house effort. That it is by Jonathan is clear since it was signed 'Abraham Lowell'. His younger brother Abie was named 'Tobias Abraham Lowell Jamie'. *In Dublin*, 17 March 1988

Of course, such was the obviousness of his talent that, had I not been fortunate in encountering him, he would inevitably have been spotted by someone else. On the other hand, I do know that he had been around the place a little and had already had a number of flat rebuffs. Even at that stage he had a certain capacity to evoke an immediate response, one way or another. In any event, I was his editor at *In Dublin* between late 1985 and about the end of 1987. The privilege was entirely mine. He had come in to me a short time before while I was editor of Vincent Browne's doomed *TV Guide*, and we had had a brief conversation. He had already had a few outings on television, but I was unaware of having seen these and cannot imagine that I would have forgotten if I had. I was, of course, immediately struck by him. Who was not? He was in every way extraordinary. His first entry into the office where I worked was like a warm breeze moving suddenly across a jaded and stuffy room. I felt immediately an absence of guile, a profound type of innocence which I have never otherwise encountered except in children. And yet he had the mind of a most intelligent adult, an extraordinary instrument of perception and analysis. And of course he was brimming with confidence and good humour. I told him I was about to leave the *TV Guide* to begin editing *In Dublin*, and he promised to look me up as soon as I got there. He arrived a short time after I started.

My time at *In Dublin* was remarkably successful in terms of circulation and much of this was down to Jonathan's contributions. It is the only time in my life I have had the opportunity of experiencing the kind of emotions which might have been felt by those who watched the early development of a Georgie Best, a Hurricane [Alex] Higgins or a Tiger Woods. He was truly gifted, having no need for the usual apprenticeship in writing skills or journalistic technique. He had this remarkable capacity to strike up an equal relationship with virtually anybody, and talk to them about their work and their lives. Although I always felt that he was in some ways wasted on journalism, he was in another sense the perfect journalist. In those days he did an enormous amount of work, often writing more than half the magazine. He also had a virtually unlimited range, although I seem to remember that he had a blindspot concerning sport. (Strange then, that the people I have compared him with are all sportsmen!). His versatility meant that he was the first writer I thought of for virtually anything. He was, on the one hand, deeply thoughtful and serious – I remember he wrote a quite brilliant piece about the obsolescence of work around an interview with Professor Ivor Browne. On the other, there was nobody more capable of writing an entirely frivolous article while maintaining perfect pitch in terms of humour and tone.

If you liked him, which I very much did, his appearance would transport you from even the blackest of places. He was, as I said, innocent, and effervescent and very, very funny. There was a warmth about him that touched your soul in the way a cup of tea can sometimes touch the cockles of your heart. He had what seemed to be an almost limitless capacity for affection. Of course, he did, as you so succinctly put it, divide the jury. Some people seemed to take an almost instant dislike to him, which at the time I found almost incomprehensible and, in a strange way, unjust. He and I, having come from entirely different backgrounds, differed and disagreed a great deal about politics and all sorts of things, but this never seemed to matter with Jonathan in the way it often mattered with others.

I remember you and I once had quite a long telephone conversation about Jonathan. He had been working for *In Dublin* for some time, and his fame was starting to spread. You called me expressing a degree of disquiet about Jonathan's sudden ascent to national celebrity, and the effects it might be having on him. I remember you saying that, whereas Jonathan gave the impression of complete confidence and self-assurance, this was not the full story. You felt he was much more vulnerable than he might like people to think. I was struck by your concern for him, which resonated with deeper feelings of my own. I had already had a sense of his naiveté – in certain respects – and felt extremely protective of him. We had developed a very close and warm relationship and I had come to regard him in a kind of elder-brotherly way. I gather from others that he did an impressive impersonation of me in my absence, but only regretted that I never got to see this. I sought a few times to have serious conversations with him about the necessity for him to develop the serious side of himself alongside the more light-hearted elements of his already strongly emerging professional personality. But he, for his part, would hear nothing of restraint or caution, and very much led his own advance from the front.

IN DUBLIN 300 BEST OF DUBLIN!

BEST ROCK VENUE

Olympia Theatre

The Olympia has finally come into its own, with performances there by everybody from the Fleadh Cowboys to John Hiatt and Rory Gallagher. Plush seats, private boxes, and three bars. What more could a body want?

BEST EXAMPLE OF WHY CELEBRITIES SHOULDN'T BE ALLOWED TO DO FOOD COMMERCIALS

Seán Kinsella saying 'I'll be using it' *or* Stephen Roche pretending to cycle along in front of a film of hundreds of other people cycling along as he explains why he eats Galtee cheese, and as he talks he gets bigger and Bigger and BIGGER.

BEST RECORDED SILENCE FROM JONATHAN PHILBIN BOWMAN

None so far.

BEST VIEW OF THE CITY (INLAND)

Three Rock Mountain

The mountain itself is not much to look at since they put the radio masts on it, but when you're on it you don't have to look at it but can gaze at the extraordinary view of Dublin and its bay. Start from Glencullen.

14 APRIL 1988 IN DUBLIN 19

In Dublin liked to jest at Jonathan's expense. Note the reference to him in their 300 best things about Dublin. Of course it is always possible that he wrote the reference himself, *In Dublin*, 14 April 1988.

We more or less lost contact when I left *In Dublin* in late 1987, but we nonetheless remained friendly for several years. He was particularly generous in his praise and support at the time of the publication of my first book in 1991.*

We subsequently fell out, rather badly. It was not over a trivial matter, certainly nothing to do with the kind of differences and rivalries which often arise between journalists, and it resulted in our continuing estrangement at the time of Jonathan's death. While he was alive, I judged his behaviour in this particular matter inexcusable. Since his death, I have come to see it as human. As time passes, the incident recedes and acquires what I suspect is its proper perspective as part of the shadow of a life lived in the light of sincerity and innocence.

I greatly feel the loss of your lovely son and regret the differences that occurred between us. He was a good and loving boy. He lit up the earth for a while. For a time I adored him and for a time I thought I hated him. I feel that, had he lived, we would eventually have put our differences behind us. They are trivial indeed in comparison with your loss. I recall that at the funeral you asked people who felt that Jonathan had hurt them to forgive him as he would have forgiven them. It is not a question of my forgiveness of Jonathan, but rather my inability to retain the larger truth about us. He lived life to the full and had not the slightest consciousness of the kind of caution or reserve which others experience as the dominant forces of existence. There was no way of knowing him except at the outer limits of human possibility, good or ill. I knew him both ways.

Fragment from Jim Cogan cartoon in *Sunday Independent*, February 2000. The flowers being delivered 'To Susan, XXX' was a reference intended for one reader only as a thank you to Susan Towers for her kindness in New York after his mugging in January 2000.

SUSAN TOWERS, now a writer and editor in magazine publishing in New York, was a contemporary of Jonathan's. She remained a close personal friend from his earliest *In Dublin* days when she was a student at UCD.

Jonathan's Rule No.1: You can never send too many flowers. To too many people. Ever. Jonathan Philbin Bowman, *In Dublin*, 28 May, 1987.

Jonathan loved to give people flowers – he'd arrive at lunch or dinner clutching a bunch and be delighted at your response (and to an extent, with himself!). There never needed to be a reason – he just thought we should all have something to brighten our day. He once arrived to have lunch with me and another one of his many girlfriends clutching an actual bucket of flowers – how we lucky recipients appreciated those spontaneous gestures of

* This was John Waters' best-seller, *Jiving at the Crossroads*, Belfast, 1991.

Jonathan with Susan Towers at the Trinity Ball, 1987. *In Dublin* cover, 28 May 1987

affection and love.

He expounded this rule in an article that appeared in *In Dublin* in May 1987. We'd been friends for a while and the two of us had posed for an article he was writing entitled 'The Guide to Social Success'.* It was funny to walk down Grafton Street that week seeing the two of us on the cover displayed in the windows of the newsagents – him with his hair flying, wearing his customary bow-tie and me in a red ball gown. Over the years, Jonathan gave me many flowers and on Valentine's Day 2000, I was sitting at my desk in New York when I was delighted to receive a beautiful bouquet from him. When I called him to thank him he told me to be sure and read his column from that week's *Sunday Independent* – there was a little message for me in there. It was only after he died that

JONATHAN PHILBIN BOWMAN'S
UNIQUE SECRETS OF
SOCIAL
SUCCESS

Like sex and riding a bicycle, Social Success comes best when you don't try too hard. Perhaps the rule should be 'Make no effort unless you want to, in which case make as much effort as you like'.

1. Places to go and things to do there.

* *In Dublin*, 28 May 1987.

his editor at the paper got me a copy and there we saw that the illustration for his weekly column had a bunch of flowers with a note saying 'to Susan' – he liked to send me little messages that way.

When my mother died on October 11th, 1998, Jonathan was distraught – the two of them got on brilliantly – when I was younger he used to sit in our kitchen in Sydney Parade Avenue and have great chats with her. I would get infuriated when he took her side in arguments over the length of my skirts but he'd always temper such support with a big wink for me. I loved Jonathan's conspiratorial winks – they were inclusive – you were in on the joke. A couple of weeks later after I had returned to New York, Jonathan called me – he knew I was grieving and from one of his many 'offices' about town, faxed me an article he'd found which he thought would bring some comfort. Entitled 'Return Appearances', it pondered the phenomenon of the dead appearing to the living, as in that not uncommon experience in which a recently departed loved one appears in what might be called a 'real dream'.

In the early stages of grief in which we feel the absolute absence of the departed subside, when the mind begins to sink into the heart, there arises a sense of absolute inseparability for that person that may well be the two-way bridge across which our dreams are exchanged. 'If after I died I dreamed with all my heart that I brought you a huge bouquet of flowers, what might happen? And how did you like the card?'

In the last years of his life, Jonathan had been on a spiritual journey – he had met Catherine Ingram, a spiritual teacher, who he felt really understood him and who showed him a love he sought. Today, as I write this in New York in the aftermath of the worst terrorist attack imaginable, I am reminded more than ever of the fragility of life and how we should all, like Jonathan, use our voices, our time and our energy to make this a better place to be. As we traverse our one-of-a-kind journey – one we never truly complete – we pass on to others the meaning and specialness of our lives. For me that meaning in regard to Jonathan is love. I'm expecting the flowers any day now.

> '*...he who kisses the joy as it flies,*
> *Lives in eternity's sunrise.*' – WILLIAM BLAKE

LUCY MADDEN, who with her husband Johnny Madden runs Hilton Park, a country house hotel, in Scotshouse, Co. Monaghan, wrote a letter of sympathy, including this memory of Jonathan which confirms his love of an audience and his capacity to hold one.

I remember many years ago being somewhere in Dublin – it was a public place, I forget where – and hearing a man's voice coming through a door and, from time to time, the most raucous laughter from an audience. I peeked in and recognized from television a very young Jonathan surrounded by a group of say a dozen people who were helpless with mirth and merriment at his stories. Much later when he stayed at Hilton Park, I anticipated that he would be very precocious but he turned out to be totally delightful, funny, considerate, full of charm.

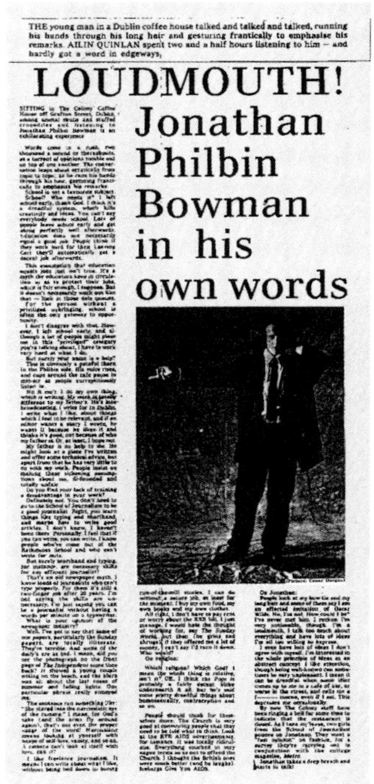
THE young man in a Dublin coffee house talked and talked and talked, running his hands through his long hair and gesturing frantically to emphasise his remarks. AILIN QUINLAN spent two and a half hours listening to him – and hardly got a word in edgeways,

LOUDMOUTH! Jonathan Philbin Bowman in his own words

Ailin Quinlan, 'Loudmouth!', *Cork Examiner*, 12 November 1987

ALAN CROSBIE, chairman of Examiner Publications in Cork, wrote:

Thankfully, none of us are one hundred per cent anything. We are all made up of a little bit of this and a little bit of that. When I first saw Jonathan Philbin Bowman on television, he really annoyed my conservative bit. I thought: 'Who do you think you are, prattling on like that?' and I agreed with the profile in the *Examiner* that called him a media brat. Then I met him for the first time in the Shelbourne Hotel, in the room off the foyer where people take tea in the afternoon. He came over to my friend and me, all loud and opinionated and my conservative bit kept saying: 'Shut up, you fool, everybody is looking.' However because none of us are one hundred per cent anything, I also have a liberal bit which is just as big as my conservative bit. My liberal bit loved JPB. It kept saying to him while he was on television: 'Good on you, about time somebody said that.' When I met him in the Shelbourne, my liberal bit was saying: 'That's right lad, talk louder; this place needs shaking up.' That's what he used to do, he made my liberal bit argue with my conservative bit and they are still at it but JPB is gone. They both miss him.

TREVOR WHITE, publisher of *The Dubliner*, was three years younger than Jonathan and was aware of him by reputation.

Like many people who grew up in Dublin at the same time as Jonathan, I knew him in passing. Only three years separated us, although he almost seemed much older and impossibly brainy? I remember his boisterous manner at local parties, and something I mistook for arrogance. I particularly remember one day in the late 1980s in the Coffee Inn on South Anne Street. The proprietor, David Wine, had printed new menus and in pride of place was something called a Bowman Burger which was described as two pieces of toast

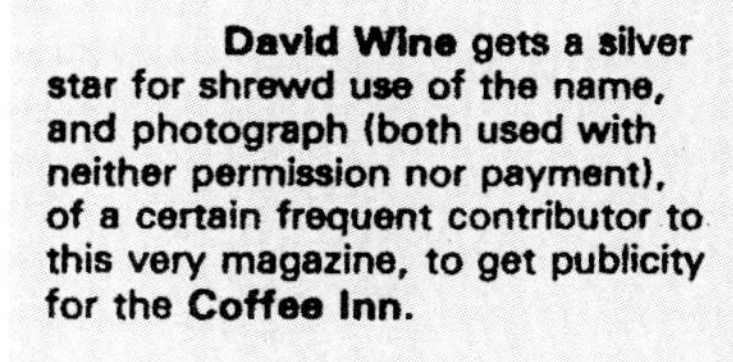
David Wine gets a silver star for shrewd use of the name, and photograph (both used with neither permission nor payment), of a certain frequent contributor to this very magazine, to get publicity for the **Coffee Inn.**

Jonathan's comment on David Wine's menu in the Coffee Inn. *In Dublin, 1987–1988 Annual*

> separated by…hot air. Instead of taking offence, Jonathan was positively delighted to be honoured thus, and promptly declared the Bowman Burger – BB – as proof of his genius! At the time I grudgingly acknowledged that he was all the things we feared he was: exceedingly charming, a little cantankerous and desperately bright.

YVONNE HAMILTON-TARLETON wrote that she was in Jonathan's company 'for no more than five minutes' but she had never forgotten him.

> It is hard to describe but my best shot is that Jonathan was alive with knowledge, charm, wit, confidence – but much more than that for one so young. He had 'the plot' of who he was, life, people. For many so wrapped in what is not and never will be important – trivia with which they fill their lives – he was the one who in my humble opinion was ahead of his time.

MARK O'CONNELL, barrister and journalist, was a young reporter for the *Irish Press* when he met Jonathan during this period.

> When I think of Jonathan Philbin Bowman the image that comes to mind is of a young cherubic face, wild hair, hands in the air, beautiful female company – and his full voluble voice. I used see him around the campus in Trinity now and again but I didn't actually meet him until around 1988. I had begun working as a journalist in the *Irish Press* and got invited to the launch of some new bottled beer, an attractive marking for any young news reporter in those days. The venue – and I could be mistaken – was the Judge Roy Bean's restaurant on Nassau Street. Jonathan was there holding court. He was by that stage an established Dublin character; everyone knew him and he appeared at all major social functions. My feelings towards him ranged somewhere between being irritated by him and being in awe of him. I remember him coming up to me and introducing himself. A bit like giving blood for the first time, it wasn't as bad as I thought it would be. In fact, he was extremely friendly and pleasant. I was quite taken by how much he appeared to know about me. He had read my modest writings in the pages of papers in the *Press* group and was able to quote back some material – more than I could myself! I was impressed and charmed by this.
>
> Thereafter, I would bump into him frequently – at press launches and in pubs like Toner's, Mulligan's and the Shelbourne Bar. We'd chat about different issues. I recall he had strong views on almost everything: the implications of the Beef Tribunal, the

winner of the new radio franchise, the IRA's latest atrocity, or the quality of the coffee in Bewley's. I challenged him about his view of formal education. I knew Jonathan may have eschewed a university education but I was impressed, not only by how extremely well-read he was, but by the quality of the argument he put forward in defence of his decision not to take the conventional route through the Leaving Cert and beyond.

Despite his difficult relationship with Newpark, Jonathan would have been amused to see himself listed in the *Sunday Times* review of Irish schools as one of Newpark's distinguished alumni. 'Parent Power', supplement with *Sunday Times,* 12 November 2000.

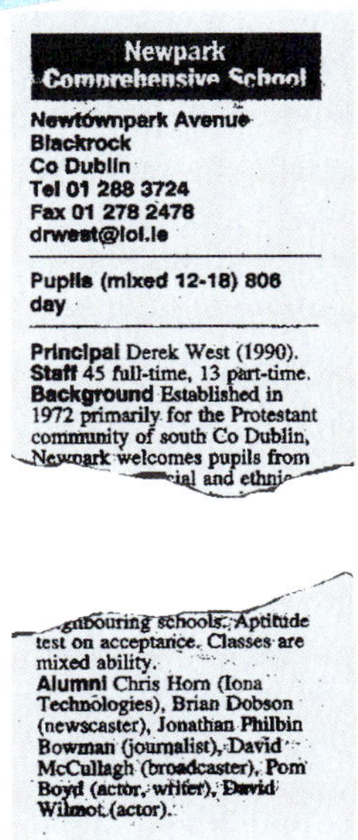
Newpark Comprehensive School

Newtownpark Avenue
Blackrock
Co Dublin
Tel 01 288 3724
Fax 01 278 2478
drwest@iol.ie

Pupils (mixed 12-18) 806 day

Principal Derek West (1990).
Staff 45 full-time, 13 part-time.
Background Established in 1972 primarily for the Protestant community of south Co Dublin, Newpark welcomes pupils from ...cial and ethnic

...ghbouring schools. Aptitude test on acceptance. Classes are mixed ability.
Alumni Chris Horn (Iona Technologies), Brian Dobson (newscaster), Jonathan Philbin Bowman (journalist), David McCullagh (broadcaster), Pom Boyd (actor, writer), David Wilmot (actor).

Jonathan often expounded his views on education. He was even invited back in 1989 by his old school, Newpark Comprehensive, to talk about education to the pupils in Transition Year. Among those pupils who remembered his lecture was LOUISE EAST, journalist with *The Irish Times*. In the *Education Times* supplement she published this account when Jonathan died. She reminded her readers that Newpark had been one of the first schools in the country to try out the 'weird, new-fangled' idea of Transition Year. By the time she was a pupil, it had been 'fairly well established in the school, as were the rumours that earlier Transition Year groups had done everything from live on a boat for a year to tend goats in the Himalayas. Sadly, when I reached goat-rearing age, Transition Year had been watered down into a more manageable formula that worked well'. Yet it was still experimental and, she reckoned, not thoroughly approved of by parents.

It was fun, but at the time it didn't seem life-changing. For a start there was far too much in the way of academic studies to be truly revolutionary – who could really rebel, when they had to get back for a 2.30 p.m. class in Irish? Then there were all those lectures, hour-long sessions with a diverse collection of speakers, spent lolling in rows, pretending not to listen.

Jonathan Philbin Bowman was invited back to speak at one – a remarkably courageous or foolhardy move given that Newpark was the school he so publicly left at the age of sixteen. Typically he managed to raise hackles and laughs in almost equal portions, but finally endeared himself to most of us by staging a mass walkout. We only got as far as the chipper, for want of anywhere better to go, but his rabble-rousing speech was typical of the insidious, impressive and enduring way in which Transition Year so radically does change your life.

An hour after his speech I was back in my seat, feeling a little sheepish at my earlier behaviour, but eleven years after his speech, I still remember it. I remember hearing, as if for the first time, that school was going to end one day, that it wasn't the be all and end all, and that the most important thing was to be a good, and if not good, then an impressive, person. It was a message that was repeated in various forms and guises throughout Transition Year, if never quite so eloquently. That year was the first time I began to realize that there were several sides to every story, several ways of looking at everything and several people who were more interesting than you would ever give them credit for. This hugely valuable information wasn't drummed into my skull by constant repetition, was never written on a blackboard and if I now know it by heart it's because I learned it to be true rather than learned it by rote.

'Winging it: taking a year out to mature',
Education Times Supplement, *The Irish Times,* 18 March 2000

4

'Under the laughter, under the fluent comic talk, under the jokes and the satirical swipes, was a totally private contemplative.'

– BRENDAN KENNELLY

In 1987 Jonathan was commissioned to write a regular column for the *Sunday Press* newspaper, then concerned that its readership was ageing and that its circulation had been overtaken by its historic rival, the *Sunday Independent.* The idea seems to have been that Jonathan would appeal to his own generation. However the editorial team at the *Sunday Press* had not recognized how unbiddable Jonathan could be. MICHAEL KEANE was then editor of the paper.

Sunday Press promotion announcing one of its new columnists, 13 March 1988

> In many ways the debate on whether he was the kind of columnist we needed mirrored the nationwide debate. This centred on whether he was a modern, day 'brat' who was making a show of his decent parents, or whether he was a wonderful breath of fresh air which was so badly needed in the stuffy atmosphere of Irish society. We had hired him to write a column to reflect what was happening in the capital which was then just becoming one of the 'in' cities of Europe. We knew he was out and about, eating in the trendiest restaurants, partying with the 'in' set, meeting young writers, actors, artists – the kind of people we wanted to read about in the paper. So where were the 'in' places, who was the hottest young writer, who held the best parties, where were the best holidays these days? That was the plan. Jonathan, as ever, had other ideas. Lots of them. Ideas were what Jonathan was all about and he had strong opinions on every topic. Some of them drove people mad and again it was a generational thing. Young people loved his columns: older people hated them. Nobody ignored him. He was wonderful

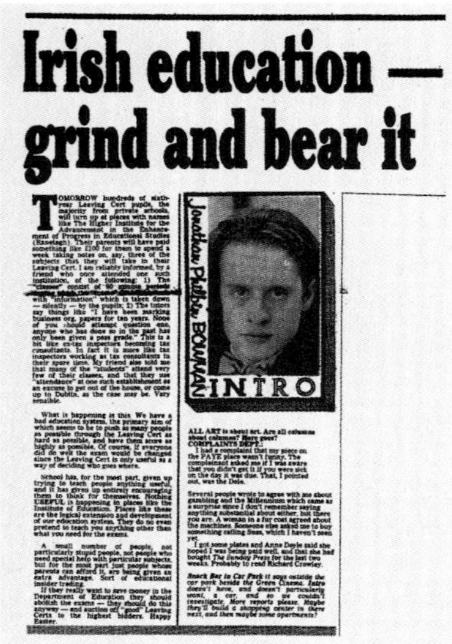

Irish education — grind and bear it

Jonathan Philbin BOWMAN

INTRO

The *Sunday Press* had hired him to be a young man about town, not a polemiscist on the education system. *Sunday Press*, 27 March 1988

to deal with, personable, always cheerful and funny about life and the people he met on his daily travels.

Because of his somewhat nomadic lifestyle, Jonathan sometimes found himself separated from his computer. He had not yet reached the stage when his briefcase carried all he needed to give himself a portable office from which he could work anywhere in the world. At that time he would occasionally make an urgent phone call to borrow my old back-up portable typewriter. EANNA BROPHY recalled that he sometimes presented his copy typed on 'what must have been the most ancient of typewriters which made holes in the flimsy paper he used, and which drove the printers bananas – especially when subbed with extra biro scribbles.' He found that Jonathan was invariably 'amused by our protestations, confident that his every word was a gem, for which we should be grateful even if he brought it in on Ogham stones – and sometimes he was right.' Eanna was a staff writer on the *Sunday Press* who also wrote an excellent humorous column which had been much enjoyed by Jonathan as he was growing up.

At that time, to those who had not met him, and who knew him only through the odd television appearance, Jonathan may have seemed cocky and precocious – but on even the briefest acquaintance such prejudices were melted by his sheer charm and wit – and his genuine warmth and interest in other people. I witnessed this occurring on several occasions in Burgh Quay. I do remember that the editor was not always pleased with what Jonathan chose to write about. He may have been hired to be our 'young man about town' but Jonathan simply declined to be strait-jacketed. He also on one occasion wrote a piece sending up a *Sunday Press* editorial decision to 'spike' one of his more outrageous efforts – and at that young age he was capable of being quite baffled when this in turn was 'spiked' – and we still had the actual spikes in those days.

I recall that after some piece he wrote he received a nannyish letter from a woman staffer of his acquaintance in *The Irish Times* deploring how he was being 'exploited' by us crass Burgh Quay types. She did not know that he was very much his own man, and that the piece he wrote was his own idea. Jonathan, of course, joyfully showed us all the letter.

FRANCES O'ROURKE was Jonathan's commissioning editor at

the *Sunday Press*. Coming back from an editorial meeting she sometimes found him sitting at her desk, 'feet up, chatting to my office colleagues. Just eighteen, he was loud, irreverent, disrespectful and good fun.' I recall that Jonathan always spoke affectionately about her even when she was attempting – unsuccessfully – to prompt him to write about subjects which did not interest him.

> The fact was that Jonathan was much too individual to write 'voice of a generation' stuff. His choice of topics was eclectic – he was passionately anti-smoking, curious about new age spirituality, and iconoclastic about established religion. One breezily rude column about the meaning of Easter sparked a row, and was toned down. He had no interest at all, it seemed, in rock music. His young fogeyish persona wasn't popular with everyone in the *Sunday Press* office: hard-bitten male reporters in particular were often immune to Jonathan's charms, although they couldn't always resist his wit. But he was the pet of pretty well all the women who met him – because of his genuine, affectionate interest in us, no matter what our age. And he was generous in his interest in other journalists: he had grown up reading Eanna Brophy's humorous columns, and seemed genuinely impressed that he was now writing for the same paper. The late 1980s was a time of great flux for the *Sunday Press*, and Jonathan's column, along with others, was discontinued in 1988 – just a few months before the birth of Saul. Sitting in a café on Burgh Quay with him to say good-bye, I felt uncomfortable, knowing the difficulties the loss of his *Sunday Press* income could cause him. But always a gentleman, Jonathan was charming – regretful, but not bitter, and candid about his plans to take care of his new baby in a few months' time. His unfailing good humour didn't desert him, even when the going was getting tough.

On 6 January 1988, Jonathan's nineteenth birthday, we planned a dinner to celebrate the fact that we were all still living under the one roof in relative harmony and that Jonathan seemed happy and stimulated in his work. We booked a table at Patrick Guilbaud's, inviting Eimer's parents, Eva and Jack Philbin, who could take some of the credit for getting us this far. By the time we arrived, Jonathan was already sipping champagne.

There was little routine to Jonathan's life. Every day was full of surprises. And what Jonathan knew that evening but did not tell us until some week's later was a surprise for which we were totally unprepared. Coming into our bedroom one Saturday morning, he opened the conversation by saying: 'Remember, Father, when you

Eimer's parents, Eva and Jack Philbin, with Jonathan, their first grandchild

Jonathan with CaraIosa Mehigan
1988

once said to me that whatever news I ever brought you, that you'd always love me?' I asked myself, what's coming here? He then told us that CaraIosa Mehigan, his girlfriend, whom we had met on a couple of occasions, was expecting their baby in about six months. We both thought of Jonathan as just about on the verge of taking flight, impatient to be free of obligations and almost neurotic about how he spent his time. We could not envisage – nor did we imagine he could – his coping with the responsibility of both a baby and a long-term relationship. CaraIosa was only eighteen and we had a number of anxious meetings with her equally concerned parents. Jonathan, however, from the first moment, was buoyant and optimistic and spoke enthusiastically about the challenges ahead. Shortly afterwards CaraIosa and he moved to a small apartment on Leeson Street.

In April 1988 CaraIosa was briefly a patient in the Mater Hospital in Dublin. Jonathan visited her daily. One of the ward nurses, MAIREAD GLEESON, recalled in a letter that he would come out to the nurse's station if one of the patients was looking for assistance. She remembered one night discussing the role of student nurses.

> He thought we worked very hard. I was of the opinion at the time that the plight of the student nurse in this country would never improve until the traditional approach to training was abolished. He then told me that whilst he would not decry the benefits of education, he felt experiential learning was much more beneficial.

I disagreed and told him that I felt the Mater Hospital was a totally autocratic, bureaucratic organization, with student nurses as pawns and was not conducive to learning. He then asked me what I learnt from life and what I did in my spare time. I replied that I was like every student nurse in Dublin – we either go to the pub or to a party. He was shocked that I had never been to a play. I went on holidays and when I came back Caralosa had been discharged. Jonathan had left me a book. It was a play by Brian Friel – *Philadelphia, Here I Come!* There was a note with it saying: 'Read this, you will enjoy it and if you ever get the opportunity, go and see it.' I read it and really enjoyed it. It came to the Abbey the following summer and I went to see it.

I subsequently went to UCD to take a masters degree. When working as Assistant Director of Nursing at a teaching hospital, part of my remit was to lecture student nurses. I always tried to convey to them the benefits of exposure to a wide range of experiences. My encounters with Jonathan were minimal and yet I feel he was somebody who really made me think. This is why I decided to share with you the significant impact which he had on me nearly twelve years ago.

'Jonathan had left me a book. ...There was a note with it saying: "Read this, you will enjoy it and if you ever get the opportunity, go and see it." – Mairead Gleeson

Saul was born in Holles Street Hospital on 6 July 1988, to the immense joy of both his parents. Having been present at the birth, Jonathan celebrated at lunch with his grandmother, Eva Philbin, and his godmother, Deirdre Dargan. We returned from France two days later in time for yet another celebration dinner, the first of many such occasions for Saul in Pembroke Lane. From babyhood Saul was taken by his parents on adventures. Jonathan experimented with what were then a new range of pouches, slings and buggies which enabled parents to transport a baby. He liked to take Saul everywhere. THERESA MILLEA from Youghal, Co. Cork recalled one encounter with him and a three weeks' old Saul on a train.

He was struggling with baby, pram, carry-cot and the 'travelling doctor's shop' that usually accompanies a small baby. When it became obvious that he was unaccompanied I suggested that if I held the baby it would be easier for him to manage everything else. His expression of gratitude and delight was unbelievable. You'd have thought I'd given him the Lottery.

JOE CARROLL of *The Irish Times* remembered queuing up to interview some author in the Shelbourne. 'I was holding a tape-recorder. He was holding his baby son. I did not know what to think and I'm sure the author was just as non-plussed.' Another

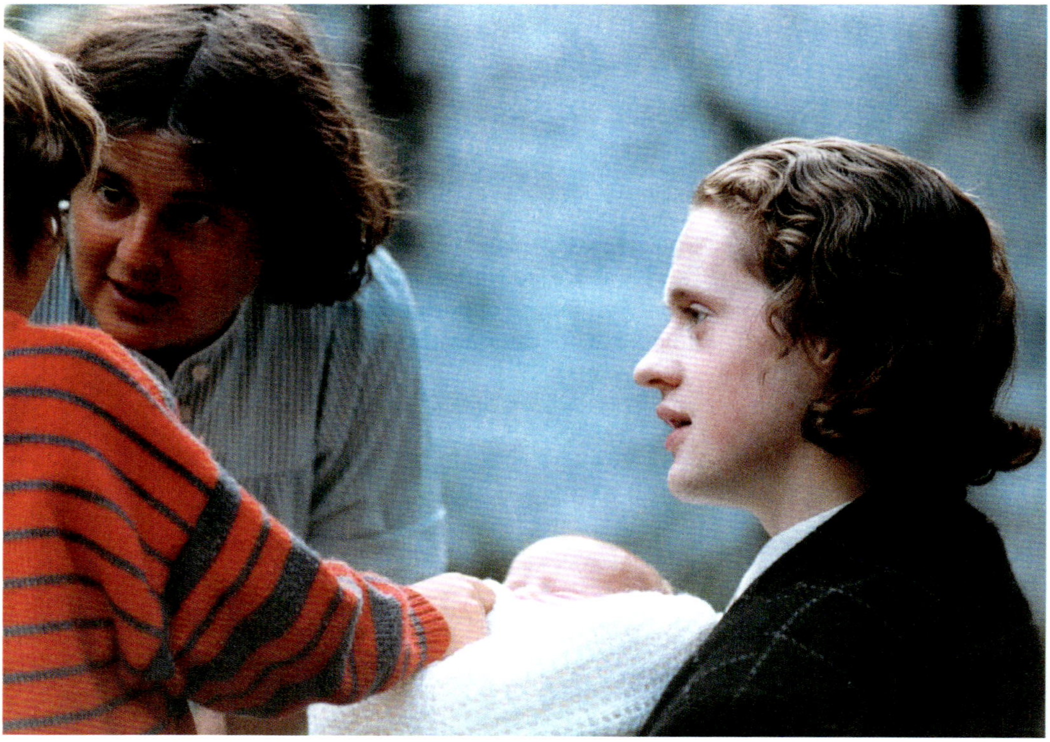

At the earliest opportunity Jonathan brought Saul to visit us. He is three days' old in these photographs

journalist, MAVIS ARNOLD, recalled Jonathan at a press conference sitting in the front row with Saul on his lap 'sucking away' at his bottle. 'He simply did not care what people thought. That was the aspect of his character that I admired most – he could irritate some people and enchant others but he was always absolutely his own man.' PROFESSOR JOHN BONNAR of Trinity Medical School recalled Jonathan at a press conference, one of thirty journalists, the other twenty-nine being women.

> He was the life and soul of the conference with his combination of shrewd questions and amazing sense of humor. In this coterie of women journalists he was highly respected and the centre of attraction for his knowledge and wit.

ELEANOR FEELY worked in the theatre in Dublin in the late 1980's when she first noticed Jonathan with CaraIosa and Saul as regulars in Bewleys.

> They looked together like an exotic creation of J.M. Barrie. I always remember meeting him in the Shelbourne Hotel with his customary white linens and curls and responding to our enquiry about Saul's well-being (all women are clucking hens!) saying that Saul had zillions of teeth. He was unique. Most importantly, he gave those of us who live our lives differently to the accepted social rhythms – and we artists can be very isolated and lonely at times – a sense that we were not alone and that individuality, a love of intangible things, and a different way of seeing, were virtues. We were not alone.

SISTER MARY LORETO MCGRATH wrote from the St Louis Nursing Home in Monaghan recalling that her sister and herself had been in Bewley's Café in Grafton Street when Saul – with Jonathan at the next table – was still a small baby in his pram.

> Jonathan was very busy, settling the baby's bottle – the devoted father even then! However, through the years, his writings have delighted so many of us. There is no need to stress that. Is it any wonder so many loved him? So now, in the loneliness of old age, your final words at Jonathan's requiem touched me deeply. They are so true, he was, and will always be, your 'lovely boy'. Be sure of all my prayers and remembrance for a dear soul as long as I live.

Around Easter 1989 it became clear that Jonathan and CaraIosa were feeling the strain of being such young parents so early in their relationship. They each spoke to Eimer about the difficulties they were having. And she noted in her journal how

...overwhelming CaraIosa finds the responsibility of being such a young mother; before becoming pregnant the plan was for her to go to France and she described how she kept thinking she'd wake up one morning and everything would be like it was when she was seventeen. She loves Saul, thinks him wonderful and fears not seeing him growing up. But commented: 'I don't think Jonathan would let that happen.' Jonathan for his part realizes how difficult it would be for CaraIosa to be living separately from Saul but, given the tensions in the relationship, understands her need to be independent and finish her education.

My response to both of them is one of sympathy. I talked to CaraIosa about how much she had achieved in a year and a half coping with pregnancy and the demands of motherhood. Saul was clearly a happy baby and loved by both of them. I said that if they continued to make him their priority they should be able to work things out. Jonathan at present seems capable and motivated to rear Saul and seems to be able to combine it with his work but would need her support to do that. I suggested to CaraIosa that she work out a plan for herself and although it was extremely difficult in Irish culture for the mother not to be the primary carer she must not think badly of herself for that. I told her that I would always make sure Saul knew how much she loved him and that while Jonathan could manage now, someday he might go through a crisis and she would have to take over.

Gradually a plan evolved: one of the benefits for Saul's extended

(PREVIOUS PAGE) When Jonathan and CaraIosa brought Saul to visit their friend, the photographer Conor Horgan, he took this impromptu photograph. Saul is one week old.

Saul with his maternal grandfather, Patrick 'Ogie' Mehigan

family on both sides was that they enjoyed his company regularly. Scarcely a week went by that he did not spend time with his grandparents, Ogie and Eithne Mehigan, or CaraIosa's sister Caoileann and her children. He was always sure of a bed, often at short notice, with my sister Deirdre Dargan and her family. And when Jonathan's unpredictable lifestyle demanded instant substitute care – often for a few days at a time – he turned to Chloe Blake for whom the word 'No' did not seem to exist where Saul was concerned. Saul has always regarded himself as an honorary member of the Blake family.

After his *Sunday Press* column was dropped, Jonathan began writing occasional pieces for the *Sunday Tribune* and was then offered a contract by the then editor, Vincent Browne, who was also publisher of *Magill* and who had acquired the *In Dublin* title from John Doyle. Jonathan worked from home but his visits to the office – often with baby Saul in tow – 'caused happy mayhem' according to one staff writer there at the time. HELEN LUCY BURKE recalled the first day that Saul arrived into the office. She noticed Saul's teeth: he noticed her open sandals.

> Although I skipped out of range he continued towards me, then followed me behind a filing-cabinet, and around the desks, with a single focus of objective amazing in one so young – about eight or nine months I would guess. Jonathan at some point noticed my alarmed squeaks. Turning first to me he said majestically: 'Show no fear.' 'But I am afraid,' I moaned. He bent to Saul, and told him to desist. I think his exact words may have been 'This behaviour is not appropriate.' Confident that parental authority had been exercised in a non-judgmental manner he returned to his conversation with the editorial staff. And Saul returned to my foot. By this stage he had me cornered and sank the sharpest teeth I have ever experienced into my instep, changed direction slightly and followed the first strike with another on my big toe. I screamed with pain, hopping on one leg, and tried to shake him off. From the other side of the filing-cabinet I heard again the parent's voice: 'Show no fear. It only encourages him.' Just as Jonathan came around to investigate I had shook Saul off; and Jonathan's adjurations to him on observing the blood streaming from my wound were almost severe. But the bulky retreating bottom was now crawling towards a target even worthier of his steel – the electric plugs under a desk. A yank from the baby's fist and the computers fell silent. Saul Philbin Bowman had annihilated the complete next Sunday's edition of the newspaper.

VINCENT BROWNE has known both Eimer and myself all our adult lives; and he had known Eimer even earlier since they had both been at Irish College in Colaiste na Rinne in 1955 and later at UCD in the 1960s.

I was intrigued by Jonathan for I had known Eimer and John for a long time and admired them both. He seemed to have in abundance the intelligence and assurance of his parents, entirely without their reserve. As I remarked on the night of his death, perhaps he had been too intelligent, too early. Some time in early 1989 he was at a loss journalistically and came to see me in the *Sunday Tribune*. *Magill*, in its first incarnation, was then around and the *Tribune* had bought the *In Dublin* title from John Doyle.

I thought Jonathan was an exceptional talent and recruited him for *In Dublin*. After a few months there, the editor said she would go or Jonathan had to go. I brought him into *Magill* and asked him to get together the photographs of the 1980s for publication in the December 1989 issue of the magazine. Kevin Myers had collected the photographs of the 1970s for the December 1979 issue of *Magill* and it had been successful. Jonathan agreed. This was in October 1989.

In November the Berlin Wall fell. Jonathan said he was going to Berlin for *In Dublin*. I said I was relying on him to complete the photographs project. He agreed not to go. A few days later, he left a note on my desk telling me how far he had got with the photographs, how someone else could complete the project – and that he had gone to Berlin. The December 1989 issue of *Magill* had to be cancelled.

The next I saw of Jonathan was at the *Tribune* Christmas party. I told him that I never wanted to have any association with him again, not personal, not social, not professional. My next sighting of him was outside the accounts office of the *Tribune* in late January 1990. I asked what he was doing and he said he had come in to collect his monthly cheque from *Magill*. I enquired why he thought he was entitled to be paid, since he had not been around for almost three months. He said he was still employed by the magazine. I had the cheque cancelled.

Jonathan sued me and won. The judge found that had I fired him at the Christmas party I would have been entitled to do so but that, as I merely had expressed a personal preference, I had to pay up. My memory here may be partly mistaken for clearly he was entitled to payment for his lengthy piece for *In Dublin* on Berlin.

I saw him a few times afterwards in pubs. He sought to buy me

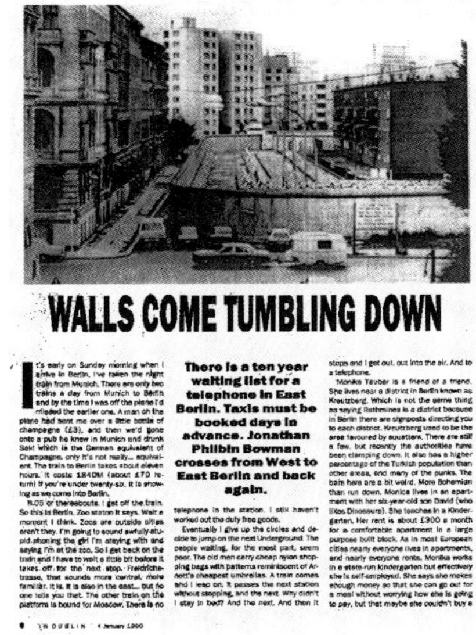

WALLS COME TUMBLING DOWN

It's early on Sunday morning when I arrive in Berlin. I've taken the night train from Munich. There are only two trains a day from Munich to Berlin and by the time I was off the plane I'd missed the earlier one. A man on the plane had sent me over a little bottle of champagne (£3), and then we'd gone onto a pub he knew in Munich and drunk Sekt which is the German equivalent of Champagne, only it's not really... equivalent. The train to Berlin takes about eleven hours. It costs 184DM (about £70 return) if you're under twenty-six. It is snowing as we come into Berlin.

8.05 or thereabouts. I get off the train. So this is Berlin. Zoo station it says. Wait a moment I think. Zoos are outside cities aren't they. I'm going to sound awfully stupid phoning the girl I'm staying with and saying I'm at the zoo. So I get back on the train and I have to wait a little bit before it takes off for the next stop. Freidrichstrasse, that sounds more central, more familiar. It is. It is also in the east... but no one tells you that. The other train on the platform is bound for Moscow. There is no

There is a ten year waiting list for a telephone in East Berlin. Taxis must be booked days in advance. Jonathan Philbin Bowman crosses from West to East Berlin and back again.

telephone in the station. I still haven't worked out the duty free goods.

Eventually I give up the circles and decide to jump on the next Underground. The people waiting, for the most part, seem poor. The old men carry cheap nylon shopping bags with patterns reminiscent of Arnott's cheapest umbrellas. A train comes and I leap on. It passes the next station without stopping, and the next. Why didn't I stay in bed? And the next. And then it stops and I get out, out into the air. And to a telephone.

Monika Tauber is a friend of a friend. She lives near a district in Berlin known as Kreutzberg. Which is not the same thing as saying Rathmines is a district because in Berlin there are signposts directing you to each district. Kreutzberg used to be the area favoured by squatters. There are still a few, but recently the authorities have been clamping down. It also has a higher percentage of the Turkish population than other areas, and many of the punks. The bars here are a bit weird. More Bohemian than run down. Monica lives in an apartment with her six-year-old son David (who likes Dinosaurs). She teaches in a Kindergarten. Her rent is about £300 a month for a comfortable apartment in a large purpose built block. As in most European cities nearly everyone lives in apartments, and nearly everyone rents. Monika works in a state-run kindergarten but effectively she is self-employed. She says she makes enough money so that she can go out for a meal without worrying how she is going to pay, but that maybe she couldn't buy a

8 IN DUBLIN 4 January 1990

Jonathan presumably reckoned he was still on the payroll because *In Dublin* had published his article on his visit to Berlin, 'Walls come tumbling down' in *In Dublin*, 4 January 1990

> a drink but I wouldn't have it. When he died, I was struck by the warmth, by the affection and, above all, by the multitude of tributes to him. I regretted, not so much my expression of anger at that Christmas party, but regretted not seeing beyond that impulsive recklessness to a generous, funny, and often lonely, man. I regretted, too, not telling him that any young journalist worth his salt should have craved to be in Berlin during those momentous days and perhaps he was right to have gone. Most especially, I regretted also not joining the voices assuring him of his worth.

At about this time Jonathan visited Oxford with his friend Glen Timmermans, then a postgraduate student at Magdalen College who was hoping that Jonathan might become a mature student at Oxford. Among those whom he met was PROFESSOR ANTHONY SMITH, President of Magdalen. He wrote:

> I met Jonathan only twice, once in Oxford and once in Dublin, but spoke to him on several other occasions. He was first brought to see me by a South African graduate student at Magdalen, Glen Timmermans, who was working on modern Irish literature. Glen's idea when he introduced him to me was to get Jonathan to Magdalen. His singularity and vivacity would have gone down well here, but Jonathan's new commitment to fatherhood at that moment persuaded him not to take the matter further, though we remained in touch. When I came to Dublin a year or so later there he was. He took me on a memorable tour, and we ended up meeting John Boorman, whom I had known in the past (in the BBC and as Governor of the British Film Institute) and various other of Ireland's current celebrities. But Jonathan was at this time a television celebrity in his own right, recognized everywhere in Dublin. He was an engaging companion, deeply Irish, international, voluble, proud to be known in every bar, full of sociological insights. I wish he had had the chance to settle down to write a book.

Questioned about earning his living, Jonathan once answered: 'Anything legal considered.' He was an occasional lecturer on media training courses. He was also augmenting his income with copy-writing and accepted some invitations from advertising agencies to attend brain-storming sessions or to write for a particular campaign. KATHY GILFILLAN recalled this part of his work.

> I worked as a copywriter when the Celtic tiger was just a kitten. Jonathan was looking for work and thought he would be ideally suited to the world of advertising. I thought so too. Over a long

lunch, we discussed the idea of Jonathan the copywriter. Part of the appeal for Jonathan was the fact that advertising people in those days took long lunches and could chalk them up to gleaning time. Back I went to the agency and broached the notion of a new writer. 'We need another writer and I know just the person.' The Creative Director was receptive. I started to describe Jonathan without naming him. 'He's terribly clever, very quick mentally, a thousand ideas a minute – so funny and very loyal, can talk up a storm. And enthusiasm, you never met such enthusiasm.'

'Stop, right there', said the Creative Director. 'Is this Jonathan Philbin Bowman you're talking about?'

'As a matter of fact, it is...up to a point, yes.'

'No way, pal', said the Creative Director, 'he'd drive us all nuts. It'd be like having Tigger in the office.' And so Jonathan continued as a journalist – to advertising's great loss.

Jonathan was twenty when he met the actress and journalist JEANANNE CROWLEY. Under the title 'Travelling light' she wrote this personal account of their friendship after he died. It was introduced in the *Sunday Independent*: 'He fixed her broken heart, and their time together was rich and exciting, and the basis for an extraordinary friendship. But at a critical juncture in their relationship, she lost her nerve. In this memoir of the JPB she knew and loved, she ponders whether she let convention ruin the love of her life.'

He breezed into my life and blew me over. One of the truest best souls I ever knew. And I was only one of many. I hugged him to myself when first we met, delighted to encounter such a bright curly head. He was twenty years old. I couldn't believe it. 'Jonathan,' I said, 'this is ridiculous. It's not so much that you can't remember where you where when Kennedy was shot, it's the fact that you weren't even born that's giving me pause for thought.' He dismissed it with an airy wave. 'I can remember where I was when John Lennon was killed, won't that do? Besides,' he added ' You presented *Printout* with my father and I used to stay up to watch that.'

Maybe it was because I fancied he reminded me of myself in those early days when I felt woefully misunderstood that I came to the conclusion that JPB and I were cut from the same cloth, and wanted, if I could, to alert him to some of the difficulties. Effortless grace and remarkable self-confidence can carry the young a long way, but there's a phrase that used to haunt me from a Tom Murphy play: ' Too far too fast JJ. Too far too fast.'

To make a big impact early on is both a blessing and a curse,

(FOLLOWING PAGE)
'Jonathan,' I said, 'this is ridiculous. It's not so much that you can't remember where you were when Kennedy was shot, it's the fact that you weren't even born that's giving me pause for thought.' – Jeananne Crowley

particularly when one is innocent in the ways of the world. Unspoken rules do exist and you break them at your peril. Now here I was faced with a lad far more gifted and quite as impatient as I'd been at his age and I hadn't a clue what to do about it. Jonathan told me all about Robert Louis Stevenson. How the author had come across a widow and her highly eligible daughter somewhere and how the widow thought it was her daughter the great author was interested in, only it wasn't; it was the woman herself. I laughed, refusing to countenance what he was trying to say. I was unpacking all my beloved books at the time and he'd come round to help. Every so often I'd stop to weep and he would put his young arms around me with such tenderness that I nearly began to believe that all men aren't bastards after all.

I'd come back to Dublin with a badly broken heart you see, back to a nice house but no money to furnish it and no notion of how I was going to make a proper living. I hadn't expected to have to start all over again. Amazing how helpless strong women can feel sometimes, but Jonathan seemed to understand completely. His company was so cheering it was impossible to wallow in self-pity for longer than it took him to laugh me out of it.

I loved him, too, because he wasn't in the least predatory. There was a fluidity to his loving and giving. Jonathan never set out to 'score'. I realized quite early on that whatever he did and wherever he went, Jonathan was one of those souls born to add to the gaiety of nations. But then people said that about me. Ex-fiancés mostly, as they waved me goodbye.

There was a crucial difference though. Jonathan had a baby. That was unusual, and more to the point he was in charge of this baby and appeared to be doing a fine job. It anchored him to have to deal with nappies and early-morning feeds and he never once complained of the difficulties he faced in taking care of such a small child. He was living in a mews house in a lane behind Leeson Park at the time, with books and the baby and very little else in the way of creature comforts.

Jonathan had that same great capacity for delight whatever the circumstances. He loved good food and good company and at least I could provide that. And the fun we had when friends would visit. The plan was that he would keep them vastly amused while I prepared a delicious meal. All sorts of folk mostly from a world he hugely enjoyed entertaining. Even people who took themselves ever so seriously ended up in fits of laughter. When a rather pompous BBC man admitted he lacked computer skills Jonathan quick as a flash shot in: 'Oh you mean you can't type?' And when on occasion I'd tell him to stop interrupting he'd answer: 'I'm not

interrupting, JA, I'm only providing the vocal backing.'

Many a Sunday after a long lazy lunch he'd organize games which went on well into the night. His absolute favourite was a word game, *Ex Libris.* Well it would be, wouldn't it? Down came the books from their shelves and he'd pick one, and, having given us the blurb and a quick résumé, write out its first sentence. Then we'd all have to write what we thought the first sentence might be. His parodies were so deft they'd easily have fooled the authors themselves. The only time I reduced him to tears was when he popped in one day and found me crouched over the typewriter drowning in crumpled paper. He couldn't believe I didn't have a computer. Well I did. There was a second-hand Apple Mac in the corner that I hadn't dared plug in, never mind turn on. 'Think of all those rain forests you're wasting,' he said. 'You're mad you know.' He offered to teach me how to use the damn thing there and then and reluctantly I accepted. Hours passed and I simply couldn't get the hang of it at all. His tears were purely of frustration at my complete inability to follow what he was doing so easily and so well, but, God bless him, he persevered.

From a contact sheet after a session in Conor Horgan's studio

God did bless Jonathan with a wealth of talent and an intellect that never threatened to overwhelm his compassion. But even though both of us believed – with Einstein – that the universe is friendly, the society we live in still leaves a lot to be desired in that department. I could see difficult times ahead for him, exciting but difficult, and I shall regret till the day I die that at a critical juncture in both our lives I lost my nerve.

Partly it was to do with money: both of us spent it like water and partly the fact that gradually I began sounding like his mother. Well, not his mother but a mother. You know what I mean. 'Pick that up, Jonathan, this is a house not a hotel.' 'Those dishes won't wash themselves, you know.' 'What did your last slave die of?' Day-to-day stuff that neither of us cared to assume the responsibility for. Being more experienced, I should have seen I was well capable of providing the structured environment we both needed in order to really thrive. This might sound stupid but I think (with the 20/20 vision hindsight brings) that I was offered a golden opportunity to create a new way of living with JPB, unconventional, to be sure, in that it would naturally have had to include a built-in Right to Roam. Of course he could do Life without me. And he did brilliantly.

But all the same I am left with a sense of failure and of unaccountable loss. I was far too concerned about stupid things, like what society would think when to Jonathan that meant nothing at all. I took a different road and it wasn't the road less travelled by. That was the one he offered, and wherever it may have led I'm so sorry now that I hadn't the imagination to take it.

Sunday Independent, 19 March 2000

ELEANOR O'HIGGINS, psychologist and lecturer in business ethics and strategic management at the Smurfit Graduate Business School at UCD, had first met Jonathan when he was five – his articulateness 'already manifest'. Subsequently their paths crossed on a number of occasions.

A vivid incident was my visit to Jonathan's flat when Saul was just beginning to walk in 1989. This was a time when I had first started teaching at UCD. Jonathan had contacted me a few weeks earlier. He had heard about a computer stockmarket game I was running with my first year Commerce class of 300-plus students and wanted to learn more about it. He was intrigued by the competitive aspects of the game, because the class was divided into teams of six and there were sponsored prizes for the first, second, and third place winners.

Jonathan wanted to describe the game and the kind of competition it set up among the students, as part of an article he was writing for a magazine about political game-playing in business. Interestingly enough, there has been a recent resurgence of interest in 'political game playing' in corporate life. Anyway, to suit Saul's timetable, Jonathan had requested that we talk about his planned article in his flat. So we discussed 'high finance' while Jonathan catered to Saul's needs. I was amazed at what a natural parent he was, given his own tender age at the time.

GLEN TIMMERMANS, then working on a PhD thesis on Brian Friel at Magdalen College Oxford, met Jonathan at this time.

My memories of Jonathan? Simply that he was immensely charming and impressive in his youthful success. Walking down Dublin streets with him was always amusing for this was the first time that I saw, close up, the gentle hand of Irish fame: people would stop him in the street and say 'Howareye, Jonathan?' or whisper 'Dere's dat Jonathan Philbin Bowman'. That he was well-known and admired there can be no doubt. I remember him as resembling a slightly scruffy cherub with a hint of wickedness; though that wickedness was often more a physical trait than anything else. I recall being a little taken aback by his rather puritan attitudes towards some subjects, especially sex, I think, for to look at, there was definitely a strong hint of dissolution. But, as I said, I imagine here, looks were deceptive. Of course, he was much younger than was reasonable to be, given his public success; and one had sometimes to remind oneself of his youth at the time.

Another friendship which developed from our summers in Ballymaloe and Shanagarry was with the potter STEPHEN PEARCE whose terracotta pottery we have used since we were first married. On our visits to Shanagarry, we would call to Stephen for a cup of coffee and, usually, add to our collection. Stephen has always been delighted with the interest shown by young children in pottery and welcomed Jonathan and Emma into the workshop whenever they visited. He wrote:

> I always felt an empathy for Jonathan as I felt we were cast in very similar moulds. Jonathan was what I never had the balls to be. He really said it like he saw it. I think you all deserve medals for putting up with the never-ending magic years because for me that must have been his way of checking your credentials; had you even blinked an eyelid he might have felt less safe to really be himself. I often wondered how many people saw through the brittle exterior to the loving, shy, searching young man.
>
> Jonathan's relationship with Saul was incredible. For me it was 'in the raw', what all parent-kid relationships are but without the polite trimmings. There was a terrible television show, *Play the Game,* and somehow my ego allowed me to do it. I scored the lowest marks ever on the show but got the highest TAM ratings. Jonathan scored the highest points ever and always wanted me to do the show with him. I considered myself very lucky to have escaped with my life the first time. As soulmates it always amazed me that Jonathan could never see the amount of fear and embarrassment I felt around that show. I always felt very protective of Jonathan; it was a strange and unique emotion, part son and part brother, but it was like our spirits were one. The sheer style of the guy. The last time I saw him was sitting at a café on the pavement with a girl and holding court like he owned the place. I had always looked forward to his maturing years because when he felt ready, some amazing material would have issued forth.

The Shelbourne Bar 'suited him for its sense of gentility and decorum, and as a child-friendly zone. There he could be a minding father, working journalist, poseur, *flâneur*, bloody nuisance, well-bred gentleman at play.' – John Stephenson

JOHN STEPHENSON had been a controversial figure in Dublin artistic and media circles before migrating to London in the 1980s where he directed the 'Sense of Ireland' exhibition. It was on his return to Dublin that he first met Jonathan.

> From the first moment we met, I envied him his mental and verbal facility, but also recognised the hurtful notice-box in myself, and loved him for that shared flaw. I had been warned as I returned from spending the Eighties in London that there was another monster on the block. Another over-educated, over-opinionated, over-confident, over-the-top performance artist had hit the scene. Anyway, nothing had prepared me for the first encounter with JPB.

My Black Knight stumbled before his Red, and I never battled him again. I felt no better than a Floyd Patterson to his exquisite Cassius. He was formidable.

He was the kind of modern Irishman that our own earlier generation of Dublin 4 upstarts aspired to, as if we could all be like that – although Geldof was not unlike. I loved and admired JPB for his sheer brilliant cheek, yet always with the heavy cavalry in reserve. He was an absolute brat who wouldn't hurt a spider, but could and did fell giants. Nights, I have witnessed his fearless and hilarious upbraiding of the powerful, the corrupt and the pompous at the Shelbourne Bar, and his kindly familial gatherings in the front lounge there by day. It was the home I knew him in. It suited him for its sense of gentility and decorum, and as a child-friendly zone. There he could be a minding father, working journalist, poseur, *flâneur*, bloody nuisance, well-bred gentleman at play. And he was at play at work, and there were plenty of boars to the slaughter. Most of all I cherish a marathon performance of political and social satire, mimickry, poetry and bizarre insight delivered at breakneck speed and with enormous genius to a bunch of us over lunch in Spiddal after the Galway Arts Festival in, I think, 1991. Never have I experienced such excruciating hilarity. It was my second tentative year back in Ireland. In a moment I knew why I had come home.

CHARLES LYSAGHT, lawyer and writer, is a family friend. It was at my invitation that he wrote about Jonathan as he had remembered him growing up. His first memory was of Jonathan aged fifteen arguing in our house about why he should go to England for the CND Aldermaston march at Easter 1985. 'What a precocious and angry child.' He also recalled Jonathan on the *Late Late Show* when he had left school and recalled that many adults 'who should have known better were taking offence because he was bumptious and opinionated – "an arrogant pup" was often the phrase from people who should have been more understanding and amused.' He felt some sympathy with Jonathan as he thought that 'in a lesser key' he himself may have been similarly regarded at the same age.

I recall meeting him in town when he was less than twenty-one and being invited to tea in the Shelbourne. I was dazzled by the way he had thought out positions on so many matters. He wanted to pay for the tea and I had to insist that students were not expected to pay for anything. I recall that he complained to me that either you or Eimer or both were not such liberals as you pretended when it came to the point. I cannot remember exactly what you had done or said to deserve this assessment.

His difficulty was that he was hyperactive and many of his defects, such as being so easily bored, derived from that. He was clever enough to be able to avoid the hard grind. It was looking as if he would never settle down sufficiently to realize the potential of his brain-power. Perhaps he was not sufficiently self-critical about his work. He was full of generous impulses, almost recklessly so. I liked that very much as I did his openness, honesty and affectionate nature. He was full of interest yet he may have thought he was even more interesting than he was. I am not sure whether the best days were over when he died or whether he would have realized his potential. I hope you will not consider that I have been too frank in what I have written. I am conscious that I could be wrong in some of my assessments but I think you would want to have them for what they are worth.

The architect MARTIN REYNOLDS was a friend – and sometime generous and patient landlord – to Jonathan. He wrote:

Jonathan could be an awful strain, as he was so demanding. His mind was in overdrive always, and words poured out, thoughts exploded on the other party to a meeting. He had a wonderful vocabulary, astonishing for his age. His range of interests and topics always astonished me. It could be architecture, drama, education, politics, religion. He had some knowledge of each subject and a view on each one, often an unusual view, and usually a controversial one. He sought to shock people, and his views were at times very extraordinary. He could be regarded as a champion of every lost cause; and of course, some went on to be won.

His appearance was also shocking. It was designed that way. His hair could be long, very long, or suddenly short. Maybe a beard, maybe none. Shirts striped, jackets maybe based on the loose linen jackets favoured by his father. Ties, again maybe from that stable. But always a rainbow of colours. Jonathan knew he was a celebrity. This was for a number of reasons. He had shocked middle-class society by a declaration on television that he was leaving school, as he could not learn anything else there. Many agreed with him, in secret, but few had the courage to leave. He had a forceful personality, serious, but in fun, a wry way of smiling, an appealing pair of eyes.

Jonathan could take photographs and took some for me and they were excellent. He had an artist's eye for composition. He could write very well, about anything, or even about nothing. I often read some article he had written impressed by the style and

the choice of words. Maybe later I wondered what it had been about. When I knew Jonathan I was having small dinner parties and drink parties in my home. The people invited ranged from artists to architects, writers, political personalities and school friends, many of whom were architects and a bit Bohemian themselves. For mischief, I would add on the printed invitation cards, by pen: 'A surprise celebrity guest will attend.' This could have been an artist, a writer, a politician; but Jonathan always assumed it was himself. In fact it usually was, as he was a celebrity and a most colourful personality, and he entertained many guests, had them in stitches. Jonathan loved gadgets, from a complicated penknife to a tiny television set or recorder or an electric bottle opener. He also knew how they worked, and he used them all the time. In a sense he was akin to one of the gadgets, intriguing, complicated and effective.

'Jonathan could take photographs and took some for me and they were excellent. He had an artist's eye for composition.' – Martin Reynolds.
Jonathan disliked posed photographs, preferring to work without the subject being aware of the camera – as here in our garden.

The wine writer TOM WHELEHAN knew Jonathan from meeting him occasionally at wine-tastings and 'also in the gregarious, mildly Bohemian atmosphere of the Arts Club'. He recalled that he himself had been 'brash and opinionated' in his twenties, his parents feeling it pretentious for such a young man 'to be posing as a wine expert' rather than drinking pints with his own generation. Tom found in Jonathan 'some of the posturings' of his own early days when he admitted that to win credibility and overcome his deficiencies he had cultivated a high profile. He found 'two sides' to Jonathan.

> The first mirrored the above reflections. He liked attention; enjoyed an argument or debate; enjoyed even more coming out on top – which he usually did. He was so highly intelligent, articulate, incisive and witty. His ability to bounce balls and bowl googlies* came from an agile mind which challenged any adversary. What did not come out in his columns or television appearances was his deeper side. Here one found a naturally thoughtful, well-mannered, generous soul who was serious and searching. Such moments shared always left me with a deep respect. Though few, these quieter moments could leave me in awe. These were some Philbin and Bowman genes working towards the surface. It is sad that we will never see their flowering.

Journalist and broadcaster ANN MARIE HOURIHANE had known Jonathan since the 1980s.

> Perhaps it's best to start with a joke from Jonathan. He certainly thought it best to start that way. One day, about six years ago, Jonathan came to visit me when I was at the height of my enthusiasm for gardening. It is true that Jonathan never bothered with suburban pursuits. I said something about my clematis, pointing to it out the window, and Jonathan replied 'Darling, most men can't even pronounce clematis, let alone find one'. That still makes me laugh.
>
> Jonathan was very kind to both my mother and my late friend, Gerry MacNamara, obtaining mobile phones for them when they were staying in hospital for long periods and when mobiles were a luxury. He loved to be helpful. I know you can always say this after a death but in Jonathan's case it is literally true: there was nobody like him. From what was said at the funeral and from what Jonathan said of himself, I think Jonathan was born as he was, all of a piece. He talked of himself when he was three years old exactly the same as he talked of himself when he was twenty-three. The tenses aren't quite right in that sentence, appropriately enough. You

* googly; an occasional slow ball bowled in cricket which looks like it will turn as a leg-break but which the bowler has disguised by sleight of hand to surprise the batsman by turning it in the opposite direction.

will know whether the extravagance, the recklessness, the brilliance, the interest in religion, the great wit, and a sort of innocence born of a ruthlessly logical brain were always there in him. The love of risk. The loneliness of being unusual. He was a conspicuous person, a feature of Dublin street life. Everyone knew him. He gave up his anonymity very young – of course, he loved attention – and later on I think he missed it.

I didn't see much of Jonathan in what turned out to be his final years. Jonathan lived fast and you had to be able for him. Sometimes he just drove me mad. I remember him from the time Saul was quite small. I once babysat, when the two of them were living in Pembroke Street. Jonathan was the only person in the world to make me feel as if I was tidy. I remember him from the time he went out with my good friend, Sarah Foot who loved him so well. One day he came to collect Saul from this house in a horse-drawn carriage. I remember Jonathan telling me several times how much he loved the lunches he shared with John – 'we have a lovely time'. How hard times must be for you now, with that complex, brilliant, infuriating, funny, chaotic, demanding and generous boy gone. I always think of Jonathan as a boy, although he lived a man's life from such an early age. I am more sorry than I can say.

Jonathan brought Saul to art openings, press conferences and into the office, whether it was *In Dublin*, the *Sunday Tribune*, or to the 98FM studios for whom he did some early morning broadcasts in the early 1990s. This was before he was recruited by FM104 as a presenter on *The Rude Awakening*. Many of those who wrote recalled seeing him carrying Saul on his back, on his bicycle carrier, or – one witness insisted – under his arm hurrying through St Stephen's Green, with a briefcase in his other hand. The economist KIERAN KENNEDY wrote of his abiding mental picture of him – 'a combination of energy and serenity pushing Saul in the baby carriage around the Baggot Street area, going at a rate of knots, and unconscious of the notice he attracted.' Incidentally Jonathan himself was carried in what I believe was the first MacLaren buggy to be brought into Ireland when its innovative design – it could be collapsed in seconds from a four-wheel buggy into little more than a shooting stick – was still a wonder. We bought it in Edinburgh just after it had been launched. He liked to think he was the first 'graduate' of a MacLaren buggy to wheel his own child in a MacLaren! CAROLINE WALSH, staff writer and now literary editor of *The Irish Times*, also remembered the buggy.

Coming home on the bus the other night and passing the

Jonathan setting out with Saul in tow, September 1989. Saul was then fourteen months old

Shelbourne Hotel I got a sudden flash of how Dublin is diminished without him. He so loved, as I do, pounding those south-side city centre streets, Dawson Street, Kildare Street, Grafton Street. The Shelbourne brought back memories of one of the funniest times I ever had with him. We had all gone there, nine or ten years ago after some book launch, and were having a fine time until Saul's buggy suddenly collapsed. Saul was desolate and wheels and screws were rolling across the floor, until suddenly a businessman from another table raced over. He was a director of MacLaren buggies and MacLaren buggies shouldn't collapse like this! He'd worked his way up through the company, he said, and he'd fix it in a jiffy. Next thing he's down on the floor in the Shelbourne – to Saul's delight – doing a major refurbishment of the buggy, assisted by some of his colleagues – in town for a conference on, no doubt, perambulators!

HILARY BLOXHAM worked at Miss Carr's Nursery, then in

Leeson Park, a pre-school playgroup which Jonathan passed every day when he lived in Sibthorpe Lane. Indeed the staff there 'were accustomed to seeing this distinctive young man, customarily suited and bow-tied, curly poet's mane bobbing in time with his jaunty gait', pushing Saul along in the buggy. Later Saul enrolled in this play-group before his third birthday. Hilary wrote:

> I remember Jonathan as being an appalling time-keeper, invariably arriving late to collect Saul, but his engaging manner and natural charm made it impossible to remain irritated with him for long. In dropping off Saul in the mornings, he nearly always seemed to be in a hurry, rushing off to the next pressing engagement. However, in the evenings he would take the time for a chat and his conversations ranged from politics to lunar eclipses. I learned from these chats that he was a great proponent of father's rights and his devotion to Saul was never in question. It was evident that they enjoyed a wonderful father-son relationship. Jonathan was well supported by his family in bringing up his son and he must have inspired great devotion in Aunt Didi, who would collect Saul whenever he was unable to. It was, no doubt, an unconventional upbringing but possibly all the richer for that – Jonathan clearly provided a secure and loving environment for his son.
>
> I remember one particular occasion which, for me, demonstrated Jonathan's sense of fun and ability and readiness to immerse himself in his son's world. The pre-school group were already playing with modelling clay when he arrived with Saul. Father and son joined the party, Jonathan cutting an amusing figure, seated on a child's chair not a few inches off the floor, long legs outstretched. I was called away briefly and was happy to leave Jonathan in control of his small charges, confident that he would be up to the task of keeping them entertained. I was not to be proved wrong! On my return the children were obviously delighted by something and shortly after Jonathan had left I discovered what it was. He had sculpted a model aeroplane from the clay and had suspended this from the light fitting on the ceiling, to the great amusement of his enrapt young audience. Jonathan was a unique individual but more than this he was a loving father to his son and that is how I will remember him.

Poet and Professor of Modern Literature in Trinity College Dublin, BRENDAN KENNELLY knew Jonathan for many years.

> The first time I heard Jonathan was when we were both taking part in a radio programme discussing 'compulsory Irish'. I remember he was lucid and passionate in his views; his loathing for the term

Brendan Kennelly, Pat Rees and Jonathan on the *Late Late Show* discussing the nature of sexual attraction, 3 May 1991

'compulsory' came across with a special intensity and lent fire to his words. He left me with little to say. I was content to listen to him.

The direct opposite of that passionate, articulate intensity was hilariously evident to me one day in Bewleys of Grafton Street when, with my daughter Kristen, we shared several cups of coffee with Jonathan. I can honestly say that I have never heard such a mastery of comedy, of mad, incisive, intelligent, outrageous fun as I did on that afternoon; the stream, rather the *torrent* of comedy, ranging from sceptical analysis of politics and politicians, to the secure insanity of marriage, to the callous ambitions inherent in our educational system, to coffee itself, to hard work, to the delights of idling, to the happiness and horrors of sexuality – all these were dealt with in a speedy, sharp, mercilessly funny language, a language that belonged to Jonathan alone and which he shared in a spirit of mischief and generosity. I often think of that day. My daughter often mentions it still, with sad, laughing gratitude.

And yet, what is to me the deepest aspect of Jonathan emerged on several occasions when we bumped into each other, and walked the streets for a while, talking, of all things, about education. He was fascinating to listen to on this topic, dear to my own heart and mind. And his thoughts on education were quite inspiring. Essentially, he saw it as a disciplined journey towards freedom, a conscious odyssey towards self-realization and self-liberation. And, in Jonathan's eyes – as in mine – it should be available to everyone. 'There's no freedom without discipline', he said once, 'and there's no real discipline without the sense of freedom.' It is my honest belief that Jonathan would have made a first-class academic, a dynamic teacher, a philosophical scholar, a humane, challenging colleague. He gave me the feeling that I would be honoured and privileged to work with him. Under the laughter, under the fluent comic talk, under the jokes and the satirical swipes, was a totally private contemplative who brooded much on individuals and society, on politics and the media, on relationships and the hope of happiness – and on education. He was one of those rare people with whom even a brief encounter on a city street is a moment of deep and fruitful learning.

Jonathan had by now become involved in media training courses at Carr Communications. He was especially interested in honing the skills of interviewees attempting to cope with an unsympathetic or idiosyncratic interviewer; and this was the challenge on one occasion facing the five headmasters of the Jesuit schools in Ireland. FR BRUCE BRADLEY SJ, sometime headmaster of both Belvedere and of Clongowes Wood College, recalled the encounter.

The headmasters of the five Jesuit schools in Ireland were involved in the training course and the afternoon session was to comprise a televised mock-interview with each of us in turn on a subject of our choosing but, in one way or another, related to education. Jonathan, whom we had not met until he bustled into the room, was to be the interviewer. He was quickly introduced to the group, the first candidate took his seat opposite Jonathan, and the interview began. All Jonathan needed to know was the topic. Then he launched into a ferocious, quick-fire interrogation, a caricature – as he assured us afterwards – of any interview we might actually ever have to undergo, but a *tour de force* of humour, intellectual agility and remarkably sure-footed grasp of the issues presented to him at point-blank range. Each headmaster retired, reeling from the lists, to the safe end of the table, where his colleagues – smug or apprehensive, depending on whether they had been 'done' yet or not – were sitting safely out of the camera's reach. Meanwhile, having enquired what the next subject was to be and after the

> briefest of pauses to focus his mind, Jonathan was launched once more, effortlessly switching gear and nailing another victim good-humouredly to the wall. He was brilliant and, although with more than a tinge of sadness because he is gone, we talk and marvel at it still.

TERRY PRONE is managing director of Carr Communications and her husband, TOM SAVAGE, is a senior consultant and teacher there. They both gave Jonathan many opportunities to exploit his ability as a teacher of media skills, especially in his early years when he was a struggling freelance.

> From the first day we met him, Jonathan constantly brought us happiness. I know of nobody else of whom that could be said. He swamped us with affection and fun and trust, inundated us – in person, on the phone and online – with insight and ideas and wisdom. He adopted waifs and strays and made us adopt them, too. All the time, he was growing, and all the time he was open, especially to people he didn't instinctively agree with. Quite apart from being literate, quick-witted and so lucid, he displaced air when he walked into a room. Because he seemed more alive under his skin than anyone else, because he was always buzzing with ideas and marvellous, wondrous talk, he attracted every eye, and, in the coming decades, would have been an unmatched force in any area of communication. He was unusually good at friendship, surrounding those he loved with a fiercely active loyalty and love. We were blessed to have known him, and will never cease to grieve for his loss.

Shortly after he had become twenty-one, Jonathan moved to one of the most neglected and magnificent streets in Dublin, Henrietta Street. Of all Dublin's Georgian architecture it was John Betjeman's favourite street. To get to Jonathan's flat-warming party, we had had to step over missing planks as we climbed the magnificent staircase. Eimer described the experience as 'like attending a Harold Pinter play on a Sean O'Casey set.' IAN LUMLEY, the architectural conservationist and campaigner for Georgian Dublin, was involved in saving the house in question. He described Jonathan's address at number 12 as 'scruffy'; it was more akin to a 'crash pad, than a place of residence' but Jonathan had made it 'in his own unusual way' home.

> At that time, number 12 was, as a number of other houses in the street still are, a nest of artist's studios in conditions that have barely altered since the once aristocratic houses were converted into

'Henrietta Street', an etching by Brian Lalor

tenements in the nineteenth century. Such details as wiring were elementary, and plumbing was of the cold water type, and shared. If a casting director were looking for a modern-day film setting for a *La Bohème* production, then 12 Henrietta Street would have been the ideal place. Those working there included Cecily Brennan, who came punctually from nine to five, boiler-suited like a Polish steel-worker, producing her huge canvasses. Others, such as Eamon O'Doherty, were more erratic in their activity with lights blazing all night to big deadlines like the production of the full-sized wax model of the 'Floozie in the Jacuzzi', which had to be sawn in half to bring it out through the front door. Jonathan initially inveigled himself on the doorstep as a writer and journalist looking for a quiet room to work and write in. He got the small second-floor room, painted battleship grey by an architecture student. Before taking possession of the room, he gradually hinted that he would be living there and then it became obvious that Saul would be part of the arrangement also.

The house was owned by an old-fashioned absentee landlord working in London and only in Dublin for the occasional weekend. However, there was the memorable moment of Jonathan's mother Eimer arriving at the house for the first time and being confronted by the obvious lack of anything that could be described as domestic comfort or convenience. Jonathan and Saul arranged the room as a child would, with everything spread out on the floor and vaguely defined sleeping, work and play areas. It may

'Jonathan initially inveigled himself on the doorstep as a writer and journalist looking for a quiet room to work and write in. Before taking possession of the room, he gradually hinted that he would be living there and then it became obvious that Saul would be part of the arrangement also.'
– Ian Lumley

have looked like chaos, but there was an order to it all. Saul was still at the nappies stage, and how practical domesticity was handled was baffling. Their comings and goings would be very much erratic, some nights there, some not; but it would be a familiar sound in the early hours of the morning to hear the two of them going up the stairs exchanging their own little private language and patter. Both were always spruce and well-turned out for the outside world and there must have been other friends much visited with bathrooms to make this possible.

Over those couple of years, there were very few evenings when both of us would be in the house together, but one has a particular memory. This was an occasion when a couple of people were visiting and Jonathan and a girl whose name can't be remembered burst into the room full of sociability and the demand for a party. Immediately the whole scene became a nineteenth-century parlour game re-enactment. Jonathan would start each game, first charades, imitating by gesture and mime a play, book or film title. Everybody else was brought along by his gregarious enthusiasm.

What is striking about this whole period is how memorable the relationship between Saul and him was. He was a perfect parent, and, indeed, others said later that if Jonathan can be said to have a stroke of genius, then it was best exercised in his talent for being a parent.

When he got his house in Harold's Cross, it was a great surprise to see him move from such Bohemian chaos to property-owning respectability. However, a first visit to the new house showed that he simply replicated the spread across the floor mode of living of Henrietta Street. Both the collection and the payment of rent was an erratic business in Henrietta Street in those days; but the rent was, in time, paid fully and gracefully.

In 1990 Jonathan first made the acquaintance of the Irish historian, OWEN DUDLEY EDWARDS, professor of history at Edinburgh University. He had known Owen by reputation as an expert on Sherlock Holmes, as a commentator on Scottish politics and culture and as one of the scholars who figured in my own researches on twentieth-century Irish history. Jonathan had been press-ganged into becoming a proofreader of my writings from time to time. Owen reckoned that the 'arrival of a letter from Jonathan Philbin Bowman, introducing himself and asserting his dissimilarity from his father, was clearly inevitable.' Jonathan was twenty-one when he was welcomed as a guest to the Edwards household during the 1990 Edinburgh Festival. Jonathan had come to report on the Festival and he enjoyed it 'with the excitement of

a first day at the seaside.' Owen wrote:

> Jonathan, I suppose, was a post-modernist answer to John: *un*reliable, *un*fair, *un*clear, even *un*intelligent, when he wanted to be; and in his sense of his duty to refuse the safe option of replaying the paternal card, there was an integrity in his defiance of the admirable paternal tradition. His love for his father was absolutely evident at any point: but its expression depended on being officially his antithesis, albeit a more subtle, and no doubt in some respects unintentional reaffirmation of him. Jonathan in repose, Jonathan enjoying a not very hurtful irony, sounded and looked very like John. But let the blood be up, and let Jonathan conceive art or criticism or journalism or integrity or something demanded *vive la différence*, and gone was the Johannine legacy to every imaginable wind.

I used to telephone my only surviving aunt on Sunday afternoons after my parents' death, and for some weeks a frequent theme with her was the depravity of Jonathan Philbin Bowman. I expressed respect, even admiration, for his father. This was firmly, even snappishly homologated. But, she thundered, Jonathan

When I was being interviewed for the *Sunday Press* in the aftermath of Brian Lenihan's gaffe on *Questions and Answers* during the closing stages of the presidential election campaign of 1990, Jonathan dropped in – 'by chance', he insisted. It was only after he died that the interviewer, Brenda Power, confirmed my suspicions that he well knew she and the photographer were visiting me and he conspired – with their approval – to be part of the interview and photograph. *Sunday Press* photograph, 30 December 1990

Philbin Bowman when broadcasting on the various media was impertinent, offensive, flippant, ill-judged, conceited, rude, inexperienced, ill-mannered, troublesome, unsound, egregious, vulgar, and above all utterly deficient in any respect for persons of greater ages than himself.* My aunt indeed went on about him so long that I perceived he had become a great favourite, and that denouncing him had for a time even taken precedence over her normal reprimands for her living relatives and reproofs for her dead ones.

Whatever else my aunt had led me to assume about Jonathan Philbin Bowman, it wasn't innocence: but that was what I found. It was an innocence determined to declare itself iconoclastic and incisive and independent and informed and inevitable, but innocent it remained. And I began to realize that while this was Festival Jonathan, and while with all emotions *crescendo* around him his would be *sforzando*, he had achieved the happy state of preserving and enlarging innocence in a rabbit-warren of street-wisdom.

HELENE MONTAGUE, the actress and her daughter Lucy, lived with Jonathan and Saul in 1990-91. They stayed first at Jonathan's flat in Henrietta Street.

We flew home together after the [Edinburgh] Festival of 1990; and after the ritual upgrading on Aer Lingus, champagne, and a lesson in the rules of backgammon, I was introduced to the beauty and squalor of Jonathan's apartment in Henrietta Street. How useful it was that I had been immersed since early teens in the theatre and literature of the eighteenth century. At least I wasn't shocked by the lack of hot water and after two weeks of hard cleaning I found the floor. Jonathan's mother Eimer always said she thought the room looked like a stage set but she was uncertain whether it was best suited to a play by O'Casey or Beckett; to me it was pure *La Bohème.* Our resources were meagre at first and we kept house with a mixture of frugality and devilmaycare – five loaves for one pound from Moore Street, red wine, Italian cheese. I cooked lamb over the open fire at Christmas; we got up one night at 3 a.m. and went to Leeson Street for free champagne; another night a glass of water froze beside the bed. There should have been mice but they must have found somewhere warmer.

Fortunately we did not progress to the fourth act of *Bohème* but moved to the relative civilization of Merrion Square. A big

* Owen recalled the 'pleased, not unduly conceited' smile with which Jonathan greeted the recital of his aunt's criticisms.

bathroom with hot water, a proper cooker; children's parties in the park; I started a new play and Jonathan a new job writing the social diary for the *Evening Herald.* When I open my diary for 1990-91 amidst the vivid colours of memories of the summer are many admonishments to self – not to ask him where he was going or, more critically, when he would be back; a sad reflection on the fact that partnering with children and the hours of a gossip columnist do not mix well.

In September the leaves began to fall in the square and I moved on, although we stayed in touch a long time after. We won't be able to laugh again about that extraordinary year, and with mixed sorrow and happiness I recall the phone-call that began it: Jonathan ringing me from Dublin while I was in Edinburgh and playing the whole third act of Gluck's *Orpheus and Eurydice* over the phone.

The poet THEO DORGAN was also living at 46 Merrion Square when Jonathan was a tenant there in 1991.

The house had been built by a Scottish brewer, was ample as all the houses in the square are, but bare, somehow, mean in its ornamentation, minimally maintained by its then owners. Jonathan moved in with Helene Montague, her daughter Lucy and young Saul, in a flurry of books, boxes, assistant movers of many kinds and much climbing and descending with wine bottles. We thought he might help to lighten the sepulchral gloom of the house, and I suppose he did, in a way. More often out than in, he proved to be mainly a staircase apparition, bustling up or down, occasionally stopping to share a word.

Like all autodidacts, Jonathan had a merciless streak with those he considered slow. He had a way of sizing you up in conversation, estimating how much of his time you were worth, how dull you were, giving you a few words and passing on. On good days this could be amusing: no harm at all, turning forty, to be reminded that to the rising generation you were already beyond redemption. On bad days, with the wind whistling up the stairs and rain battering at the ill-fitted windows, the sharp-tongued pup on the landing could be a lot closer to a punch in the mouth than he realized.

Jonathan lived for the social world, for techie toys, for the cut and thrust of a quick thought pungently expressed. His writings were often jejune, the quick, dismissive opinions of that curious right-wing radicalism the *Sunday Independent* fostered. He was the centre of his own universe, would stop you in Merrion Square to show you his new Psion organiser, bow from the waist to you, swivelling on his heel to conduct you past when met on the street, the eyes blank, faintly dismissive. Most days, met on the stairs or in the street, he would be brisk; curt sometimes, at other times possessed by some nameless impatience, talking at speed as if speech itself were a form of urgent breathing. He seemed to me devoid of emotional curiosity, quickening only to rapid thought, endlessly eager for verbal combat. Sometimes we'd spark for a moment or two and I'd feel a start of sympathy, a sense that with the bullshit knocked out of him his would be a large and serious soul. Mostly I found his bumptiousness irritating and juvenile.

The flat we had then, at the back of the house, had been hacked out of a single room; a staircase led from the minuscule hall out over the main stairs and up to the kitchen and bathroom, a half-height wall giving privacy of a sort. Because this wall didn't reach the ceiling of the main stairs, you could hear people talking as they came up and down through the house. I was standing in the kitchen one evening, waiting for the kettle to boil, when I heard Jonathan and Saul come in. As they climbed slowly, bags rustling, bottles clinking, Saul was asking questions and Jonathan was answering him slowly, clearly, with considerable patience and thought. I should of course have felt guilty at eavesdropping; what I felt, instead, was a kind of wonder and a kind of shame. Few people assume, as Jonathan was assuming, that children are intelligent and expect sensible answers to sensible questions. Perhaps fewer offer their children the kind of intelligent love I heard, or overheard, that evening. I knew I would never think of him in the same way again, and I was ashamed at my own glibness, at the easy, unthinking reaction I'd had to him until then.

Of course he could still infuriate. I have no wish to sentimentalise either his or my own memory, but the many times after that I encountered him with Saul I would balance my occasional irritation with what I knew of this unseen side of him, and little by little, as time swept on, the irritation dropped away. I began to notice how ferociously hard he worked. I began to notice his growing interest in a more ample, perhaps spiritual, dimension to life. I began to see thoughtfulness in him, a fugitive wistfulness sometimes. Do I project it on to his memory, that deepening gentleness I saw whenever I met him with Saul? Perhaps, though I don't really think so. We were never friends, simply chance acquaintances, but when I heard he'd died, I felt the sudden, savage stab of genuine grief.

In 1991 Jonathan was offered the job of being social diarist for the *Evening Herald.* It was the idea of the then editor, Michael Denieffe. But the commissioning editor to whom Jonathan

Masthead for his *Evening Herald* column

worked was FRANK COUGHLAN. He had little faith that the new recruit was going to prove a success.

To be honest, I didn't know what I would make of him. And to be even more honest, I would have wagered that I wasn't going to like him much, if only because the demands of writing a daily diary for an evening newspaper are as much to do with discipline and stamina as they are to with the ability to turn a phrase on a sixpence or light up a page with a barb that makes a reader want to come back for more the next day. And I reckoned he didn't have what it takes, even if my editor had a hunch that he might. Whatever about stamina – he always seemed to have buckets of that when I saw him on television – I doubted that the demands of coming up with five yarns a night, written to a precise length and always (always) delivered on time, would be to his taste. I was right too. But, over time, so was the editor.

At first Jonathan didn't take much notice of me. His copy, like himself, breezed in whenever it was ready. It didn't seem to care a jot who it blackguarded and a story pencilled in as a 300 worder often sat on that scales at an obese 3,000. It was, initially, at least the stuff of nightmares. My nightmares. Jonathan, I'm sure, slept soundly. The diary – 'Ad Lib' as it had been known since John Feeney put bums on seats back in the 1970s – had to be off the stone by 9.30 a.m. and I came in at 7.30 a.m. to make sure that it was. Jonathan's copy (all 6,326 words of it) regularly sneaked in the backdoor an hour late, which gave me little time to untangle what Jonathan himself later described as his 'stream of semi-consciousness'.

We had words, most memorably in the canteen one day, when I laid down the law. To my astonishment he promised to be good and asked, with a poignant quiver in his voice, if I would try to like him then. Disarmed and embarrassed, I said I would. He was true to his word and things got much better. The words turned up in the correct sequence and on time – well, near enough – and he began to deliver on his promise. The more serious he got about his work, the funnier 'Ad Lib' became. I was true to my word too and, as seemed to happen to everyone, I began to like him. And he must have begun to trust me, because he left little Saul and a box of crayons sitting on my desk on an occasional afternoon while he swept himself off with a Wildean flourish into the strange world of ligs and liggers.

Then one day, in September 1991, he upped and left. I think he turned up next on radio on 98FM doing the cornflakes shift. A reputation as one of the nation's favourite writers was a little bit away yet. I could take no credit for turning him into the fine columnist that he eventually became, but a little for teaching him that newspapers are, first and foremost, unforgiving word factories that can only indulge the talented after they've learned to keep time. Our paths didn't cross very often after that, although we did sometimes bump into each other in that short corridor that bridges the vast cultural gulf between the *Herald* and the *Sunday Independent*. When I published a novel a few years back, Jonathan sought me out to see what he could do to help. Grateful for his interest, I promised him a pint sometime soon.

But I didn't see him again until a fortnight or so before his tragic death, when he regaled me with some delicious office gossip. Again I promised him that drink. I'm sure, if we had ever got around to it, we would have recalled old times. He might have forgotten most of them by then. I never could.

FRANK CALLANAN, barrister and historian, had first noticed 'the barely adolescent' Jonathan on South Anne Street – or rather his girlfriend had. 'By performative loquacity he demanded attention and slyly coaxed affection: it was his characteristic double move.' In recalling Jonathan, Frank found that 'chronology is difficult, because in retrospect everything seems to have happened more or less simultaneously.' He had seen 'a fair amount' of Jonathan, and of Saul when Saul was a baby.

They called to the mews I lived in. Jonathan had a place at the back of Wilton Road where I recall visiting him. I was exiled to a bleak concrete garage when I lit a cigar. In spite of his predilection for techno-futuristic handbooks, which I used to annoy him by referring to as 'sci-fi', Jonathan had all the cultural reflexes of an entirely liberal education. In writing about him, I have to make a confession. He and I had fallen out, or at least I considered that we had. Writing a column for the *Evening Herald*, Jonathan had slipped in something rather slight that I had told him, and told him also (though admittedly only afterwards) that he could not use. Perhaps pompously, I felt that a show of umbrage was called for. After that I was marking time until the imaginary sentence had expired. This impasse did not preclude my appearing as counsel for him in an action against *Magill.* Mr Vincent Browne stated that he had not fired Jonathan at the *Magill* Christmas party. He had merely told him that he never ever ever wanted him working for any publication of his in the future. The President of the Circuit Court, the late Frank Spain, determined in his droll and elegant manner that Jonathan was entitled to regard whatever had been said as constituting his dismissal.

Jonathan was and endures as both an irrepressibly modern figure and as something older, something antiquely urbane and gregarious, rooted in the city-state of Dublin. Jonathan's turbulent and unflinchingly extroverted journey towards inner quiet – which included a magnificent sabotage of a Zen weekend, provokingly conducted from a perfect lotus position while still adhesively attached to his suit – has been brutally foreclosed. All who knew Jonathan feel a terrible sense of abridgement, of something brought to an absurdly premature end, which goes beyond an ordinary sense of deprivation, and falls outside conventional lamentation.

I remember Jonathan as I first saw him. He is, by some process of enchantment, gathered up into *Ulysses.* He is Aeolus, one of the unnamed newsboys who break in upon the stasis of the conversation in the office of the *Freeman's Journal.* He is in Scylla and Charybdis, the scene set in the National Library, a cherub in stucco grimacing irreverently as Stephen Dedalus sententiously propounds his theory of Hamlet.

Architect SAM STEPHENSON was among a loose circle of friends who formed a lunch club at the Unicorn restaurant on Saturdays. Jonathan would have grown up with Stephenson's buildings pointed out to him as landmark buildings in Dublin. I have always taken an interest in architecture and all my children have noted – and sometimes complained – that I could not pass a major building when they were small without attempting to interest them in its architecture. Sam had organized a special lunch in Jonathan's memory on the Saturday after he died. Invited to contribute to this book, he replied that he had 'found it difficult to have to write in the past tense about Jonathan' so his response took the form of a letter addressed to Jonathan himself.

Dear Jonathan, This is the first letter I have written to you. I find it difficult to realize that you will no longer be breezing in and out of my life as you did over the last decade. One of my earliest and enduring memories was of you playing with Saul in the Phoenix

Park. I was so impressed and moved by the affectionate care and attention you lavished on Saul when little more than a baby. He and you were more like companions than parent and child. He would be with you in the Shelbourne lounge, Buswells and around town like pals. I remember you and Saul in the mews behind Fitzwilliam with the mountainous piles of newspapers, books and magazines in some kind of abundant but seemingly chaotic order.

Abundance is a word that fits you well. You had it in gifts: talent, personality, spirit and soul. You were like a breeze. You had a refreshing and sometimes startling effect on all and every company that you joined. You were full of chat, enthusiastic about ideas and with a flow of instant opinions, on top of the latest news or happening. You could be very critical and dismissive of other opinions at times, but never personally offensive. If any hurt was taken, you were ready to rectify and apologize if necessary. I feel you are looking over my shoulder as I write this letter, saying that I have got it all wrong. You could always take the opposite position for the sake of a good argument. I still miss you coming into the Unicorn on Saturdays and I feel sad to have to write to you like this. As your dad put it so poignantly at the funeral service, he never thought he would be giving the eulogy on 'his lovely boy'. I cannot say it any better. Kindest regards and best wishes. I hope to bump into you again some day, it would be just great. Sam.

Jonathan sometimes commented on the Unicorn Saturday lunch in his *Sunday Independent* diary log, 18 July 1999

Saturday

SING ho, for the new AG Michael McDowell turns up in the Unicorn, in a Ralph Lauren baseball cap. He has mothballed his barrister's wig for a while, one supposes. Later we are joined by Adrian Hardiman.

As the afternoon progresses McDowell gets up to help little old ladies manoeuvre their cars out of the little laneway off Merrion Row. If it weren't for the baseball cap, he'd make a convincing lock-hard.

Still, it's not every woman driver who gets direction on her driving from a freshly anointed Attorney-General — you can only assume she parks her car in Dublin southeast at night.

CIARAN MACGONIGAL the museum curator and art critic, was also part of the Unicorn Saturday lunch circle.

I will always remember his tremendous energy and bounce and look back on many a lunch with Bride [Rosney], Angela [Douglas] and *tout le gang*, days full of laughter, fun and great merriment. He will be greatly missed, not least for his irreverent sense of humour, his rapid-fire conversation and his hugely interested approach to life and living. The great disputations of the day could be anything from tying a tie to where to get the best cod fish or books or whatever subject occupied his mind at a given time. We bet one day on two flies on a wall: which would fly away sooner?

Because of his interest in food and restaurants Jonathan was an appropriate choice for a charity fund-raising event when he was invited in the early 1990s to be a waiter for an evening. The dinner was held in Jennifer MacDougald's restaurant, Octopussy's Garden in Blackrock, Co. Dublin and it was in aid of the Dun Laoghaire Lifeboat. Jonathan had been asked as a media personality, but no doubt he raised some extra laughs based on his lifelong observation of restaurant life. JUSTIN KEATING, academic, former Minister for Industry and Commerce, broadcaster and always a man interested in food and wine, recalled that he was another of those persuaded to accept the challenge of being a waiter for the night.

> The idea behind it was that the waiters would not be professionals, but persons like Jonathan and myself who, for one reason or another, were known to the public. We took the orders from the customers, transmitted them to the kitchen and served the food when it was ready. This developed, as was the intention, into a good-humoured interchange between diners and waiters. A certain amount of wine was consumed, on all sides, and, as the cliché has it, the craic was mighty. Looking back I believe that this sort of occasion provided an opportunity for people to see and appreciate those aspects of Jonathan's personality which made him so remarkable and so widely loved. He gave out an infectious happiness which, because it was so unforced and natural and truly part of him, easily spread to others.
>
> He was innocent in the best sense of a misused word – curious, without guilt, open-minded, not judgmental, presuming that everyone was as good and decent as he was. He knew that humans were neither perfect nor hopelessly mired in original sin. So he knew too that the world was a place happy and beautiful if we made it so, and he was able to inspire this belief in others. We all behaved better for knowing him, and for that, rightly, people loved him. He was a fountain of joy and goodness and decency. We remember that night for his radiance at the centre of it.

One of the diners, CAROL DONOVAN, recalled the evening. Her husband had telephoned her from the office suggesting they meet at the restaurant where a charity dinner was being served by celebrities.

> Lo and behold your lovely son Jonathan and Justin Keating joined forces to help that charity. I would like you to picture Jonathan emerging from the kitchen, napkin over arm and a most mischievous look in his eye. Firstly doing a twirl after which we thought everything was on the ground, but no, Jonathan held on and the rest of the night was just 'tears of laughter all round'. Of course, everybody wanted to be served by Jonathan, which was impossible. Our luck was with us that night. The fun and laughter he created was absolutely marvellous. My husband has since died and very often I think back on that night – it truly does help me to cope with my great loss.

From *Celebrity Pot Luck*, RTE, 17 November 1999. Tony Gregory TD and chef Terry McCoy are taking their work seriously while Jonathan prefers to flirt with the presenter Alison Comyn

MÁIRE GEOGHEGAN-QUINN, Fianna Fáil TD from 1975 to 1997 and former Minister for Justice, is currently the Irish member of the European Court of Auditors.

He was just wonderful company, intellectually stimulating and exasperating at times. Life in Dublin will be the poorer without him. Even though he was a proud and devoted father to Saul, he was still in so many ways a big child. We were friends for a long time, which many of my former colleagues found hard to understand. 'That fella', friends would say, eye-rolling. He would get launched, needing your appreciation and your laughter, but also willing to laugh at himself if you weren't in the mood to be his audience. Once, he annoyed me so much I ordered him away from me at a public reception and he went, looking more crestfallen than he felt. A friend who witnessed the row was later surprised to see the two of us in riotous good humour, bouncing insults off each other.

'I thought you'd fallen out with JPB?', she asked.

'I wouldn't know how to fall out with him', I said. 'I might kill him. But I'd never fall out with him.'

The writer BEN KIELY wrote:

He was a wonderful young man. We became friends from our first meeting, in the Shelbourne, many years ago. All I can do, alas, is extend to you my useless sympathy, but also let you know that my memories of being in Jonathan's company are all wonderful happy memories and will stay with me. Fifty years, or so, divided us in age. That was of no account. In the waterholes or restaurants we deigned to honour with our presence we ended up always sharing the same table. What did we talk about? The usual subjects, I imagine: books, politics, the general goings-on of the Dublin bourgeoisie. But what I remember vividly is the feeling of ease and happiness that was part of Jonathan's company. It said, '*Carpe diem*', and we did.

The poet PAUL DURCAN wrote that he 'had the great good fortune to meet Jonathan a few times over the years, and each time, he charmed and delighted the cockles of my freezing soul.' Jonathan incidentally wrote a parody of a Paul Durcan poem during our last birthday dinner with him to mark his thirty-first birthday in January 2000. I cannot remember how this came about but midway through the dinner Jonathan uncharacteristically lapsed into silence and began scribbling. He soon produced a parody of a Durcan poem. His brother Abie could only recall the concluding lines:

When outside the wolves are barkin'
Would that I were Philip Larkin;
But bein' Paul Durcan
Beats workin'.

When Paul heard about this he commented that he was 'touched and uplifted' more than he could say that Jonathan was 'in the business of Durcan parody. No higher compliment have I received.' He added that it was precisely because 'he was such fun, he was the most serious of us all.' He added this memoir of Jonathan.

I was simply one of the hundreds or thousands of people who happened to meet Jonathan at an intersection along the road. There were several bumpings-into, across streets, in hotel lobbies. But there is one clear-cut, vivid memory for me. It was the summer of 1992, the Dublin International Writers' Festival in the National Concert Hall in Dublin. You can imagine all the egos flying about and indulging themselves and I dreaded going along there. But being a participant I had to put in an appearance every day. One day as I trudged along Earlsfort Terrace with butterflies teeming in my stomach, I spotted Jonathan on the steps of the Conrad – the Festival hotel – with a group of people. Prejudiced, I assumed that he'd add to the chorus of disapproval that happened to be engulfing me at that time. I had said something and in public and

'He was sporting a wooden tie; literally, wooden. He demonstrated its virtues to me, for my benefit alone.' – Paul Durcan

people didn't like it one bit. Unfortunately, I cannot now remember what it was; it may have been my defence of Seamus Heaney in the face of Desmond Fennell's anti-Heaney pamphlet; or it may have been a statement in defence of Charles Haughey's arts policies – a literally life-and-death matter with me – but I cannot be sure at this stage.

I heard a shout of at once greeting and support from the steps of the Conrad and I realised it was emanating from Jonathan. His group and other groups and myself and other stragglers by now were commingling on the footpath under the Conrad before crossing the road to the National Concert Hall for the next session. There were little islands of accidental encounter in one of which I found myself in the same little knot as Jonathan. He was sporting a wooden tie; literally, wooden. He demonstrated its virtues to me, for my benefit alone. I was thrilled by the sheer ingenuity of the actual necktie but also by Jonathan's courteous matter-of-factness. It was just *so refreshing*. Ireland had jumped from 1958 to 1992 without hysteria or fakery. He was so full of simple integrity. I expressed some reservation about my public position on Heaney or Haughey and what then amazed me was Jonathan's quiet but totally confident advice to stick to my guns.

Now that I press my memory, I think the reason for my unpopularity with the mullahs on the day in question was that the day before in the Concert Hall I had made a statement to the festival in session that had it not been for Mr Haughey's arts policies I would not have been still alive. I was in all too deadly earnest. A speaker from the floor, a well-known teacher and bibliophile, had made an Ayatollah-like attack on Mr Haughey and on Aosdána in particular. I then rose in a trance of fear to my feet and made a Danton-like reply. It was on that speech that Jonathan was advising me to stand my ground. And boy – did his support lift my spirits.

Growing up in Pembroke Lane, Jonathan had been within walking distance of St Stephen's Green. In the four years since leaving home he had moved even closer; first to Leeson Street, then Merrion Square, Sibthorpe Lane, Pembroke Street, South King Street – and via Henrietta Street – back again to Merrion Square. A non-driver, he got to know the city by living and walking in it and this suited his Bohemian lifestyle. But Saul was by now coming up to his fourth birthday and the prospect of school loomed.

Since Saul had been born we had been encouraging Jonathan to save for a house of his own. His finances were so precarious and his attitude to money so eccentric that this was difficult. But for a number of years we had been putting regular small amounts of money into a building society account in our joint names and Jonathan's so that when the time came he would have a deposit for a house. Although he managed to access it on a couple of occasions for current spending he seemed pleased that it was there and by now was not uninterested in the idea of becoming a houseowner. We thought that the responsibilities of a mortgage would encourage him to save. Eimer started looking at properties and soon came across No. 1 Fitzgerald Street, a corner house in a Victorian redbrick terrace in Harold's Cross. It was snugly located a few minutes' walk from the Grand Canal and, more importantly, a few minutes' walk from St Clare's National School. Jonathan was very taken with it and negotiations began. The house was being sold by private treaty and I can recall the negotiations as the only occasion since he had been about fifteen on which he was content to play second fiddle to me around what I may call the choreography of the deal. When Jonathan was arranging the mortgage, he met the financial consultant JOHN LOWE, who found him a 'free spirit' more concerned with his work than with his finances.

> At that first meeting, the various mortgage options, the mandatory life cover options and the income he needed to show in order to justify a mortgage went over his head. Not because he could not understand, but it was as if he was saying: 'Listen, you're the mortgage man, I trust you, get the best deal you can'; and a deal was done.

In September 1992 the house was purchased. There was 2p left in his account. He had taken on the responsibility of a mortgage and Saul was enrolled in St Clare's. Jonathan's attitude to schooling was unorthodox: there was not only his own well-publicised premature exit from secondary school but he led a Bohemian lifestyle – in which Saul participated – so that punctuality and attendance were not always highest on their agenda. And he liked occasionally to bring Saul on what he called 'adventures' instead of attending school! Such a parent poses an obvious challenge to any school principal: and while only ever hearing in a fragmentary manner of how MARIA SPRING – the principal of St Clare's throughout Jonathan's time there – handled this situation, I was always impressed by her combination of flexibility, discipline, humour and common sense. Moreover, what I heard of this relationship between principal and parent came from Jonathan or Saul – who

With Saul in Fitzgerald Street

presumably were talented spin-doctors when this was called for. When Saul was enrolled, Maria Spring can only have guessed at the challenges ahead before he would graduate, reluctantly and with many happy memories, eight years later. She wrote this account of Jonathan as a parent after he died.

My first encounter with Jonathan was on 1 September 1992 when he made an appointment to see me to enrol Saul in St. Clare's. He had just moved into the area and our school was only a short distance from his home. He arrived on time for the meeting – the first and only time he was punctual! He talked so fast – enthusiastic about every detail about school and eager to ensure that his beloved Saul would settle in and enjoy school. 'Tell me everything about St. Clare's', he uttered. 'How long have you been here? Do you like it?' Like any parent he was overjoyed as he brought Saul to school on his first day.

Saul's new agreements with Daddy about homework, bedtime, playing, adventures and fun, television, videos etc.

1. Bedtime, Sun -Thur: 8:00 Light out: 8:30
Fri-Sat: 9:30 Light out: 10:00

2. Homework: After Snack finshed by 3.00/4.00
Show Homework to Dad, or
Eimer, (or Ogie on Mondays)

3. Playing and other adventures wait til after homework, unless specially agreed with dad

4. Videos. Saul can record programmes whenever he likes so long as dad does not need to use the video for work.

5. Television. Saul can watch TV up until 6:00pm

6. Saul must check the video in the machine before recording. He can only use tapes with his name on them. Dad must also check the tape in the machine and is not allowed use Saul's tapes.

7. Fun. It is fun to use dad's computer, but Saul should ask dad before using it, or inviting his friends. One day per week we will agree for dad to allow sauls freinds use the computer, too.

8. Adventures. Dad will bring saul on adventures from time to time. Saul agrees to be good, and dad agrees to pay for everything like ice cream. toys etc.

Saul's agreement with Jonathan on homework, television, computer access and adventures.

It is a tradition in St Clare's that Santa Claus visits the school the day before the Christmas holidays. Jonathan willingly agreed to be Santa for the children one Christmas. Saul was in first class at the time. Santa was to arrive at 1.30. For obvious reasons I begged him not to be late. 1.50, no sign of Santa! I was beginning to panic. Phoned Jonathan on his mobile (Jonathan had a mobile when no one had a mobile) – 'Where are you?' 'On my way!' 'The children are waiting for Santa, Jonathan, hurry up!' He continued to joke. 'I've heard all the jokes by now, Jonathan. Get here now'. Taxi pulls up outside the school door. Santa had arrived. The excitement was magic. He responded enthusiastically to the children. As he gave them their presents that day he was transported back in time to his own childhood. I was mesmerized. He was gentle and caring with them – totally absorbed in their world of make-believe. We recalled that afternoon on many occasions afterwards. Saul even reminded me of it last year.

I remember on one occasion when I was trying desperately to make contact with Jonathan, I learned of his whereabouts from my husband, who had heard him on RTE radio on the *Gay Byrne Show* telling the nation of his latest adventures – on a weeklong survival course somewhere in the west of Ireland. I could have killed him for not letting me know. His answer was: 'You heard it first on the GB *Show*.' He could defuse a tense situation with his humour and wit.

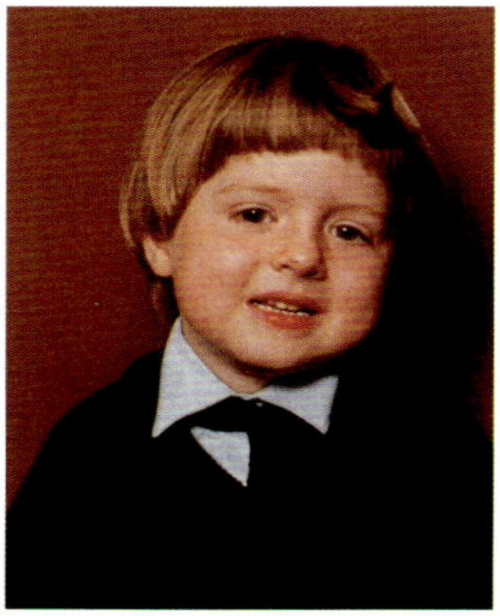

Saul spent eight years at St Clare's, documented here by Tom Godson, the official school photographer

His total love of Saul was evident – he attended every concert and school event. He was so proud of Saul's achievements. But he was not entirely preoccupied with himself and Saul. He was elected a member of the parents' association when Saul was in senior infants. He was generous with his time and he had the interest of the school at heart.

Over the years Jonathan and I both grew to understand each other better. He once told Chloe Blake *[Saul's principal minder]* that he was the only parent in the school that dared call me Maria in public and get away with it. His wit and sense of irony were sharp. There wasn't a malicious bone in his body. He always looked for forgiveness and one more chance. We had a very good relationship. I miss seeing him striding along the avenue with his mobile phone to his ear always in a hurry and late. I miss hearing his voice as he rushed in to collect Saul. Those beautiful eyes. That smile. Jonathan was unique.

Although Jonathan had by now a very high profile as a broadcaster, he had yet to be employed *presenting* his own programme. It is greatly to the credit of FM104 that it was the first radio station to employ him in this capacity. DERMOT HANRAHAN is the founder and chief executive of FM104. Jonathan had a friendly if sometimes robust relationship with him. Dermot does not recall any 'serious rows' but on one occasion when 'there was a little mild turbulence', Jonathan mischievously 'invited Michael Noonan on to the show and had great fun at my expense by asking Noonan – a former teacher of mine in Limerick – to talk about what I was like as a schoolboy.' Dermot also praised his ingenuity and courage.

To the best of my knowledge Jonathan is probably the only radio presenter in the world to have persuaded a sitting prime minister to do a review of a rock concert. The station was promoting the Whitney Houston concert and we were looking for somebody to review it for us on *The Rude Awakening* the following morning. Jonathan, never being shy, contacted Albert Reynolds who was alleged at the time to be a fan of Whitney Houston. He asked Albert to be our guest at the show and to review it on air the following morning. To everybody's amazement he complied. It was a great piece of radio and would not have happened were it not for Jonathan's 'bottle'.

Indeed at the conclusion of the Taoiseach's 'review', Jonathan even invited him to repeat the words: 'This is Albert Reynolds reporting for *The Rude Awakening* from the Point Depot.' The Taoiseach obliged. SEÁN DUIGNAN was then government press secretary.

He liked Jonathan, believing he had 'that magic gift of making one's day brighter just for having bumped into him' – but on this occasion he was wary. Knowing Jonathan's editing skills he elicited a promise from him that the sign-off would not be mischievously re-edited for a programme ad to suggest that the Taoiseach had been recruited to the programme's regular team of reporters!

ALBERT REYNOLDS, was leader of Fianna Fáil and Taoiseach from 1992 to 1994.

> On a professional level Jonathan was an insightful and intuitive journalist. During my political career I have been interviewed and profiled by national and international journalists. One profile – by Jonathan – I remember was uncannily accurate; such was its accuracy that my wife, Kathleen, joked that it was she who supplied the information. Jonathan examined my direct approach to business and politics and its pitfalls. There was one section which suggested that I would jump straight to the top of a queue without realising one existed. Something, I confess that has happened. On a personal level I always enjoyed meeting Jonathan at social events as you were guaranteed cutting political analysis, witty story-telling and sincerity.

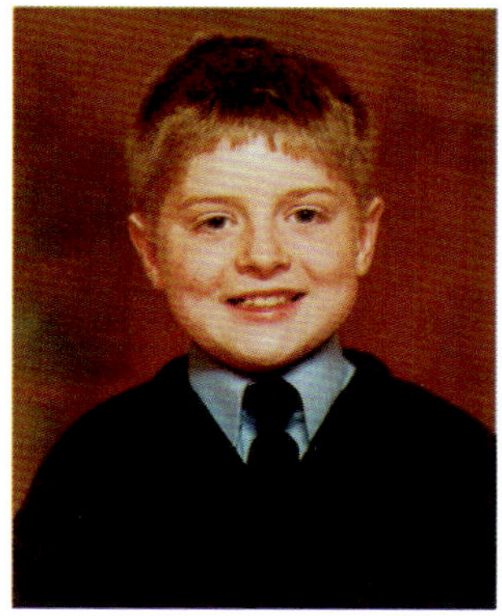

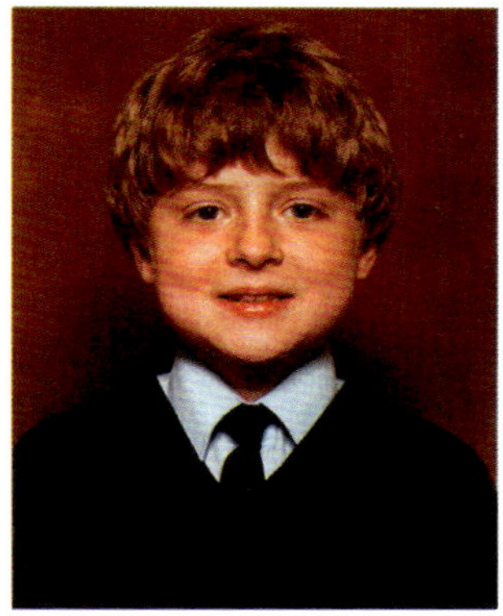

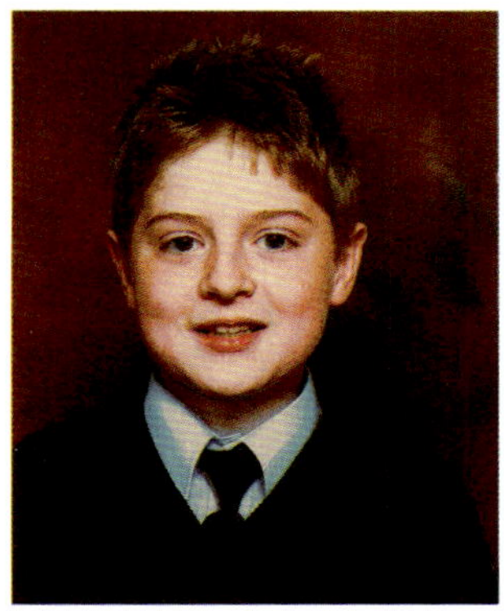

Albert's wife, KATHLEEN REYNOLDS, associated Jonathan with 'big smiles and warm hugs' – she always enjoyed meeting him.

> It didn't matter where it was or who he was with, I always got the same welcome. I remember going into the Shelbourne with Albert one miserable night. The place was packed with nowhere to sit. In an instant Jonathan was over to say he had found me a chair and the tea was on the way! Everyone who was anyone in Irish politics was there that night and I'm sure Jonathan could have got a lot of work done. Instead he kept me laughing for hours telling me stories and refilling the tea.

ANDREA REYNOLDS, one of Albert and Kathleen's daughters, initially found Jonathan 'loud and opinionated' and somebody who might worry you as to what he might say next. Before meeting him she had listened to him on *The Rude Awakening* and read his columns in the *Sunday Independent*.

> I was a big fan so needless to say we hit it off immediately. It wasn't long before JPB was top of the Christmas party list. I can remember him holding court in our kitchen; a sing-song broke out at one stage with Jonathan giving a running commentary. The Christmas after he died we decided the party wouldn't be the same without him so after toasting Jonathan everybody gave a raucous rendition

of 'Always Look on the Bright Side of Life'. This will become a tradition every year, as Jonathan was too big and beautiful a character to ever forget. I miss him

High jinks in *The Rude Awakening* studio with Scott Williams

BARBARA MCKEON as a fellow journalist met Jonathan at press receptions and on occasional foreign trips.

Jonathan brought laughter to thousands of people. And when he made you laugh, it was like being tickled to death. You would have to beg him to stop, because as soon as he saw you giggling he was laughing at you laughing at him, while still going on with whatever story or accent was making you laugh. He was a great practical joker and he found an outlet for this talent on FM104 when he did something called *The Rude Awakening* making early morning hoax calls to the public, and he really could make you believe as many as six impossible things before breakfast.

We also had our not-so-serious altercations, like the time I emptied a pint of stout over his head in the Shelbourne's Horseshoe Bar! But we remained friends and much later when the *Irish Press* closed down, he offered to help in any way he could in getting me work elsewhere. Jonathan was a firebrand whose flare was quenched too soon.*

'The curly-headed cherub' was the headline given to a *Sunday Independent* interview in January 1994 with MARY O'SULLIVAN, then writing under the *nom-de-plume*, Carmel Monahan. She admitted that most people's image of Jonathan was that of 'a precocious teenager annoyingly spouting off' on the *Late Late Show*.

Now twenty-five, a house owner and single father, Jonathan still has the cherubic face, the mop of curls, and he still spouts off, but these days, as co-presenter of FM104 's *The Rude Awakening*, he's paid to do so and this time around it appears people enjoy what he's doing. On air in the Dublin region between 7 am and 10 am, Monday to Friday, Jonathan and his co-presenter Margaret Callanan deliver a three-hour mix of music and entertainment, including wacky interviews and candid telephone calls in which Jonathan, assuming bizarre accents, telephones unsuspecting members of the public with far-fetched scenarios which, for some reason, they fail to see through.

A recent call to an insurance company revolved around his insurance claim for Bertie, his dead goldfish. The insurance people were sympathy itself as he sobbed uncontrollably over the telephone and even when he telephoned back with the glad tidings

* Based on a letter of condolence and interview on RTE Radio 1, 11 March 2000.

Jonathan and Saul at home in Fitzgerald Street, January 1994

that Bertie was, after all, still with us, they couldn't have been pleasanter.

Whatever about the effect these calls have on the people at the other end of the telephone (and most appear to be reduced to blithering idiots) they're going down very well with Jonathan's listeners, as is the rest of the programme, something which pleases Jonathan hugely. 'There's a great feeling of satisfaction when you get feedback. First people say: "I hear you on the radio, occasionally"; then "I hear you every morning"; then they quote something you've said. It's very satisfying to be entertaining.'

Mind you he still provokes some mixed reactions but it's not something that bothers Jonathan too much – that's what happens when you're 'witty, provocative, stimulating.' And in any case 'women like me more than men like me, which is nice because I'm heterosexual.' But he does claim to have mellowed somewhat; 'naturally I got toned down by lots of things, getting older, having a child, a mortgage.' The mortgage is on a little old red-brick end-of-terrace house in the Harold's Cross area, which he shares with his son Saul, who at five can already read very fluently, and if his three pounds winnings are hard evidence, can also play a mean hand of poker.

Just about the only trendy object in the room is a black wire magazine rack from Presents of Mind. Interestingly, the most prominent magazine on it is *The Oldie.* 'I am old', he laughs. And there's no doubt that he cultivates an impression of maturity with business suits quite unlike the traditional garb of the young broadcaster-journalist. 'I nearly always wear a suit and I always, always, wear a shirt and tie. It's a professional thing. I'm comfortable like that.' Then he laughs: 'They know I'm bloody mad, so I have to do as much neutralising as possible.'

But he's very sane when it comes to Saul, his life and his house. For example he doesn't waste time tidying. 'I can't do everything. I could tidy up for one and a half hours and five minutes later with the child it would all be just as bad; I might as well have spent an hour and a half reading. I do so many other things that I do well that are more important, like minding Saul. We knock great fun out of each other, it's a mutual thing.'

One slightly soft sentimental thought expressed and Jonathan is on to a new thought immediately. 'I've a new philosophy,' he announced gleefully. 'I was sitting in the kitchen worrying about life when I got a huge insight: 'nothing matters'. I've even got a name for my philosophy: futilitarianism. We're having the first annual meeting in the Point. It's not so much where's the point, but what's the point?'

Though capable of being downhearted – 'sometimes it's a look at the bank statement and that's all it takes, your week's ruined.' – Jonathan appears quite content at the moment. Professionally things are good: 'It sounds like I want to be Miss World, travel the world and help people, but it's an honour and privilege to entertain. And suddenly it has become alright to like me and it's a growing band.'

Personally things are rather nice too. 'People think I'm always out but I'm hugely cocoony and domesticated. It's nice sitting in my own room, yer man upstairs asleep, drinking small glasses of wine and reading a book and being very quiet which is basically the point of having a house.'

Now is that the JPB you all know and ...love?

Sunday Independent, 23 January 1994

5

'And what was Jonathan like?'

– PHILIE SHEEHAN, a fellow participant, on the question everybody asked her after the *Gay Byrne Show* survival course

As already mentioned, TOM DOORLY had seen Jonathan on his *Late Late Show* interview on why he had left school. Initially irritated by him, he ended up cheering him on against his 'small-minded, unimaginative, parochial' critics. Tom Doorly recalled that when they had first met, it was still 'the age of the long lunch' – and Tom was working in public relations. Later when he became restaurant critic of the *Sunday Tribune,* Tom often brought Jonathan as his guest, finding in him 'an ideal companion: amusing, intelligent, armed with interesting gossip and, above all, a terrific decoy. The kitchen would be told, doubtless, that JPB was at table seven or whatever and nobody would look at me at all.' Tom Doorly wrote:

> I still associate Jonathan with lunch – lengthy, leisurely affairs. This is largely because he supplied me with lots of quirky ideas for the client which I acquired late that year: Durex. Jonathan's fee was always lunch, in the restaurant of his choice. This tended to be either Cooke's Cafe or The Park which, in those days, Colin O'Daly ran in Blackrock. When we launched 'The Durex Report: Ireland', Jonathan was a great supporter. Carr Communications burnished the Durex spokesman, who even by his own admission was a little wooden, at Jonathan's suggestion. He gave the event such prominent billing on the radio and in print that the good old London Rubber Company ran to lunch at Le Coq Hardi.
>
> I certainly didn't realize at that stage that he would end up being one of the funniest, brightest, engaging people that I would ever meet. I made the mistake of thinking him much stronger than he really was. I had glimpses of his vulnerability from time to time but I suppose I was taken in by his breathtaking energy. Jonathan wasn't always good company. There were times when he was in

Jonathan aged 25,
photograph by Tony Maxwell

very low spirits and while he could entertain a group, a one-to-one chat was a very different matter. His brief flirtation with cocaine intensified these episodes of depression, I think. I remember telling him that JPB at normal speed was quite enough for most people to handle, but JPB under the influence of coke was more than the strongest constitution could take.

I remember talking to him about the cocaine habit and saying that Johann and I cared about him and wished he would give it up. And he did. On reflection, it was a privilege to have seen the sad side of Jonathan; it was something he concealed very well from most people. And there was never anything sad about his greeting. Jonathan was forever hailing me from a café table, through the window of a restaurant, from an escalator... I still expect to see him on Dawson Street or sitting outside Cooke's Café with his fingers a blur over the laptop, the very latest in mobile phone technology at his side.

Actually, I think it was quite a privilege that Jonathan would often allow himself to show his inner self to me – the sad side which was so much at odds with the extrovert entertainer. His interest in other people was remarkable; he would try to find their strengths and urge them to work on them – indeed he poured so much of his energy into other people that sometimes there was not much left for himself. His sense of justice and fairness was unflinching and, of course, his ability to deflate the pompous was legendary.

I miss him still, wish I could phone him on the mobile and suggest a bite to eat. Not just because he was so funny, so quick-witted, so incisive. But because he was kind and generous (he would squirm to hear himself so described). Not to flatter or to ingratiate. No, Jonathan's kindness and generosity was most fully expressed in his dealings with people who were not in a position to further his career. Shortly after he died, I was at a meeting in London and ended up talking to an American woman who was pleasant but distinctly homely – not Jonathan's type at all. She told me that she had spent a few weeks in Dublin and had been devastated to hear of Jonathan's death. Did I know him? It turned out that she had been standing on Grafton Street looking at a map when Jonathan came up to her and said, 'Forget the map, I'll show you Dublin.' And he did, for two days. 'He was one of the most amazing people I ever met,' she said. I couldn't have put it better myself.

Despite the popularity and ratings success of *The Rude Awakening*, Jonathan and FM104 could not agree a renewal of his contract. This probably had a greater effect on his income than he admitted at the time. He was invariably optimistic about the prospect of more work and liked the challenge of remaining a freelance. Even when he was under pressure financially he would blithely turn down work if he thought it unsuited to his ability, or if he thought it was underpaid. And such was his lifestyle – he could spend extravagantly even when his bank manager was hounding him – he was not always easy to help.

As those who attempt to earn a living from freelance journalism and broadcasting will attest, it can be a precarious existence, especially when one is young. I can recall telling Jonathan of the advice Seán O Faoláin once gave me at the same age: that to a freelance the ten guineas one was paid every week was more important than the occasional thirty guinea fee. It is now clear – although we did not know it at the time – that Jonathan's finances after he left *The Rude Awakening* became somewhat precarious. And I recall being non-plussed by his acceptance in May 1995 of an invitation from the *Gay Byrne Show* to participate in their survival course. We did not know about his involvement until he had already set out on the course. We were concerned that his lack of any interest in outdoor activities would tell against him in such a five-day endurance test.

It is also the case that participants enrol on the same basis as those who sign on for an adventure holiday. RTE's commitment to the participants is that the programme budget pays the organizers the brochure price for the 'holiday'. Given that Jonathan was, in effect, a celebrity participant, I thought it was naïve – and, I may say, uncharacteristic of him – to accept such terms. But I now think that he had another agenda. Aware of how much he had been stereotyped as somebody incapable of meeting such a challenge, I think he was to some extent 'reinventing himself' and was determined to prove the begrudgers wrong. And I recall him saying as much at the time. He may also have hoped that the experience would mark the adoption of a healthier lifestyle.

The week-long endurance test was in the west of Ireland. One of the producers on the radio programme, BARBARA JORDAN, was a fellow-participant. She recalled the experience in this article in the *Farmers Journal* which she entitled 'Surviving Jonathan'.

> In May 1995 Jonathan Philbin Bowman and I were selected as participants in the notorious *Gay Byrne Show* survival course. The survival course is a very particular type of experiment. Members of the selected group agree to submit themselves to the plans and whims of another for six full days. Contact with family and friends is banned. Links with routine life are severed: there is no job to go to, no cosy bed, no food, no shelter, no cigarettes, no alcohol. It's an extremely tough experience – an experience I would never repeat voluntarily.
>
> The public predicted failure for Jonathan. The view was that he was too much of an urbanite to withstand such total exposure to the countryside. Callers to the programme urged Gay to give him hell. Some suggested that for the other seven members of the group, surviving Jonathan would be the greatest task of all. By the end of the week many were forced to change their minds. Yes, JPB was arrogant, quarrelsome, opinionated and mocking – but there was more. He was also comic, loyal, affectionate, kind and extremely generous with his time.

On our last day we stood on the pier in Spiddal looking on to Galway Bay and across to the north coast of Clare. I was a stone lighter, exhausted mentally and physically. A mobile studio had been set up by RTE, and one by one we queued at a microphone to speak to Gay for the last time on radio. Every man and woman in the group paid tribute to Jonathan for his contribution to the experiment. Jonathan had poor fitness and suffered more than anyone. His mental strength, however, was Olympian.

His sparkling conversation and brilliant mimicry kept us sane and good-humoured. It was like having a good radio station switched on for the week. Typically, Jonathan had bucked the trend. He coped admirably with privation and the general misery of the week.

Farmers Journal, 18 March 2000

'Yes, JPB was arrogant, quarrelsome, opinionated and mocking – but there was more. He was also comic, loyal, affectionate, kind.' – Barbara Jordan

Barbara Jordan said on radio that the week had proved to be 'a brilliant experience' for Jonathan personally and that he was 'easily the person most able mentally for what we went through.' On that final morning Jonathan joined the other participants in a link-up to the *Gay Byrne Show* on Radio 1.

GB: You certainly seem to have come up smelling of roses out of all of this anyway. You're 'Mr Popularity 1995', a most unusual situation for you to find yourself in, I must say. But there you are.

JPB: Well, that's kind of nice; but it's far less unusual than people might think. I mean I'm fairly unpopular with people who don't know me. One of the things I like doing is entertaining people and

'I decided that arguments and moods were just like the weather. They just came and went. And we should be grateful for the sunshine and try and hide under a rock when it's raining' – Jonathan on the lessons of the survival course.

it's something that I'm fairly confident that I can do. Although at one point Barbara was in some funky mood about four days ago and the rain was pouring down, and I caught up with her and she said: 'For God's sake, say something funny and make me laugh.'

GB: And what's this blonde woman that you saw?

JPB: Ah now listen. That's not fair…

GB: I have a note here to say that you like blondes.

JPB: Not especially. Well I don't dislike them, nothing against them. Send them along, fine. Now isn't that terrible? You might make a casual comment to Barbara Jordan and she'd tell the world, but that's the nature of life. But we were walking and you see a car and you get very excited. Or at least some people got very excited. But at one point I said: 'Oh, look a blonde! We haven't seen one of those in five days, that was all.'

BJ: Gay, ask Jonathan about the lamb incident.

GB: Tell us about the dilemma about the lamb, Jonathan.

JPB: I didn't particularly have a dilemma. We were walking over a mountain. I was getting very hungry; a few others were very hungry and I looked ahead and I saw either Eileen or Phil had a lamb and I thought great, dinner! But no, they were helping it out of a bloody bog. So that was fine, a little disappointing. So the next thing we find an even bigger lamb, not a lamb just stuck in mud but clearly a lamb that was on its last legs. In fact not even on his legs, but on his knees. And we stop and look at it, and I said well is he dying, would it be all right for me to help him along? He's probably in pain, shouldn't we put him out of his misery? Wouldn't that be the compassionate thing to do? Somebody courageous like Barbara said she would like to eat. And wouldn't roast lamb be lovely? But no, she wouldn't like to kill him or see him being killed. And I said: 'Go over there.'

GB: And hide your face.

JPB: But Doug immediately snapped out: 'We were told on day one …'. I think we were told lots of things on day one, including that our rucksacks would be safe, so I wasn't too concerned about the legalities of day one, but I was very concerned about eating.

GB: You would have done the lamb.

JPB: I would have done the lamb, thank you very much; not too well done now, but I would have done him anyway.

* *Gay Byrne Show*, RTE Radio 1, 26 May 1995

The survivors unkempt and unwashed on the *Late Late Show*, 26 May 1995

The survivors must have been hoping for an end to their ordeal on that Friday morning. But there were no hot baths in prospect until midnight because that evening they were to appear, unkempt and unwashed, still in their survivor's gear on the *Late Late Show*. What follows is Jonathan's contribution to what was a discursive and wide-ranging discussion.

GB: Jonathan, young fellow, as I said this morning, you came up smelling of roses. But the doctor says – and she's just been working on your feet – she says you're not smelling of roses, by any means.

JPB: We were all in a certain amount of disarray. We met people along the way sometimes when we were crossing a road and they said – they'd heard us on radio – 'you're making it sound awfully easy'. And I think what happened was that no matter how miserable the night had been, it had been raining hard and then you'd get into bed and that would be okay for about ten minutes – and it would be wet and it was horrible. And then you wouldn't sleep, you'd wake up and be miserable and then you'd light a fire. But the first good thing that happened in the morning was the van would appear to get you to a phone and there were people in the van who had eaten; and they were adults and they were speaking to one another. So we were actually all generally in pretty good shape or good humour when we spoke to you on the radio. I think if you had a show going out at eight o'clock in the evening, it would have been a very different programme. Generally I stayed in good enough spirits. Wednesday we all hated because it was miserable – and there were one or two days that were very heavy and there were squabbles and things. But since yesterday afternoon I was in good form.

GB: Well I can tell you that your mother and father are very angry with you because you went away on this and never let them know. So you have a lot to answer for.

AUDIENCE QUESTIONER: What did you all learn from the whole week?

JPB: I think a whole lot. You don't get one blinding flash of insight and say great: now I can write that down, put it on the wall and it will be true for ever. I think there was a lot of observation. I think also it crushes you into a space where you're intensely with yourself and intensely with other people; and therefore a lot of the good stuff and the bad stuff in your personality and the way you behave comes up. And you get a lot of feedback about it as well. And you give a lot of feedback. You also get a sense of what's important and what isn't. I think we all learned different things. What I'm interested in now is the next couple of weeks as I reintegrate into the real world: what comes up and what looks relevant. But specific things: one was argument and mood. It's very interesting watching people because if you feel miserable and rotten, everything is terrible and it's not worth going on and that's all you feel. But if you watch somebody else who was very happy twenty minutes ago, and then you see them very despairing, I decided that arguments and moods were just like the weather. They just came and went. And we should be grateful for the sunshine and try and hide under a rock when it's raining, you know. But I think we learnt different things.

RTE, *Late Late Show*, 26 May 1995

Another participant on the survival course, PHILIE SHEEHAN, wrote to us recalling the experience.

It was a difficult week for all of us but I remember it fondly due to the quick-witted, funny and so intelligent conversations with Jonathan. I really enjoyed listening to him and arguing with him on many points. Anyone I spoke to after the week said: 'And what was Jonathan like?' and I am so glad that my answer always was:

> 'He's a really genuine lovely guy – and so intelligent.' I hadn't seen him since that week but had often thought of him. I just feel it is so sad, so pointless and so wrong that all of you and all of us have lost such a special person. He added such a spark to company and had such a clever way. I will miss what he had to give. I listened to all his *A Living Word* broadcasts and I cried at the loss.

SINEAD IMPEY had first come to Jonathan as an occasional baby-sitter in January 1994. She was then doing her Leaving Certificate. She had also tried to help him organize his research files and papers. He had come to rely on her help and had taken an interest in her career. She recalled his response to the experience of the survival course.

> Jonathan was a bit annoyed with the whole survival course. When it was first suggested, he was reassured that they could all bring one rucksack. So he'd gone to a specialist outdoor shop and he'd bought himself the right boots, some wet weather clothing and some survival food. And on the first day just when they were getting on a small boat, they were surprised to be told they had to leave this gear behind. He thought this unfair but the organizers said the change of rules was a further test so the gear was taken off them.
>
> I don't think he was paid; and he was annoyed about that because he was a professional; he felt he was being put up there as a name, to get interest. And he said he'd never do it again. They were all given a voucher of a weekend away in some hotel chain. He gave it away to someone. He was a bit depressed after that and I remember him eating the survivors' rations he had packed in the rucksack in the days that followed.

What is also now clear – and what was then clear to Sinead – is that Jonathan's usual financial problems were deepening. Sinead Impey wanted him to open all his post. She could see there were 'more and more' bills coming in.

> I told him they're not going to go away. And I said we'll put them in two piles; personal stuff and bills stuff. At this stage he hadn't opened any of the bills in four months. He had his head in the sand when it came to practical things; and sometimes I'd slip some of the unopened bills into his personal post, hoping he'd come upon them by mistake. Then one day we opened all the bills and there was so much to pay. And there was the crisis with his mortgage. He was so laid back about it. He was saying about the building society: they either take the house or they don't.

In June 1995 – one month after Jonathan's survival course – we

Jonathan sometimes wrote about his difficulty in handling money. Wendy Shea provided this illustration for the *Sunday Independent* diary, 4 October 1998

were at a public dinner when Frank Feely, then Dublin City Manager, slapped me on the back saying: 'I see Jonathan's in the headlines again. But he'll be okay, he'll bounce back.' We did not know what he was talking about until he explained that the *Evening Herald* had, that afternoon, reported that a building society had, in court that day, won possession of Jonathan's house because he was in arrears and had not appeared in court. JOHN LOWE, who had arranged his mortgage with First National Building Society, wrote:

> When Jonathan first moved into his Fitzgerald Street home he paid the monthly mortgage repayments. After some time repayments dried up and he was frequently sent reminders from the credit management department. Eventually the patience of First National ran out and Jonathan received a court order for repossession. Unfortunately he chose to ignore this at the time and I, as his branch manager, did not receive communication from the department – as was the practice at the time – that a customer of mine was about to have his home repossessed.
>
> Gerry Murphy, a director of the building society at the time, had also formed a friendship with Jonathan – they went on some self-development courses together – and became aware that Jonathan's home was about to be taken away from him only when he read about it in a Sunday newspaper. The order for repossession was granted to First National but before it was executed Gerry met with Jonathan and myself to discuss the issue. At the time, I had just started writing for a free Dublin publication called *Lifetimes*. I

was also enormously busy and had spoken to Gerry about the column. It was Gerry's idea to do a quid pro quo with Jonathan by paying him for helping me with my column in *Lifetimes* and lodging that money directly against his mortgage account. It was a win-win-win situation – Jonathan kept his home, First National was paid and I was given help with my column. Jonathan remained a very loyal friend not only to Gerry and myself, but also to First National. The writing support was not needed for too long because, with Jonathan's help, I myself became proficient at the art of writing and am currently writing for five publications in my role as managing director of Providence Finance Services. I have Jonathan to thank for setting me on the literary road. Subsequently Gerry left financial services and now works largely in the social economy, renewing his home village of Churchtown in north County Cork. He's been named Cork Person of the Year for his efforts – Jonathan would have approved. As for Jonathan, his home was never again at risk. He became the model mortgage customer and at the time of his passing, he was actually in credit with the mortgage.

SINEAD IMPEY recalled Jonathan's delight at the manner in which John Lowe and Gerry Murphy had sorted out this crisis. 'He said: "I told you it'd be okay." And that even made me more annoyed.' Sinead was hoping that the episode would teach him a lesson.

Being freelance his money was not always regular. He got to a stage where he was hiding the post from me because I'd be hassling him about his bills. He was one of the worst people I know in handling money. He'd even borrow money off me sometimes, one time he borrowed a hundred and twenty pounds; he had important people to meet at lunch, important for his career. And he came back late; he'd been drinking and he was delighted to show me that he had bought an expensive Allessi gas lighter. I was furious. The gas had been cut off some weeks before! He did me bad turns and good turns. But I don't think he could help himself.

When I was finishing my Leaving I stayed overnight one night as I was babysitting on the eve of my English exam. Jonathan came back very late and forgot to set the alarm. I slept it out and was twenty-five minutes late for that exam. I was really wound up about this and I had a fierce row with him. He was telling me I'd be fine; exams weren't that important, skills were important. I had just finished secondary school and I didn't know what I wanted to be. I thought of doing a computer course in the College of Commerce in Rathmines.

Jonathan had about three computers in the house, so he put me on one of them. He told me he'd teach me the basics so that I'd have a head-start. He insisted that shorthand was old hat; that a computer and a dictaphone – and he gave me one and showed me how to work it – would cover all eventualities. He taught me on an Apple Mac; he took me from A to Z on computers and showed me everything. When I was babysitting he would tell me to come early for a lesson and I'll show you. He understood computers; he was great with any new gadgets. Sarah Foot, who was editing *Irish Tatler* at the time, needed an assistant. And he encouraged Sarah to hire me. Before that I was just doing anything around the office; she brought me in and let me write a few pieces for the magazine. He would correct my early efforts. He'd go through them for spelling mistakes. And he could be quite tough: 'This is what you should have done here; and this line is not funny; this is really bad; this is how it should have been done.' Sometimes I had to laugh because he was so anti-teacher but here he was being hard on me; and he was a very good teacher too. I wouldn't be the best speller in the world; and he'd give me lines; to spell it out correctly five times. I'd never do that; so he taught me how to use the spell-checker; and how the computer had further tricks, it wasn't just a machine, it could also test your grammar, it could question your sentences. I was only young. I didn't know what I wanted to do but he had said to me that journalism or magazine work was an option. I'm not saying I had the ability, but he encouraged me to try. And then I decided that I was more interested in design and layout than writing.

I went on to *IT* magazine and then a design position came up for just three months, and with Jonathan's encouragement I bluffed my way into getting it. I struggled a bit but that's how I established my career in print design. If I had a problem during that three months I would phone him and he'd get me to call into his house on the way home; and he wouldn't know the programmes I was using but he'd tackle it with me and figure out how to solve the problems. He was very good; he understood the logic of the computer; he'd just figure it out.

SARAH FOOT, the writer and magazine editor to whom Sinead refers, recalled her friendship with Jonathan, especially during her years in Dublin in the mid-1990s when she was editing *Irish Tatler*.

I am so sorry and saddened by Jonathan's death. He was a very good and dear friend to me. We met in Ann Marie Hourihane's kitchen when I had just moved to Dublin. I had not heard of him and my first thought was that I had encountered a phenomenon. I miss him terribly. He was a genius and over the years always

These two pages, a satire on the Keane Edge, Terry Keane's column in the *Sunday Independent*, was entitled 'Not the Keane Edge, Teasing Teasie', *Irish Tatler*, October 1996

> extravagantly generous to me with his ideas. He gave me so much help when I was editing *Irish Tatler* and he edited much of the novel I am now working on. To me, one of the most extraordinary things about him was that he did not see life as a balance sheet. So much of the time he seemed to be in another dimension to most people. One of my dearest memories is of him collecting me at the airport and rushing towards me with outstretched arms holding a cauliflower because I had told him that on *Vogue* magazine we had a phase of being given designer vegetables as 'thank you' presents. Jonathan had to ask the greengrocer what a cauliflower actually looked like.

Jonathan, as has been seen, had a somewhat unorthodox attitude to money: when he had it, he spent it or might even give it away; but when he hadn't got it, he tended not to allow this to interfere with his lifestyle. Consequently, he was difficult to help financially. On one occasion while he sailed in the Caribbean we looked after his leaking roof. In general, we preferred to declare a budget which could be spent only on home improvements. On birthdays and at Christmas, which for Jonathan came close together, we tried to think of practical matters – imperatives, but matters which Jonathan might not get around to doing himself. His kitchen was small and in need of modernization. Eimer thought this might encourage him to cook more at home; and at Christmas 1995 she proposed that we would finance a make-over of the kitchen. Jonathan seemed delighted. We called on a friend of ours, SUE KEATINGE, expert not only in interior design but in tuning in to her clients' needs and evolving simple but effective solutions to their problems. Sue recalls:

> I didn't know what to expect but went to that first meeting reckoning that I'd never be trendy enough for such a celeb and wondering if it was indeed Jonathan or the two of you who thought his kitchen might be in need of a make-over! I needn't have worried – for although like all mothers, Eimer, you had your own viewpoint – you were very careful about expressing it and Jonathan was very careful about listening to it. He was surprisingly open to advice, and at the same time somewhat amused by the two of us! It took me a while to take in the space at first, but he quickly broke the ice by offering us coffee from his beloved Italian coffee-maker and I gradually started to take in the room: tiny, with the entrance to a steep staircase splitting it in two. It was also my first meeting with Saul as he hopped up and down that staircase, discussing this and that with his dad. Jonathan seemed well able to give him his fullest attention, whilst listening to my questions and, if I remember rightly, answering at least one if not two mobiles at the same time. It was clear straight away that he liked to cook and had certain specialties, so he was keen on the hob area and his pots and pans. Not quite so concerned about the sink and all that tends to pile up around it; and the storage definitely very haphazard, with books and papers taking over every available nook and cranny. He really seemed in need of a larger counter space where he and Saul could perch for a second or two in mid-flight to somewhere or other. The alterations were made, a new floor laid and the kitchen completed. It was time to give the space back again. There was no need, but I was very touched to receive a lovely and enthusiastic letter from him. I shall always delight in the memory of having 'kitchened' for him.

Jonathan, I thought, had learned a lesson from his mortgage fiasco. And there seemed to be some improvement in his approach to spending. But it was only after his death that the full scale of his reform programme became apparent. HARRY ALLEN of the credit union in Independent Newspapers provided some of the explanation:

> The late editor of the *Sunday Independent,* Conor O'Brien, always said to me that 'a good journalist cannot handle money'. This certainly applied to Jonathan. I first met him when he bounced into the managerial accounts department, with baby Saul strapped to his chest. He wanted to know why he had not yet been paid for an article he had written. To an office consisting of five men, this was a most unusual sight. He explained that he was a single parent and he needed the money. No further explanation was necessary.
>
> In the years that followed he often returned with Saul and gave

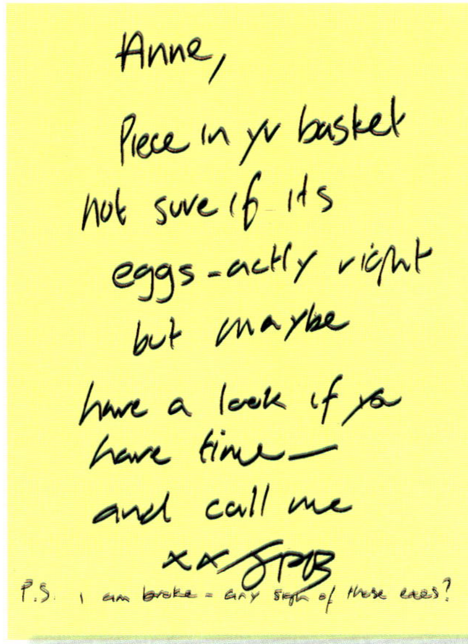

A memo to Anne Harris with a postscript: 'I am broke. Any sign of those expenses?'

us little snippets of what was going on in both their lives. He was a strange mixture, with his cultured accent, dandy manner of dressing and a general air of confidence; yet underneath we felt he was just like the rest of us. He had his highs and lows, both in his journalistic and broadcasting careers. This struck a chord with us.

I remember getting a phone call from Anne Harris, asking me to talk to Jonathan about the Credit Union. I arranged to meet him in the canteen. He explained his predicament. He had exhausted his credit with the lending institutions and needed a loan from us to begin sorting out his finances. But before we could help him, I had to ask him to sign the application forms and to put some of his next salary payment into his shares. As he was now earning money regularly, we would be able to take his deductions from his salary. Before the credit committee could sanction any loan, they also insisted he join the budget scheme for paying his mortgage, electricity and phone bills. This was to prevent the same situation developing again and was designed to bring reality home, but still leave him with enough to live on. I am sure it was a bitter pill for him to swallow, but he handled it with good grace. The Credit Union looked on Jonathan as one of its success stories and we were delighted to have been of some service.

Jonathan appreciated being bailed out when he was in financial trouble. But he was also compassionate about others who were too poor to have ever managed to even get into debt with the lending institutions. The chief executive of Superquinn and independent senator, FERGAL QUINN, knew him over many years.

Jonathan was caring and most compassionate. He would move mountains for someone in trouble. And frequently rang me when he came upon situations where he thought I could help. On one occasion he told me he had no shame in asking for my help and others whom he knew were able to help; indeed, he was delighted to use his position in every way possible. It may sound like a cliché but to me Jonathan was the champion of the underdog.

In the mid-1990s Jonathan was still exploring new career paths. Publisher MICHAEL GILL recalls receiving a proposal from him: he had an idea for a book.

A couple of days later over coffee in the Shelbourne he talked enthusiastically about his plan to write an insider's guide to

> Dublin. It would be rude and irreverent but it would be real. He certainly had the credentials and the knowledge to write such a book and I encouraged him. Some weeks later he sent me a synopsis of what he proposed. It was still promising and we met again, this time to discuss in detail what would be involved in actually writing such a book. But I could sense his enthusiasm waning as I outlined the extent of research that was needed and emphasised the importance of supporting opinions with incontrovertible facts. The idea withered then, suffocated by the imperatives of other deadlines and – to be frank – the need to earn a living which the royalties from an irreverent Dublin guidebook could never have provided.

LYN GELDOF, who had known Jonathan for many years, wrote from Geneva.

> I really knew Jonathan and Saul as one, introduced to me years ago by Jeananne [Crowley], ever the facilitator of congenial company. Jonathan was a favourite son to many, transfixing us with his precocious and undisciplined intellect and his glorious mischievousness. When I was staying with Jeananne, he'd hear me 'working' the phone. He told me that he'd never met anyone like me for addressing high and low in the same direct manner. I had never noticed that before – and I think he had a bit of that in himself – which, I recall, landed him in the street on a few occasions! The last time I met him – eighteen months before he died, I gave him my brother's [*singer and television producer Bob Geldof*] telephone number in the fond expectation that his star would soon shoot to its natural dizzy elevation in the firmament. Instead, it has gone out, leaving us all dumbfounded and bereft.

Jonathan never drove a car – and, I think, never intended to. He rode a bicycle for only a couple of years. He alarmed me when he purchased his first adult bicycle and announced that he trusted Dubliners and didn't intend to be encumbered with a lock! His next bike, purchased soon afterwards at a Garda auction, came with a lock and lasted somewhat longer. But thereafter he walked or taxied everywhere. That he walked so much suited him because he liked meeting people. I have often heard it remarked that those who live in small towns without a public transport system enjoy a much richer social life because of chance meetings with friends and neighbours. Jonathan thought of Dublin – and especially the south inner city – as a small town and treated it as such. Indeed in many ways his lifestyle belonged to another age, before public transport and our love affair with the motor car had the effect of insulating us from our fellow citizens as we move about the city. DAVID NORRIS, formerly of the English department in Trinity College Dublin, Joycean scholar and independent senator for Trinity in Seanad Eireann, was one of those who often met Jonathan when walking through the city.

Mister Ten Percent

Shortly after the ruling by the European Court of Human Rights that the Irish government must now legislate for the decriminalization of homosexual acts in private between consenting adults, JONATHAN PHILBIN BOWMAN interviewed David Norris – who has been pursuing the matter through the courts for eleven years, first in Ireland, and since 1983 in Europe – about his homosexuality, Lotto, Family Solidarity, James Joyce, and the Winchester verdict.

Jonathan interviewed David Norris, 'Mister Ten Percent', *In Dublin*, 10 November 1988

> I still find it difficult to contemplate his final absence from the daily round in Dublin. I do remember my many casual encounters with him, often accompanied by Saul. I would be ambushed in various places. Grafton Street was a particular favourite where Jonathan – followed by Saul – would launch out of Bewleys already talking at high speed about all kinds of subjects and clutch me by the arm and demand my company over a cup of coffee. But it was always worthwhile stopping and chatting with Jonathan. The only disadvantage was that he was an even greater gabber than I am. We both had to learn that it was necessary for one of us to stop the flow of verbiage in order to let the other one in occasionally to keep up the interplay.
>
> In the weeks after his death I was stopped in the street by a number of people who knew that I had known and been fond of Jonathan. Each of them had their individual story. One was a woman who said that Jonathan had helped change the tyre on her car. I could hardly believe it but she swore it was true. Then there were tales of friends who had been depressed about their job, the sickness of a relative, whatever, and got home miserable only to find their apartment full of flowers all arranged by Jonathan. I found out that Jonathan could not only be a talker of great brilliance but also a listener of considerable sensitivity who, when his friends needed it, was able to provide the balm of his interest.
>
> We shall all miss him; not just his company which was such a stimulant to those of us privileged to know him, but for us and the wider public there will always be a gap in the *Sunday Independent* on that page where he used his Swiftian satiric talents to poke fun and lampoon all forms of Establishment, Irish, American and European. It's a strange thing but even as I write this I can feel the shadow of his presence come once again into my life.

Editor of *The Dubliner*, EMILY HOURICAN, first met Jonathan through the magazine she was then working for, *Himself*, to which Jonathan was an occasional contributor.*

> We had spoken on the phone a few times, and always had lively,

* Based on a letter of condolence and editor's note in *The Dubliner*, February 2001

amusing conversations. Jonathan insisted we meet up, which we did, and hit it off instantly. Even in a bad mood he was amusing. He was so clever and well-read. His library was amazing and his interest in people other than himself unusually keen. The special effort he always made to have conversations worth having, to make the hours spent in his company memorable, was maybe the most endearing thing of all. It was impossible just to *like* Jonathan; he was too demanding for that. You actually had to love him.

My older brother told me of a friend of his – a fairly rough character who spent several years in Mountjoy Jail for armed robbery when he was younger – who told him that Jonathan had been his hero, in those words. He saw him first on television years ago, and thought him 'a useless ponce', but quickly grew to respect and admire him because, as he put it, 'he had guts. He stuck to his guns and was always the same.' He met Jonathan once, in Galway, a few years ago; Jonathan greeted him very warmly when approached and they chatted for quite a while. This interest in and ability to connect with people from any type of background, on an emotional rather than intellectual level, was maybe Jonathan's greatest charm. He really wanted to know all about everybody he met. I know the friend in question and I know he is not given to sentimentality or even easy friendship with others, yet his encounter with Jonathan touched him deeply. He recalls it with much pride and affection.

The editor of the *Sunday Independent,* AENGUS FANNING, remembers Jonathan as 'the most brilliant and irritating person' he has ever known.

He never returned my phone calls; the only way I could get him was to ask Anne Harris to ring him, whereupon he would call back promptly. Anne was his strongest supporter from even before he joined the *Sunday Independent.* I shared her admiration and respect for his talents, although there were times when I couldn't stand him: he couldn't resist showing off, and his penchant for demonstrating to all and sundry that he was more clever than me, and his sheer nosiness, were to put it bluntly, a pain in the neck. His eyes were drawn, as to a magnet, to any legal letters lying on my desk; he would almost break his neck trying to get a peek at them over my shoulder, unaware of how annoying this was to a libel-phobia sufferer like me. I found that Sir Anthony [O'Reilly] and Gavin O'Reilly greatly appreciated his creative genius – they often said so to me. But many fellow journalists, I discovered, found Jonathan hard to take; probably they were envious, and at a ratio of about two-to-one, they were inclined to rubbish him if they could. I ignored them.

Jonathan was a brilliant mimic and his take-off of Charlie McCreevy was hilarious; he occasionally rang me with his latest McCreevy impersonation and I did my best to hold my end up with a 'take' on Bishop Eamonn Casey. Once on *Morning Ireland*, Charlie McCreevy praised Irish voters: 'They were sophisticated', he said, 'they always made the right decision.' Some listeners misheard this as 'they were so *phisticated* they always made the right decision.' Jonathan mischievously took this interpretation; the line went into legend and gave him fodder for one of his most hilarious send-ups. Jonathan had what Charles Wintour, *Evening Standard* editor, called the 'divine spark'. I defer to no one in my respect for his talent; and he brought a unique spark to the *Sunday Independent* which I like to think of as a pretty sparky newspaper. I miss Jonathan and, like the whole world, it seems, I loved him too.

JOHN HORGAN teaches journalism in Dublin City University and is also a journalist and historian. He too appreciated Jonathan's capacity as a mimic.

I met Jonathan on only a handful of occasions. Like many others in the same category, I know that I won't forget him: his impromptu impersonation of Eoghan Harris made me laugh until I cried. Even a brief encounter with this *enfant terrible*, however, underlined two telling aspects of that particular gift. One was that his mimicry was not just of his subject's accent and facial expressions, but of their thought processes as well. The other was that it was informed, and buttressed, by an underlying seriousness which gave it an extra, hidden charge. I'm glad he never chose to exercise this gift at my expense.

The novelist and *Irish Times* writer MAEVE BINCHY wrote:

Whenever I saw him we always greeted each other cheerfully, though I never remember anyone introducing us or anything. I think I managed to avoid telling him what a cute little baby he was in the pram. I hope so because he actually *was* very cute. He always talked as an equal in age which is immensely pleasing to a middle-aged woman when it comes from a very young man. He wore his own fame and public attention well, never being over-elated by success; nor put down by criticism. He didn't seem to believe his own publicity which is an easy mistake to make; instead he took his work seriously and himself not seriously at all, which is hugely satisfying when you meet someone. Anytime I did meet him he seemed happy and surrounded by a big circle of friends. But I had no idea until after his death how very much loved he was by so many people and how central to so many lives he had become. I realized that I had hardly known him at all and yet when somebody told me that he had always liked me the day lit up and I hope he knew, and knows, I liked him too.

MARK O'CONNELL, barrister and former political correspondent of the *Sunday Business Post,* recalled 'many lively discussions' on Northern Ireland with Jonathan in the mid-1990s.

> My view was that the main players were going to have to take a chance. I don't remember talking to him about the issue of censorship but I recall him expressing difficulty with the Hume-Adams initiative. He was insistent that before Sinn Féin was to be embraced as agents in the process, the IRA would have to call a halt to its campaign. I told him that it should be the other way around: if Sinn Féin was encouraged to participate in the preparation of a solution, then a ceasefire would more readily follow. We returned to the conversation regularly and he maintained the same view. I suppose I did too but it didn't affect the relationship we had. We respected each other's point of view, even though I must say I sometimes found him quite strident. But that was the way he was and his many qualities made up for his sometimes overly energetic manner. Even though he might at times annoy me, he would always provoke fresh thinking on whatever topic was under discussion.

Despite having a national television profile it was not until 1996 that Jonathan first *presented* a programme on television. This was when he was invited by Andy Ruane of Like It Love It productions to host the quiz show *Dodge the Question.* When he was preparing for the series I gave him one piece of advice: 'Keep trying to play second fiddle and the balance between contestant and quiz-master will come out just right.' I knew that second fiddle was not Jonathan's favourite role. I feared that he mightn't know how. But that is exactly what he did. And his natural sense of fun, mischief, courtesy, wit and flirtatiousness – when the opportunity offered – was, I thought, perfect for that programme. It was not a very difficult programme. It was prerecorded; errors could be excised; but he did it exceptionally well, and to the surprise of the critics and some others. ROBERT DUFFY from Hacketstown in County Carlow was a contestant on *Dodge the Question.*

> I spent some time sharing *Monty Python* moments with him and when it came time for the cameras to roll Jonathan helped me

relax and enjoy the experience. I found a friend that day and now I wish that I had known him better.

An earlier encounter with Andy Ruane, *Scratch Saturday*, RTE. 18 November 1989

DJINN GALLAGHER wrote a profile of Jonathan for the *Sunday Tribune* to coincide with the launch of the series. It was entitled: 'Boy genius with attitude learns to play the game'.

Jonathan Philbin Bowman is the closest thing to a genius that you're likely to meet this side of the Nobel Prize. Ferociously, fiendishly clever, his nimble mind always skipping along two steps ahead of his interlocutor, making outlandish connections and spewing out comical ideas with the rapid-fire intensity of an adrenalin-fuelled AK47. He laughs in staccato bursts, his voluptuous mouth curling at the corners like a corrupt Botticelli angel, and he talks so quickly it's often difficult to figure out what he's saying. After an exhausting half-an-hour in his company, you may find yourself wishing he was just a little bit less brilliant.

JPB, as he calls himself, navigates his social life with a thundering lack of finesse, leaving behind him a trail of resentful people who feel patronized and ridiculed. Those who know him well, love him dearly, but he treats most people as if they were a lot slower than he is. And over the years Jonathan-watchers have often wondered why, if this guy was so intelligent, he couldn't figure out the basics of human relationships.

Why couldn't he let us take it on trust that he was smarter than we are, and stop rubbing our noses in it? Where was he hiding when they were handing out the diplomacy and tact? For all his

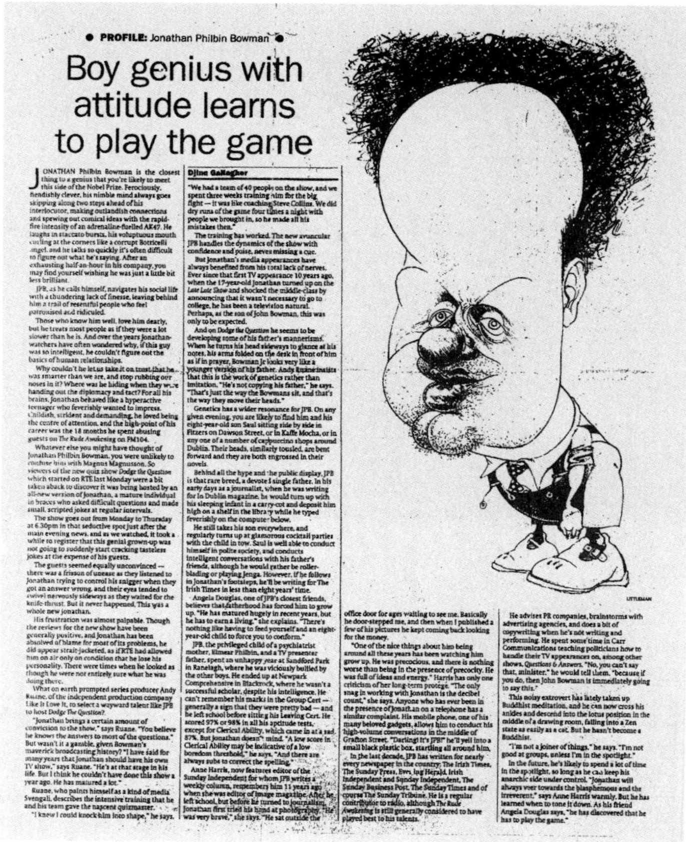

● **PROFILE:** Jonathan Philbin Bowman ●

Boy genius with attitude learns to play the game

Djinn Gallagher

JONATHAN Philbin Bowman is the closest thing to a genius that you're likely to meet this side of the Nobel Prize. Ferociously, fiendishly clever, his nimble mind always goes skipping along two steps ahead of his interlocutor, making outlandish connections and spewing out comical ideas with the rapid-fire intensity of an adrenaline-fuelled AK47. He laughs in staccato bursts, his voluptuous mouth curling at the corners like a corrupt Botticelli angel, and he talks so quickly it's often difficult to figure out what he's saying. After an exhausting half-an-hour in his company, you may find yourself wishing he was just a little bit less brilliant.

JPB, as he calls himself, navigates his social life with a thundering lack of finesse, leaving behind him a trail of resentful people who feel patronised and ridiculed.

Those who know him well, love him dearly, but he treats most people as if they were a lot slower than he is. And over the years Jonathan-watchers have often wondered why, if this guy was so intelligent, he couldn't figure out the basics of human relationships.

Why couldn't he let us take it on trust that he was smarter than we are, and stop rubbing our noses in it? Where was he hiding when they were handing out the diplomacy and tact? For all his brains, Jonathan behaved like a hyperactive teenager who feverishly wanted to impress. Childish, strident and demanding, he loved being the centre of attention, and the high-point of his career was the 18 months he spent abusing guests on *The Rude Awakening* on FM104.

Whatever else you might have thought of Jonathan Philbin Bowman, you were unlikely to confuse him with Magnus Magnusson. So viewers of the new quiz show *Dodge the Question* which started on RTE last Monday were a bit taken aback to discover it was being hosted by an all-new version of Jonathan, a mature individual in braces who asked difficult questions and made small, scripted jokes at regular intervals.

The show goes out from Monday to Thursday at 6.30pm in that seductive spot just after the main evening news, and as we watched, it took a while to register that this genial grown-up was not going to suddenly start cracking tasteless jokes at the expense of his guests.

The guests seemed equally unconvinced — there was a frisson of unease as they listened to Jonathan trying to control his snigger when they got an answer wrong, and their eyes tended to swivel nervously sideways as they waited for the knife-thrust. But it never happened. This was a whole new Jonathan.

His frustration was almost palpable. Though the reviews for the new show have been generally positive, and Jonathan has been absolved of blame for most of its problems, he did appear strait-jacketed, as if RTE had allowed him on air only on condition that he lose his personality. There were times when he looked as though he were not entirely sure what he was doing there.

What on earth prompted series producer Andy Ruane, of the independent production company Like It Love It, to select a wayward talent like JPB to host *Dodge The Question*?

"Jonathan brings a certain amount of conviction to the show," says Ruane. "You believe he knows the answers to most of the questions." But wasn't it a gamble, given Bowman's maverick broadcasting history? "I have said for many years that Jonathan should have his own TV show," says Ruane. "He's at that stage in his life. But I think he couldn't have done this show a year ago. He has matured a lot."

Ruane, who paints himself as a kind of media Svengali, describes the intensive training that he and his team gave the nascent quizmaster.

"I knew I could knock him into shape," he says. "We had a team of 40 people on the show, and we spent three weeks training him for the big fight — it was like coaching Steve Collins. We did dry runs of the game four times a night with people we brought in, so he made all his mistakes then."

The training has worked. The new avuncular JPB handles the dynamics of the show with confidence and poise, never missing a cue.

But Jonathan's media appearances have always benefited from his total lack of nerves. Ever since that first TV appearance 10 years ago, when the 17-year-old Jonathan turned up on the *Late Late Show* and shocked the middle-class by announcing that it wasn't necessary to go to college, he has been a television natural. Perhaps, as the son of John Bowman, this was only to be expected.

And on *Dodge the Question* he seems to be developing some of his father's mannerisms. When he turns his head sideways to glance at his notes, his arms folded on the desk in front of him as if in prayer, Bowman Jr looks very like a younger version of his father. Andy Ruane insists that this is the work of genetics rather than imitation. "He's not copying his father," he says. "That's just the way the Bowmans sit, and that's the way they move their heads."

Genetics has a wider resonance for JPB. On any given evening, you are likely to find him and his eight-year-old son Saul sitting side by side in Fitzers on Dawson Street, or in Kaffe Mocha, or in any one of a number of cappuccino shops around Dublin. Their heads, similarly tousled, are bent forward and they are both engrossed in their novels.

Behind all the hype and the public display, JPB is that rare breed, a devoted single father. In his early days as a journalist, when he was writing for In Dublin magazine, he would turn up with his sleeping infant in a carry-cot and deposit him high on a shelf in the library while he typed feverishly on the computer below.

He still takes his son everywhere, and regularly turns up at glamorous cocktail parties with the child in tow. Saul is well able to conduct himself in polite society, and conducts intelligent conversations with his father's friends, although he would rather be roller-blading or playing Jenga. However, if he follows in Jonathan's footsteps, he'll be writing for The Irish Times in less than eight years' time.

Angela Douglas, one of JPB's closest friends, believes that fatherhood has forced him to grow up. "He has matured hugely in recent years, but he has to earn a living," she explains. "There's nothing like having to feed yourself and an eight-year-old child to force you to conform."

JPB, the privileged child of a psychiatrist mother, Eimear Philbin, and a TV presenter father, spent an unhappy year at Sandford Park in Ranelagh, where he was viciously bullied by the other boys. He ended up at Newpark Comprehensive in Blackrock, where he wasn't a successful scholar, despite his intelligence. He can't remember his marks in the Group Cert — generally a sign that they were pretty bad — and he left school before sitting his Leaving Cert. He scored 97% or 98% in all his aptitude tests, except for Clerical Ability, which came in at a sad 87%. But Jonathan doesn't mind. "A low score in Clerical Ability may be indicative of a low boredom threshold," he says. "And there are always subs to correct the spelling."

Anne Harris, now features editor of the Sunday Independent for whom JPB writes a weekly column, remembers him 11 years ago when she was editor of Image magazine. After he left school, but before he turned to journalism, Jonathan first tried his hand at photography. "He was very brave," she says. "He sat outside the office door for ages waiting to see me. Basically he door-stepped me, and then when I published a few of his pictures he kept coming back looking for the money.

"One of the nice things about him being around all these years has been watching him grow up. He was precocious, and there is nothing worse than being in the presence of precocity. He was full of ideas and energy." Harris has only one criticism of her long-term protégé. "The only snag in working with Jonathan is the decibel count," she says. Anyone who has ever been in the presence of Jonathan on a telephone has a similar complaint. His mobile phone, one of his many beloved gadgets, allows him to conduct his high-volume conversations in the middle of Grafton Street. "Darling! It's JPB!" he'll yell into a small black plastic box, startling all around him.

In the last decade, JPB has written for nearly every newspaper in the country: The Irish Times, The Sunday Press, Evening Herald, Irish Independent and Sunday Independent, The Sunday Business Post, The Sunday Times and of course The Sunday Tribune. He is a regular contributor to radio, although *The Rude Awakening* is still generally considered to have played best to his talents.

He advises PR companies, brainstorms with advertising agencies, and does a bit of copywriting when he's not writing and performing. He spent some time in Carr Communications teaching politicians how to handle their TV appearances on, among other shows, *Questions & Answers*. "No, you can't say that, minister," he would tell them, "because if you do, then John Bowman is immediately going to say this."

This noisy extrovert has lately taken up Buddhist meditation, and he can now cross his ankles and descend into the lotus position in the middle of a drawing room, falling into a Zen state as easily as a cat. But he hasn't become a Buddhist.

"I'm not a joiner of things," he says. "I'm not good at groups, unless I'm in the spotlight."

In the future, he's likely to spend a lot of time in the spotlight, so long as he can keep his anarchic side under control. "Jonathan will always veer towards the blasphemous and the irreverent," says Anne Harris warmly. But he has learned when to tone it down. As his friend Angela Douglas says, "he has discovered that he has to play the game."

LITTLEMAN

Djinn Gallagher's profile, *Sunday Tribune*, 14 July 1996. The caricature is by Littleman – Michael Drake

brains, Jonathan behaved like a hyperactive teenager who feverishly wanted to impress. Childish, strident and demanding, he loved being the centre of attention, and the high point of his career was the eighteen months he spent abusing guests on *The Rude Awakening* on FM104.

Whatever else you might have thought of Jonathan Philbin Bowman, you were unlikely to confuse him with Magnus Magnusson. So viewers of the new quiz show *Dodge the Question,* which started on RTE last Monday, were a bit taken aback to discover it was being hosted by an all-new version of Jonathan, a mature individual in braces who asked difficult questions and made small, scripted jokes at regular intervals. The show goes out from Monday to Thursday at 6:30 pm in that seductive spot just after the main evening news, and as we watched, it took a while to register that this genial grown-up was not going to suddenly start cracking tasteless jokes at the expense of his guests.

The guests seemed equally unconvinced – there was a frisson of unease as they listened to Jonathan trying to control his snigger when they got an answer wrong, and their eyes tended to swivel nervously sideways as they waited for the knife-thrust. But it never happened. This was a whole new Jonathan. His frustration was almost palpable. Though the reviews for the new show have been generally positive, and Jonathan has been absolved of blame for most of its problems, he did appear straight-jacketed, as if RTE had allowed him on air only on condition that he lose his personality. There were times when he looked as though he were not entirely sure what he was doing there.

What on earth prompted series producer Andy Ruane, of the independent production company, Like It Love It, to select a wayward talent like JPB to host *Dodge the Question*? 'Jonathan brings a certain amount of conviction to the show,' says Ruane. 'You believe he knows the answers to most of the questions.' But wasn't it a gamble, given Bowman's maverick broadcasting history? 'I have said for many years that Jonathan should have his own TV show,' says Ruane. 'He's at that stage in his life. But I think he couldn't have done this show a year ago. He has matured a lot.'

Ruane, who paints himself as a kind of media Svengali, describes the intensive training that he and his team gave the nascent quiz-master. 'I knew I could knock him into shape,' he says. 'We had a team of forty people on the show, and we spent three weeks training him for the big fight – it was like coaching Steve Collins. We did dry runs of the game four times a night with people we brought in, so he made all his mistakes then.'

The training has worked. The new avuncular JPB handles the dynamics of the show with confidence and poise, never missing a cue. But Jonathan's media appearances have always benefited from his total lack of nerves. Ever since that TV appearance ten years ago, when Jonathan turned up on the *Late Late Show* and shocked the middle-class by announcing that it wasn't necessary to go to college, he has been a television natural. Perhaps, as the son of John Bowman, this was only to be expected.

And on *Dodge the Question* he seems to be developing some of his father's mannerisms. When he turns his head sideways to glance at his notes, his arms folded on the desk in front of him as if in prayer, Bowman Jr looks very like a younger version of his father. Andy Ruane insists that this is the work of genetics rather than imitation. 'He's not copying his father,' he says. 'That's just the way the Bowmans sit, and that's the way they move their heads.'

Genetics has a wider resonance for JPB. On any given evening, you are likely to find him and his eight-year-old son Saul sitting side by side in Fitzers on Dawson Street, or in Kaffe Mocha, or in any one of a number of cappuccino shops around Dublin. Their heads, similarly tousled, are bent forward and they are both engrossed in their novels.

Behind all the hype and the public display, JPB is that rare breed, a devoted single father. In his early days as a journalist, when he was writing for *In Dublin* magazine, he would turn up with his sleeping infant in a carry-cot and deposit him high on a shelf in the library while he typed feverishly on the computer below.

He still takes his son everywhere, and regularly turns up at glamourous cocktail parties with the child in tow. Saul is well able to conduct himself in polite society, and conducts intelligent conversations with his father's friends, although he would rather be roller-blading or playing Jenga. However, if he follows in Jonathan's footsteps, he'll be writing for *The Irish Times* in less than eight years time.

Angela Douglas, one of JPB's closest friends, believes that fatherhood has forced him to grow up. 'He has matured hugely in recent years, but he has to earn a living,' she explains. 'There's nothing like having to feed yourself and an eight-year-old child to force you to conform.'

JPB, the privileged child of a psychiatrist mother, Eimer Philbin, and a TV presenter father, spent an unhappy year at Sandford Park in Ranelagh, where he was viciously bullied by the other boys. He ended up at Newpark Comprehensive at Blackrock, where he wasn't a successful scholar, despite his intelligence. He can't remember his marks in the Group Cert – generally a sign that they were pretty bad – and he left school before sitting his Leaving Cert. He scored 97 or 98 per cent in all his aptitude tests except for clerical ability, which came in at a sad 87 per cent. But Jonathan doesn't mind. 'A low score in clerical ability may be indicative of a low boredom threshold,' he says. 'And there are always subs to correct the spelling.'

Anne Harris, now features editor of the *Sunday Independent* for whom JPB writes a weekly column, remembers him eleven years ago when she was editor of *Image* magazine. After he left school, but before he turned to journalism, Jonathan first tried his hand at photography. 'He was very brave,' she says. 'He sat outside the office door for ages waiting to see me. Basically he door-stepped me, and then when I published a few of his pictures he kept coming back looking for the money.'

'One of the nice things about him being around all these years has been watching him grow up. He was precocious, and there is nothing worse than being in the presence of precocity. He was full of ideas and energy.' Harris has only one criticism of her long-term protégé. 'The only snag in working with Jonathan is the decibel count,' she says. Anyone who has ever been in the presence of Jonathan on a telephone has a similar complaint. His mobile phone, one of his many beloved gadgets, allows him to conduct his high-volume conversations in the middle of Grafton Street. 'Darling! It's JPB!', he'll yell into a small black plastic box, startling all around him.

In the last decade, JPB has written for nearly every newspaper in the country: *The Irish Times*, *Sunday Press*, *Evening Herald*, *Irish Independent*, and *Sunday Independent*, the *Sunday Business Post*, the *Sunday Times* and, of course, the *Sunday Tribune*. He is a regular contributor to radio, although *The Rude Awakening* is still generally considered to have played best to his talents.

He advises PR companies, brainstorms with advertising agencies, and does a bit of copywriting when he's not writing and performing. He spent some time in Carr Communications teaching politicians how to handle their TV appearances on, among other shows, *Questions and Answers*. 'No, you can't say that, minister,' he would tell them, 'because if you do, John Bowman is immediately going to say this.'

This noisy extrovert has lately taken up Buddhist meditation, and he can now cross his ankles and descend into the lotus position in the middle of a drawing room, falling into a Zen state as easily as a cat. But he hasn't become a Buddhist. 'I'm not a joiner of things,' he says. 'I'm not good at groups, unless I'm in the spotlight.'

In the future, he's likely to spend a lot of time in the spotlight, so long as he can keep his anarchic side under control.' Jonathan will always veer towards the blasphemous and the irreverent,' says Anne Harris warmly. But he has learned when to tone it down. As his friend Angela Douglas says, 'he has discovered that he has to play the game.'

Sunday Tribune, 14 July 1996

ISEULT O'DOHERTY was the contestant co-ordinator on *Dodge the Question*. She recalled the early production meetings when 'we did a lot of thinking' about who the presenter should be and lots of different names had been suggested.

Andy Ruane came up with Jonathan's name. I must say that we were all a little dubious – untried on television, very young, unpredictable. But Andy was convinced. So Jonathan came on board. He was bursting with enthusiasm, anxiety, opinions. But he

On the *Dodge the Question* set. I gave him one piece of advice: 'Keep trying to play second fiddle and the balance between contestant and quiz-master will come out just right.' I knew that second fiddle was not Jonathan's favourite role. I feared that he mightn't know how.

threw himself into it all and managed to keep all his other jobs going at the same time – the master juggler. He hopped in and out of the Like It Love It production company's office, did test runs, argued and discussed everything – a mixture of certainty and doubt. The actual recording was gruelling. As far as I remember we recorded four programmes a day, back to back. He seemed to cope well and was the picture of confidence. Cracked jokes at the appropriate moments on screen, put the contestants at their ease and was generally the master showman. He also seemed to have acquired a world-class collection of braces for his trousers. Every day he would come in with about four different sets of exotic braces in all sorts of colours. Great! He brought Saul in one day to see the show being recorded. He was so good with him, paid him real attention. The little fellow was agog with all the shenanigans.

After a few shows had been recorded Jonathan came up to me and asked: 'Was that any good?' I realized a few things then. Nobody was giving him any feedback. He had no idea of how he was doing and his air of bravado hid all his doubts. In some ways his ability to appear supremely confident was also a handicap. I don't think that the people there realized that he did need reassurance and he was vulnerable. So we ended up chatting about how he was doing after takes. I think this was the only positive feedback he got – bloody ridiculous when you think about it. Whatever happened to 'minding your talent'?

ANDY RUANE had been responsible for selecting Jonathan as presenter of the programme.

I looked up to Jonathan. So did lots of other people, they mightn't say they did, but they did. Everywhere he went, he shone. Sometimes too brightly. He was my guest in 1990 on the live television show I presented, *Scratch Saturday.* A mystery guest. Literally. He was my guest on a few *Lyrics Boards* where his best performance was off camera, but that's another story! I always said he should have his own TV show. And he did. We did two series of *Dodge The Question* and he loved it. And we loved him. First year, pain in the arse to work with but I'm sure they probably say that about me as well! Second year, the perfect host. Wow ! Where did that come from? Jonathan knew that what we had gone through on the first series was worth it because by the end of the first run he had mastered the discipline of recording five shows a day. Not easy for anybody - especially Jonathan. Actually we got up to six shows one day! First year we almost had to tie him into the chair to get the shows recorded. And I'm not joking! Now he had settled down and was even settling the guests and putting them at ease while we recorded. Wonderful. We did a lot of TV together. He had just got a new agent in the UK. We were pitching him and the show there. We talked about it in Kielys pub in Donnybrook just two weeks before he went away... Miss you. Big Hug. x

FRANK FEELY, former Dublin City Manager, first met Jonathan in the hospitality room when they were both guests on the *Late Late Show.** This was in January 1986. 'He looked even younger than his age. He could not wait to get on. He spoke enthusiastically about the subject of his appearance which, as best I remember, related to photography.' In fact it concerned the recently launched generation of video cameras for the domestic market. The *Late Late Show* had loaned a camera to Jonathan to test what an amateur could achieve with this technology. Frank's letter of condolence emphasized what he believed was Jonathan's potential as a television broadcaster – and specifically as a chat show host.

It seems to me that there is an almost indefinable quality, which makes for excellence in such a role. It is a combination of appearance, personality, and knowledge and requires that he or she

**Late Late Show*, 17 January 1986.

be articulate, prepared at times to take an unpopular stand but at the same time concerned for the guests. It can help if he is slightly zany when the mood requires. Jonathan seemed to me an ideal candidate for such a role and I was convinced that someday this would be recognised. I met him one night after *Dodge the Question* was finished. We were leaving the Gaiety Theatre at the end of a performance. I told him that I thought that he would make an excellent host of such a chat show programme and that he should pursue the possibility. I felt he liked the idea. I will always remember his response. He smiled and said: 'Frank, you will be my first guest.'

OUTRAGEOUS WASTE

In your current issue we read of how stubbly cartoonist Thomas Mathews travelled to sunny Portugal. How can you justify the outrageous waste of resources involved in sending this lousy drunkard abroad, and worse, furnishing him with a return ticket? Why couldn't you have sent that nice young *Gentleman*, Jonathan Pigskin Whatsit instead? I'm sure the resulting article would have been far more socially responsible, and he would have drunk a lot less.
Yours etc,
Terry O'Neill.
P.S. How are you? I'm terrible. I'll tell you what, will you call me back tomorrow?

'He was a funny man and our friendship was full of laughter' – Tom Mathews. Jonathan is the author of the spoof letter mocking Mathews, *In Dublin*, 17 March 1988.

The cartoonist and writer TOM MATHEWS knew Jonathan from the time when they both worked for *In Dublin*. They remained friends.

> Much of our time together was spent casually insulting one another and trying to top one another's jokes. Over the years I think we both became better listeners; but we remained rivals with lots of meaningful stuff like which of us did the better Peter Cook as Sir Arthur Streeb Greebling being discussed. Our plan to go into business together – he to think up the cartoons, I to draw them – came alas to nothing, principally because he didn't think of any. He was a one-off, an infuriating charmer, envied for his energy and ambition in a town not noted for either. More than once I took his part when his hard won success was begrudged. I remember a friend of mine who went on his TV quiz determined to dislike him, telling me afterwards how thoroughly professional and how likeable he was. Of course he was. He was a funny man and our friendship was full of laughter; but he was a deeply serious man too. And he had a sort of innocence. I never knew him to treat anyone unkindly. I was very glad to know him.

Jonathan received many invitations to contribute to charity auctions, school debates and student meetings in universities throughout the country. One such invitation was to chair a *Questions and Answers* event in a large secondary school for girls, St Paul's in Greenhills in west Dublin. The school principal, TRIONA GLACKEN wrote:

> Not only did Jonathan respond promptly: he also injected the event with his own unique cocktail of vitality, brilliance, meaningful debate on contemporary issues, superb wit and finally – but perhaps most importantly for the school – *fun*. Our panelists included Mary Harney [leader of the Progressive Democrats and

local TD], Bishop Eamonn Walsh [Auxiliary Roman Catholic Archbishop of Dublin], John Connolly of the *Irish Times's* Education and Living Supplement and subsequently successful author, Helen Carroll, a researcher from *Kenny Live*, and a staff member. For us it was the highlight of the two-day festival to mark th 150th anniversary of the school. This brief encounter with your son has left all of us here with what now might be called bitter-sweet memories.

At a personal level, I would like to add that I have thought a lot about this since Jonathan died. One after the other, each of my own friends and family members (including my mother of 80-plus living in Ballina) has talked about how sad they feel at the loss of such a vibrant and delightful character. In a sense, I suspect that, as your daughter has said *à propos* your own family, there is perhaps, in *everyone* a bit of Jonathan, or at least, a deep down desire at times to throw all convention aside and *live* life more. As a principal, I can honestly say that I applaud Jonathan's critique of second-level schooling as repeated in the tribute programme to him on radio. His challenge to the system is even more pertinent today.

Questions and Answers debate, St Paul's College, Walkinstown, Co. Dublin. 'He injected the event with his own unique cocktail of vitality, brilliance, superb wit and *fun*' – Triona Glacken.

JOHN MINIHAN, chairman of the Progressive Democrats and a pharmacist by profession, met Jonathan when he was researching an article on Mary Harney. They met in the Rochestown Park Hotel in Cork during a selection convention for the 1997 general election. Later John Minihan's wife and Mary Harney joined them at the bar.

He entertained us for the evening with his impersonations of various political figures, particularly Charles Haughey and Brian Farrell. By the end of the night he had insulted everyone, their feelings, their egos, their views and their policies. Anyone else would have got a dig in the mouth but Jonathan had us all eating out of his hand. It was as if he could insult you and sympathise with you at the same time. No one took offence and we were all left wondering did he admire Charles Haughey or loathe him?

Thereafter we became acquaintances, and he started to call to my pharmacy when he visited Cork. He stayed in the Imperial Hotel quite near me and dropped in for toiletries or the odd gift of perfume. He would also come in taking off Charlie Bird saying something outrageous about Mary Harney, customers staring, then laughing and he would be having a right go at me. So it was always a laugh and he could carry it off and get away with it; and to my own surprise, I enjoyed it and could take it from him. His presence in the pharmacy was never quiet or discreet; it was like a tornado. He came in with a bang and created havoc. The only difference was, unlike the tornado, everyone felt the better for his visits. These were infrequent and unpredictable. You could see him twice in a month, then not for three.

When I wrote to you after his death, I did not know what to say. Even though I could not classify him as a close friend I felt part of my life was gone. I knew I would miss those visits; I knew I would no longer see those articles which I enjoyed; and that I would no longer benefit from his infectious personality, which was such an inspiration. I had to write, I wanted you to know that I appreciated him and maybe it was my way of saying good-bye. I think the gift he had is he saw things through his own eyes, eyes that were not tinted by the views of others. He was a natural, pure in thought and he lived life openly and honestly and was bereft of the hypocrisy that shrouds so many of us to different degrees.

MARY HARNEY, in her first election as leader of the Progressive Democrats, recalled the disappointing results which her party had suffered in the 1997 general election. They had won ten seats in 1992 and, having suffered two defections during the course of the 27th Dáil, saw their number of TDs further reduced to four in the 1997 election, She recalled her arrival home late on the night of the results.

Physically and mentally exhausted I dragged myself towards the hall door to answer the unrelenting ring of the doorbell. It was Jonathan. There he stood, arms full of flowers, his face quizzical and smiling. It was so typical of him to be there when I most needed human kindness and at a time when others might have instinctively stayed away. Friendship with Jonathan was full of brightness and energy – always unpredictably spontaneous and such fun. He was keenly aware of the political scene, understanding all its nuances. His impersonations of some of our better known public figures would have fooled even themselves! His death has left us with many questions, none more than what that extraordinary potential would have gone on to achieve.

FARREL CORCORAN, Dean of the Faculty of Humanities at Dublin City University and former chairman of the Radio Telefís Éireann Authority, recalled one encounter with Jonathan and also offered some insights on grieving.

I met Jonathan only once, a few years ago. I was standing with a friend at the bar of my local on a warm Sunday afternoon a few summers back, watching the bubbles settle in two pint glasses, chatting about some innovation in computer power just announced in the papers. Jonathan, also waiting for a pint nearby, piped up and topped our news with his own, in an enthusiastic three-minute treatise on computer markets yet to come, just around the corner. The memory for me is one of personality, ebullience, social fearlessness, mental exuberance, total focus on the subject. Then he was gone, as quickly as he had appeared. The anguish you feel must be great. But there is a psychic rhythm to the process of grieving, I believe, unique to each one of us but patterned across the human species. There are stages to be passed through, moods to be endured, memories to be sifted through, rushes of intense emotion to be experienced, material things to be dealt with, support for others to be reassembled, future projects to be re-focused upon, motivation for going on to be found – and a lot of cathartic crying to be done. None of us can ever prepare for this, whether the loss takes place in the glare of publicity or the seclusion of the micro-world of the family.

BERNADETTE GUERIN, mother of the distinguished *Sunday Independent* crime correspondent Veronica Guerin, who was murdered by a criminal gang on 26 June 1996, wrote:

A short time before Veronica's death, Jonathan was instrumental in giving her some magazine award for having sexy legs. She told me about it on Friday, 21 June 1996. She was wearing a tracksuit with Graham's rugby socks up to her knees, we laughed so much as she sang 'If he could see me now'. On the following Friday Jonathan stood in tears shaking my hand in sympathy and then I thanked him for giving us the last good laugh together, he put his arms around me and said: 'Thank you for telling me.' I've always admired your son, but because he left me with that memory, I've loved him. We can only hope that both of them are sharing a laugh and gossip as I write.

DAVID O'CONNOR was a distant relative of Jonathan's through the Maddens of Roscrea. John Madden 'Jack' Philbin, Jonathan's maternal grandfather, grew up in Roscrea. His wife, Eva Philbin, was professor of Organic Chemistry in UCD and Jonathan was their first grandchild, Saul their first great-grandchild. Jack died suddenly in July 1997 and Eimer concluded her oration to her father in Donnybrook Church with the words: 'My mother has lost her greatest admirer and Jonathan has lost his greatest fan.' David wrote:

His gentleness and warmth made a profound impression on me at Jack's funeral. This was reinforced when he was telling me how Eva was getting on [*then recovering from a serious motor accident*]. The previous week Jonathan had researched a question on some arcane reaction between two chemicals and had posed it to Eva. The delight and pride with which he told me how lucidly and authoritatively she had rattled off the answer again impressed and moved me deeply. Their admiration was truly mutual. I loved my occasional short chats with Jonathan. He fascinated me and impressed me on many levels. Life can never be easy for one so gifted, which makes his gentleness and softness all the more memorable.

RAY BATES, Director of the National Lottery, was abroad when Jonathan died. Jonathan had a keen interest in statistics and had participated in a number of debates when the Lottery was launched about how very long the odds were on winning.

While my contacts with him were all too infrequent, Jonathan came to all our National Lottery game launches, and added to the events that particular quality of bonhomie that he radiated. I would have seated him at my table, by my side, every time, but my PR people rationed our togetherness on the basis that when I sat beside him I generally ignored everyone else at the table. Even though we didn't meet regularly, I feel I have exchanged more ideas with him than I have with some of my life-long friends. He had an extraordinary mind and I believe he was, an extraordinary person. The last time we were together I remember kissing him good-bye – not usual for a 'Christian Brothers boy'! – I can still remember the feel of his designer stubble. I was in California on business when I got the awful news and I stood in the lobby of a San Diego hotel with tears running down my face.

EGERTON SHELSWELL-WHITE, owner of Bantry House and musician, had never been introduced to Jonathan but had seen his programme on television and recalled one 'very vivid' memory from 1998.

I was having coffee in the Shelbourne – I go to Dublin once a year in November for my trombone lessons – and Jonathan was sitting on the arm of a sofa in the middle of the room talking on his mobile. I then noticed a rather odd thing: everyone who came in seemed to make straight for Jonathan and his sofa as if he were entertaining guests in his own house. And I thought: here is all of Dublin, its spirit, its atmosphere, its literature, its history, embodied in this little gathering of young Dubliners in its most famous hotel.

CHARLES BRADY is a member of the bar staff in the Shelbourne Hotel. He wrote that it was only in the past three or four years of

Jonathan's life that he had come to 'know and like' him.

I must confess that wasn't always the case. For a long time, I pretty much ignored him, finding him just too brash and loud for my taste. Then, several years back, he wrote a piece on the film 'Crash' for the *Sunday Independent.* This was at a time when the media were throwing their collective hands up in horror at the thought of such a film being released here. Jonathan had seen the film in Australia and his article was one of the few sensible appraisals to appear in Ireland. On the spur of the moment I bought him the little B[ritish] F[ilm] I[nstitute] Modern Classics study of it, scribbled a rather self-conscious note and handed it to him the next time he came in. You would have laughed had you seen the look of puzzlement, surprise, then pleasure as he looked at this barman who had always been faintly hostile!

After that he would often drop in, especially on a Tuesday morning when the bar would be empty and we could chat about whomever he was due to interview, or what his latest enthusiasm was – and there was no shortage of them. I began to look forward to his visits, and can truly say that I came to like and admire him a great deal. We were opposites in most ways. However, we were both ferocious book-lovers; also, neither of us was interested in the pseudo-macho posturing that usually takes place when men gather in bars. I don't suppose I need to tell you that women loved Jonathan, and it didn't take long to see why. Jonathan liked women, and I don't just mean in a physical sense. I mean that he really *liked* them. He listened, and was totally at ease in their company. There never seemed to be an agenda with him.

However – and here I may be completely wrong – I thought that there was a loneliness at the heart of Jonathan that was hard to define. I didn't know him well enough to know why, but I felt that if you scratched far enough beneath the surface you would find a strange sadness there. He often surprised me with small acts of kindness. Several months ago I was having lunch in Fitzers of Dawson Street with my girlfriend when we saw Jonathan holding court. We exchanged small talk but in my mind I resolved to ask him out for a drink sometime. But, I thought, there's plenty of time for that. It is a matter of just plain grief to me now that I never took the opportunity to get to know him better than is possible across a counter.

6

'They were like this pair of loveable vagabonds who needed nobody but each other.'

– SARAH BINCHY on Jonathan and Saul

GREG COLLINS, Jonathan's English teacher for one term at Sandford Park – when he was twelve, remained a lifelong friend. He recalled that on one New Year's Eve, their wedding anniversary, he and his wife, Eileen, met Jonathan when they were walking towards DaVincenzo's restaurant on Leeson Street. Spontaneously they invited him to join them.

> An evening of much hilarity and high spirits followed. At some stage in the roistering, Jonathan left us only to return some time later with a bottle of champagne to toast the occasion and with flowers for Eileen. That's when he gave me a plastic toy which he called 'the see-saw of life' which sits in my study – a constant reminder of that hilarious night. On New Year's Eve we returned to the scene to celebrate Jonathan's memory.
>
> For a number of years he always rang to invite me to his birthday – 6 January. The occasions were usually attended by a small group of friends. Ironically, his last birthday was not celebrated in this way: he rang to say he was going on retreat! This didn't surprise me. Behind the 'face to meet the faces that you meet' (one of his Eliot quotes) there was a lot of self-doubt and confusion and he wanted to get away, as we all do at times, to contemplate. I sometimes had from Jonathan a vague impression of sadness, as if he wasn't quite happy with his mode of life in the media world. He was many-faceted and complex and did not confide in people easily or talk about his emotions. Behind the image he conveyed of 'the man about town' lay a sensitive soul who sought answers to many of life's imponderable problems and, like

Jonathan with Saul, 1988

Wordsworth, listened for the 'still sad music of humanity'. His talks for *A Living Word* recorded shortly before his death convey for me the real Jonathan.

In 1997 when I retired from Sandford there was the usual final assembly of boys and staff. You can imagine my surprise when in the midst of the proceedings Jonathan suddenly appeared, made a short speech in my honour, proceeded to hug and kiss me Russian-style, presented me with a bunch of sunflowers and left as quickly as he appeared! Here, yet again, was the thoughtful Jonathan who took the time off to be there and remembered our jokes about Van Gogh and his sunflowers!

JOHN GORMLEY, the Green Party's TD for Dublin South-East, wrote about many different encounters with Jonathan, including a 'vitriolic exchange on the radio' on the possible health risks of mobile phones shortly before his death. They had not met since that encounter.

But I know that had we met there would have been plenty of good humour and banter and our row forgotten about. Jonathan was quick to have a go, but equally quick to forgive. I saw the kind side of Jonathan a few months after I was elected to the Dáil. He rang my office in an agitated state a number of times, because he'd come across a homeless girl outside the Central Bank. He was deeply upset by her plight and wondered if anything could be done. Unfortunately, by the time I got to the bank, she was gone. Jonathan had a social conscience and he was a good man.

SEAMUS SCALLY, former general secretary of the Labour Party, was a friend of Jonathan. Seamus is interested in religion and its place in Irish society.

Jonathan and I spoke a lot about religion – especially about socialism and the Catholic faith. Those talks reminded me of many lengthy conversations I had had when travelling on the road with Conor Cruise O'Brien during the 1973-77 coalition government when I was one of the government's press secretaries. Jonathan was cheeky, assertive, provocative; and he was restless – a friendly free spirit. He was not in any way snobbish and was mature beyond his years. I liked his style. He was a wonderful encourager. He believed in Dana's campaign for the right to be a contestant in the 1997 Presidential election. Jonathan was a true liberal. He thought the media had been unfair to her and he felt that, in justice, she should be a contestant. And at her party after the election he brought the house down when he sang a parody with her based on *All Kinds of Everything*.

BREDA O'BRIEN is a secondary school teacher, broadcaster and columnist with *The Irish Times*. She had previously written a column for the *Sunday Business Post* in which newspaper she also published an interview with Dana during the 1997 presidential campaign. She recalled that at the time Dana 'was not talking to many journalists'. Jonathan telephoned her.

He began the conversation with some outrageous flattery saying that he was a fan of my column. I replied that I doubted that very much, except that I think I expressed it in slightly more robust terms. He admitted that his real reason for ringing was that he was intrigued by Dana. Since I had been granted an interview, he thought I might be able to put him in contact with her. I did so, and there was an instant rapport between them. That might surprise some people but it was absolutely typical of Jonathan. He was at once a very complex person and very simple. He trusted his instincts. He liked her, he believed her to be a good person, and that was enough. Also, he had an unerring eye for star quality. While other commentators were still sneering, he had seen that Dana was the real story of the campaign.

Everything in Jonathan's life happened at high intensity. I got to know him very fast, saw him regularly over a period of months, and then he moved on. If that makes him sound like a butterfly, in

> some ways he was. In others, he was the most deeply loyal of friends, maintaining relationships over years, and even though he was not in regular contact towards the end, I knew that if I ran into him in RTE or on the street we would pick up a conversation as if it had never been interrupted.
>
> He was incredibly generous. The first time I was to appear on RTE's *Questions and Answers* I was riddled with anxiety, so he told me he would help me prepare for the price of a pint. Again, looking back, it was a very funny session as he became his father before my eyes. Though it has to be said, that dad was nowhere near as challenging as son was, so most of my nerves were misplaced. It was part of him to enjoy the fact that his father would not know that Jonathan had helped me.
>
> It is stating the obvious to say that Jonathan was extremely bright. At first I found this intimidating, but as time went on I challenged him right back. He forced me to clarify my thinking in many ways, to justify things which I thought were self-evident but with which he did not agree at all. Although Jonathan was the soul of kindness, he could also wound, and wound deeply with an acerbic comment. I know that I was cut to the quick on more than one occasion, and yet it was impossible to hold it against him. He was a searching soul, too impatient sometimes to find the answers which he so much desired. He found someone like me hard to understand in many ways, rooted as I was so deeply in one tradition. When I pointed out to him once that the Dalai Lama and the Pope had had a wonderful dialogue when they met, he said loftily that the difference was that one was judgmental and the other was not. When I pointed out that that was an extremely judgmental comment in itself, he had the grace to laugh. Laughter and friendship and challenge – my memories of Jonathan, who lived more intensely in the brief few years he had than most of us do in ninety. I miss him. I expect I always will.

Jonathan as a boy had taken a very keen interest in television, especially humorous, comic or satirical programmes. He was especially interested in the early satirical programmes from the BBC – some of them first broadcast before he was born – but which he had seen as repeats or on video: *That Was The Week That Was* and *Not So Much A Programme More A Way Of Life*. Later he liked *Monty Python's Flying Circus* and tried to persuade his school friends and teachers to watch it. NED SHERRIN had been among the pioneers of this genre in the BBC and when he was in Dublin with the stage play *Jeffrey Bernard is Unwell*, Jonathan interviewed him. Sherrin wrote:

> I met Jonathan during a brief visit to Dublin to preside over the one unsuccessful production of *Jeffrey Bernard is Unwell.* I think Dubliners felt that they had enough witty drunks of their own without importing ours. My vivid impression of Jonathan was of a lively mind, an all-embracing sense of humour and an almost puppyish exuberance. I last waved to him on the stairs as I left the first night party which had not yet turned into a wake.

On RTE Jonathan was an early fan of Dermot Morgan's work and could do a 'Fr Trendy' sermon from a cold start at the age of ten. It was one of his party pieces: he liked to test his impromtu skills by asking us to complete the opening line of a Fr Trendy sermon: 'Life is like a…'. We would add 'burst balloon' or 'a rained-out cricket match' or whatever and Jonathan would be off. It was the extemporaneous dimension to these performances which was so striking at that age. ARTHUR MATHEWS, co-author of the highly successful *Father Ted* television series, met Jonathan only once – at Dermot Morgan's funeral. Dermot died suddenly in London in March 1998 having just completed the filming of the last series of *Father Ted.* Arthur remembered having a lengthy conversation with Jonathan that night:

> I remember that we talked about many things; amongst them your work as a broadcaster and historian, his son Saul, and his love of classical music. I mentioned that, although I didn't have a vast knowledge of it, I particularly liked a piece by Gluck* which I listened to quite a lot. This caused Jonathan to launch into a detailed, knowledgeable and enthusiastic appreciation. I also told him that I thought he'd done a very good job of presenting a quiz show on RTE which I had seen. It seemed a role particularly suited to the unusually unselfconscious and gregarious Jonathan. He made a deep impression on me on that sad day of Dermot's funeral, and afterwards I felt glad that I had met him. Like Dermot, his death was shocking in it's suddenness.

DON MORGAN, son of Dermot, wrote that his own earliest encounters with Jonathan were unsatisfactory. This was because Jonathan was among a number of Dermot's friends who would spontaneously join him when he was having lunch with his two eldest sons, Don and Bobby, on his occasional visits to Dublin. Dermot's marriage had broken up and he was then living in London with his partner and their child Ben. Don coveted such

*Christoph Willibald von Gluck 1714-87; his *Orpheus and Eurydice* was one of Jonathan's favourite operas.

visits from his father and 'absolutely and completely' hated it when others joined their table. He admitted that he must have greeted Jonathan on such occasions with 'teenage sullenness'. He remembered meeting him at his father's funeral.

> He happened to be one of the people I remember the night of the removal in the pub opposite the church. Jonathan was having a good time, taking something of a slagging from my friends and, from the little of the night I can remember, giving it back admirably. He was just there, and we began to appreciate him properly. A while later, he took us to the theatre, to see the Reduced Shakespeare Company's *The Bible (abridged)*, a show our dad no doubt would have liked to have seen. It cheered us up a great deal. There was a lot more to Jonathan than our initial meetings could possibly gauge. Certainly how I felt about him when I first met him is violently at odds with how I felt about him when he died. You couldn't help but like him, but for that you had to get to know him a bit better. There is one thing he did which I must mention: when Bobby, Ben and myself wrote a book for our dad, he brought flowers with him to the launch; not for the authors, but two bunches – one bunch for our mother and one for Ben's mother.

Sunday Independent
◆ March 15, 1998

The greatest story ever told quickly

The Reduced Shakespeare Company takes things like the Word of God, cuts it down to the essentials, adds some topical humour and comes up a little gem, says Jonathan Philbin Bowman

Sunday Independent, 15 March 1998

The Reduced Shakespeare Company's production referred to by Don Morgan had first been seen by Jonathan in England. He had written a favourable review. He saw it a number of times during its week in Dublin. On another night he took Don and Bobby Morgan. ABIE PHILBIN BOWMAN recalled:

> Donny [*the family's pet name for Jonathan*] phoned me one Monday to invite me to see The Reduced Shakespeare Company's *The Bible, the complete word of God (abridged).* I was in the middle of my 'Atheism is the One True Faith' phase so I was delighted to go. But at such short notice, Donny couldn't round up anyone else, despite having four complimentary tickets.
>
> When we arrived at the Gaiety there were, predictably enough, a couple of God Squad guys outside doing their 'this show is sinful and blasphemous' routine. Donny, in typically mischievous form, asked them if they had seen the show. No, they hadn't, but an English associate of theirs had, and had subsequently sworn an affidavit that it was blasphemous. 'Wait a minute. If I hadn't read the Bible, but I went round swearing that it was bollocks because a friend of mine had said so in an affidavit, what would you tell me to do?' The Lord's representative conceded that he would tell Jonathan to read it for himself and make up his own mind. 'So come and see the show!'

Let me just tell you this is a fast and witty production, well worth not missing. It hasn't attracted a Fatwah yet, though it may manage the odd (very odd) picket and it's one of those things which everyone should experience once in a lifetime — in your case, reader, that means next week at the Gaiety.

Poster for Dublin performance, *The Bible: The Complete Word of God (abridged)*, Gaiety Theatre, Dublin, March 1998

This argument went in circles a few times, and we got some tired looks from other patrons, but eventually – assured that the tickets were complimentary and that the affiliates of Satan would in no way gain financially – the two protestors relented and came in to watch. As the four tickets were in Donny's name we were all seated together.

When the show started, both men tried to remain solemn, but sporadic smiles and laughs kept breaking out. At the interval Donny asked one of them how he was enjoying the show. 'Well it's all right so far but I've heard that the second half is much worse!' Near the end, one of the two walked out in order to resume his picket ahead of the heathen multitudes. But a minute later, one of the actors bid the audience farewell by concluding: 'Well, if you liked the show, tell both your friends. And if you didn't like it, hell – tell those guys outside.' The remaining protestor beamed with pride and self-importance.

Throughout the show Donny kept pulling out his latest gadget and typing notes on a tiny illuminated screen. I found out afterwards that he was writing extra gags for the show. I asked him why, if he'd written nearly all the Irish gags, he didn't seek a writing credit. 'Because then all the reviews that say "excellent local references" would be derogatory instead.' Afterwards we met up with the three-man cast and spent hours swapping stories, Radiohead interpretations and *Life of Brian* moments. It was a great night.

JOHN POHLHAMMER, an actor and writer with the Reduced Shakespeare Company, recalled Jonathan's involvement with the Irish production of the show.

Jonathan wrote a wonderful review of our show *The Bible: The Complete Word of God (abridged)* when he saw us in London and asked if he could be of any help on our upcoming trip to Dublin. We always include local references in our shows, so I asked him to tell me as much as he could about local politics, scandals, or anything else we could use to get some laughs. He was such a wealth of helpful information that together we rewrote about half of the 'Ten Rejected Commandments' and several lines in the 'In the Beginning Blues' for the Irish audience – one line that comes to mind is: 'Do you really want to live in a country where it takes two referendums to legalise divorce while your Taoiseach lives in sin?'! Jonathan obviously had his finger on the pulse of Dublin because his suggestions were right on the money; those lines got some of the biggest laughs of the entire tour.

But Jonathan was far more than just a great resource to us; he was a terrific host and our strongest supporter during that week and stands out as one of the best friends we made on the tour. There was a lot of controversy upon our arrival – some misguided Bible-thumpers were trying to have us put away for blasphemy – and I think Jonathan loved being a part of it all.

Another of the company, RICK BLAND, befriended Jonathan during that week, having first encountered him in Bromley, Kent where Jonathan had seen the production prior to its week in Dublin.

About ten days before our time in Dublin Dermot Morgan had passed away suddenly and because of his past as a comic who used religion as one of his foils, our show, which was causing a lot of controversy, became linked to him for a short time. Jonathan brought two of Dermot's boys to see the show. After the show we went for a drink and we had a good laugh. I kept looking at them marveling how they were in grief but you couldn't tell by looking at them. Jonathan and I proceeded to have a long chat about death because in late 1994 and early 1995, four friends died very suddenly, one of whom had moved to Dublin in early 1994. She died in Dublin in early 1995. Eileen Farrell was her name and she was one of the most amazing friends one could ever wish to have. She was a very special, gentle, kind and fiery girl. When she danced people marveled at how amazing she was. She was a rare kind of dancer who explored her emotions through dance. While in Dublin I felt her presence and went to see where she had lived. I thought of her all week and because of her and the death of Dermot Morgan, Jonathan and I had a long conversation about death.

The day after our conversation, Jonathan came to the show and gave me a book called *Your Loved One Lives on Within You*, by Alexandra Kennedy. I read segments of the book and eventually put it on a shelf. Jonathan told me how he'd read it to help him cope with a death at one point in his life. I left Dublin and never had the pleasure of talking to Jonathan again. In June 1998, while on tour, I received a message that my father had suddenly died. I flew to Canada for ten days to attend the funeral. During that time I thought back to being in the bar the night that Dermot Morgan's kids came to see the show. I suddenly knew how they felt, full of sorrow on the inside, and yet somehow able to move forward in life carrying this sadness with you. And of course I thought of the beautiful Eileen Farrell who died before her time. Soon after I came back from Canada I rejoined the tour and began to read the book Jonathan had given me. It helped me cope with the sorrow I felt.

Cast of the Reduced Shakespeare Company

* 'The greatest story ever told quickly', *Sunday Independent*, 15 March 1998.

I thought maybe you'd like to know that this book was a book that Jonathan turned to at one point in his life to cope with a loss. I will always treasure it and will probably find myself reading it again as I get older.

DJAMEL SOUALHI is an Algerian and represents the liberal Algerian opposition party, the RCD, in Scandinavia, Britain and Ireland. In 1998 he invited Irish journalists to visit Algeria to attend the annual conference of the RCD. Jonathan alone accepted.* Djamel had first known him twelve years before.

I used to see Jonathan a lot in the Colony Café in Johnston's Court off Grafton Street in the mid-1980s. It was then among the trendiest cafés in Dublin. Of course Jonathan didn't discuss matters; he made statements and speeches. He was the master. He had his own court – followers, admirers, fans. To me, he was just a kid – spoiled, loud, a show-off and, above all, unconscious of the trap of life ahead. In fact Jonathan left no-one indifferent; you either loved him or hated him. You just could not ignore him.

Twelve years later, in 1998, Algeria was going through the worst time of its history with daily massacres of innocent civilians taking place. For many it was a 'no go' area. Foreign ministries in the western world were advising their citizens not to travel to Algeria under any circumstances. The RCD party was holding its national conference which took place every four years in March 1998. I had invited Irish journalists and politicians from across the divide to attend the conference. As it turned out, for one reason or another, no one could attend except for Jonathan.

En route to Algeria, I introduced him to a number of French journalists and personalities forming part of our delegation. During the flight Jonathan was full of chat, cracking jokes and engaging in conversation right up until we landed. There was no bother on him despite the dreaded destination! In the car travelling from the airport to the hotel, some thirty kilometers west of Algiers, Jonathan became very inquisitive, asking me all sorts of questions about Algeria as he was memo-photographing the landscape and taking notes; he wasn't wasting any time.

During the three days of the conference Jonathan was on his own talking to delegates, doing interviews, attending the party's daily news briefing conference. At times he would seek my help for some translation. He managed to make friends with French journalists and local politicians; he took to people like a fish takes to water. During this experience I discovered the coming of age of Jonathan. I discovered the man, the talented, professional

* 'Algerians say "We have no other country"', *Sunday Independent*, 1 March 1998.

journalist – uncompromised. He was brave, warm, friendly, full of integrity but, above all, objective. Misunderstood during his teens, he was now acclaimed and appreciated as an adult.

Occasionally during his early years at the *Sunday Independent*, Jonathan's articles would be illustrated by the paper's cartoonist and caricaturist JIM COGAN. From September 1998 when Jonathan was writing his diary he would liase with Jim every week.

As the cartoonist for Jonathan's weekly diary in the *Sunday Independent* my Thursdays revolved around chasing him – leaving messages at numerous contact points to ring me! As the day wore on, more and more people knew less and less about his whereabouts. Eventually Jonathan would contact me; crackling interference would be explained by the fact that he was ringing me from inside the tent of an Outer Mongolian yak farmer. 'What are you doing there?' I would ask. I am interviewing Ludmilla Lush the super-model, she's promoting Bulgarian yogurt at the Ulan Bator Trade Fair.' 'Did the *Indo* send you?' I would enquire. 'No, I'm supposed to be in New York to do a profile on Ivana Trump, but that's another story.' Indeed it was another story – maybe next week's diary. Jonathan's diary reminded me of some strange Marx Brothers adventure: 'A night at the opera way out west with duck soup.' As a result I drew some very weird cartoons. 'Could I fit in the forty-seven vodka-drinking Uzbeki acrobats, he had met on the Trans-Siberian Express?' he'd ask before interference on the line cut us off.

Jonathan's untimely death shocked and saddened me. It took from us someone who in his unique and hilarious manner would have gone on to chronicle the new century and its bewildering technology. His enthusiastic and inquiring mind was tailor-made for the task. Sadly, others, less funny and engaging, must fill the vacuum.

The Progressive Democrat TD and minister LIZ O'DONNELL had met Jonathan shortly after she had been first elected to the Dáil in the 1992 general election and remained a close enough friend to be invited to a dinner party for his 30th birthday.

Jonathan literally bounced into my life at a reception in Trinity in 1992. I was a newly elected TD; he a sparkling young journalist and broadcaster. He introduced himself with laughing eyes and tousled curls. A romantic feminist, Jonathan loved and admired many women; I was privileged to be one of them.

He had a childlike capacity for unconditional love. Once on the list, one was assured of swooning attention, lavish praise and bouquets of encouragement. Though he sought attention rather than approval himself, he knew the value of the latter. Our friendship over the years sustained long lapses in contact. Then, out of the blue, a rapturous phonecall – of teenage girl duration – would reaffirm the bond. When I say telephone I mean mobile. His youthful enthusiasm for gadgets and technology meant that he was master of the text message long before anyone else. At one point he commandeered my slumbering and underused mobile from the depths of my bag and fixed it so that all his contact numbers could be accessed by my simply pressing seven. Frequently thereafter my phone would beep with text messages to which I couldn't reply, not being a texter.

There were occasional lunches and regular hysterics and high jinks in the Leinster House Bar where he was a regular visitor when we were awaiting votes on late sittings. Jonathan was obsessively interested in politics – even more so than me. I just did it. He dissected, devoured and contemplated current affairs. Often, he would call me late at night, rousing me from my bed, to outline a wonderful idea or concept which couldn't hold. His brain was highly charged, rat-tat-tatting ideas as fast as he could speak and even unraveling them while the listener played catch-up.

His quest to fill the spiritual 'hope' left by the Christian God in his life was a constant. I was honoured to be invited to a small dinner party to mark his thirtieth birthday. We were a very diverse group, strangers awkwardly drawn together by our friendship with Jonathan – in retrospect, it was reminiscent of his unforgettable funeral.

The journalist and author MARY KENNY knew Jonathan only 'in a social kind of way'.

Middle-aged women are not always the most scintillating company for a young person – I remember quite well thinking 'boring old trouts' when obliged to strike up a conversation with someone of my age, at his age – but with Jonathan, it was as if there was no generation gap. He was genuinely responsive to everyone he met. It wasn't put on. He had a tremendously lively mind, unclouded by the prejudice nowadays known as 'political correctness' – he didn't think in rigid categories of what was officially approved of, and what was not – but was open to paradoxical and elliptical thinking. He also read texts thoroughly: it is surprising, in the media business, how many people just read headlines. If he felt enthusiastic, he showed it. He was involved.

I think he drank too much, but so did I, at his age. I could have had a thousand mishaps like Jonathan's, but I was luckier.

That's the only difference. A thirst for liquor can be a kind of rage for life, for experiencing the highs and lows it delivers. He would have corrected this excess with maturity: but he would not have wanted a prim kind of life as a young man, and he took the risks and he will always be remembered fondly by those who encountered him.

As with so many people, Jonathan's strength could also be his weakness. His ability with words, his quick-fire wit could evoke such mirth and instant approval that it could encourage him to the point of becoming tiresome. And he wasn't always the best judge of ensuring that others too did some of the talking; nor did alcohol make his judgement any better. The *Sunday Independent* writer BRIGHID MCLAUGHLIN was among those who had a difficulty with Jonathan in this regard. After his funeral she published accounts of two quite different encounters with him a year before, in the spring of 1999. She admitted that she had found his funeral difficult.

> Last night, lying in bed with a brandy throbbing in my skull, I tried to be calm. Funerals are traumatic affairs and for me, Jonathan's was the worst. Yes, the worst. Sitting among hundreds of those who loved him, I tried to gather his life's traces into a hard, tiny knot of understanding. It was horrific. Horrific to see his wonderful father hold back the tears. It is with the greatest shame I tell you I missed a lot. Jonathan used to drive me crazy. That is why I proceed timidly, cautiously, fearing I know not what, because I know now, too late, that he was sad and splendid.

She then gave the accounts of her two meals with Jonathan the previous year. The first was when she was meeting Jim Kebel, travel writer with the London *Evening Standard*.

> We met in the bar of the Fitzwilliam Hotel. As Jim was reviewing the restaurant, he invited me to dinner. Suddenly Jonathan appeared between us, jauntily dropped his briefcase onto a barstool, and perkily introduced himself to Jim. He was as high as a kite with the awful hysterical voice that frequently made my heart sink. Within seconds, the conversation evolved into an elaborate treatise on newspapers and whom he knew in the *Daily Telegraph* and the *Sunday Times*, 'Did Jim know . . . etc, etc?' Jonathan had a hot line to everyone. Kebel was intrigued.
>
> 'Shall I ask him to dinner?' he whispered when Jonathan darted to the bathroom. 'That's up to you,' I said, 'but he'll wear you out within the hour.' I am not proud of this memory. Jim, being kind,

asked him anyhow. Jonathan was delighted. The compliance he drew from people was astonishing. It was as if Jim knew at once that he was in the presence of someone who could not be judged by the standards he had hitherto employed in relation to most journalists. 'Brighid minds me joining you, I know it,' he said, 'but she will get over it.' Jonathan was mischievous. He knew I did mind. Very much.

Jonathan ordered the most expensive bottle of wine on the list with great aplomb. He knew his wine. I was horrified. Even the sommelier was embarrassed and declared Jonathan's wine out of stock. Jonathan ordered another. Then Jonathan's mobile phone rang, each time, a Tara, an Eva, a Julia. His voice was shrill and unbearably loud. I felt sorry for the poor couples nearby trying to have a romantic evening out. 'Brighid's embarrassed, what do you think, Jim?' I smiled uncomfortably while Jonathan drank his way into Edward Leardom, and then he lost his way to the bathroom. I ordered a taxi. Jonathan was boisterously assertive. 'I don't want a taxi!' But he got one anyhow. 'I see what you mean,' said Jim after dinner. 'A bit of a nightmare, eh?' That was an understatement.

Brighid McLaughlin recounted this experience to Anne Harris, who explained it – as did Jonathan occasionally – as due to his suffering in winter from SAD syndrome, seasonal affective disorder. In latter years Jonathan believed he needed some winter sun to help him cope with this condition. Anne Harris suggested that Brighid McLaughlin meet Jonathan again.

This time Jonathan was completely different, sandals and bare feet, beads that looked like coffee beans wound around his neck, an open shirt. Unshaven, he seemed earthed and quiet. We weaved our way to the Bridge Bar. We sat outside on the canal wall and Jonathan tried to convert me to Buddhism. 'You've suffered, Brighid, I know that, and I have.' We talked about a German philosopher called Feuerbach,* ECT, depression, Saul, a mutual friend who worked for an American TV show and whom Jonathan thought was beautiful. Delighted with himself, he told me they had a bit of a thing going on.

In the sunshine, we puzzled over 'reality' in a world outside of work, like children. It was a place presumably where people could be happy. He insisted I read over a passage he had marked in some Buddhist book five times. I told him it didn't do anything for me. He said it would. The Hari Krishnas couldn't have been more

* Ludwig Andreas Feuerbach (1804-1872), German philosopher and theologian who argued that Christianity was 'nothing more than a fixed idea'. Influential with Engels and Marx.

intense in conversions. But I was already converted. To Jonathan. He was so, so much different from the Jonathan I knew before. I felt a redemptive chemistry between us; it was one of those moments that cannot be assessed in words, that live on in memory. Like the magic and magicians he was so fond of, he had executed an instantaneous personality change, as quick as one would change costume. I now realize that, despite the super-confident walk, the super-abundant brightness of his mind, the toothy smile, the curly brown hair falling from a high forehead, Jonathan was quite fearful and closed.

I wish I had been more patient and kind to Jonathan. It will always be a massive regret. I try to imagine him in a happy place, a conjuror in top hat and tails, unveiling his true heart, that innocent, wonderful, irritating mind, while a chorus of beautiful girls remain on hand to witness his class act, as he snatches new silk banners from the depths of a happy soul. I miss all that I should never have missed and more. His death has provoked me to give my life some sort of better shape. A kinder shape.

Sunday Independent, 19 March 2000

PATRICIA DEEVY was a colleague of Jonathan's on the *Sunday Independent* but had known him first as 'a preternaturally confident young man' who was a regular in the café in the Arts Block in Trinity in the mid-1980s. Jonathan never confined himself to the company of his own age-group. When he was still at school, he regularly gate-crashed the Trinity College Games Club, to play anything from chess to a fad of the time, 'Dungeons and Dragons'.

I didn't know what to make of him but thought he was fascinating. A decade later I finally met him – when he mistook me for my colleague, Eilis O'Hanlon, at a *Sunday Independent* party. Jonathan, being Jonathan, quickly made it seem like he had made a most fortunate mistake. I was delighted by him then, as I was ever after. Over the years it has been a privilege to have known him. His heart, his humour and his intelligence were rare and dazzling. And his kindnesses were quiet and comforting. When I was hospitalized after a car accident in the UK two years ago, one of the first voices on the line from Dublin was Jonathan, full of jokes and encouragement. It was a wonderful breath of life at a time of distress.

I sometimes think that fear turns us into pale imitations of what we might be. But Jonathan had the courage to be utterly himself. At his funeral when Emma talked about finding our 'inner Jonathan', it crystallised a thought I had had about transforming this tragedy into something good and lasting and worthy of his life,

> which was a resolution to try to remember and be inspired by the way he went through the world, stripped of artifice, sometimes in chaos, but always in truth, in love and in fun. Just as it was an honour to know him in life, so it was an honour to share in a farewell that was so beautifully and fittingly composed. But I realize that the farewell is just a moment in an infinity of loss, which defies language.

CAROLINE FURNEY ENGLISH met Jonathan in Dzogchen Beara, the Buddhist retreat centre in Allihies, west Cork which he occasionally visited in these years, sometimes accompanied by Saul. She especially 'enjoyed his sense of humour and how he was never afraid to challenge anyone – including visiting lamas whom everyone else was in awe of.' DEIRDRE GLEESON also remembered 'great fun' on these occasions: 'He sent the place into a whirl, with lots of questions and debating and got everybody thinking.' URSULA HALLIGAN, who had formerly worked in print journalism and with RTE's *Prime Time* current affairs programme, is now political correspondent of TV3. She frequently met Jonathan in the environs of Leinster House. Although she thought of herself 'as more of an acquaintance than a close friend', she still felt 'a huge sense of loss' when he died. 'He was always stimulating and dynamic company. In a world so often glum and serious, his cheerfulness regularly lifted my humour and made my day.' JOANNE BYRNE works in public relations and knew Jonathan both personally and professionally. She found him at times the bane of her life. He could be 'cheerful, exasperating, annoying and flirtatious – all in the one phone call!' Saul, she wrote, was the cause of her first near heart attack

> ...when he wandered around a priceless Picasso exhibition bouncing what appeared to be a gigantic basketball with Jonathan in the background telling me not to be worried! He was truly a unique character capable of great affection, great feeling and great emotion – often over a myriad of different subjects. He will really be missed by a huge number of people – from his close friends and acquaintances to the waiters and taxi-drivers you mentioned at his funeral. My abiding memory of Jonathan is sitting in a taxi driven by Tommy Valentine, 'The singing Frank Sinatra taxi-driver', and listening as the two of them absolutely killed 'The Girl from Panama' – that was truly an instance when Frank Sinatra was trespassed against.

DEBORAH MARTIN is managing director of the

Communications Partnership, a specialist firm in public relations. She first knew Jonathan professionally as an occasional advisor on public relations or advertising campaigns.

> Jonathan spent quite a bit of time in my office. He would often arrive unannounced, and simply open my office door and sail right in. Sometimes he and I would work together thrashing out ideas. For bigger projects I would organize a larger brainstorm session and Jonathan would end up leading it. As you know, creativity was one of his strengths and he was particularly clever with words – he would have made a very good copywriter in an advertising agency. I really enjoyed his visits to the office. Not only was he a valuable contributor when formulating ideas and proposals for existing and potential clients, he was a wonderful observer of life and we would spend much of the time simply discussing politics or business. He was brilliant in his wit and observations of public life. We all know how well he could impersonate Charlie McCreevy, Charles Haughey, Mary O'Rourke – and sometimes an innocent secretary or receptionist on answering the phone to Jonathan would be completely taken in by his impersonations and tell me Michael Noonan was on the phone for me!

After Dana Rosemary Scallon's creditable performance in the presidential election of 1997,* she was approached by some of the political parties in 1999 to consider running for the European Parliament in Connacht-Ulster, the most conservative constituency in the country. In the event she ran as an independent and defeated Noel Treacy, who had been considered a certainty by Fianna Fáil to hold their second seat in Connacht-Ulster. RONAN MULLEN, a Galwayman then working in the press office of the Dublin Roman Catholic Archdiocese, wrote that he had met Jonathan on only one occasion in Galway at Dana's victory party after the European elections.

> At the end of the night it was announced that the campaign had debts to pay and that they were going to sell the campaign posters as souvenirs. Jonathan was in the crowd watching. When Dana's brother announced that they were going to auction two of the posters on the night, Jonathan naturally volunteered to be the auctioneer. What followed was quite memorable. For about twenty to twenty-five minutes he gave a high-octane, fast-talking, barn-storming auctioneering performance. He generated excitement

* Dana Rosemary Scallon came third in the presidential election with 13.82 per cent of the vote, almost double what the Labour candidate, Adi Roche, received. And in Connacht-Ulster, Dana won 17.68 per cent of first preferences.

'a high-octane, fast-talking, barn-storming, auctioneering performance…laced with wit and wicked asides.'
– Ronan Mullen

and fierce competition where none existed before, and his comments were laced with wit and wicked asides. I particularly remember some close bidding (at about one hundred pounds) between a man and a woman in the crowd for the second poster. Jonathan, of course, invited the man not to do as Noel Treacy had done by allowing himself to be beaten by a woman! It was great too to see how everyone was enjoying the fun and wit. Even the older – you might say traditional – members of the Dana bandwagon laughed heartily at some of the more risqué interventions that Jonathan made. As a bit of a talker myself, I was full of admiration – and a touch of envy – at Jonathan's extempore powers, the speed and the wit.

EITHNE HAND knew Jonathan throughout his career in journalism and broadcasting, recalling that he was a celebrity by 1987 when they shared an *Indo* page on 'My favourite Valentine' – a 'wonderfully cringemaking' page.

He was part of probably every programme I was involved in but mostly Pat Kenny's programmes on the radio during many summers in the late 1980s when Jonathan would bounce nonchalantly into the Radio Centre and, having talked in complete circles in the coffee bar or over your shoulder as you wrote the brief, would launch into an articulate precís of whatever topic he was covering once the 'live' moment came in studio. Talking to him over the years socially at all sorts of events – it was almost always like talking to a number of people at the same time. He balanced that 'Yes, I am listening intently to you' sense with the 'Hey, look who's just walked in the door' moment with ease. When I moved to Century Radio he was a weekly contributor to the mid-morning programme and he became more of a rock of sense in an increasingly mad world. He seemed to deal with crises very well – in a shrugging of the shoulders sort of way. I liked the sense of calm he seemed to have and the right amount of world-weariness as well. He was incredibly loyal. Later, back in RTE, he would come in to chat, pitch ideas and fill me in on the seventeen things that were going on. He was always honest about what he needed right now, so if he was in a tight spot financially he would be able to just say: 'Look things are tricky – I've been thinking of an item on such and such – what do you think?' Nobody else was that honest and realistic. I always cared about whatever was going on with him whether it was heartache trouble or work trouble or this-bloody-country trouble. You know, I wish I wasn't writing down any of this. I wish he wasn't gone from all of us.

The radio and television producer and journalist SARAH BINCHY was a close friend of Jonathan's in 1999.* She likened him to 'a cannonball of energy and love and personality; and when he left the room, his personality seemed to linger on like a scent.'

I first met Jonathan when I was editing his column in the *Sunday Independent* where I used to work and he rang up to hear how it was going, and I told him he was a dreadful speller but a wonderful writer. And the next time I met him was in The Bailey in town, it was the day before his thirtieth birthday and I was with a friend and we sat down beside him. And he was a bit despondent because he said I'm getting mature now, I've got to grow up and I'm going to have to start doing sensible things, and be responsible and get a pension scheme, and go to bed at ten o'clock at night. And I can't have flings with women anymore; I'm going to have to have serious relationships. But I think I'd like another fling. And a few days later, he turned up on my doorstep. He found out what day I had off and turned up about three o'clock with two bottles of wine and he stayed all day and Saul was delivered later and they stayed for days, weeks and months after that.

Jonathan was so good – most of the time. He always reminded me of that line from Yeats – 'For the good are always the merry.' There was such merriment surrounding him. He could make a dull day a thrill by just arriving. I loved the way he didn't so much enter

* Her comments are based on letter of condolence; and contribution to RTE Radio 1, 11 March 2000.

a room as happen to it – and the way Saul would be delivered in the evenings – like an exciting parcel. They were so alike.

Jonathan was such fun, he was so dazzling; and he was also very maddening and he was a bit of a bolter. He'd come for lunch and say I will see you tonight and you'd get a call from London or Los Angeles – or Lourdes, on one occasion! And that time he'd gone to Lourdes for Easter with Saul, and I got a call from them on Easter Sunday night and they were all excited. They were en route from Lourdes to Paris and Saul put on Jonathan, and Jonathan said: 'I've decided that Saul needs to see Paris; I'd like to take him up the Eiffel Tower and all that. We're going to stay for a few days but I'm running out of money, so I'm going to have to wire home for some tomorrow.' And I said I've got a credit card and I've got a few days off, so I joined them the next day. Saul was on roller skates; it turned out that he had lost his shoes somewhere and neither of them thought this was the remotest problem and it turned out not to be a problem. You know, a little bit awkward getting in and out of restaurants and cafés and up and down the Eiffel Tower, but it was just so typical of the pair of them. They were like this pair of loveable vagabonds who needed nobody but each other.

There were so many things about Jonathan that I liked. He could make me cry with laughter. He was terribly wise and fair-minded about many things. I loved his unorthodoxy: it was just so rare, and precious. If you

Anyway, we are having dinner when Saul decides to take a toilet break. This totally fabulous waiter, Julio, who spends much of his time dragging girls off the street and asking if they need a boyfriend rushes over to me and asks for the name of one of Saul's friends at home. I have no idea what he's at, but I tell him Daniel. "Hokay," says Julio, who reminds me a little of Gene Wilder, and a little of that Oscar-winning Italian clown. "What is the name of the hotel where he stay? I get him with the telephone." Julio says something else about a flood and I presume that he's going to tell Saul his room is flooded — which wouldn't faze Saul, but the scene is set.

Saul returns to the table. A few moments later the phone rings and Julio rushes to answer it. "Saul! Saul! Eees there a Saul here? Hotel Mercure? Rheum thew-oh-five-ah. Saul! Eees for yew. A Daniel on the phone?"

Saul is slightly disbelieving. "How the hell did Daniel know I was here?" He asks me but I shrug, and he scoots over to take the call. "Hello?" he says. "Hello?" And then he receives an earful of freezing cold water, delivered forcefully enough to make him jump. Julio and Saul are now friends for life — he won't eat anywhere else. "We have all kinds of tricks at the bar," Julio tells me. "Ess-plodehing muss-tar! Ev-hairy-thing!"

Sunday Independent, 11 April 1999

perceived that an orthodoxy was growing about somebody and that they were getting a raw deal, he would seek them out, write about them, befriend them. And he was genuinely affectionate. I remember Jonathan using the phrase 'the other three hundred girlfriends' if I was giving out about something. He'd say: 'The other three hundred girlfriends never had a problem with this.' And I thought it was just a turn of phrase but as I began to discover around town, it probably wasn't; it probably was literal! He was always fascinated to know what I liked about him. I always said – it was true – 'your rakish charm'. Of course this gave him a great out clause: if I were distressed about some rakish idiosyncrasy he would say, 'What were you attracted to? My rakish charm. What are you now complaining about? My rakish charm. Darling, you are not being very logical.'

Sarah's father, WILLIAM BINCHY, Professor of Law at Trinity College Dublin, wrote about his first meeting with Jonathan in March 1999.

I first met Jonathan on St. Patrick's Day. He came to our home in the afternoon with our daughter Sarah and Saul. Oddly, it seemed entirely reasonable for us to decamp to the garden, sitting on kitchen chairs drinking wine from huge glasses. Within five minutes, Jonathan declared that he liked us very much. I know that I had already formed the same view of him. After our glasses had been refilled many times we adjourned to the dining room. Food was not a great priority. We played games – precisely what ones I can't quite remember, but they involved races to dredge up the names of Russian rivers and South American presidents, dismantling anagrams and drawing pictures of abstract nouns. If these were trivial pursuits, Jonathan had not been informed. He played as though there were no more important purpose in life, his mind working laterally at huge speed. When leaving late that evening, he proclaimed even more strongly that we were his friends, as indeed we were. Jonathan's unique quality was to cut through the reserves that normally exist in human relationships. His drawbridge was permanently down, allowing access for all. He delighted in the experience of life, willing to share its joys and frustrations with others, with the enthusiasm of a young child. He affirmed human existence with a simplicity and depth very rare to behold and impossible to forget.

DAVID BEGG, then chief executive of the international development charity, Concern Worldwide, wrote of a commitment which Jonathan had made to him. Despite his fondness for good

Paris, Easter 1999

living, he was capable of enduring hardship – as he had proved on the survival course – and he had the courage to embrace a challenge, such as that suggested by David Begg.

> In the course of our conversation he offered to travel with Concern to any developing country and to write about the experience. I fully intended to take up this kind offer but did not get around to it by the time of his death. Nevertheless, I was very grateful to him. It shows that he had a strong commitment to social justice and was willing to use his talent as a journalist to promote it. In my experience very few people are willing to engage to this extent.

EAMON Ó CUIV, Fianna Fáil TD for Galway West and then Minister of State at the Department of Arts, Heritage, Gaeltacht and the Islands, wrote:

> I met him a few times and remember one particular occasion when we had a lively debate about the Irish language. He was sceptical about it and was surprised to learn that I did a lot of my constituency work through Irish. However he very readily took up my offer to allow him accompany me while doing my clinics in Connemara. Sadly now he will never have what I feel would have been a new and novel experience. His great humour and willingness to argue his case were most attractive and stimulating.

Although very well known through television, Jonathan by the age of thirty had only ever been presenter on one television series, *Dodge the Question*. When its first series had just started, one senior executive in RTE met me in the corridor and said: 'John, you have a star.' I gave my response without thinking. 'No', I replied. 'You have a star. Use him.' I think it was the only occasion that I allowed myself to be his advocate in RTE. When he died, Ed Holt, television critic of *The Irish Times*, complained that 'elements in the media seemed to encourage him to act precociously and prattishly, perhaps fastening him to a persona which, in truth, he knew he had outgrown.' In 1999 Jonathan recorded a pilot programme with Shay Healy, broadcaster and independent television producer and one-time host of the innovative and successful *Nighthawks* programme on RTE's second channel in the late 1980s and early 90s. That programme was live, included some sketches and 'happened' in a night-club setting with Shay Healy drifting from table to table where he would be both a prompter of conversation and an eavesdropper. There were also dozens of 'extras' on the set to provide atmosphere and to authenticate the club setting. Such a programme attracted aspiring broadcasters. Jonathan was an occasional guest on the show – his appearances were limited by his expectation of a fee higher than *Nighthawks* liked to pay, which was often nothing. A decade later, in 1999, SHAY HEALY teamed up with Jonathan to investigate the possibilities of making a television series.

Our independent production company got money from RTE to make a pilot for a series called *The GUBU Files*. This was a putative series on anomalies in Irish life, and Jonathan was our ideal candidate for presenter/reporter. We reckoned his combination of puckishness and incisiveness was ideal for putting civil servants and prevaricators to the sword. For our pilot story, we chose to examine the wrinkles in a little known Act called Section 19. Under Section 19, people who own houses of architectural or historical interest can avail of generous tax breaks in return for opening their houses to the public on a set number of days every year. Many who covet the tax break consider visitors a nuisance and do little to encourage them. We decided to pay an unannounced visit to one such house and so it was that I found myself with a camera in my hand following Jonathan to the front door. He rang the intercom and a disembodied voice crackled back over the speaker. 'Who is it?' 'We'd like to look around the house.' A woman of about fifty opened the door to us and for the next twenty minutes she showed us around the house. Jonathan turned on his full charm and was engaging and humorous, without ever being disrespectful. It was a hugely enjoyable twenty minutes and Jonathan's charisma worked to such an extent that at no stage in the proceedings did our host ever enquire as to why she was being asked so many questions. Even more extraordinary, she never enquired as to why there was a camera following her around her own house! When the tour was over, Jonathan asked for the price of our visit. 'One pound', she said. He handed over the pound, never paid for the cameraman and the two of us exited laughing into the sunshine.

The pilot is, for me, Jonathan's finest hour, a combination of his mischief, his astuteness, his precocity, his tenacity, his puckishness and his beguiling charm. He was effortlessly brilliant throughout the making of the pilot and his fearlessness, composure and sense of devilment made it a joy and a great bit of fun for us to make. I agonized over when would be the right time to send this video copy to you, but I realize now there will never be a perfect time, because I have no doubt that, no matter when I send it to you, to watch it will make you cry. But I hope it will also make you laugh and draw comfort that in his short life, the star that was Jonathan was truly incandescent with the blinding light of pure talent. Even as I write this, I find myself shedding my own tears at the memory of him.

With Shay Healy on *Nighthawks*, 25 October 1988

Jonathan was engaged in another pilot programme for RTE television that summer. When Pat Kenny switched from his *Saturday Live* chat show to host the *Late Late Show* on Friday nights, RTE adopted the experimental formula of inviting a different presenter each Saturday to host a *Saturday Live* chat show. To audition potential hosts for these broadcasts, RTE ran a dummy pilot programme in which three or four 'guests' with a story to tell would be interviewed in turn by each aspiring presenter. The actor ALEXANDER DOWNES was among these guest interviewees. This formula had the merit for RTE that they could not only assess the presentational skills of each aspiring host but could also evaluate what each host had managed to glean from the same collection of 'guests'. Alexander wrote:

> In August 1999, I was interviewed by Jonathan as part of an RTE screen-testing. Every year RTE gather a group of potential presenters, who have popped up in various areas of broadcasting, and gives them a shot at fronting a mock-up chat show. I knew Jonathan as Emma's brother, and he me as Emma's friend. We knew each other in context if not in detail. I was admiring, if not a little wary. There were seven or eight other presenters that day, and to say that Jonathan was curly hair and bow-tie above the rest would be something of an understatement. True, he had presenting

experience but two interlinked qualities set him aside from the others. Firstly, Jonathan could talk for Ireland. Where most of us combine word and thought during speech, Jonathan's mouth played catch-up with his thoughts; 'stuck for words' and Jonathan never met. Secondly, and more importantly, Jonathan was truly interested in people; their lives and their quirky patterns. It seems too obvious to state, but a good interviewer needs to be curious about his/her subject, and less interested in their own ego. They need to have the confidence to probe and the humility to facilitate. They need to listen so that they can explore avenues not mapped on their clipboards. An interviewee is like a muscle; their performance is enhanced when they are relaxed, and Jonathan had an ability to put people at their ease; he could remove that ease fairly sharply also! I left RTE that day knowing that it was only a matter of time before Jonathan would pop up on our screens again. In fact, I looked forward to it. I never saw him again.

The comedienne, actor and novelist PAULINE MCLYNN was interviewed by Jonathan when her first novel, *Something for the Weekend*, was published.

It is always daunting to have someone you know interview you. The worry is that they know too much and will steer you into uncomfortable territory while wearing their journalist's cap. This is how I felt on one of the last times I spoke with Jonathan. He was interviewing me for the *Sunday Independent*. I expected a nerve-wracker. I didn't get it. Instead, the man I knew to be precocious and thorough was sweetness itself and one of the most encouraging people I met around that time. He was calm, generous and happy with a friend's (perceived) success. And I should not have been a bit surprised because I had seen him in action before.

At a launch of a Murphy's Cat Laughs Comedy Festival, Jonathan arrived to interview Paul Merton, who was there to do the honours. After a while, the length it would take to do the job, I insinuated myself into the conversation and found they were deep into a discussion on depression, possibly not the expected subject for the kick-off of a comedy project, but there you had it; Jonathan and a man he had only just met, opening up to one another. The following Sunday's paper had a great article, admitting he had worked without notes, because the scant ones he had taken were in another jacket as he wrote his copy. And it was wonderful, capturing exactly the humanity of the moment and the laughter that had been shared too that afternoon.

But a tangent to when I first spent time with Jonathan some years before – a friend had partnered me with him for a television

Pauline McLynn at Jonathan's funeral

Rich vein of humour

Paul Merton is too kind, too intelligent and too funny to dislike, even though he makes £10,000 per episode of his hit TV show, says **Jonathan Philbin Bowman**

It's not that there's no ego there at all, but just that the ego isn't always at the wheel.

Encounter with Paul Merton, *Sunday Independent*, 3 May 1998

quiz and, squirm as I tried, I could not back out. I was terrified on many levels. For starters, I had seen him in action on the box and knew he was opinionated and quick. I felt neither on the fateful day. We did badly, because of me, and I'm fairly sure he told me as much. Now, in these days of 'Millionaire' and 'phone a friend', I would have to have him on my list, at least for the sureness of his answer, right or wrong. So, if he's up for it, so am I. The call will just be a longer distance than I'd like.

The writer SUE TOWNSEND first met Jonathan in October 1999. When he died, she wrote of their first encounter and subsequent friendship.

Jonathan fell in love once a day. He fell in love with me in the lounge of the Shelbourne Hotel on a Friday in October 1999. He came (reluctantly) to interview me about my new book. He had been allocated half an hour by Michael, my publicist. The other people in the lounge stared at him when he came in. A beautiful woman in an eccentric hat came over, and tearfully disclosed to him the latest melodramatic happening in her life. He gave her some advice and made her laugh, and when she'd gone he gave me a waspish and hilarious account of her life and loves. It was obvious to me before he'd even sat down that it was Jonathan who was the star.

He talked faster than anyone I'd ever known. Words spat from his mouth like the bullets from a machine gun. He was only thirty-one when he died, but he must have clocked up as many words as a man three times that age. At the end of our conversation I was due to catch a train to Belfast. Jonathan decided to come. On the train we deconstructed the buffet-car menu which had been written by somebody who had only a passing acquaintanceship with the English language. Jonathan sent an e-mail complaint to the perpetrator on his electronic organizer.

In Belfast I went on a TV show and was asked by the chat-show host about two past abortions. Jonathan was outraged on my behalf. He told me I needed media training. I was due to go on *Question Time* in two weeks. I told him I was terrified. He travelled all the way to Leicester and sat in my kitchen and pretended to be David Dimbleby in order to help me. He was immensely kind and very funny, and I am absolutely furious that he is dead.

Sunday Independent, 12 March 2000

EUGENE MCELDOWNEY, author and night editor in *The Irish Times,* first spoke to Jonathan when he received a telephone call in

May 1999. Jonathan was looking for a colleague's phone number which was supplied. They got talking and this is Eugene's account.

'You write novels, don't you?', Jonathan said.

'That's right.'

'When's your next one coming out?'

'November.'

'Give me a call and I'll do an interview for the *Sunday Independent*,' he said and was gone.

I've met a lot of people in my career who are long on promises and short on delivery, so I didn't hold my breath. But when *The Faloorie Man* was duly published, I decided to take Jonathan at his word. I rang, and he remembered.

'We'll have lunch,' he said.

We agreed a venue and a time. I was delighted. An interview with Jonathan in Ireland's largest-selling newspaper was quite a coup. His column had a wide following. It was sure to bring the novel to the attention of thousands of readers. If even a fraction of them bought the book, *The Faloorie Man* was bound to be a best-seller.

When the day came, I hurried along to Browne's Brasserie on St. Stephen's Green for my appointment. I got there early, studied the menu, told the anxious staff that I was expecting a guest and waited. And waited. And .... waited. Finally when I could wait no more, I rang Jonathan's mobile. I could hear the sound of laughter and clinking glasses in the background. Jonathan was apologetic. He had got the dates mixed up and was attending the annual ESB media awards. Crestfallen, I made another appointment and lunched alone.

Sunday Independent, 26 December 1999

the most of Christmas present

A novel venture

Behind every successful man is a good woman — so says popular gospel. And in the case of writer Eugene McEldowney, there's a woman with a good story. **Jonathan Philbin Bowman** meets the novelist and his wife Maura

On the second occasion, I was determined not to let him escape. I rang in the morning to confirm our lunch appointment in Nico's restaurant in Dame Street. This time, Jonathan turned up. We started our meal but he insisted on regaling me with funny stories about well-known Dublin hacks who had crossed his path, complete with impersonations, for he was a brilliant mimic. Any attempt at an interview was quickly abandoned and I surrendered to Jonathan's hilarious stream of delicious, if scandalously libelous, anecdotes. We parted on a high note, but with still no interview done, I made yet another appointment.

This time, I invited him to my home in Howth. I think in the back of my mind, I had the idea of holding him prisoner and only releasing him when the interview was successfully completed. He came out on the DART and

I met him at the station. He didn't want any lunch but succumbed to my wife Maura's offer of beer and pork pies. Out came the notebook and, at last, Jonathan got down to the interview. It continued for hours. He had read the novel and enjoyed it, but he didn't like the cover. He thought it was too garish. But he had done his homework. He had a list of questions and insights that truly astonished me. He went into every little nook and cranny. Why did you say this? Why did that character do the other? Why this? What that? When he finally closed his notebook, I felt like I had just spent two hours in a confession box with a Redemptorist preacher at the Limerick confraternity. He talked about Saul, and Maura gave him a bag of books and gameboys that my own son, Gavin, had long grown out of. That evening we got a phone call from Jonathan. He had Saul on the line to thank us. It was the last time I was to speak to him.

Jonathan kept his promise. The interview duly appeared.* It was a brilliant piece, honest and perceptive. I didn't like all of it, but interviews are not publicity puffs and no one should know that better than another journalist. That's how I will remember Jonathan – as someone who went out of his way to do me a kindness. He didn't know me and he didn't have to do it. But he did and it made a difference to my life.

An individual to whom Jonathan was greatly indebted was his accountant in the last couple of years of his life, FRANCES BRENNAN. She complemented the efforts of the credit union in Independent Newspapers, estimated his probable tax liabilities and arranged for appropriate deductions in anticipation of his annual tax demand. I like to think that all his parents' admonitions over the years to sort out his finances may have been of some influence in this turnabout. Parents are invariably over-involved in giving such advice. That it is not immediately acted upon is scarcely surprising: in Jonathan's case he seems to have eventually taken such advice – but from others. Our response after his death when we discovered that his finances were in such good order was a mixture of disbelief and admiration; and bemusement that he had never bothered to tell us about his reform programme. Rather had he allowed us to continue giving the old advice without letting us know that it had become redundant. Frances Brennan had met him first in a professional capacity but – as tended to happen with Jonathan – they became friends 'by building trust'. She wrote:

* 'A novel venture', *Sunday Independent*, 26 December 1999.

I received an e-mail from JPB about two weeks before his death to arrange lunch. It read: 'We're going to Guilbaud's, 12.45 on the basis that we may eat, drink and be merry, and tomorrow we may die and I'm paying and you are love itself. XXXX JPB. P.S. I may have to leave earlyish to collect Saul. XYZ JPB. [*As was often the case with Jonathan, there were some late changes in the arrangements: the lunch was at Bruno's restaurant in Kildare Street and Saul arrived too.*] I met JPB and Saul and while Saul was not having lunch, he still managed to choose what he wanted and have it served to him as if it was the only worthwhile thing on the menu. JPB 's starter had a slice of hard-boiled egg sitting on top and Saul asked if he could have whole eggs. JPB quickly summoned the waiter to ask if there were eggs in the kitchen. When Saul asked for four, the waiter suggested three which duly arrived perfectly timed and were consumed with a can of coke! It struck me then that most fathers might have dismissed the request from a child but not JPB – and he asked the waiter in such a way that one couldn't refuse him. Part of our conversation related to alternative medicines and while in the middle of lunch JPB got on the phone to the *Sunday Independent* cartoonist Jim Cogan, and asked him to get started on an image of himself being pampered by every kind of treatment imaginable which I observed was in the following edition of the newspaper as an anchor for his piece. This seemed to me to reflect Jonathan's own search for an anchor in his life at a time following a retreat at Christmas which wasn't very successful and fell short of his expectations.

Over the short period of about two years of knowing Jonathan, his generosity and 'giving' ability was always to the fore. I have several gifts from him – one being a house-warming present he gave me in a taxi late (or early) one morning. This is a bronze plaque which now hangs on my livingroom wall: '"Bidden or not bidden, God is present" – Carl Jung.' This is something I will always treasure. When Jonathan sent that e-mail saying he was leaving 'earlyish' – how right he was, but I have met him in many guises since and his devilish ways live on.

Another of his financial advisors, GERRY MURPHY, also became a personal friend, despite the fact that his initial role in Jonathan's life was to 'knock some sense into him about his mortgage'.

My interest in the alternative spiritual side of life also brought me into contact with Jonathan when we attended a number of courses together. Jonathan certainly added much to these events with his rapid-fire verbal challenges and mostly I felt for the presenters who had no hope against his intellectual capacity.

Jonathan's library reflected his growing interest in spiritual matters. M. BURKE* worked in a Dublin city bookshop and remembered him as a regular customer. This letter was written some months after Jonathan died and was posted from Nicaragua.

> The last time he paid a visit was during my last week at Christmas. I recall the moment with clarity and humour. Jonathan had purchased quite a few books from the mind, body and spirit department. The total came to one hundred and twenty pounds and rather than the usual credit card, he pulled a bundle of crumpled notes from his pocket and we all began to count them. The queues were frantic and tensions were high, manners few but I clearly remember your son assisting me in packing his bags, lifting them, carrying them – a small gesture but with weeks of tense clients, public service can be difficult. I just wanted to say I remember your son, for his empathy, manners and above all courtesy to me as a shop assistant. It is a rare happening these days – so few that you recall them with clarity.

JOE DUFFY met Jonathan just before Christmas 1999 in Dawson Street in Dublin.

> We were yapping and having coffee, and we began talking about what the kids were looking for, for Christmas – what Saul wanted and what my kids wanted. And at that stage it was about four days before Christmas, I was in a frenzy trying to get Pokemon gameboys for my three. They were the Christmas craze. Off I went scouring the shops of Dublin, unsuccessfully, I hasten to add. When a few hours later, Jonathan rang me on the mobile and he said I've tracked them down, how many Pokemon gameboys do you want? I need an answer now, I've a friend on the other line. 'Three', I shouted back. 'Where is the friend?' The friend was not in Dublin or in London. The friend was in Manhattan, New York! He had persuaded a pal of his living in New York – and remember he had friends everywhere – to go down to Fifth Avenue to queue in F.A.O. Schwartz [*New York's biggest and best toyshop*] for these gameboys which were not available in Ireland for love or money. And he got three sent to Dublin, arrived two days later, just in time for Christmas Eve, just in time for Santa's sack.

Sometime in early December Jonathan and Saul were having

* Probably Mary Burke. I am indebted to Eoin McHugh, General Books Manager, Eason-Hanna's Bookshop in Dawson Street for making enquiries and noting that an ex-Hodges staff member recalls that Jonathan was on 'very friendly terms with a "Mary" who, coincidentally, was looking after the Mind, Body, Spirit section in Hodges & Figgis a little while back.'

dinner with us on Sunday evening. We started to talk about plans for Christmas. Jonathan surprised us by saying that he was considering going on a Buddhist retreat and Saul began to protest. We sensed that perhaps Jonathan wanted to avoid the temptation of too much partying and drinking over the holiday season. Saul then asked: 'Can I come here on Christmas Day?' to which Eimer replied: 'Of course you can choose to do whatever you like. Christmas is for children.' And so it was settled.

On 22 December Jonathan talked on radio with PAT KENNY about his plans for Christmas and the Millennium celebrations.

JPB : I'm going to be in a Buddhist monastery in Scotland. I'm heading off today. I've never really been a huge fan of Christmas and the pseudo-Millennium, absolutely not. So I'm getting away from it all. I will be somewhere very quiet, meditating and doing strange things and probably drinking herbal tea and eating lentil soup.

PK: Until?

JPB: Until 4 January.

PK: From now until 4 January seems quite a retreat, doesn't it?

JPB: Yeah, I'll be very quiet. I'll be untypically quiet. I'm told that last year – I'm in a place called Samye Ling which has been a Buddhist community for twenty or thirty years – and they wrote me this really sweet letter. And the whole retreat was going to be led by a lama who was terribly prestigious in Buddhist and God knows what terms. And they wrote me a letter, and basically the lama got a better offer, I think, to fly to the sun. And they wrote a really nice letter saying – you see the Buddhists love the word auspicious – he had this auspicious opportunity to receive special teachings somewhere hot! So therefore the retreat was going to be led by somebody else. I'm told that last year the power went out and the lama got sick and everyone was snowed in, and there were no lights, so I mean I'm bringing my Millennium candle with me.

On Christmas Eve Jonathan's girlfriend Joey arrived unexpectedly at our house, laden down with beautifully wrapped presents for all of us and for Saul to be put under the tree from Jonathan. Usually his presents – if wrapped at all – had been covered in old newspapers and we presumed that Joey had been responsible for the presentation. But it turned out that Jonathan had done them all himself before leaving for Scotland. Saul's present, a Dreamcast computer console, was difficult to come by that Christmas and was to be a big surprise. Jonathan seemed to be even more excited

Jim Cogan's comment on Jonathan's plans for Christmas 1999

about it than Saul and from the retreat centre he telephoned throughout Christmas Day to keep abreast of events. He might as well have been with us. He wanted to experience Saul's response when Saul opened the parcel. And he did.

7

'These guys live awful lives and I live a great life. In terms of life expectancy, they're probably going to die at thirty-five.'

– JONATHAN on the two men who mugged him in Washington, D.C., January 2000

It became apparent from his calls on Christmas Day that Jonathan had 'flu and, since the Spartan conditions of the retreat centre were unlikely to help him recover, Eimer suggested that he consider coming home. He flew back to Dublin on 26 December from where, on antibiotics and nursed by his girlfriend Joey, he greeted the new Millennium.

Because we were away until 7 January and missed both his and Emma's birthdays, we had booked a table to have dinner with both of them and Abie on 8 January. Jonathan, who was the last to arrive, looked washed-out and seemed somewhat morose. He smoked, the first time he had ever done so in our company. Jonathan had been anti-tobacco all his life, but had begun to smoke only at the late age of twenty-seven. He listened to my occasional appeals to him to quit, always based on the grounds that he well knew the risks since he had for so long preached them to others. That he was morose we put down to a post-'flu state, but as the evening progressed his mood lightened. What we did not know that evening – and did not learn until after his death – was that he had been feeling depressed since his return home and had, a few days previously, called at short notice on a psychiatrist friend of Eimer's who had prescribed some medication for him. What he had not disclosed to her or to anyone apart from a couple of close friends was that from early December he had been drinking too much. His original decision to spend ten days at the Scottish retreat centre may have been his way to avoid the Christmas round of parties.

Emma, home for a Christmas break from Devon where she was looking after the kitchen garden in Gaia House, a Buddhist retreat centre, sensed Jonathan's dejection; her concerns prompted Eimer to telephone him some days later to ask more direct questions. He acknowledged 'a touch of SAD syndrome' but, typically, said it in an upbeat way. She suggested he might take a leaf out of the lama's book and go off for a week in the sun – offering to fund it. However when he phoned back a few days later it was to say: 'I'm off to Washington tomorrow.' Confirming that he had no warm coat (he tended to mislay them in other people's houses for months at a time) she suggested that I might lend him mine if he promised to bring it back. The following morning he dashed in, tried on the coat and, delighted with it, made his exit to a waiting taxi. It was his last visit home.

He arrived in Washington on 11 January 2000 to interview Patch Adams* prior to his visit to Dublin. That interview was published in the *Sunday Independent.*

> "What kind of a doctor are you?"
>
> "I'm the kind of doctor who likes to read books and stay up all night talking."
>
> Patch wants the whole you. That way you get the whole Patch. That is why he insists that initial meetings with patients last no less than four hours. After our interview he expressed regret that he hadn't learned a lot about me but he promised he'd do it another time.
>
> *Sunday Independent*, 30 January, 2000

When Jonathan died, PATCH ADAMS published an account of their short friendship.

> We hit if off from the starting-gate, like brothers separated at birth. He showed up at my apartment with an impish fire in his eyes and a crisp wit that told me this was not the typical journalist I had grown to avoid. He had read my books and he brought an intelligent enquiry that made me want a long interview because I knew it would be challenging and stimulating. He brought a

* Patch Adams is founder of the Gesundheit Institute, dedicated to a more personalized approach to medicine. His career was featured in Universal Picture's *Patch Adams* in which he was played by Robin Williams.

probing agenda that I could see and feel came from deep within, much larger than his role as a journalist. Sparks flew on the subject of health, particularly mental health, that had us both tickled for long after, that carried us toward a quick deep friendship. He loved me and I loved him. We were both wacky, intense cerebral eccentrics that cared for our world. I passed his rigorous intellect and rested in the garden of his friendship. Afterwards, over several weeks before my visit to Dublin, he called many times at all hours to pick up where we'd left off, like mathematicians swimming in theorems.

Sunday Independent, 12 March 2000

On his last night in Washington, Jonathan was mugged when walking home late to his hotel, which was in a leafy suburb near Dupont Circle. The roads are tree-lined and relatively dark at night. This was his own account in his diary column in the *Sunday Independent*. He first mentioned that his attentive readers would have noted that his column had been absent the previous Sunday.

For this absence we must pay thanks to two Washingtonian gentlemen of the coloured persuasion, who sadly must remain nameless. The reason they must remain nameless is that they neither told me their names nor produced any form of official I.D. Instead their approach was more informal and initially from behind. It may have had socio-anthropological subtleties which were lost on me but essentially it initially involved knocking me to the ground. When I turned around still on the pavement both of these gentlemen were standing over me with their legs apart. A posture one generally associates with authority, and especially with NYPD Blue cops when they have just nabbed a rapist/murderer/hold-up guy/crack dealer.

Unfortunately these fellows were on the other side of the law. While one of them produced a syringe full of a reddish substance which might have been Chateau Kirwan '78, or more hazardously might have been HIV-infected blood, his companion demanded my worldly goods in a colourful language which I believe is called Ebonics. The essence of the communication was: 'Give us your fuckin' money, you fuckin' mother-fucker.' Though my memory of the event is far from perfect and they may not have been quite as polite as that. Strange indeed what thoughts go through your head when you are in a critical situation. I raised both my hands in what I hoped was an international and inter-racial gesture of surrender, and as I did so I realized it is also what paediatricians call the 'morra reflex'*. Clap your hands in front of a baby and the chances are he will raise both hands, outstretched, elbows bent, and facing outward.

So anyway, I reached into my back pocket and threw my entire wadge of American play money at the crack-heads. To my relief they were so delighted with the quantity of money involved that they snatched it up and ran like the clappers without so much as a 'Thank you, mother-fucker.' As I raised myself properly from the ground, a little shaken, and got my bearings, I realized I was only a few hundred yards from my charming hotel. It was only when I arrived at the hotel that I discovered I was also missing my key, lost somewhere in the scuffle presumably. I explained my situation, and they couldn't have been nicer. They let me into my room, and asked if I needed anything, which frankly I didn't. I took two of the sleeping tablets I had been saving for my return overnight flight and fell into a fitful slumber.

Sunday Independent, 23 January 2000

On RTE's *Liveline*, after he had published the above account, Jonathan told JOE DUFFY about what had happened following the assault.

Four people I was able to call and say look this has happened, I have now no money, and I couldn't pay my hotel bill. I explained to the hotel and said I'm not running away, but I have to go to Western Union to collect some money. And they understood. I have a little computer – my Psion – that has all my telephone numbers in it but it had been damaged in the attack. So anyway I got up to New York and didn't have my friend Susan Towers's home number; so I went into Fitzpatrick's in Manhattan and I checked myself in. And they couldn't have been nicer. Because I'd escaped the threat of AIDS, that so overshadowed any feelings of anger; and then a few days later you're thinking these guys live awful lives and I live a great life. In terms of life expectancy, they're probably going to die at thirty-five. I mean okay, maybe they had a great night or a great weekend on me and I'd prefer they hadn't, but I have to say – I know it sounds horribly Christian and compassionate – I didn't have that much anger. I found funny things. I will always try to be kind to people. I found myself consciously going out of my way to be kind and attentive to

* Eimer telephoned Jonathan to correct this to 'Moro reflex'. He intended making some humorous acknowledgement and spoke to her about it later in the week when she discovered that he had misspelt it again. This was so unlike him that Eimer commented: 'If there is such a thing as post-traumatic dementia, I think you have it' and he laughed.

people, just the guy serving you the food on the train or the person in the ticket queue or wherever on the basis that you don't know what kind of day they've had either. You do find yourself slightly more paranoid, keeping an eye on your bag. I still have little flashes of anger, but I have also to say that food has been just tasting better. It's quite remarkable. Then when I came home and collected Saul from school – and when I've been away it's always great to see him – there was a huge surge of joy and happiness there.

Liveline, RTE Radio 1, 25 January 2000

LIZ O'DONNELL TD recalled a telephone call – her last conversation with Jonathan – after his mugging in Washington.

> He had been traumatized by it. He had often spoken to me of his abhorrence of male violence. His flamboyant personality meant that sadly he was frequently on the receiving end of the aggression of limited males, who felt threatened in some way by him. He was too clever and sparkling for this rough world. I worried about him and tried to advise him and protect him. I looked forward to his growing up and being happier. It never happened.

Over the years we had sometimes worried that Jonathan's personality and pacifism might put him at risk of physical assault. To our knowledge, until the mugging in Washington he had never been seriously attacked. However, late on Friday night, 4 February in Dublin, when he was walking from the Gresham Hotel to a taxi rank two young men recognized him and one of them punched him, cutting him just above the eye, saying: 'Take that, you Brit-lover.' This was presumably because of his consistent opposition to IRA violence. That evening he had gone to see the film *American Beauty* in the Savoy Cinema with his friend DEBORAH MARTIN. She wrote:

> Once the movie was over, we went back to the Gresham for a drink. A kindly older waiter struck up a conversation with him and we discussed how he had been attacked in Washington. Jonathan was touched that this waiter was supportive and interested in his welfare. I had to leave just before midnight as my car was in a nearby carpark and I had to get home to my babysitter. When we parted at the Gresham we agreed to meet up next day for coffee. He assured me there would be no problem getting home as there were lots of taxis around and O'Connell Street was busy. The next morning he called me and informed me that he had been attacked on O'Connell Street. Apparently, some young man accompanied by two others, approached him, confirmed it was Jonathan and hit

him in the face. I cannot remember what this man actually said to him but he made reference to the fact that Jonathan had been attacked in the States. He told me this as he was in a taxi going somewhere that Saturday morning. I was shocked but he was very calm about it, didn't seem particularly bothered by it. I didn't see him for several days and when I did, and saw the bruising on his face, I was very shocked and upset as he had down-played the whole incident.

Jonathan did not tell us about this incident. The following Wednesday Eimer was in the Peppercannister Gallery when Antoinette Murphy, the owner, mentioned that she had seen Jonathan with a black eye, 'looking awful', the previous evening. When Eimer reached him on the phone he made light of it; he was pleased that he had had it checked out at the hospital and talked about how friendly the staff had been. She ended the call by asking him to tell us himself if anything like this were to happen again, because it was so much more upsetting to hear of it from third parties. He promised he would.

EDDIE O'CONNOR, founder of the alternative energy company Eirtricity, had known Jonathan since O'Connor's 'long, bruising public relations battle' with the then government over his future as managing director of Bord na Mona. He had then found Jonathan fair-minded. The last time he spoke to him was during lunch to discuss an article Jonathan was researching on wind energy.

He was in bad shape. He had been attacked twice, once in Washington and once while walking in O'Connell Street. He bore the scars of the O'Connell Street attack. I guess a doctor might say he was suffering from post-traumatic stress. He was having panic attacks, having trouble sleeping and even coping with ordinary chores like writing his articles. There was a luminous quality to his pain. I felt he was reaching out to be understood but counterbalanced with a deep understanding of wounded people everywhere. He did not condemn his attacker or seek my reassurance that the attack was unjust. Then he was dead. What a terrible tragedy.

The poet JOHN MONTAGUE wrote:

I read of your son's death in a day-old *Irish Times* from a news stand in New York. Only a month or so before, my partner Elizabeth [Wassell, the novelist], and I were travelling back from London and found ourselves on the same plane as Jonathan. But he was on some journalistic junket and travelling first class whereas the poet and his mott were cramped in economy. Nettled by the seeming injustice of this, he deployed a battery of charm that I have rarely seen equalled, and had us moved up to the seat behind him. When we thanked him profusely he just smiled, with that Cheshire Cat grin of his. Perhaps he was thinking of the irony of those lines of poetry woven into the seat designs, while the living poet suffered in steerage. Meeting him over the years in the hostelries of Dublin, we were always struck by his brightness – those piles of well-thumbed papers and books under his arm! – and his generosity; it was always difficult to buy him a drink back. So we remember him smiling at us across the Horseshoe Bar at the Shelbourne, as though delighted to greet a kindred spirit in that corporate shark tank.

We were aware that he was drinking too much, for reasons beyond our ken. But we thought, hoped, that he was young and lithe enough to evade the old-fashioned Irish death wish, which has lured us all. My impression was that he was too smart, too bright, had too low a boredom threshold, to learn the litany of *taedium vitae*, the daily grind.

Jonathan was travelling back on that occasion from a British Airways function to which he had been invited by BILL O'HERLIHY, public relations consultant and broadcaster, who was also on the flight. He too recalled Jonathan's lobbying on behalf of John Montague and Elizabeth Wassell on the journey home to Dublin.

I remember his agitation when he discovered they were travelling economy. I remember, too, his asking me if I could arrange an upgrade, or more pointedly, would I object if he pointed out their status and advocated their case – which is what happened. He was chuffed when he succeeded but what remains most vividly in my mind is his insistence on waiting in the airport for their luggage to be unloaded and ensuring they got a taxi. Jonathan had no luggage on that day trip and refused our lift because waiting for John and Elizabeth was, to him, in the presence of such talent, almost a duty. On that trip he was loud, argumentative, misunderstood, generous, memorable and decent. He dominated the day utterly and wrote of it with a wicked wit.* To say he was unforgettable would not be an overstatement.

DEREK FREEDMAN, who had been interviewed by Jonathan for *In Dublin* in 1987, had watched his subsequent career 'with interest

* *Sunday Independent*, 6 February 2000.

and affection'. The Freedman family had remained friendly with him in the intervening years.

> For all the ups and great times, there was also a dark side; too often subsumed in alcohol. This is the side few saw, but those who did, saw him tackle the excess and take measures to moderate it. When his problem touched other people, he was the first to let them know in a sensitive way. The stress of being assaulted as you walk down the street is never appreciated. Perhaps this made him turn back to alcohol for ease. We can only speculate. What is for certain is that for anyone who knew him, his loss has turned out a light and we all feel the loss of a truly exceptional, gifted and different person who enchanted us with his presence and continues to flicker in our memories.

Professor Ivor Browne had been one of Jonathan 's earliest subjects for interview in his *In Dublin* period. This may partly have been because Eimer had been a student of Ivor's – and later a colleague. In one of his conversations with Eimer about Patch Adams, Jonathan described him as 'like R.D. Laing without the drink'. Sensing the extent to which Jonathan was influenced by, and seemed in need of, the Patch Adams message, she commented: 'But doesn't Ivor Browne fit that picture, too?' This prompted Jonathan – as we later discovered – to telephone Ivor and invite him to lunch, ostensibly to talk to him about the forthcoming workshop but really to talk about himself. During the lunch Jonathan disclosed his anxiety following the mugging and his tendency to become depressed. Ivor told him that medication was not the answer and that before seeking any kind of therapy he would have to stop drinking. Jonathan promised to think seriously about it. IVOR BROWNE wrote:

Ivor Browne photographed for Jonathan's interview with him, *In Dublin,* 18 September 1986

> I miss Jonathan. I used to look forward to meeting him as I approached St. Stephen's Green which is where we usually bumped into one another. Sometimes when I pass the places where he was likely to pop up I have to admit that he is gone. Sometimes he would drop in. I miss his creativity, his keen intelligence and good humour. Above all, I miss the way he made me feel. Maybe that was the key to Jonathan, his consciousness of other people as human beings. To Jonathan I was not merely a psychiatrist, a colleague of his mother's, or simply an old guy he sometimes met. I was Ivor and he gave me the feeling that he understood and accepted me as I am, better than people who have known me much longer and more intimately. Jonathan had an innate humanity which was in no danger of spoiling. He liked people and treated

everyone the same. I was grateful for his affection. The last time we met was in the Shelbourne and I asked him how he knew the waitress's name. He looked surprised: 'It's on her blouse,' he said, 'I like to know who people are.' And you could see that the young woman appreciated that he related to her. It was not just a matter of using her name.

But perhaps he gave too much of himself and went into overdrive. Then exhausted, he became depressed. I felt that because of this his drinking was getting out of hand. As a friend, for he was never my patient, I told him so. He promised he would think about this. A week later he was dead. Perhaps I could have done more?

I remember when he first appeared as a child on the *Late Late Show* I thought him a bit precocious, but when I met him discovered that his brightness was a delight. He would tackle any idea and made a great fist of understanding my ideas on psychiatry. He had been beaten up in America and I think that had shaken him more than he admitted, and he seemed bewildered by the experience. No matter what, violence would never have been his way. He adored Saul and was a great single father, grateful for the support he got from his family. He talked to me a lot about spiritual matters, but he didn't fancy my own method of meditation and continued his search.

CATHERINE O'FLAHERTY, who works in the independent film sector, could remember 'vividly' the first time she had met Jonathan. They were both seventeen. She had met him occasionally in the intervening years but what she termed the next memorable meeting was on Valentine's Day 2000 – this was to be within three weeks of his death.

> I was a little wary of him as a journalist because last year when my dad resigned [*her father is Hugh O'Flaherty, a former justice of the Supreme Court*] some journalists weren't too kind, so I never told him who I was. I think he knew anyway because the first thing he asked me was, was I a barrister? (which I ain't). Anyway this 'wariness' lasted about two seconds with Jonathan. When we were leaving I told him I loved his article on Patch Adams. He was delighted and insisted that I meet Patch, who loved Jonathan – and Saul was there too and it was such a great evening – although Pokemon ruled. The next day we went to Patch's workshop; I'd never been to anything like this before and practically everyone I met was there because of JPB's article.

When Jonathan died, PATCH ADAMS published this account of the seminar in Dublin.

Saul with Patch Adams on his Dublin visit

> In February, I met up with him late at night in a hotel celebrating a rugby game with his energetic, funny awake son Saul and a mosaic of new and old friends. He treated me like an old important friend, over-enthusiastic for ideas we had shared. I began to understand his presence and how involved he was with people and Ireland. He took my workshop the next day on living a life of joy. Saul was there along with seven hundred people, possibly half of whom came because of his sweet article of our meeting. I remember throughout the workshop his rapt attention and smiles given to me as if to his oldest and dearest friend. I write this tribute to those eyes: they burn in my memory, thinking we would have many years together in pursuit. Alas, dear friends, now I shall have to feast on that memory. Our brief moments together will forever keep me on course with my passions, knowing you might be watching. I love you, Jonathan.
>
> *Sunday Independent*, 12 March 2000

A couple of Jonathan's friends suggested to Patch Adams that he advise Jonathan to give up alcohol for a period. On the Tuesday after the workshop, speaking to Eimer on the telephone, Jonathan out of the blue announced that Patch Adams had suggested that he give up drink for a year. What did Eimer think? She replied that she thought it would be a great idea and would allow him to focus on his career plans. He then disarmed her, saying he thought he'd start on 1 April since he thought it better to wind down and not do it overnight. When we discussed it together later, we thought it had to be a good sign that he was telling us in advance but, perhaps naively, we did not question Jonathan further.

BRENDAN BALFE the broadcaster also met Jonathan in

February. It was in the bookshop Book Stop in Dun Laoghaire Shopping Centre 'a week before his death'. Brendan was accompanied by his own son.

> We talked of radio and things and he left with two bags of books. When I went to pay for my own book, the cashier told me that the previous customer had left a present for me. It was a little book by Richard Carlson called *You Can Be Happy No Matter What – five principles for keeping life in perspective.* The book was gift-wrapped and was inscribed 'For Brendan, with love, JPB'. The following lines may be of some consolation:
>
> LATE FRAGMENT
>
> *And did you get what*
> *You wanted from this life, even so?*
> *I did.*
> *And what did you want?*
> *To call myself beloved, to feel myself*
> *Beloved on the earth.*
>
> RAYMOND CARVER – *Last Poems.*

MARGARET NELSON, an executive with FM104, had always championed Jonathan's cause as a broadcaster and was critical of the failure of himself and FM104 to keep *The Rude Awakening* on the air. They regularly had lunch together, the last occasion being on 25 February.

> I have so many wonderful memories of the fun-filled times we spent together – the last being the Friday before his fatal accident when he arrived for our lunch date complete with the usual flowers and the latest book he wanted me to read; we always joked about the fact that I called my first baby after him.

JAMES DYSON, inventor, entrepreneur and chief executive of Dysons, manufacturers of Dyson vacuum cleaners, had been interviewed by Jonathan in Dublin in February. It was to be one of Jonathan's last interviews. They lunched in Bruno's restaurant in Kildare Street. James wrote:

> It was the most wonderful and emotional lunch imaginable. Jonathan sent an e-mail shortly after and I was about to respond when Polly Devlin told me of his tragic death. Our conversation swung wildly across an extraordinary range of subjects – arts, business, books, affairs, people. Our topic of inner confidence typifies Jonathan's emotional warmth. At a nearby table, Caroline

Errington, another Dyson employee, was having lunch with an Irish distributor. I confided to Jonathan that Caroline, charming, hardworking, intelligent and sensitively aware of others' feelings, still lacked inner confidence. Jonathan had spoken earlier with Caroline and immediately said 'if you pay for my flight, I will spend a day or two with her to help her'. He jumped up and brought Caroline back to our table and gently asked her a series of questions in a warm and sympathetic way. All with that infectious smile and enthusiasm. Caroline looked a bit frightened, not least because this was being conducted in front of me, but quickly warmed to the offer. I asked her afterwards why she had agreed to trust her emotions to a complete stranger. Caroline said that Jonathan was thoughtful, perceptive and intriguing. He offered help in an open way. Although it was an unusual thing for a stranger to do, she instantly trusted his generosity.

The final letters in this book refer to the last days of Jonathan's life. On Tuesday, 29 February he recorded his ad lib talks for *A Living Word*, he being in the RTE studios in Dublin and the producer and commissioning editor of the talks, Jacqui Corcoran, being in RTE's Waterford studios. JACQUI CORCORAN wrote:

I had met Jonathan a few times when I lived in Dublin. It was in the most superficial way at various functions. 'Hello, nice to meet you. Good-bye.' It was only a few weeks before he died that I had a conversation of any length with him, when I asked him to contribute to *A Living Word*. 'You're a very brave person,' he said. 'Isn't that the one where you start off with something like: "Life is like a tree…?".' And that was the start of our very short friendship.

On Tuesday Jonathan, accompanied by Saul, came in to booth 2 in the RTE Radio Centre in Donnybrook to record the pieces. He eventually got connected to the Waterford studio and we were off.

Recording the broadcasts with him was a wonderful, memorable, at times funny, at times moving experience. He was so full of ideas and so, so able to articulate them in the given time slot. The pieces speak for themselves. He was charming and flirtatious in the most easy, inoffensive and contagious manner. Later I told him about a play that was on in Waterford that he should bring Saul to see. 'Right, we'll get the train,' he said. 'Not tonight. I have to go to an RTE public meeting in Kilkenny.' 'Perfect', he said, 'We'll be there. Come on, Saul, we're going on an adventure.' I was temporarily living with my parents and don't generally invite people to visit, but somehow I found myself agreeing that he could come and stay. The events of those days merge

From Jonathan's last column, comment on being invited to record *A Living Word*, *Sunday Independent*, 5 March 2000

Tuesday

The reason I am in RTE is that, in a moment of atypical premature dementia, they asked me to to do *The Living Word* — a thing that goes out at about 7.20am. I ask if I can be relieved of the scriptwriting thing and instead wing it. And God bless Jackie/Jacqui Corcoran (I've hugged her and don't even know how she spells her name), for she lets me improvise . . . and we make not the required five, but 27 "Thoughts for the Day" — that's right!

And then — what the hell — I hie myself and the boy down to Waterford. CIE may be suffering from post-scandal disorder, but it hasn't affected their service, which is still (as Keith Floyd might say) "top".

Cartoon illustrating Jonathan's last diary column for the *Sunday Independent*, 5 March 2000

into one. There was happiness, goofiness, silliness, quietness, energy. The four of us – Jonathan, Saul, my son James and I – shared moments of mischief, lots of laughter, and serious moments too. We played charades. James and Saul put on a puppet show for us. When we decided to go for a walk to the seal-caves, Saul wasn't interested. He and James had been up to the back-field playing and had gone into the caravan we were minding for a friend of my parents. Saul wanted to stay in the caravan. Jonathan was trying to persuade him that he would enjoy the seals. 'We're going to the seal-caves, Saul; we might see some seals!' 'Dad', came Saul's reply, 'I can see seals in the zoo at anytime.' Jonathan was lost for words. He gave in. We left Saul for a bit, but didn't go to the caves, which are some distance. We went first to the cliffs which are overlooking Kiely's Cove directly across the road from my parents' house. We sat, mainly in silence. It was a peaceful, beautiful few minutes. We went to another favourite spot of mine along the cliffs; then to the top of the path looking down over the boatrock moorings. Jonathan in wellies is not an image that comes to mind when people speak of him. They quite suited him!

We all went to the play [Red Kettle's production of *All in the Head]* the following night. Again it was great, great, fun. The few days were totally relaxed and comfortable. He said he wanted to spend more time and, as you know, asked could they stay another night. To my deep regret I said no, a decision I have questioned over and over, wondering if things would have been different if I had agreed. Jonathan asked could they come back the following weekend as Saul was going to Galway with CaraIosa that weekend. I said I would be delighted with that. Sadly that was not to be. I would so like to have been his friend for longer.

This letter is, I know, a little disjointed and I have already said much of it in the number of conversations we've had since Jonathan died. I think I just wanted you all to know and remember that, in contrast with the terrible drama of his death, some parts of the few days beforehand were peaceful and happy in a very simple, down-to-earth way that centred very much on Saul.

Although we had many telephone conversations with Jonathan in February, we were aware that we had not seen him since his fleeting visit en route to the airport to fly to Washington in mid-January. In late February Eimer had invited him to accompany her to a lecture on 1 March in Trinity College entitled 'Educating the Brain'. It was to be given by Professor Ian Robertson. Phoning him on the day to confirm the arrangements, Eimer discovered that he was in Waterford with Saul.

He filled me in on having been requested by RTE to record *A Living Word.* I thought it was inspired of them to ask him and told him so. At the end of the call he asked me to pick up any handouts at the lecture as he might like to interview Professor Robertson on his return. The following day, Thursday, we spoke at length a couple of times. Over the previous month or so, without articulating it, I had a sense that Jonathan seemed vulnerable. Since Christmas there had been an unusual number of long calls to both John and myself. While not aware of the extent of his depression in January and February or that he had been taking medication, I began to wonder during these last conversations was he now becoming too high? Perhaps it was the mention of his having recorded over twenty pieces for *A Living Word* that triggered this thought; but for whatever reason I found myself trying to assess his state of mind. The difficulty with Jonathan's temperament was to distinguish his normal speed of thought from something more worrying. He was interested in psychiatry and on that day he asked me to look up a reference for something he was writing for the following Sunday's column: I found myself reading out descriptions of 'thought disorder' to him from the *Oxford Textbook of Psychiatry.* The descriptions hugely delighted him and he offered to buy me the latest edition if I would give him my own copy. His perceptive and funny comments and ability to engage with the text in an analytical way reassured me in my concerns about him.

It was only after Jonathan's death that I was able, with hindsight and the information provided by his friends, to piece together the sequence of events over those last few months. At the beginning of January recovering from 'flu he felt acutely depressed and called on a psychiatrist friend who thought that medication would help him. He did not disclose to her that he had been drinking (anti-depressants interact with alcohol and are therefore contra-indicated in this situation). Then within the next three or four weeks he had the traumatic experiences of being mugged first in Washington and then in Dublin and, while he rationalized how well he was coping with these experiences, he clearly was suffering from intense anxiety and had difficulty sleeping. By mid-February he was at a low ebb.

Around this time, over the telephone, his medication was increased and – as can happen with anti-depressants – he quickly moved up through the mood spectrum so that by the last week in February he was showing signs of being too elated. He may have sensed this himself and, perhaps also influenced by Professor Ivor Browne's advice that medication was not the answer, he stopped taking it a week or so before his death. My impression, confirmed by conversations with Jacqui Corcoran, was that during his visit to Waterford he was able to be calm and reflective and slept well. And I sense that his mood was stabilizing during that period. Sadly he was not yet ready to take the second piece of Ivor Browne's advice – reiterated a few days later by Patch Adams – to stop drinking; but by warning us of his plan to do so, we felt that he was giving us the right to intervene had it not happened. It is a matter of great regret that we did not realize how at risk he was – nor, I think, did he. But those who did know and cared for him gave him the advice we would have given. His last conversations protected me in the days immediately following his death and continue to do so.

Jonathan returned from Waterford on Thursday, 2 March. On Friday I had a long conversation with him on the telephone. It was just after midday. There was no particular agenda. At one stage I attempted a take-off of Charlie Haughey's voice – which I can sometimes 'catch'. I would not normally risk doing this with Jonathan, he being so much more accomplished. 'Not bad', he said, himself mimicking Haughey's verdict on my effort. 'But you should think of visiting the Northside a bit more. I'm still hearing a little too much Dublin 4 there.' We then got into a discussion of the characteristics of Haughey's accent. I asked him had he noticed that Haughey put a z into absurd; and a u (as in ooh-la-la) rather than a u (as in you) in document? Jonathan said he had never detailed the idiosyncrasies of individual voices in this way: he worked entirely by ear.

Then, impromptu, he launched into a mock *Questions and Answers* debate, mimicking me chairing exchanges between two panelists, Haughey and McCreevy, on the topic of whose accent was the more easily mocked; on who was the real Charlie – as in real Taoiseach. Voice from the audience: 'This is the wrong question; we must ask who is the *proper* Charlie?' He encompassed McCreevy's role as an arch-critic of Haughey in the 1980s, included envious comments from Haughey on the irony that it should be McCreevy who was now reaping the rewards of his spending cuts in the late 1980s. He threw in jokes about the tribunals, about accountants – the original profession of both men – about Fianna Fáil's attitude to RTE; and he laced it all with what he supposed were the private opinions of both men about myself. He played all three parts effortlessly – and on this occasion, for one listener only. And the more I laughed, the funnier he got until at just one o'clock, he said, 'I've finished my pieces for Sunday but must file them before lunch.' And we said good-bye with a promise that we would probably meet up at the Fianna Fáil Ard Fheis the following day. It was my last conversation with Jonathan.

The final three letters are from neighbours of Jonathan's in Harold's Cross. CIARAN EARLEY lived close by.

> There are neighbours up in Ashworth Place – two sisters – who didn't particularly know JPB but on hearing of his death they just broke into floods of tears. They appreciated the life he brought to the streets. I can still see him stop, curl the head, listen in wonderment, begin to grin, crinkle the eyes and formulate the response. He was flourishing when he died. He helped us to laugh; to lose comfortable smugness; to appreciate the good; to open chinks of compassion.

MARY FINN had known Jonathan as an acquaintance in Fitzgerald Street since he had moved into the area in his mid-twenties.

> I am a sixty-year-old woman and I loved Jonathan like he was my own son. I shared his great love of books and being so well informed. The last time I set eyes on him he was coming up the Harold's Cross Road, laden down with messages and bags from the AM-PM shop in one hand, and a book in the other, reading it as he walked along. I beeped the horn of my car, and he beamed out the biggest smile you ever saw. It would light up the entire Harold's

Cross Road, as his two hands were otherwise engaged and he could not wave as he so often did on other occasions. My friend Carmel lived opposite and they both shopped in AM-PM where my brother-in-law Paul works, and Paul simply adored him, admired his great talents as a real Daddy – anybody can be a father, but he was a Dad. He had a one-to-one relationship with Saul, as you all know, and the whole world knows too. He listened to him, corrected him in a nice way, and they were like two adults in some ways. They had a great bond with each other, a great love and a great respect.

You know, when Paul Finn rang me and said he had very bad news for me, I first thought it was my own family, and then he said: 'No, it is Jonathan Philbin Bowman.' Well my heart sank and the most terrible sadness and grief came over me and I have to admit I cried bitter tears for him; tears of regret too, regret that I had not written to him to tell him how much I thought of him, personally, and his sharp intellect, his abundance of talent, his wicked sense of humour. But also his ability to admit when he was out of line, which he indeed was from time to time, like all of us. He did not suffer fools easily, and yet he was lovely and kind to an awful lot of people and especially ladies, young and old like myself and Carmel. Sometimes when he was much younger, I could put him across my knee and give him a smack like a bold child! But he could disarm you very quickly with his charm, panache and style and wit and get away with murder so to speak. He crammed more life and living into his thirty-one all too short years than a score of people would in an entire lifetime; and I know you are so shattered now and your lives will never be quite the same again.

KATHLEEN BOLGER was a neighbour of Jonathan's in Harold's Cross and was the last person to see him alive. She wrote to us because she wanted us to know that 'on Jonathan's last journey home' he had met in herself 'a friend and long-time fan'. Jonathan had got out of the taxi some doors away from his own halldoor, and

...after initially stumbling on a green recycling box – it was pitch dark – he straightened himself up and a good conversation started up. I was chattering on; he spoke of Saul. I mentioned my friend Therese Cronin who had died last year – same age as myself. 'Oh, he said, you don't look it.' I laughed. After some time I decided he wanted to go in, so I stopped chattering and he said: 'No, we will continue at a later date.' People of all ages loved Jonathan. Neighbours were tired of me going on about Jonathan for the *Late Late Show*; he would have been perfect. I miss him around the neighbourhood. I miss him scanning headlines in the local shop or reading labels on items before purchase. I hate passing his house now. Please take comfort from the following: on Jonathan's last journey home he was a very happy man, full of lighthearted banter and affection. I wish there were more like him. He is missed around here. But all this will pass, that I know. God Bless Saul. God Bless you all. Kathleen.

In her account at his inquest, Kathleen Bolger quoted Jonathan as promising that in their next conversation they would 'talk generalities'. TOM CONATY noted this point and wrote at Christmas 2000 enclosing his poem 'Winter Solstice'. He wrote that the poem 'would not rest until it was written' and that the 'biggest struggle' had been to send it.

WINTER SOLSTICE
in memoriam Jonathan Philbin Bowman

When the winter
Sucks the last light of day
And promises to give it back
To the waning sun
The waning moon

Then shall I go down to the bower
To find something
To break the fall
And there you will appear
My 'dishevelled angel'
Barefoot on dead leaves
Giving breath to Spring.

Speak to me
Speak to me
Speak to me aloud,
So I can hear your soft curled voice
Fill the air with 'generalities'.

8

'If anything, it was like a country funeral'

— LIAM COLLINS

Jonathan's death was announced on Monday, 6 March, the day his body was found by myself, Abie and the Gardaí in his house in Harold's Cross. I had promised to meet him on Saturday at the Fianna Fáil Ard Fheis where we were both working. But not finding him in the press room on Saturday was scarcely a surprise: Jonathan could always have been waylaid or some more interesting assignment might have intervened.

On Sunday evening, Saul, who had just returned from a weekend in Galway with his mother, telephoned us to say that although the light was on in the house they were getting no reply. Did we know where his dad was? We didn't but said that we'd try to make contact on Jonathan's mobile. Saul meanwhile stayed overnight with Chloe Blake and we left messages for Jonathan to contact them. It was unusual for him not to have made alternative arrangements for Saul but we presumed there had been some misunderstanding. On Monday around lunchtime Eimer phoned Chloe just to confirm that all was well and discovered that there had been no communication from Jonathan. Now alarmed, she made a number of calls, the final one to Jurys Hotel where Jonathan and Saul had spent Thursday night, and was informed by reception that, although his belongings were still in the room, he had not returned to check out.

PHILBIN BOWMAN (Jonathan) — March 3, 2000, after a tragic accident, adored and adoring father of Saul, beloved eldest son of John and Eimer, warm and generous brother of Emma, Abie and Daniel, cherished grandson of Eva and nephew of Deirdre and Peter (Dargan) and Ann and Des (Conboy), mourned by his cousins, by Caralosa, mother of Saul, Chloe, friend of Saul, relatives and a wide circle of loving and supportive colleagues and friends. Removal from his parents' home to arrive at the Church of the Sacred Heart, Donnybrook, at 5 o'c. this (Wednesday) evening, followed by a Liturgical Service tomorrow (Thursday) at 11 o'c. Funeral afterwards to Glasnevin Crematorium.

Death notice, *The Irish Times*, 8 March 2000

We telephoned the Gardaí in Rathmines to state that we now considered Jonathan a missing person; and intended going to his house in Harold's Cross to force entry if necessary. Abie came with me and it was when we arrived at the house that we could see one Garda on the back wall with a colleague on the footpath below. We immediately gathered from their demeanour that all was not well.

They told us they could see Jonathan in the house. I cannot now remember the sequence of questions which I quickly asked, but I appreciate the professional manner in which they allowed me to make the enquiries which established that there had been an accident and that Jonathan was dead. I telephoned Eimer. Abie and I were not allowed into the house to see Jonathan since the scene had to be preserved. The Assistant State Pathologist, Dr Marie Cassidy, was called. Meanwhile photographers had arrived. Before any public announcement could be made, we had to inform Saul and other members of the family.

Jonathan's death was announced on RTE's News at 9pm.

CHARLES BRADY, a member of the bar staff in the Horseshoe Bar in the Shelbourne Hotel for the past seventeen years, has already described in this book how he had slowly come round to 'know and like' Jonathan. I include here that section of the same letter in which he described how he heard the news of Jonathan's death on the evening of 6 March.

> I turned forty-one on 7 March. I was working the late Monday shift on the 6th with head barman Seán Boyd and feeling vaguely sorry for myself when all was put into perspective by the news of Jonathan's passing. We began to hear the news sometime after six. A clearly upset Betty O'Neill from the Lounge called to confirm it. Stunned, Seán and I got through the night on some kind of autopilot. Yet – and here I'm trying to choose my words – that night became a rather beautiful testimony to the man. Many who knew him began to drift in, not the normal Monday crowd at all.
>
> 'Is it true? Is it true?'
>
> Most were women, simply disbelieving, with the exception of one girl – I had seen Jonathan in with her a couple of months before – who was visibly distressed. That night had its own peculiar hush, and felt as strange as any that I ever expect to experience. I can only say that I grew to like your son very much. For the last few years Jonathan was on a spiritual quest that my cynical nature found hard to understand. I sometimes thought of him as a spiritual magpie. He made me smile as he enthusiastically imparted the latest nugget that he had come across. At such times the words machine-gunned out of him, as if the mouth couldn't keep up with that barn-storming intellect of his. He was a man who was in a constant quest for answers. I like to think that in those last moments, as he moved from this phase of his existence, he found some of them.

That Monday night EAMONN Ó CATHAIN, the broadcaster and chef, spoke about him to VINCENT BROWNE on Radio 1. He had known him since Jonathan, at the age of sixteen, had become a regular visitor to his restaurant in Dublin in the 1980s.

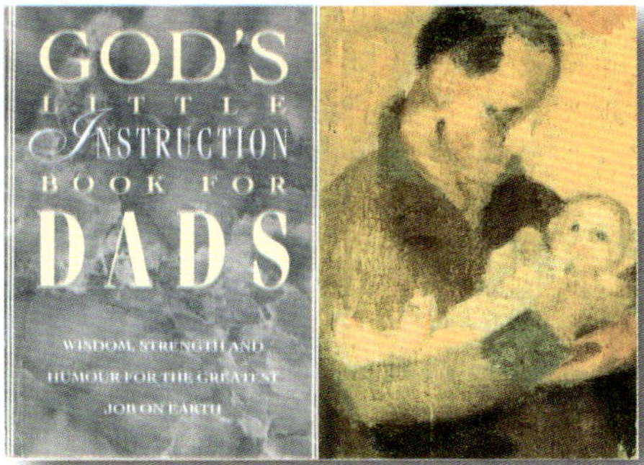

Book found by Jonathan's bedside: *God's Little Instruction Book for Dads: Wisdom, Strength and Humour for the Greatest Job on Earth.* Comprises a collection of sayings about fatherhood drawn from many writers, juxtaposed with quotations from the Bible – all to 'enable you to maximize the joys and minimize the trials of fatherhood.' Published by Marshall Pickering, London 1995.

EOC: I saw him not ten days ago in the Shelbourne Hotel. We had a mighty discussion and we would always get into these sort of intellectual rows about the North, nothing terribly serious, great fun really. We didn't share views at all. But the last thing he did to me was take me in his arms and hold me for about four minutes because I'd just told him something he didn't know: that my brother had been killed in Belfast in 1975,* and that was the last time that I spent with him. And at the time I wished that he'd let go of me, he seemed to go on forever and now I'll remember him with great pride and great sorrow as well.

VB: You remember somebody who was very considerate?

EOC: Absolutely. A lot of people don't know this about Jonathan because he could be perceived as very brash, and a bit boorish perhaps. But nothing could be further from the truth. He always had a twinkle in his eye and a smile, and a wink always for me at the height of some of our more heated rows. I always remember in 1986 in Dublin, I was laid up for about two weeks with the 'flu and this was at a time when we got very interested in technology and mobile phones together, me probably more than he did. I suppose I taught him a lot. But I remember in the middle of that he was sending me text messages on the mobile and berating me for not getting up and having dinner; and not believing that I was unwell. He eventually realized that I was and he arrived at the door with what can only be described as a veritable hamper of necessities – food, and soaps, shampoos, all sorts of things. It was very kind, very considerate. I was really taken aback that night. He put so much thought into what a person who was bedridden could possibly need. And it's a memory I'll always have of him.

VB: He was remarkably clever, and in a way that was often irritating to others, but it didn't obviate the fact that he was genuinely clever.

EOC: Oh, he was genuinely clever, there is no doubt about that. I think the only thing irritating about him was that he would outsmart me on many occasions, and leave me speechless. I suppose that would irritate many people because they couldn't

*Kevin Kane, aged eighteen, was killed by the Protestant Action Force in a bomb attack on McLaughlin's Bar, Antrim Road, New Lodge, Belfast on 5 April 1975.

Jonathan was interested in information technology; he was fortunate that so many innovations in this field coincided with his working life.

keep up with him; they couldn't argue with him because he had out-argued you because he was so clever and devastating in doing that. But I loved listening to him. I adored his company, and, as I said earlier, a lunch would become a dinner, a dinner would become a feast, and it was a feast of the mind as well as anything else. Just listening to him talk to you and share his ideas with you, and also convert you, change your mind – that's what was so enthralling about it. And he had such a vocabulary, and was such a delight to listen to, never boring, and, as I say, Dublin will be a sadder and a poorer place.

VB: Eamonn Ó Cathain, your last words about him?

EOC: Well, I want everybody to remember Saul tonight, and on many occasions he played games on my computer, and I'm devastated. I just cannot believe that I am making this broadcast. I'm so sorry to hear the news. I saw Jonathan ten days ago standing in front of me as live as anything. Until I saw the RTE News tonight and those photographs, and the house that I visited... I just cannot believe this news. I'm deeply shocked.

VB: Eamonn Ó Cathain, thank you for being with us.

Tonight with Vincent Browne, RTE Radio 1, 6 March 2000

GAY BYRNE had also contributed to Vincent Browne's radio programme on Monday night. He emphasised how Jonathan had always been 'ready to burst the balloon of pomposity', something which in Gay's opinion, Irish people tended to resent in youngish people. 'They see it as precocious and something to be discouraged. And that is why, for a time, he was disliked by a good number of people. But eventually he won them over, because he had great charm and great style about him.' The following morning Gay spoke about Jonathan to MARIAN FINUCANE on Radio 1.

MF: You were really fond of him, weren't you? Apart from a professional relationship, and knowing his parents, you really liked him, didn't you?

GB: Absolutely. Because we had known him growing up and when he was going through that particular period when people in Ireland thought he was a bumptious, outrageous young fellow. Kathleen was very good to him through that period and, as she said yesterday, amidst her tears, she always made a huge fuss of him when they met and she is so grateful now that she did. Kathleen had come home to be greeted with this news, and she was just utterly, completely overtaken with upset.

MF: And you went over last night?

GB: Yes, we went over last night – and I don't want to invade the privacy of the family – I'll only say that Eimer, to me, seemed to be coping extraordinarily well* and John was overcome with sadness, overcome.

MF: There's a lot of talk now about fathers and parenting and all that. I think he was twenty when Saul was born and he soon took on complete responsibility for him.

GB: Jonathan did a most heroic job with Saul. When you say it's heroic, it's only in the context of so few fellows of that age would even contemplate doing it. I know there are young girls and young women who have to do it all the

Mary Carr's appreciation: *Evening Herald*, 7 March 2000

Evening Herald, TUESDAY, MARCH 7, 2000

'JONATHAN, WE WILL ALL MISS YOU TERRIBLY'

Always a friendly, irrepressible presence

Bowman died after fall

*Since none of us had been permitted to enter the house, Eimer spent that evening negotiating permission to see Jonathan's body and to see exactly where he fell so that we could attempt to make sense of what had happened. It was finally agreed that when the pathologist's examination had concluded, she could be accompanied to the house by the Gardaí. After spending a little time in silence, she was then able to discuss with the Garda forensic experts the possible sequence of events. It was a great comfort to us that one of us had been able to see Jonathan's body where he had fallen, rather than read a description of it at a later stage.

time and do it, but he was quite extraordinary. It was an unusual set-up and because, in the minds of many people, Jonathan was the sort of flibbertigibbet that he was, they didn't think that it would work out so well.

MF: That he would stick with it basically.

GB: Absolutely. But indeed he did and he showed that everybody who had that opinion was absolutely wrong. It was a terribly, terribly united father-son relationship and to see Saul last night, your heart would go out to him: the ferocious unity of the family – that is Jonathan's younger brothers gathering around and minding him and so on and the whole lot of them just united. It's just terribly sad. And he was so bright, he was so sharp.

MF: Do you think he was bright? Because people used to think he was a bit of a notice-box and, you know, he wasn't that bright.

GB: Well he could be something of a notice-box, alright. Of course he was, but he was very, very bright. Very well read, and because of the home he came out of, he was extremely well informed on politics and current affairs. He was terrific.

MF: A good guy.

GB: A good guy. A really good guy. He would be astonished at so many people now saying so many nice things about him.

MF: I suspect he would, yes.

GB: Because he would have seen himself as a bit of a renegade and somebody who was not particularly well liked by the mass of people. But he was terribly charming, and terribly sharp, and terribly smart.

Marian Finucane, RTE Radio 1, 7 March 2000

Sun, 9 March 2000

PADDY CLANCY, in his column in the *Sun* published a personal tribute.

6 THE SUN, Thursday, March 9, 2000 2R

Paddy CLANCY

Star Jonathan shined brightest for his son

SPARE a thought today for little Saul Bowman.

He's the 11-year-old boy left without a father after Jonathan Philbin Bowman's tragic death.

Friend .. Gay Byrne

Brilliant

Guest .. Marie Cassidy

He was always his own person – and usually had a witty one-liner to put his detractors in their proper place. Anyone who bothered to get to know him – and I'm so glad that I did – couldn't fail to warm to him. He was witty, so articulate, brainy and marvellous fun. And he was just as much at ease among Dublin's destitute as he was sharing cocktails with its socialites in trendy cafés. I know that when I heard the news one of my first thoughts was that a bright star had been extinguished. For Jonathan was a star. Perhaps the brightest of his generation in Ireland. He would, without doubt, have been a superstar had he lived even a decade longer. Of

Sunday Independent ♦ Sunday, March 19, 2000

RADIO DAYS: Jonathan in studio

I started out hating him and ended up adoring him

Jonathan could turn the scariest event into something hilarious, and life just won't be the same without him, writes **Ciara Dwyer**

JONATHAN Philbin Bowman dead. It's just not right. Someone so full of life as him.

I had been reading Jonathan's column aloud to my father. I did this a lot. And usually I tried to imitate Jonathan as I'd do it; trying to imagine what fresh chune he was creating, whether he was trying to get money out of the bank or complaining about not being able to use his Psion 5 on a plane.

Only Jonathan could turn a syringe attack into hilarious copy. As the thugs approached him in Washington, Jonathan speculated that the syringe could have been full of HIV positive blood or on the other hand, it could have been Ribena. He made it sound so funny that I assumed he was fine. Just another dramatic day in the life of JPB.

I first met Jonathan at a *Sunday Independent* features meeting. He poked fun at others, questioned everything and picked up on each colleague's suggestion. Some were not amused. They squinted in his direction for creating

newly-crowned Miss Ireland, Emir Holohan Doyle, and her family. They left, and I spent the afternoon with him. I should have gone home to write up the interview, but instead I stayed with Jonathan. He had that effect on people. You just

Sunday Independent, 19 March 2000

course he already was a superstar to Saul. Not because he was as famous as the celebrities he wrote and broadcast about. But because he truly was a loving, dedicated, great father.

Sun, 9 March 2000

Under the headline 'I started out hating him and ended up adoring him', CIARA DWYER wrote the following account of Jonathan as a colleague in the *Sunday Independent*.

Jonathan Philbin Bowman dead. It's just not right. Someone so full of life as him. I first met him at a *Sunday Independent* features meeting. He poked fun at others, questioned everything and picked up on each colleague's suggestion. Some were not amused. They squinted in his direction for creating such chaos, for the hard-to-take decibel level and the incredible confidence. I found it all adorable. Then there was the day I dragged him in to my pal who waitressed at the Shelbourne and made him apologize for his bad manners. He was full of remorse. When I first met him, I told him that he really annoyed me on his *Rude Awakening* radio show. But when the programme stopped, I really missed him annoying me in the mornings. Like a lot of people, I started out hating him and ended up adoring him.

The last time I met him was in the Clarence Hotel. I should have gone home to write up an interview, but instead I stayed with Jonathan. He had that effect on people. You just forgot what you had to do, and did what you felt like doing. All afternoon, he cracked political jokes. Not only would I not get them but he was appalled at my political ignorance. He did his Charlie McCreevy impression. And then he proceeded to read Vincent Browne's column. He didn't just read it. He performed it for all in the Octagon Bar. He did Vincent's voice, complete with wheezy coughs and then would pause to point out how Browne was contradicting himself.

Cycling around town last Tuesday, I kept expecting to see Jonathan. The booming voice. The fresh adventure. He was generous, intelligent, loving and very, very funny. Dublin will not be the same without him.

Sunday Independent, 19 March 2000

Card with flowers at Jonathan's funeral

The actress and broadcaster, JEANANNE CROWLEY, spoke about him to GERRY RYAN on 2FM.

JC: It's difficult to talk about Jonathan in the past, because he was gregarious and lively and the most marvellous friend and companion. A lot of my friends in England used to come over to visit, and I'm not name-dropping, but people like Michael Grade [*former head of Channel 4 and Controller of BBC2*] and John Birt [*former Director General, BBC*], both said to me and to Jonathan: 'You're wonderful; you should be at the BBC, you should be running programmes.' They were absolutely impressed by his breadth of knowledge. He was a consummate reader. You always met Jonathan with a new book under his arm and he was dying to share the information with you. He made friends of all ages. Everybody who met him had a reaction to him, and most people adored him.

GR: What will you remember him most for?

JC: His delight in human beings and his utter love of life. His total delight in people.

The Gerry Ryan Show, RTE 2FM, 7 March 2000

In the *Sunday Independent* CONSTANCE HARRIS wrote this appreciation of Jonathan entitled 'From media brat to brilliant mind'.

It was in his nature to be true only to himself, although I think he found life – its cruelties – hard to bear. His peers loved to knock him. I think Jonathan must have found this mystifying. And deeply hurtful. There was no malevolence in him. He was bright, funny and more intelligent than most people. He never held back. Who else is that brave? Most of us are terrified to be who we are.

Everyone knew Jonathan Philbin Bowman because of Jonathan Philbin Bowman's personality. Nothing else would do. Like most dandies, there was a beautiful femininity about him, but he was utterly masculine. I remember seeing him about ten years ago with his then girlfriend and their baby, Saul. He was pushing the buggy across the road from the Ha'penny Bridge onto Liffey Street. I remember being told by people, scandalized, that he'd got a girl pregnant. When I asked what he was doing about it, I was told he was very much the parent.

I remember from that moment on I stopped thinking of Jonathan as a loud prat and realized that he clearly wasn't all talk. This was when I started admiring the adult Jonathan. Hugely.

I can think of no other person in my generation who is as brilliant and brave a thinker as he. My generation is one of political apathy, alienated from faith, overwhelmed by globalization, money-focused and fearful. Jonathan Philbin Bowman was the one person who could have helped us think our way through it, for he embraced our fast-evolving technology but also history, culture and, above all, community. More than anything, he believed in loving thy neighbour. And having fun.

We were both raised without faith and we constantly sought it. He was always prepared to love even his foes. His heart was tremendous. The final parallel (that I know of) is that we both ended up as parents alone, and very proud of our children. I believe he learned, very early on, that the only meaning of life is love. Love is God. God is love. Saul was the love of his life, as my son is mine, and I believe he knew that was the essence of life. Thank love for our children.

He was self-educated, a free thinker, a brilliant mind. He was loud and sometimes too smart. He was sensitive and loving. He was an evolved human being. I can think of no other whom I looked to, in our generation, for brilliance and inspiration, and his death has been a blow to our future. I know I was, until recently, intimidated by him. I am glad to say that we became friends. He liked me and I him. Very much. I thought we had another lifetime to get to talk about everything else, meet at street corners, television studios and parks.

I am bereft.

Sunday Independent, 12 March 2000

Jonathan had been an occasional contributor to PAT KENNY's morning radio programme over many years. Pat paid him this tribute on the morning after his death had been announced.

Well I can't let this day pass without a personal reference to my friend Jonathan Philbin Bowman, who died so tragically, and of course all our sympathies go to John and Eimer and the rest of the family at this unspeakably difficult time. Jonathan was a truly extraordinary man, the news of his death was – the only word for it is – stunning. This cannot be so; it cannot be true; it must be wrong; there must be something in the newsroom that has got this thing awry. It cannot be so because it was unthinkable that I would never be in his company ever again. It was always so exhilarating. He had a quicksilver brain, as everyone says. He was witty, he was iconoclastic, he was teasing, and he was precocious. He certainly was all that but there was so much more to Jonathan. He was generous with his time and with his probably limited enough resources. A simple example – a Christmas present for me, a book I just had to read, he said; or flowers for Rachel English on the day that she presented this programme for the very first time. These were private gestures, never meant for public notice and there are hundreds more examples of his generosity out there. He was on the *Late Late Show* twice in September and we enjoyed him for his constant questioning of the orthodox,

Card with flowers

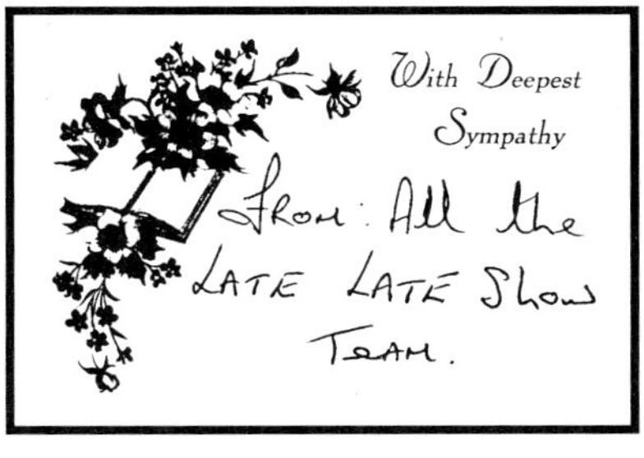

Debating with American feminist Susan Faludi on his last *Late Late Show* appearance, RTE, 12 November 1999

for his eagerness to expose humbug wherever he found it, for his energy and his sauce, I suppose. But behind the flamboyant and quite deliberately constructed public persona, there was a spiritual man. He will be missed so much.

Today with Pat Kenny, RTE Radio 1, 7 March 2000

The editor of *Marketing*, MICHAEL CULLEN, met Jonathan in the bar of the Merrion Hotel on 3 March, the day of his fatal accident. Jonathan had agreed to write a column for the next issue of the magazine.

Next month's 'Since You Ask' column was earmarked for Jonathan Philbin Bowman. Sadly, Jonathan died tragically and is now most likely up above knocking edges off the wings of angels. Articulate, brash, loud, impetuous, insightful, creative, a pain in the neck, humorous, argumentative, spiritual and incredibly kind, partly describe the man. JPB will be missed for his intellect, but more so for speaking his mind when often one-dimensional conformists fake it to win approval and get ahead.

Marketing, April 2000

Jonathan's friend ANGELA DOUGLAS spoke about him to MYLES DUNGAN on Radio One.

AD: Being around Jonathan, it didn't matter what time of the day it was, it didn't matter where you were, that was where it was happening. He attracted people from all over the place; and of every age. He got on with six year olds, sixty-five year olds. He had a wonderful intellect; he was bright, smart. Women absolutely loved him. He had no difficulty with women at all; he got on extraordinarily well with them. He was just a wonderfully kind person.

MD: He was always an entertainer wasn't he? That seems to have been what he wanted to do all the time.

AD: It's what he wanted to do a lot of the time. He didn't want to do it all the time. There was a serious and spiritual side to Jonathan which was more obvious in later years than it had been. He loved entertaining. And he used entertainment as a method of showing you things as well. It wasn't always just for the quick laugh. If you read a lot of his diary logs in the *Sunday Independent* especially, some of the funniest stuff makes very serious points. And Jonathan did know that if you make people laugh, they'll see the point in half the time with a tenth of the effort.

MD: What could he have done? What might he have gone on to do?

AD: Well he should have been here in RTE with his own programme a long time ago; that's the first thing he should have done.

MD: I think he could have done a lot better than that.

AD: Well he could have started here. I was in his company with John Birt when he was head of the BBC who more or less said, 'What are you doing here? Why aren't you working for us?' And I know that Michael Grade was somebody who expressed amazement that Jonathan hadn't gone an awful lot further. Now he hadn't gone a lot further in some ways because of his own personality. He wasn't the easiest person in the whole world; but neither was he half as difficult to handle as he has possibly been portrayed. There was a lot of begrudgery, a lot of nastiness where Jonathan was concerned – directed at him in a fashion that I absolutely never understood. He was annoying and exasperating at times. There were times when I wanted to —

MD : To strangle him...?

AD : Absolutely, but he was never bad. He was a wonderful guy. I'm going to miss him an awful lot.

Five-Seven Live: RTE Radio 1, 9 March 2000

On 7 March the phone-in programme *Liveline* devoted that day's edition to Jonathan; most callers had met him once and recounted various acts of kindness on his part. EOGHAN HARRIS, the writer and television producer, and a friend of Jonathan, spoke about him to JOE DUFFY.

EH: There's something very poignant about a middle-aged man making a friend in middle age. He was the only friend I made in my middle years. I met him in 1994 on *The Rude Awakening* and I walked out in a daze. We just had this meeting of minds and I walked out on to the street and rang the *Sunday Times* and I said you've got to get this guy, he's amazing. What I was really struck by were the calls on *Liveline* from the general public with no special knowledge of him, the way they got his character, the sweetness and the kindness. You know the old Irish phrase, that he had 'great nature'. You see an awful lot of people now will be hiding out but the fact is he got a terrible press for a while and he had a terrible image of being a brat and being a know-all. Ordinary people are never affected by media image; they read into the character of the person, they know exactly what you're like and you can't PR or spin it. But he was just so, so loving. You'd see him on the steps talking to down and outs, you'd hear people ringing him up with terrible problems, and he was so unlike his public image. He was no angel or anything; he was like a dishevelled angel, you know the golden hair, the incredible brain, radiating. I just miss him so much. And I honestly don't think there's anyone like him and I don't think he's replaceable. And all that talent, everyone felt there was great things ahead of him, didn't they? We all wondered why he didn't have his own chat show for years; why wasn't he doing the stuff on the screen and on radio? You'd wonder about why people didn't see his talent. He was a private person but he made himself vulnerable and I think that's why people loved him. Everyone loved him because he never protected himself. If he was in a pub or in a conversation, he ran terrible risks. He didn't hide his feelings; he didn't care.

JD: Jonathan wasn't a politician; and he hadn't written books. In terms of trying to remember him – even the debate in here today – how do we properly remember Jonathan?

EH: He caught a lot of things about modern Ireland, things that didn't make him popular in certain media circles. He wasn't a reflex kind of socialist when everyone else in the media is: Jonathan was a compassionate conservative. He was very much into competition. A lot of socialists confuse competition with conflict. Jonathan wasn't for conflict, he was for competition, he liked to be first, he liked to be best. He hated this thing of the parish priest saying – we used always talk about this – he'd say imagine Sonia O'Sullivan wins a race and the parish priest says I'm only sorry there's not a prize for everyone, after Sonia has done the training seven nights a week! He hated that mendacious, politically correct, posturing. He hated that; that everyone who stayed in bed every night should get a prize as well. And he was so funny about that sort of laziness. He was also very tough on Sinn Féin. He hated anti-semitism; he hated racism. You said rightly that he never said a bad word about anyone, but he was absolutely merciless against racist ideas. Small-minded, naturally mean-minded people saw straightaway that he was a problem.

JD: I think people are going to be surprised over the next few days…

EH: The outpouring?

JD: The outpouring, and the network of people who did not know each other but that he was so close to.

EH: Yes, and he had that Kipling thing, he could 'walk with Kings – nor lose the common touch.' Jonathan was always looking for underdogs, looking for people who were losing, to give them the little edge, to let them get back into the game of life. He was a massive version of Dean Swift; he had that savage indignation against injustice. And that he got from his parents, and that he passed on to his son. It's like losing a son, the whole country feels like that. If there were two people that were deeply loved in Ireland that nobody knew it, one was Conor Cruise O'Brien, the other was Jonathan. Everyone gives out about Conor Cruise O'Brien: at some profound level everyone knows he was like a father to us and Jonathan was like a son. You mightn't agree with your father but he was there to set standards, and Jonathan was there to take risks for us. And to do all the things that we wanted to do when we were young but were afraid to do and he had the courage to do.

Liveline, RTE Radio 1, 7 March 2000

WAKE AND REMOVAL

Baptized a Roman Catholic, Jonathan had attended Mass in Donnybrook church throughout his childhood with his grandparents. At home when he and Emma asked questions about religion, we each tried to be honest about our own position while emphasizing that on such questions many people differed and should be respected for their beliefs. Jonathan maintained a sceptical and critical attitude toward the Church without ever being overtly anti-clerical. From an early age he had declared himself to be an agnostic: and had latterly become interested in Buddhism.

After his death we decided to bring him home to be waked in Pembroke Lane where he had grown up and where we could welcome his friends to say goodbye. We laid him out on a small Irish hunting table – also known as a wake table because its centre leaf is exactly the right size to accommodate a coffin. We also decided that we would request permission from the Church of the Sacred Heart in Donnybrook to hold a liturgical service there as part of his funeral. I appreciated that such a request – to have the funeral service in the church but without any funeral Mass – was unorthodox, and I would have understood if the archdiocese had felt unable to grant our request. Permission was immediately forthcoming.

Label from the magnum of Chateau Coutet 1975 which I had been keeping for Jonathan's fortieth birthday. It was opened instead at his wake on Tuesday night. One of the great dessert wines of Bordeaux – Jonathan liked it with blue cheese – a recommendation from Tom Whelehan. That was how we served it at his wake.

At the conclusion of the wake and before Jonathan's coffin was closed, there was a brief informal ceremony at which his sister Emma read from Derek Mahon's translation from Horace (Odes I, ii): 'How to Live'.

Don't waste your time, Leuconoë, living in fear and hope
of the imprevisible future; forget the horoscope.
Accept whatever happens. Whether the gods allow
us fifty winters more or drop us at this one now
which flings the high Tyrrhenian waves on the stone piers,
decant your wine; the days are more fun than the years
which pass us by while we discuss them. Act with zest
one day at a time, and never mind the rest.

Among those who received Jonathan's coffin when it was brought to the church in Donnybrook was Dr Desmond Connell, archbishop of Dublin, along with Professor Enda McDonagh and Fr Tom Stack. I was personally pleased too to see a number of Jesuit friends, including some from my old school Belvedere College, taking part in that ceremony. I spoke briefly.

I must apologize for the somewhat late start, Jonathan running a little late, as usual. I will be speaking about him in tomorrow's ceremony. But I just wanted to say a few words this evening to thank you all for coming to say goodbye to him.

He was a good son, and he was a wonderful father to Saul. He was a good brother to Emma, Abie and Daniel and grandson to Eva and Jack and to my late father, John. And he was a good friend to so many. We had some sense of this – his gift for friendship; but we did not know of its extraordinary extent until the past few days. And that has been a very considerable comfort to his family. Saul knew about it already, as he was so often with Jonathan sharing his Bohemian lifestyle. For myself, I have never been hugged and embraced by so many beautiful women, as in the past few days. All friends of Jonathan. Thank you, Jonathan.

STARS GATHER IN SAD SALUTE TO JONATHAN

Tears and laughter in church

The Sun, 9 March 2000

Above all, his family want to thank Jonathan for thirty-one challenging years. There never was a dull moment. He could be entertaining, mischievous, generous, exasperating; but he was never dull. I can honestly say that he made me laugh more than any other human being I have ever met.

There's one point, which I hope I am saying on his behalf. I would like to thank all those who were so kind to him: his friends from whom he could expect it. His work colleagues who tolerated over many years his sometimes eccentric working style and who gave him the space to accomplish what we did. But I would also like to thank the taxi-drivers, the waiters, the barmen – the gardaí in recent days – and many strangers who befriended him and who were so good to him. And I would ask those against whom he may have occasionally trespassed to forgive him his trespasses, as – I can tell you, and I know this – he forgave those who trespassed against him.

I will conclude with a poem, new to me but brought to my attention by our friend and Jonathan's friend, Fr Enda McDonagh. And it's from a book called *Remembrance*. It's a short poem entitled 'Farewell'. Incidentally, the author is given simply as 'Jonathan', no second name given. Because it is written on the death of a woman friend, I have taken the liberty of rewriting the last two lines, especially for Jonathan.

FAREWELL

It is with hearts of sorrow and thoughts of joy
That we stand at this gunwale to say goodbye.

The water will cleanse you
The salt will heal you

The waves will cover you
I will never forget you.

The boat sails on to leave no trace
We're glad your soul has found a resting place.

Yet we know you haven't left us, for we will always remember
Your mischief, your big heart, your charming face.

Thank you Jonathan for a wonderfully challenging thirty-one years.

We were not certain how to arrange his funeral service. While we wanted to reflect both his agnosticism and his spiritual journey, we did not wish to be hypocritical. My guiding advisor throughout the shaping of the service was Jonathan himself. At each juncture I asked myself: what would Jonathan have wanted next?

Once agreement had been reached that a liturgical service without a funeral Mass was permissible, we discussed with the family and Dr Enda McDonagh and Fr Tom Stack what the service might contain. And we included prayers, poetry and music reflecting many different traditions. This was followed by a Quaker-style service at the Crematorium in Glasnevin Cemetery. Many of those who attended the ceremony and some who could not be there have requested that the programme for the liturgical service be included in this book.

FUNERAL

Liturgical Service for
Jonathan Philbin Bowman (1969-2000)
Church of the Sacred Heart, Donnybrook, Dublin, 9 March 2000

Programme for the funeral service

Music by The Vedres String Quartet
The Last Rose of Summer: Thomas Moore
Salut d'Amour: Edward Elgar
Welcome prayer: Dr Enda McDonagh

DEIRDRE PHILBIN DARGAN, godmother to Jonathan, reads Psalm 91

EMMA PHILBIN BOWMAN

I just want to say a few words before I read this poem. I was born eleven months and a bit after Jonathan. He was the most horrendous act to follow. But I'm doing my best. I've noticed since he died that I have a sense that I, and maybe you, have a latent inner Jonathan that has been longing to get out; and get out through him, somehow. And maybe now that he is not with us in quite the same way, we find him even more fully within ourselves – I hope that's true for you all.

I'd really like – because I shared it with him – to honour Jonathan's spiritual journey and its many rich manifestations. I want to thank his many teachers and guides on that journey. I'd like to tell you that in the coffin there's a little Buddha from Joey and a picture of Ramana Maharshi, an Indian saint, who has beautiful eyes: it's a picture which I gave Jonathan at Christmas and I know he loved very much. So before I read this poem, I'd like everyone to look into my brother's eyes for a few moments and just be with him in that way.

Deirdre Philbin Dargan at funeral

Emma then read from Wendell Berry's 'The Sabbath Poems'

I would not have been a poet
except that I have been in love
alive in this mortal world,
or an essayist except that I
have been bewildered and afraid,
or a storyteller had I not heard
stories passing to me through the air,
or a writer at all except
I have been wakeful at night
and words have come to me
out of their deep caves
needing to be remembered.
But on the days I am lucky
or blessed, I am silent.
I go into the one body
that two make in making marriage
that for all our trying, all
our deaf-and-dumb of speech,
has no tongue. Or I give myself
to gravity, light, and air
and am carried back
to solitary work in fields
and woods, where my hands
rest upon a world unnamed,
complete, unanswerable, and final
as our daily bread and meat.
The way of love leads all ways
to life beyond words, silent
and secret. To serve that triumph
I have done all the rest.

Thank you, Jonathan, for being a wonderful brother. I miss you.

Chloe Blake reads from the first letter of Paul to the Corinthians

Vedres String Quartet: *Abide with me*: William Henry Monk

ABIE PHILBIN BOWMAN

Like my sister Emma, I'd like first to say a few words about Jonathan. Someone said in the past few days that Jonathan probably lived more in thirty-one years than many people would in eighty. And I think that's true. He had an amazing intensity to his life: he could be intensely generous and intensely funny and he could also be intensely annoying when he wanted to be. And he really did everything with incredible enthusiasm. But most of all I'd like to focus today on how intensely loving he could be. And I think the huge number of people here is a sign of the love that he inspired and that he felt. And I'd particularly like to mention Saul, who has been absolutely wonderful for the past few days, who has been really, really good, who is taking all this in his own way, in his own time, as he should be doing; and I'd just like him to remember that of all these hundreds of people who came to say that they loved his Dad, that his Dad loved him more than all of them put together. He loved him more than anything; and, Saul, I want you to remember that. And so, I'm going to read the lyrics of a song by someone who myself, and Emma and Jonathan, and my parents and, in time, I'm sure Daniel and Saul will appreciate: Bob Dylan's 'Forever Young'.

May God bless and keep you always
May your wishes all come true
May you always do for others
And let others do for you.
May you build a ladder to the stars
And climb on every rung
And may you stay forever young.

May you grow up to be righteous
May you grow up to be true
May you always know the truth
And see the light surrounding you.
May you always be courageous
Stand upright and be strong
And may you stay forever young.

May your hands always be busy
May your feet always be swift
May you have a strong foundation
When the winds of changes shift.
May your heart always be joyful
May your song always be sung
And may you stay forever young.

Emma reading *The Sabbath Poems* by Wendell Berry

Abie reading the lyrics of *Forever Young* by Bob Dylan

CHLOE BLAKE, on behalf of Saul, and CARAIOSA MEHIGAN, mother of Saul, read from the first letter of Paul to the Corinthians

FR ENDA MCDONAGH: Reflection

Professor Enda McDonagh quoted John Donne 'teasing' death with the question: 'Where is thy sting?' But 'in the sudden and savage death of a much-loved son, brother, father, friend, the sting is palpable'. He added: 'In this church when Jonathan was baptized, a blithe human spirit was formally joined to the blithe and sublime spirit of God, and they led each other a merry dance for some thirty-one years. Our Christian hope must be that the dance continues.'

JOHN BOWMAN: Jonathan

Jonathan and I sometimes discussed funeral services and we both agreed that they should be more informal and, above all, more suited to the most important person present. I was perhaps giving him my own thoughts, because at the back of my mind I knew that my day would come; and I confess that I sometimes regretted that I would not be able to hear what Jonathan might have to say about me at my funeral. I knew how devastating he could be. I knew his talent for throwing away lines that were intended for only four people in the audience. Anyway, I never thought that it would fall to me to be here today talking about my lovely boy.

I have tried to keep faith with what I think would have been

Jonathan's wishes in deciding the funeral service. So after this liturgical service, Eoghan Harris will talk about Jonathan at Glasnevin Crematorium, and – as in the Quaker tradition which Jonathan much respected – friends who wish to share some short thoughts about Jonathan may speak there. Before that, I want to warmly thank Monsignor Sherry of Donnybrook Church for welcoming Jonathan here. Jonathan was no longer a believer but he was baptized here just thirty-one years ago, and he was a seeker after truth. He was a very spiritual person, as Emma has told you. If you had asked Jonathan, he would have told you that he did not believe in God. But the book in his briefcase when he died was *The Encyclopedia of Gods: Over 2,500 Deities of the World.*

Another point about funerals on which I spoke with Jonathan was how the design of coffins needed to be simplified. I asked Conor Massey could we have a plain coffin of solid wood – no veneers, no handles, no ornamentation; and I thank him for that.

Jonathan once said to me that funerals should also be fun, celebrating the good that men do, favourite poems and so on. Now he didn't know this poem: but I introduced him to Noël Coward. We both admired his brilliant comic song-writing. Occasionally, for private occasions, I would attempt a parody on Coward and I really coveted, above all else, Jonathan's approval. He would tell me: 'Not bad, but it is for a *private* occasion!' Coward claimed to have – his own phrase – a talent to amuse. That's a rare talent and an important one. And Jonathan had it. I know he would have approved of this choice. I am indebted to Enda McDonagh for a loan of the book where Ned Sherrin was invited to write an introduction to poetry, prayers and hymns suited to occasions of remembrance, and Sherrin admonishes the editors for omitting this particular poem by Coward.

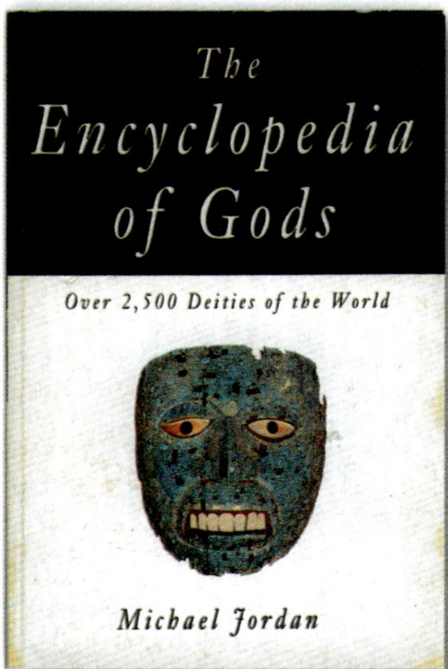

Michael Jordan, *The Encyclopedia of Gods: Over 2,500 Deities of the World,* published by Kyle Cathie, London 1974

When I have fears, as Keats had fears,
Of the moment I'll cease to be
I console myself with vanished years
Remembered laughter, remembered tears,
And the peace of the changing sea.

When I feel sad, as Keats felt sad
That my life is so nearly done
It gives me comfort to dwell upon
Remembered friends who are dead and gone
And the jokes we had and the fun.
How happy they are I cannot know,
But happy am I who loved them so.

I would like to pay a special tribute to Jonathan's work

colleagues who tolerated his eccentric working methods. And especially to Anne Harris, to whom he worked in the *Sunday Independent.* He had first met Anne – I think he had sat outside the door when she was editor of *Image* magazine. He was trying to make his way in the media; he was sixteen and he insisted she give him a hearing about a number of ideas he wanted to contribute. Anne told me later: 'One thing about Jonathan: he always had a great welcome for himself.' And I say this also for Jonathan: he was, as I have discovered, a great friend of promise. He loved to help young people and people starting out on their careers. He was very kind in that way.

Anne Harris told me: 'One thing about Jonathan: he always had a great welcome for himself.'

I've never met anyone in my life so unaware of age. As a child he loved the company of adults, as a ten-year-old he loved the company of four-year-olds, as a little audience to impress. When he was fourteen he was partly an adult, when he was thirty-one he was still partly a child. He was a very innocent person behind all the front, although some people thought he could hide this very well. When he was a child of eight or nine, he set up a magic company performing at children's parties, professional engagements. And I remember when I was researching at the British Museum trying to do about five days' work in two days' available time, that Jonathan spotted that the greatest magic shop in the world, Davenports, was just across the road from the British Museum; and he gave me a shopping list.

'The vanishing banknote box, sir; of course we have it. It's £48, sir.'

I said: 'Well it's well named anyway.'

Jonathan on his first appearance on the *Late Late Show* aged eleven, 13 December 1980

'Oh, it's best Honduran mahogany, of course, sir.'

Jonathan's line was that if he could play it with the right victims, it would soon pay for itself.

He also used his conjuring tricks on his first appearance on the *Late Late Show* where Gay – who was later a very good friend of his and from whom he received many kindnesses – was his victim. All his tricks involved money, Gay's money, and it vanished into Jonathan's pocket.

Jonathan was always keen to turn professional. And I must say I had a heartening experience, when he was requested by the RTE Saturday morning children's programme *Anything Goes*, to review a film about a boy who had hacked into the White House computer. Jonathan took it very seriously, arranged a half-day off school, went to the Carlton cinema, took his notes, went in on Saturday and delivered his verdict. And just after this a very unfortunate young woman on the production team came up to him and gave him a little T-shirt with *Anything Goes* on the front. 'What's this for?' asked Jonathan. 'Oh, that's a token of our appreciation for the film review?' After Gay's largesse, Jonathan thought RTE was rolling in money. 'I have two problems,' said Jonathan. 'First of all, I don't carry advertising without some arrangement, but more important than that I presumed this was professional work. You contracted me: Wednesday, to go to see the film and make my notes; and Saturday, the broadcast.' And she said: 'Well this hasn't happened before, most unusual, you'll have to wait back and explain this to Gerry Gregg, the senior producer, Children's Department.'

I was working in the Radio Centre that Saturday and Jonathan phoned me. He was very worried that he had to see Gerry Gregg. I told him that Gerry was a very tough man, but fair. And I also told him that he should keep one card in his back pocket: Gerry was always championing the rights of the working classes. And indeed there were some who thought that Gerry had been banished to the Children's Department because he wore those views too strongly on his sleeve. But my advice was: don't leave his presence without at least a guinea. No vouchers, or tokens or promises; it has to be money. The accounts department has to know about this. Jonathan emerged with fifteen pounds. And I would like now, on Jonathan's behalf, to thank you, Gerry.

I knew that my old age was safe, that I had a professional who knew how to argue his case. The £15 was capital for his next idea. And he put it towards a camera, and again he was mixing this up with journalism and he was still at school. David Bailey, the world-famous fashion photographer, came to town and Jonathan wanted to interview him. And again I was reassured because at the end of the interview, Jonathan handed David Bailey his camera which was a very good quality, single lens reflex – a Pentax – and he said: 'Now Mr Bailey, will you take a picture of me?' And David Bailey took two pictures of Jonathan. And I said well you are a very clever boy: Bailey charges very big money – you have two David Bailey originals and you also have the negatives.

Meanwhile, however, Jonathan's school reports had increasingly familiar comments: 'Must concentrate more; too anxious to turn the class into a debating society' and so on. I must thank Jonathan's teachers, I have met many of them in the past few days and I know how dealing with Jonathan must have been both stimulating and heart-breaking. His approach to homework was erratic. He was reading avidly but not always his school texts. I remember once trying to pin him down on the subject of homework. And he was being very evasive. Now I'm paid to get answers for a living, but this was beyond me and I can remember in a moment of exasperation complaining to Jonathan that our problem was that by now he knew more about the fifth amendment than the fourth commandment. He was disappointed that his parents' sympathies were invariably with the teachers.

He left school when he was sixteen.

He couldn't wait to get into the adult world and decided to educate himself. His parents were alarmed; but we soon accepted that Jonathan was determined to do that. We had already noticed his capacity for absorbing new information – provided the subject interested him. From childhood he had always been curious. Of course when a child is very young, a parent's answer to any question is taken as gospel; even the vaguest spoofing on a subject is satisfactory. But then comes a moment which is both humbling and marvellous when one's answers are greeted with a quizzical or sceptical look: or even with a rebuttal. And in the case of Jonathan, this happened very early. On so many subjects, very quickly, Jonathan knew more.

Jonathan was entertaining, exasperating, hugely mischievous. He loved an argument, to a fault. And could also be courteous, generous, but – one thing must be said: he was never dull. From the age of ten he was a brilliant mimic. Dermot Morgan he adored, and his character Fr Trendy. And more, he could mimic and satirize from a cold start.

He was a great practical joker. He had a number of April 1st spoofs published and broadcast over the years. One piece in 1996 was published in *The Irish Times*. Apologies to Aengus Fanning and Anne Harris, but I must admit to some moonlighting here on Jonathan's part. But since April 1st didn't fall on a Sunday that year, the *Sunday Independent* couldn't have used the piece anyway. He

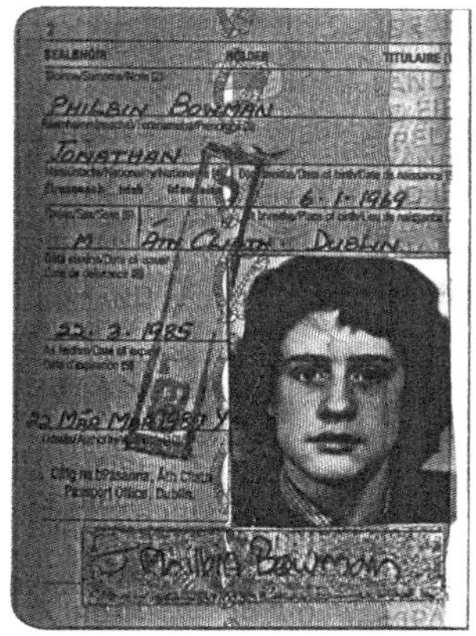

Jonathan used the David Bailey photograph on his first passport and one of Conor Horgan's photographs for his next passport.

wrote that Telecom Eireann was introducing a new policy of allowing a ten per cent discount to telephone subscribers who made their phone calls through Irish. The phone lines of customers who registered for the scheme would be monitored by a computer programmed to recognize the distinguishing sounds of the language and measure the proportion of Irish used during each call. Those interested in registering should phone Telecom that morning. It threw Telecom into confusion and was even read as a straight news report on RTE Radio 1's review of that morning's newspapers.

In Normany for the fortieth anniversary of D-Day I decided to travel the battlefields to interview as many of the thousands of veterans of all nationalities who were returning for the commemoration. Quite late in my plans I began to appreciate the scale of the challenge, so I asked Jonathan to come with me to shepherd the best talkers towards my microphone. There were no hotels available, so I purchased a small two-person tent and Jonathan and I spent the week working about fourteen hours a day interviewing the veterans. They were all so keen to talk that I quickly appreciated that it was much more productive if Jonathan harvested their recollections on another recorder. I told him the simple line of questions which I needed. And he kept to it, up to a point. Some of the veterans who recognised his CND badge were interested in a debate on that issue and that lost some time; Jonathan so enjoyed those challenges that he declined my hint that he put the badge in his pocket when we were meeting the veterans. And it was when travelling through those battlefields and cemeteries that he learned to love William Henry Monk's hymn 'Abide with me' which we heard in so many of the graveyards; and that is why I have included it in this morning's ceremony.

Abie and Daniel visit the Normandy graveyards in 1993

The April First spoof, bottom of the front page, *The Irish Times*, 1 April 1996

Card from Kevin O'Connor, who was taken in by Jonathan's April First spoof and reported Telecom's innovation on RTE Radio's *It Says in the Papers*, RTE Radio, *Morning Ireland*, 1 April 1996

Irish Times 01/04/96 1

Telecom encourages talk with a patriotic ring

Irish Times Reporter

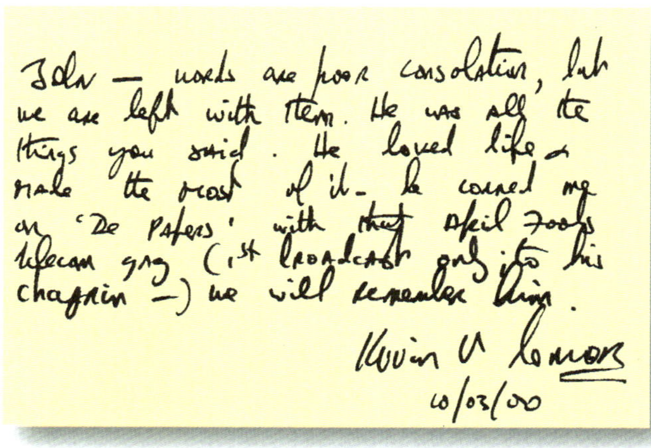

John — words are poor consolation, but we are left with them. He was all the things you said. He loved life & made the most of it. He conned me on 'De Papers' with that April Fools Telecom gag (1st broadcast only to his chagrin —) we will remember him.

Kevin O Connor
10/03/00

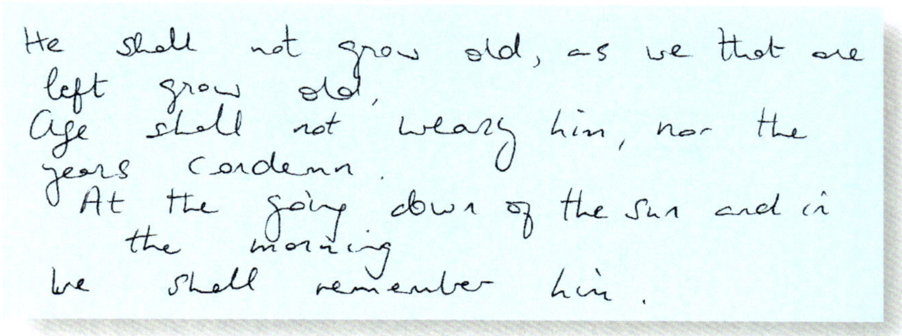
He shall not grow old, as we that are
left grow old,
Age shall not weary him, nor the
years condemn.
At the going down of the sun and in
the morning
We shall remember him.

Emma and Abie have already spoken, and Saul has chosen the reading for CaraIosa and Chloe. Daniel, while I was preparing my notes for this talk and having visited Jonathan's coffin at the wake, said he wanted played a recording he had made on the computer of a short piece of music which he had composed on Abie's guitar. He had given it the title 'A musical tribute to Jonathan from Daniel'. Abie has written an arrangement for the cello and Sandra Vedres will now play it.

Sandra Vedres, Cello: A musical tribute to Jonathan: Daniel Philbin Bowman

I will conclude now, first with another verse by Noël Coward, again recommended by Ned Sherrin.

I'm here for a short visit only,
And I'd rather be loved than hated.
Eternity may be lonely
When my body's disintegrated;
And that which is loosely termed my soul
Goes whizzing off through the infinite
By means of some vague remote control.
I'd like to think I was missed a bit.

Finally, especially for Jonathan, one late change in the printed programme. I had intended concluding with something happy, a rag by the great Scott Joplin: *The Entertainer*. The beginnings of jazz was as funeral music, as you know, and for Jonathan we thought *The Entertainer* would be a good number, and we will hear it presently. But not next. Abie insisted that, before hearing it, we should play one of Jonathan's great favourites, *Always Look on the Bright Side of Life*. But alas, because there was no arrangement for string quartet, I thought this impossible. But Abie insisted otherwise and so we are indebted to one of Jonathan's old schools and now Abie's school, Sandford Park, and to some of Abie's

I chose *Abide with me* by William Henry Monk not alone because of its relevance to a funeral service but also because of the impression it had made on Jonathan and myself when we heard it played – usually by brass bands – countless times during our four-day visit to the Normandy battlefields and graveyards: this was during the commemoration of the fortieth anniversary of D-Day in June 1984. A prayer heard so often in those graveyards – Lawrence Binyon's 'For the Fallen' was sent with a letter of condolence by one of Jonathan's readers, Lisa Tierney of Swinford.

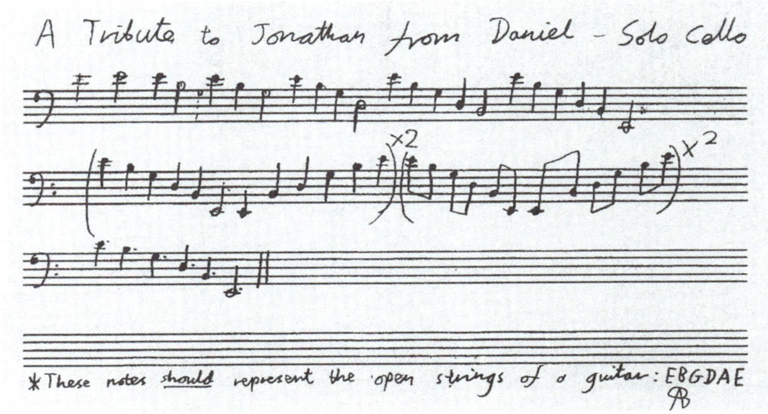

Daniel's musical tribute

friends in the music class, Manus de Barra and Edward Abrahamson, who yesterday afternoon took on the project of arranging this for string quartet. I want to thank Manus and Edward and I also want to thank the Vedres String Quartet for being so accommodating as I was attempting to fashion this funeral service for Jonathan.

So we conclude with *The Entertainer* by Scott Joplin and, before that, *Always Look on the Bright Side of Life*, from the once banned Monty Python film *Life of Brian*. I'm sure Jonathan would especially appreciate this; yet another first, I'm sure, for the Church of the Sacred Heart in Donnybrook.

Sun, 10 March 2000

THE IRISH Sun

PRINTED IN IRELAND

PYTHON TUNE HAS BOWMAN PALS IN TEARS

Emotional farewell

Vedres String Quartet: *Always Look on the Bright Side of Life*: arr. Manus de Barra and Edward Abrahamson. *The Entertainer*: Scott Joplin

In the *Irish Independent* SAM SMYTH published the following report: 'Celebration of a unique talent'.

Jonathan always had the last word but it was his father's gentle eloquence and his family's quiet dignity that helped make sense of that sparkling public phenomenon. The Philbin Bowman's are more than simply the other elements of the genetic cocktail that produced the loquacious intensity and intellectual curiosity that was such an important part of Jonathan. They are remarkable people and Jonathan was certainly a one-off, although his son, Saul, shows many of the same talents. His family shared their private memories and put the public persona in context yesterday at the liturgical service in the Sacred Heart Church in Donnybrook, Dublin.

We mourned the heart-wrenching loss, celebrated Jonathan's

Liam Healy and Gavin O'Reilly of Independent Newspapers. Gavin O'Reilly described Jonathan as 'one of the brightest talents of his generation. He engaged our conscience with his sense of justice and fairness and he entertained us with his wit, He is irreplaceable.'

unique life and it nearly made sense for that hour and a bit. It's the finality that will take time to come to terms with, and those precious moments with his family yesterday may, in some small way, help them and us through such an enormous loss. Parents burying a son, a young boy mourning his dad, siblings saying a final farewell to the eldest, yet it was more than a family funeral. Jonathan Philbin Bowman had spent half his young life burrowing into the nation's consciousness, regularly making us laugh and occasionally throw things at the radio or television. He would, of course, have loved to be there yesterday, quietly observing. Government ministers and media moguls brushed shoulders with senior politicians, eminent academics, the world's most famous poet Seamus Heaney and sports columnist Con Houlihan. There were pop stars, multi-millionaires, actors, movers and shakers from the artistic and business communities. His father said he had never been hugged by so many beautiful women in his life and, while the remark provided a light relief on a grim day, it was no less true for that.

FAREWELL

Always Look on the Bright Side of Life is his funeral anthem

The Star, 10 March 2000

The funeral was quite an occasion: religiosity was not obvious, although it was an intensely spiritual occasion and Jonathan had been a student of Buddhism. The mourners who filled the church were indeed an eclectic bunch. A young man wearing a monocle, bald men with ponytails, beautiful women elegantly dressed, schoolchildren, pensioners, and modest people who turned up to quietly pay their last respects. The Vedres String Quartet played the hauntingly beautiful Thomas Moore ballad *The Last Rose of Summer*, then Elgar's *Salut d'Amour*. Dr Enda McDonogh said a welcome prayer and Deirdre Philbin Dargan, the godmother who had stood for Jonathan in the same church at his christening thirty-one years ago, read Psalm 91. His sister, Emma, read from 'The Sabbath Poems' by Wendell Berry, his brother, Abie, read the words of Bob Dylan's song 'Forever Young' and CaraIosa Mehigan and Chloe Blake read Paul's first letter to the Corinthians on behalf of Saul. It was John Bowman, his father, who carried the day with enormous dignity and eloquence, putting his late son's talents into a fitting perspective. He read a largely unknown Noël Coward poem: 'I'm here for a short visit only…'. The Vedres String Quartet played a lively arrangement of *Always Look on the Bright Side of Life*, which John Bowman reminded us was the theme from the Monty Python film *Life of Brian*. The service finished to the strains of a Scott Joplin ragtime tune, *The Entertainer*.

Irish Independent, 10 March 2000

Sunday Independent, 12 March 2000

LIAM COLLINS of the *Sunday Independent* wrote this report on Jonathan's funeral under the title 'Tears, emotion and laughter, the funeral was classic JPB'.

Tears, emotion and laughter, the funeral was classic JPB

Jonathan turned the city of Dublin into a village, says Liam Collins, and we gathered to give him a country funeral

It was the whispering voice of the professional broadcaster, emotionally remembering 'my lovely boy.' It was the ranks of beautiful women with stricken faces and tears splashing on designer black. It was the passion in the voice of his sister Emma as she read the words of the poet Derek Mahon, 'decant your wine … Act with zest one day at a time, and never mind the rest.' It was his brother Abie repeating Bob Dylan's lines: 'And may you stay forever young.' It was his son, Saul's composure. It was the poignant hollow notes on the cello of a short composition written by his younger brother Daniel. It was very much Jonathan Philbin Bowman: entertainment, laughter, poignant sadness, emotion; it never kept to a schedule and you never quite knew where it was going. But in the end it was the saddest of things, a farewell to a young life. In the Church of the Sacred Heart,

Donnybrook, Dublin, where he was baptized 31 years ago, a typically eccentric but very spiritual service commemorated the lives and loves of Jonathan Philbin Bowman. 'See ya,' he ended his column in the *Sunday Independent* last Sunday, and twice he filled the church with the people who would never see him again. The congregation at the removal and funeral of JPB were as catholic as you could get in this city that his father, John Bowman, said he had turned into a village. If anything, it was like a country funeral. Jonathan's body was waked in his parents' house, before he was brought to the church in a plain wooden coffin, without handles or adornment, because that was the way that he wanted it. Father and son believed that a funeral should reflect the personality of the deceased. Jonathan Philbin Bowman's funeral certainly reflected his enormous capacity for friendship, and the breadth of his restless mind over 31 years.

Sunday Independent, 12 March 2000

JONATHAN

The Star, 10 March 2000

CEREMONY AT THE CREMATORIUM, GLASNEVIN

At Glasnevin Crematorium a Quaker-style ceremony was held, at which many friends of Jonathan spoke. It opened with a message which his friend and occasional teacher CATHERINE INGRAM had sent from the United States. Jonathan had been introduced to her by his sister Emma, and had interviewed her in the summer of 1997. He had since attended many of her sessions and she had become a personal friend. Emma read Catherine's message.

Blazing flame too hot to burn long in this world, I will always remember the moments of tenderness with you. The times we fell mute, holding hands and looking at the trees, immersed in the mystery. The night we stood with a group of friends in retreat under the full moon, and tears ran down your cheeks. You shyly said later that you were thinking of your grandmother and how she used to point out the constellations to you.

The pride and delight in your eyes when you spoke of Saul, your son and most favoured playmate, the only one who could keep up with you.

Most of all I will remember your uncompromising love of truth and your willingness to shout it to the heavens. You were more trouble and beauty than seems possible for one to bear. You bore it bravely.

Rest in peace, dear friend.

Seamus Heaney at the funeral

His family invited EOGHAN HARRIS to speak at the crematorium. He spoke without a script but the main themes of his address were summarized in this essay, 'Sad loss of a subversive wit', in his column in the following week's *Sunday Times.*

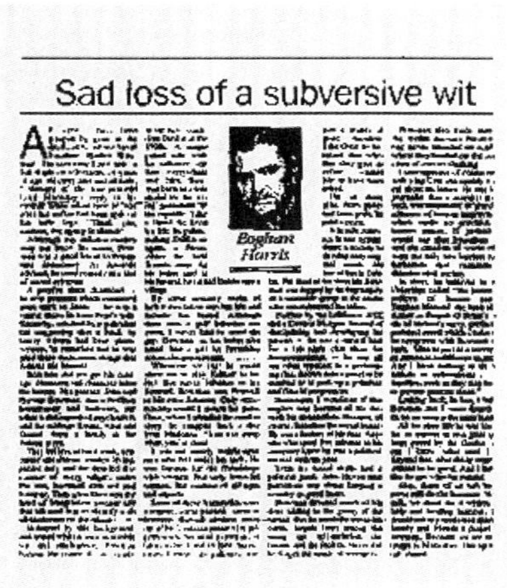
Sad loss of a subversive wit

Eoghan Harris

Sunday Times, 12 March 2000

All week I have been gripped by grief at the death, at thirty-one, of my friend Jonathan Philbin Bowman. The first time I saw him in full flight on television, fourteen years of age, all curly hair and attitude, I thought of the four-year-old Lord Macaulay's reply to his mother when asked how he was after hot coffee had been spilt on his little legs: 'Thank you, madam, the agony is abated.'

Although my unionist readers may not know his name, Bowman was a good friend to Protestant democracy. As Aristotle advised, he used comedy as a tool of social criticism. A pacifist since childhood – he sent presents, which contained guns back to Santa – he was a satiric thorn in Sinn Féin's side. Recently, rebuked by a publisher for suggesting that a book by Gerry Adams had been ghost-written, he remarked that he was glad there were some things that Adams did himself.

Bowman did not get his courage, charisma and character from the breeze. His parents, John and Eimer Bowman, one a brilliant broadcaster and historian, the other a distinguished psychiatrist, and his siblings Emma, Abie and Daniel, form a family in the Fabian style. They believe in hard work, academic excellence, modest living, public duty and the detailed discussion of every subject under the sun, leavened with wit and humour. They gave their son the kind of imaginative interior life that allowed him to identify with all traditions on the island.

Bolstered by this background, and armed with his own inimitable wit and intelligence, Bowman became the centre of café society in the new, confident Dublin of the 1990s. A single parent who took his talkative son Saul everywhere with him, Bowman became a role model for the rising generation of the republic. Like a Greek he lived his life in public, making Dublin an agora, a forum where he held Socratic court. As his father said at his funeral, he turned Dublin into a village.

By some amazing stroke of luck I was taken into his life and became his friend. Although there was a gulf between our years, I never had to mind the gap. Bowman, as his father also noted, had a gift for friendship across the generations. Whenever we met he would allow me to play Falstaff to his Hal. But never Johnson to his Boswell. Bowman was Boswell to his own Johnson. Only occasionally could I match his pace. Once, when I pleaded the need to sleep, he snapped back a line from Madonna: 'You can sleep when you're dead'.

It was not merely middle-aged men who fell under his spell. He was famous for his friendships with women. Not only beautiful women, but women of all ages and aspects. Some of these friendships were romantic, some platonic, some in between. But all of them arose out of his Yeatsian passion for pilgrim souls, his need to mentor, to tutor, to heal and to love. Sometimes I think his gallantry was just a matter of good manners. Like Ovid, he believed that whether they give or refuse, women like to have been asked.

For all these gifts, from genes and from gods, he paid a price.

It is said America is too sympathetic a society to develop truly original minds. No fear of that in Dublin. For most of his short life Bowman was dogged by the begrudgery of a miserable group in the media who misunderstood his talent. Baffled by his brilliance, RTE did a Dermot Morgan. Instead of disciplining and developing his powers – he was a natural host for a late-night chat show for thirty-somethings – he was all too often typecast as a performing flea, thrown onto a panel to be insulted or to perk up a pointless and flaccid programme.

Sometimes I wondered if this neglect was because of his distaste for nationalism. Because, of course, Bowman the social butterfly was a fantasy of his foes. Anyone who spent five minutes in his company knew he was a political animal without peer. Even his social skills had a political point. John Hewitt said patriotism was about keeping a country in good heart. Bowman devoted much of his time adding to the gaiety of the nation. But he carefully chose his comic targets from among the smug and self-satisfied, the fanatic and the foolish. Never did he forget the needs of strangers.

Bowman also made many in the media nervous because he had never attended an academy where they handed out the certificates of correct thinking. Contemptuous of conservatism with a big C, he was equally sceptical about socialism. He was less a journalist than a moralist and, as such, was suspicious of grandiose schemes of human improvement, which made no provision for human nature. If pushed, he would say that boundless love and the creation of works of art were the only two barriers to the barbarism that continues to threaten civil society.

In short, he believed in what Coleridge called 'the permanent politics of human nature'. Stephen Maturin, the Irish ship's doctor in Patrick O'Brian's novels of Nelson's navy, professes a political creed that I believe to be congruent with Bowman's beliefs: 'Man as part of a movement or crowd is indifferent to me . . . And I have

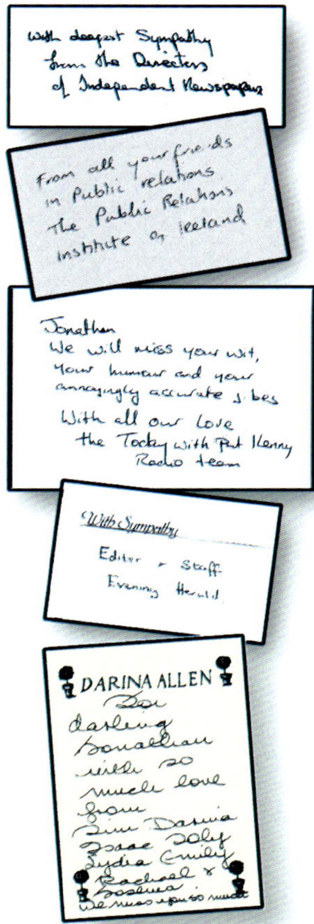

Cards with flowers at funeral

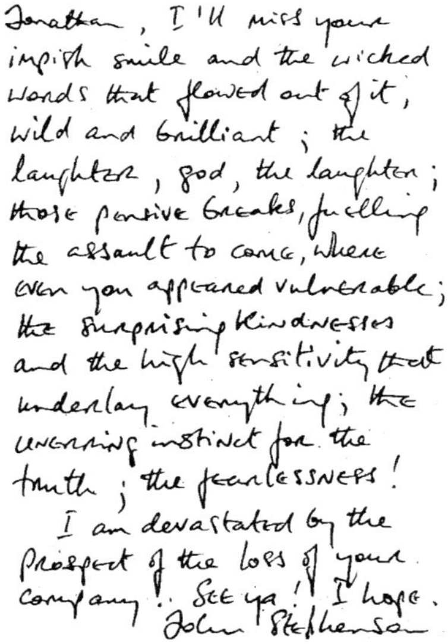
Jonathan, I'll miss your impish smile and the wicked words that flowed out of it, wild and brilliant; the laughter, god, the laughter; those pensive breaks, fuelling the assault to come, where even you appeared vulnerable; the surprising kindnesses and the high sensitivity that underlay everything; the unerring instinct for the truth; the fearlessness!

I am devastated by the prospect of the loss of your company! See ya! I hope.

John Stephenson

Card with flowers from John Stephenson

nothing to do with nations or nationalisms. My loyalties, such as they may be, are to private persons alone.'

Looking back, in loss, I believe Bowman and I were friends because we were in the same business. All his short life he was looking for an answer to two great questions posed by the Greeks: what can I know, what must I do? Beyond that, what did he want? He wanted to be good. And I believe that he got what he wanted.

Alas, those of us left behind must still do the business. Worse still, we must do it without his help and healing humour. So I would ask my readers to spare his family and friends a prayer this morning. Because we are not as tough as Macaulay. The agony is not abated.

Sunday Times, 12 March 2000

9

'... *the guy made you wince and think*'

—NELL McCAFFERTY

The DAILY TELEGRAPH in London published an obituary under the title: 'Jonathan Philbin Bowman: Irish journalist and broadcaster who treated audiences to his forthright views and sharp humour'.*

> Jonathan Philbin Bowman, who has died aged thirty-one after falling through a glass door at home in Dublin, was a flamboyant Irish journalist and broadcaster who as a sixteen-year-old claimed on television that it was not necessary to have a good education in order to get on in life, and then set out to prove it. Despite leaving school without any qualifications, the cheerful, curly-haired Philbin Bowman became one of the most noted Irish satirists of his generation, best known for his early morning performances on the Dublin radio programme *The Rude Awakening* and as a weekly columnist for the *Sunday Independent.*
>
> Philbin Bowman's forthright views and quick-fire delivery brought regular invitations to appear on current affairs programmes. In 1993 he was asked to co-present the radio show *The Rude Awakening*, where his considerable gift for mimicry found an outlet in spoof early-morning telephone calls to important people. Impatient and mischievous, Philbin Bowman was not an easy man to manage, and despite the programme's huge success, his contract was not renewed. He subsequently presented the television quiz programme *Dodge the Question* and wrote for several newspapers, including the Irish *Evening Herald.* He reached his largest audience as a social diarist and political satirist on the *Sunday Independent.* Daring and principled, he was at his most vigorous on the subject of terrorism. The sophistry of Sinn Féin was frequently his target.

* This is an abridged version, omitting some biographical facts already included in this book.

Much of his information and insight was gained as a man about town, and he was often to be glimpsed holding forth in electrifying fashion in Dublin's pubs, clubs and hotel lobbies. He would often be accompanied by his son, Saul, whom he had fathered at nineteen and brought up almost single-handedly. Philbin Bowman combined wide reading with a love of technology. He was one of the first people in Dublin to own a mobile phone, and eventually carried several. Baptized a Roman Catholic, he later professed not to believe in God, although he did embrace what he described as 'post-Buddhism'.

Daily Telegraph, 11 March 2000

In his weekly article in *The Irish Times*, DRAPIER, whose column reflects opinion within Leinster House, commented on Jonathan's death.

Jonathan Philbin Bowman met a most untimely end at the age of thirty-one, and there was genuine sorrow on all sides of the House for one of the most unusual, but basically well-loved, journalists in the country. Jonathan's eccentricities were at times very exasperating but he was completely lacking in malice. He was genuinely innocent, even as an adult, as his father remarked. His most malicious acts were conceived in a sense of fun and rarely, if ever, hurt. How especially tragic it was for a young man who abhorred violence and was totally pacifist that he should have been mugged on the street twice within two months before his death, once in the United States and once in Dublin. It is difficult to think of anyone who less deserved to have violence inflicted on him.

The reaction of many men to Jonathan, until they got to know him, was one of exasperation or annoyance. Women were different. They revered him. Older women wanted to mother him and the real grief on the faces of so many women at his memorial service in Donnybrook Church was evident to all. That fact was remarked on by his father, John, who expressed amazement at the number of times he was hugged by attractive women he did not know. At that poignant event in Donnybrook the courage and dignity of Jonathan's parents and siblings shone through. John Bowman's appreciation of his son, delivered in the most agonising of circumstances, was an extraordinary expression of love, tolerance and pride. In what, for any father, must have been a situation of the ultimate horror, John Bowman's incredible professionalism and polish saw him through with flying colours. His good-humoured courage in such dreadful circumstances was inspirational to his listeners. It is hard to imagine someone as exuberant as Jonathan and so much a man about town as a parent himself. But Jonathan's generous affection for, and care of, his son Saul was itself quite remarkable.

Rarely can such a young man have had such a profound influence for the good on so many people, even if for some he was something of an acquired taste and took some getting to know. The loss of such a talented thirty-one year-old would in any event be extraordinarily sad. His passing in such a tragic way compounded the grief that was so widely shared. Dublin has certainly lost one of its greatest characters, but Drapier hopes that the many happy memories will sustain his stricken family at this awful time.

The Irish Times, 11 March 2000

The television critic of *The Irish Times*, EDDIE HOLT concluded his column of that week with this comment on Jonathan's death.

Finally, it was very sad to hear of the death of Jonathan Philbin Bowman, a likely TV star in the making. Exasperating and (to me anyway) invariably wrong about political and social issues, he nonetheless had the kind of ego and ebullience which pleases a camera as much as it infuriates an audience. There is no point in hypocrisy at this stage: Jonathan got his start from Gay Byrne because of his background. He took it because he was bright and loved attention.

However, like a lot of young Irish media talent, he wasn't always used as well as might be hoped. He did present the RTE quiz show *Dodge the Question* with a suitably restrained panache and, for once, was favourably reviewed here for his work. But elements in the media seemed to encourage him to act precociously and prattishly, perhaps fastening him to a persona which, in truth, he knew he had outgrown. For all that, he was, like all thirty-one-year-olds, much too young to die. Tragic indeed.

The Irish Times, 11 March 2000

NELL MCCAFFERTY wrote in *Hot Press* magazine an article entitled: 'The young Lord is Gone'.

Hot Press, 29 March 2000

The Young Lord Is Gone

NELL McCAFFERTY mourns JONATHAN PHILBIN BOWMAN

JONATHAN PHILBIN BOWMAN

Some years ago, at a time of great pain, I sought to bury my troubles in a bottle of Southern Comfort. I woke up on the kitchen floor, blood pouring from a wound in my head. I had fallen out of my standing – as you do when insensate with drink. I learned a lesson the hard way.

Next day, in town, black of eye with yellow bruises around them, I ran into Jonathan Philbin Bowman. He gazed at me quizzically. I had once built sandcastles for him on the beach, and had only just written a column about his television series debut *Dodge the Question*. I had said in the column that the boy had the makings of a star, but not yet – a touch of the Brandos about his shirt braces, I remarked, velvet bags under the eyes, good delivery but not yet. The young Lord had a little more to learn, not least a touch of humility – something like that, I sermonized, but I expressed delight and excitement that the boy was finally coming good.

I reminded him of that when I met him, pointed to my black eye, remarked that youth was no protection against too much drink (for he, and others had a serious reputation in that department, as many of us did when we were young) and went on my way. A few hours later, a florist arrived with a bouquet. Not your average bunch of flowers – a big, generous, extravagant bouquet, including roses, lilies and freesia. What a boy, young Jonathan, I smiled to myself.

When he died, after falling down drunk as a Lord and knocking his beautiful head against a plate glass window (professional that he is, he had written his column before going out on the town), I learned that I was only one of a million women to whom he had sent flowers! Age, class, and creed made no difference to him. It was ironic and somewhat lovely that he was taken from his parents' home and brought to lie in state in church on International Women's Day. It may have been – I hope to God it was – some small tiny consolation to his parents to know on such a day how beloved amongst women was the young Lord. They turned out in force to say good-bye to him.

Let us not be too sentimental here – Jonathan Philbin Bowman could be a pain in the neck, all-opinionated and sure of himself. Such a pain though – at least the guy made you wince and think. And sending flowers to me was an act of pure kindness – he did not moralize, sermonize, or, as some might have, treat it as hot gossip. It was never mentioned again between us, but I understood the gesture for what it was – he had recognized a person with pain in her heart. Truth to tell, I felt dead glamorous too. There I was with a black eye, in the pits, fifty something, and a beautiful young man had sent me flowers.

I kept an eye on his newspaper column in the years since and a thing leaped out of it – he was searching for spiritual peace, through some form of Buddhism. It was brave and courageous of a young man like that to state his quest so boldly, though Jonathan probably enjoyed the sensation of going against the tide, which he most definitely was as the institutional churches crumbled, and many said 'Good riddance' and not a few of us enjoyed getting that awful religious yoke off our backs.

Anyway, his search was more sincere, open and declared. Imagine that, in this day and age. He was not alone in this search – Sinead O'Connor, his contemporary, has also made the leap for faith – and I wonder now if there is more of it out there than we have realized. He died in the middle of his leap. And I wonder if this has fuelled the extraordinary wave of quiet grief that has greeted his falling back to earth. That was another thing about Jonathan Philbin Bowman – enjoy him or loathe him, there was curiosity about where he might land when he should finally decide to settle. There goes Jonathan – again – people would think, as he made yet another foray into God knows what, God knows where. We shall never know now, we who used mutter, sometimes in annoyance, at his antics 'Give the boy time'.

That anticipation, that he would get there, one day, and it would be worth waiting on, always took the edge off the annoyance. He looked healthy and handsome in death, which added to the pain. The young Lord is gone. We shall never know what might have been. We can guess though. He would have been somebody. Kindness never fails a person.

Card with flowers at Jonathan's funeral

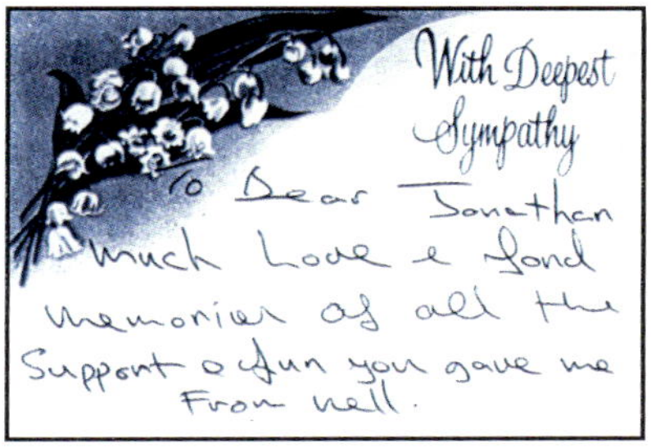

Hot Press, 29 March 2000

A LIVING WORD

In February Jonathan had been invited by Jacqui Corcoran, commissioning editor of the daily 'God-slot' talk, 'A Living Word' on Radio One to present five talks for St. Patrick's week. He gladly accepted, suggesting two preconditions: that he could choose the music which would follow each broadcast talk; and that, instead of writing scripts, he could ad lib a number of talks and allow Jacqui Corcoran to select the five she preferred. In the session he recorded over twenty. These were recorded on Tuesday, 29 February three days before his fatal accident.

Jonathan's five broadcast talks are included in Jacqui Corcoran [ed.] *A Living Word* published by Town House, Dublin 2001

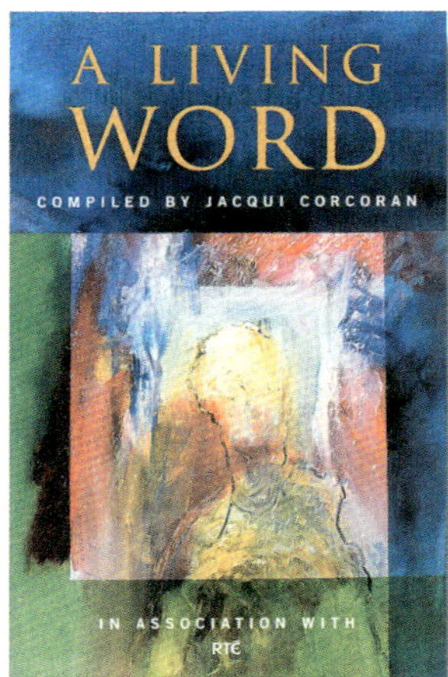

RTE requested his family's approval to broadcast Jonathan's talks as originally scheduled. We had no hesitation in agreeing as Jacqui Corcoran had selected five which she believed would be appropriate. We were invited to select the music to follow each talk and they were broadcast in St Patrick's week. They were introduced by Maxi, who presents RTE's early morning programme *Rising Time*. The five talks, as chosen by Jacqui Corcoran, follow:

How I became a journalist. It was completely by accident. I saw Quentin Crisp on the *Late Late Show*. That was when Gay Byrne used do the *Late Late Show*. I wanted to meet him. I was

living

+ business & appointments

Crisp and spry

'To be in the world, but not of the world' is for Quentin Crisp the secret of life. Consummate stylist, gentleman guru and — in his own words — England's most famous stately homo, the 90-year-old writer now holds court in New York, a magnet for the mad, the sad and the bad, his compelling presence a draw for anyone who has ever felt different. **Jonathan Philbin Bowman** spent a mind-blowing day with him

Jonathan's interview with Quentin Crisp, *Sunday Independent*, 20 September 1998

about sixteen, seventeen. So I had a friend in college who was doing a magazine and I said do you want an interview with Quentin Crisp? And he said yeah. So then I phoned up the theatre and said I wanted to interview Quentin Crisp for this magazine. It was the first interview I ever did.

Also perhaps the last interview I did with Quentin Crisp might have been the last interview he ever did, because I met him last year. I went back to check, and he said: 'Of course I don't remember you.' I said that doesn't matter. 'But it always amazes me that people are so obsessed with the idea that you should remember them. What should matter is you want to be with them and spend time with them and take pleasure in their company.'

Anyway, he used to have lunch every day in the same café in New York and we were joined by this gay, confused English kid of about twenty, and afterwards we went for some drinks in a pub called Jonathan Swift and the kid said to him: 'What's the meaning of life?' And Crisp said, 'Happiness.' And the kid said, 'What is the secret of happiness?' And Crisp said – and this is what every wise Buddha would say – after a pause: 'The secret of happiness is remaining in your mind and your body in the present moment for as long as is humanly possible.'

Music: Madonna: *American Pie*

Rising Time, RTE Radio 1, 13 March 2000

One of the two most beautiful women I ever met is called Nigella Lawson. Her father used to be Chancellor of the Exchequer under Margaret Thatcher, Nigel Lawson. She is married to a man called John Diamond who has cancer and he has lost his tongue. He only gurgles. And she can translate. Her sister died of breast cancer. Her mother died of breast cancer. She has to be screened every year. Her husband is a little older than her, and she has got two children called Cosmo and Bruno, three and five, and they are beautiful.

I was in her book-lined house, they are refitting the kitchen, and John is kinda funny about this, because he knows he won't be there necessarily to see the end of the kitchen being refitted. But he still makes his input and makes his decision. In the course of our interview she said: 'If I wanted to be rich I'd have gone into the City, but I am lucky, I like writing, and this way I could follow my interests and I can do what I like to do. I am so lucky.'

And I called up the next day and I said: 'Nigella, I know why you are lucky, I understand. But my readers will not

Nigella Lawson, quoted in an interview with Terry Keane, *Sunday Times*, 12 November 2000

Nigella also spoke affectionately about Jonathan Philbin Bowman, whom she knew slightly. He had visited her twice in London and, like all hot-blooded males, he was mad about her. She thought his tragic death and eventful life had an almost operatic quality.

understand. How can you say with your husband dying of cancer and all of that, how can you say you are lucky? And as a food writer for *Vogue,* how can you search for the right asparagus? It seems so trivial. Or is it those small things that count?' She said: 'Yes.' She said: 'I think that it is only in its tiniest moments that we most deeply experience life.'

Music: Bob Dylan: *Forever Young*

Rising Time, RTE Radio 1, 14 March 2000

One of the great things about my life, and about my work – which are the same thing really – is that I get to meet all kinds of people, people at every level and people in all kinds of businesses, actors and people who do different things with their lives.

And by chance last week I met a director of the Central Bank, pretty important job. And we chatted away about life and possibility and what you could do, and we came up with some ideas and things one might do. And he said: 'What about the people who have no choice?' He meant the little people. People who don't have a company car, people who don't have £60,000 and a big house in Foxrock. And I said: 'What people have no choice, who are you talking about?'

And he said: 'You know, people who are in jobs they hate.' And I said: 'They have a choice all the time. All the time every minute of your life, every second, you have choice.' And he said: 'No, no, no, they have to work.' And I said: 'No, no, no, they might choose to work in a job they hate and they might choose to spend what little money they have, going out on Friday together and having beer, and complaining to one another about how awful the job is, and how awful the boss is. But that's a choice. The only time you don't have a choice is when they are actually nailing you to the cross. When there are two guys hammering nails into your hands and two guys hammering nails into your feet. Even then you have a choice. Because you have a choice to forgive them. You have a choice to be a victim. You have a choice to feel the pain. You have a choice to think about your last supper.'

The FURROW

At the far reach of Christian symbolism we know that we all die that others may have life. In one of the final acts of his life just before his tragic death, Jonathan Philbin Bowman recorded a series of 'thoughts for the day'. In one he defended human freedom in the most extreme circumstances. Even as one is being nailed to the Cross one is still free to forgive one's crucifiers and refuse the category of resentful victim. It might have been his epitaph, all our epitaphs if we learn how to die for others into the completion and transformation of life.

Enda McDonagh
For What We are About to Receive

Enda McDonagh's comment in *The Furrow,* June 2000

Music: John McCormack, *Will you remember me?* from Balfe's *The Bohemian Girl*

Rising Time, RTE Radio 1, 15 March 2000

My friend Susan gives seminars around the world and she asks people to put up their hands and says: 'How many people believe in God?' Maybe half the hands go up, because these are kind of New Age types and many of them are atheists or agnostics or God knows what. But God would know what exactly. Anyway, then she says: 'OK, of all of those of you who believe in God, how many of you trust God?'

The answer is not very many. Why exactly would you need to buy insurance if you trust in God? Anyway, the whole thing about God is, I don't know why people need miracles to prove anything. It seems to me that fingernails are a miracle. The fact that if you are lucky and your child is OK they get born with five on each hand. Fingernails. Who came up with fingernails and put them just there at the end, and let them grow, and made them hard and different chemically from flesh? That's enough of a miracle. There is enough in the world to be in awe of.

Music: Loudon Wainwright III: *Sometimes I forget that you've gone*

Rising Time, RTE Radio 1, 16 March 2000

Nothing should be compulsory. Especially not Irish. And of course the secret is, nothing is compulsory. But if you've got kids in school you should give them a day off from time to time, for no reason, even when they don't ask. Go play with them; the world is an adventure. Go have an adventure. My son often says to me: 'Dad, are we going home now or can we go and have an adventure?' And we go and have adventures. You can have adventures too. Having a kid is a pretty good excuse. If you don't have a kid, have adventures anyway, but the thing is – boredom is when you're not learning.

Music: *Always look on the bright side of life*, soundtrack from Monty Python film *Life of Brian*; followed by *Thanks* sung by Bing Crosby.

Rising Time, RTE Radio 1, 17 March 2000

Irish Catholic, 23 March 2000

The Irish Catholic, Thurs, Mar 23, 2000 17

From the Heart With Pat O'Leary

PAT O'LEARY REFLECTS ON THE LIFE OF JOURNALIST AND BROADCASTER JONATHAN PHILBIN BOWMAN, WHO DIED LAST WEEK.

JPB — great humanity and generous of spirit

PAT O'LEARY entitled her column in the *Irish Catholic* 'JPB – great humanity and generous of spirit'. She wrote that in his short lifetime Jonathan had become widely known and admired 'not least because he dared to walk a different path; had dared to be different! In an Ireland described so often nowadays as 'an economy' rather than a country, where we have become obsessed with the pursuit of wealth, JPB put people first.'

I cannot help noting so many similarities between Jonathan Philbin Bowman and a young man, born way back in the 4th century, St. Augustine of Hippo. The brilliant scholar, prolific writer and master of rhetoric who also had a son, Adeondatus. And for whom friendship was very high on his list of priorities, 'whenever a man is without a friend not a single thing in the world appears friendly to him,' he wrote. And St. Augustine's whole life was a quest for the Truth he ultimately found.

'In the evening of our lives we will be judged on how we have loved' (St. John of the Cross).

SAD SINEAD'S FAREWELL NOTE TO TRAGIC TV STAR

Coroner told of glass-door horror

The Sun, 8 March 2000

The singer and song-writer SINEAD O'CONNOR wrote a personal memoir of Jonathan in the *Sunday Independent.*

Sinead O'Connor at Jonathan's funeral

Jonathan was a magician. He still is. He will always be. He is like Houdini, with whom he was fascinated, as I was myself as a child. He has made the ultimate escape. But he is everywhere still. And he would like his family and friends to know that. He would also like us all to learn and understand something from his suffering in this life. Not just his boulevardier public persona about which so much has been written.

Great souls come into this world to teach us about ourselves. Sometimes they will choose great suffering and I emphasize the sometimes, as it is not often that masters come back. Jonathan Philbin Bowman was a master. Also very human and imperfect. Beautifully so. But in his suffering, as well as in the love he gave to those suffering people with whom he identified so much, he has given us great lessons about Ireland and Dublin and how we deal with our pain in this country.

Those of us who truly knew Jonathan know that he was not always a very happy person, though he was good at fronting, as his chances of actually making a life for himself depended upon him inventing a character almost, for work purposes, which was cocky and confident and self-assured.

His suffering was in no way created by his family experience. I feel he would like his mother and father to understand this deeply. There is always such self-blame when one's child is suffering the fear that one has done or not done something. Jonathan grew up in a family, where he could not have been more adored and cared for. And I know that he knew this. Though he may not have been so good at showing he knew it while he was in his human body. He can show it now.

Around Christmastime, Jonathan often felt at a low ebb, and wondered whether he suffered from SAD (seasonal affective disorder). This year, on top of that, he had to cope with being mugged in Washington and, some weeks later, being punched in the eye in O'Connell Street, Dublin. Life, in general, I believe, is much harder for men than it is for women, as they are bound by more constraints than we could begin to imagine, and a fragile

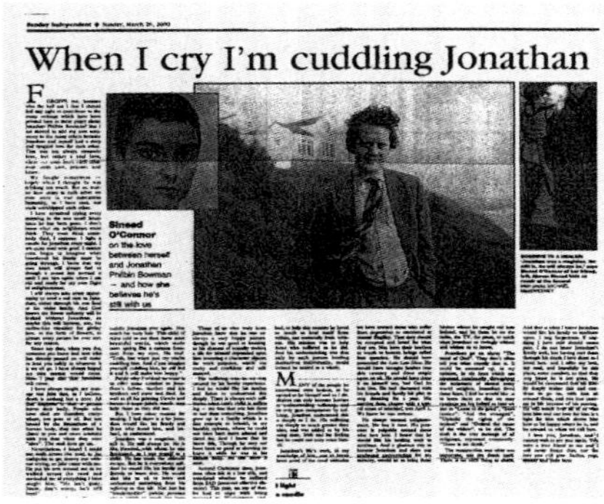
When I cry I'm cuddling Jonathan

Sinead O'Connor on the love between herself and Jonathan Philbin Bowman – and how she believes he's still with us

Sunday Independent,
26 March 2000

man is in big trouble, in this Ireland which mocks its afflicted so much. And which places so much emphasis on acting like everything is okay, even though we may be falling apart inside.

Jonathan's life's work, in my knowledge of him, was to break down some of the cruel attitudes we have toward those who suffer from depression or emotional or mental fragility. That they should be accepted and loved for what they are. Not have their intellect or worth as human beings called into question. He should have presented the *Late Late Show*. He would have brought healers into this country and done magic upon us all. He would have done it on himself too, had God let him live. He had discussed with his friends and family his plan to stop drinking for a year. His starting date, chosen with a typical sense of mischief, was 1 April. We knew he was serious.

He always wanted enlightenment. He has it now. His presence is palpable around those who love him. I know that he would like his healing work to continue. And a glorious way to honour Jonathan and show our profound appreciation for his mastery, would be to bring these healers whom he sought out into Ireland, and let them be on the radio, the TV, the press, to teach what Jonathan so lovingly wished and wishes us to know.

Preachers go on about the word of God. They don't often tell you what exactly that is. It could be summed up, in my opinion, in six lines which are repeated continually throughout the scriptures of almost every world religion. Jonathan lived these lines. I feel he would like us to learn them so that we may continue on his behalf as best we can to Learn to do good, Seek justice, Aid the wronged, Uphold the rights of the orphan and Defend the cause of the widow, as he did. The sixth is the true message of all religions, repeated constantly: there is no death.

Sunday Independent, 26 March 2000

In *The Irish Times*, ROBERT O'BYRNE reflected on Jonathan's life under the title 'The final stroll of Dublin's "unofficial boulevardier"'. The introduction described him as 'a dandy, a character, a gatherer of friends and much loved, as evidenced by his highly emotional funeral.'

> Probably like very many other people, I did not warm to Jonathan Philbin Bowman on our first meeting. We were introduced at an art exhibition opening in the mid-1980s, and what followed was not so much a conversation as a monologue with one party obliged to listen to the other. It hardly needs to be said which role each of us assumed.

In retrospect, I suspect my irritation with Jonathan was strongly tinged with envy: how was it that this sixteen-year-old was so full of confidence and so little marked by adolescent angst? How, at that absurdly young age, could he have so many opinions, and express them so well? And why was he not like his contemporaries, abashed in the company of somebody older and aware of the necessity of deference?

THE IRISH TIMES, SATURDAY, MARCH 11, 2000 — NEWS FEATURES 9

'Women loved Jonathan because he so obviously loved them . . . He was wonderfully sympathetic to them'

The final stroll of Dublin's 'unofficial boulevardier'

A dandy, a character, a gatherer of friends and much loved, as evidenced by his highly emotional funeral in Dublin on Thursday. Robert O'Byrne looks back on the life of Jonathan Philbin Bowman

The Irish Times, 11 March 2000

In fact, deference was never a characteristic of either Jonathan or his conversation. He was not a calculating iconoclast but in argument he loved to take the opposing view for the challenge this offered him. His own opinions could best be defined as liberal and were dearly held. However, he could turn into a reactionary if the opportunity presented itself because he enjoyed treating conversation as a game in which you played with whichever team you were assigned. That meant the opposition's weaknesses had to be discovered and exploited. There was nothing malicious in his verbal dexterity and habit of undermining the speech of others; he loved company and would happily meet someone with whom he had recently argued, the subject of their dispute entirely forgotten.

At the removal ceremony on Wednesday evening, his father used the word 'exasperating', among others, to describe Jonathan. He could be maddening, not just because he would never stop talking but because he was inclined to be hopelessly disorganized, late for appointments and often full of distractions when he did eventually arrive. It is a characteristic of auto-didacts that they are invariably excited by the discovery of new authors and ideas but rarely allow themselves to settle with one subject before being captivated by something else. This was very much the case with Jonathan. He relished novelty, particularly in relation to technology, and would insist on displaying the complexities of every new gadget he had managed to master. Barely had the mobile phone made its debut than this became his lifelong associate (naturally, he always possessed the very latest model).

From his late teens, Jonathan was Dublin's unofficial boulevardier, likely to be met sauntering along looking for someone to join him for coffee or something stronger. For many years, he wore bow ties, and this calculated affectation gave him the air of a latter-day dandy. He was not vain; he simply wanted to be noticed and used whatever means came to hand to achieve this ambition. But Jonathan was not entirely preoccupied with himself.

Robert O'Byrne at the old Taylor Gallery in Dawson Street with Jonathan in the background. This was their first meeting, referred to in O'Byrne's *Irish Times* piece and in his note accompanying the photograph.

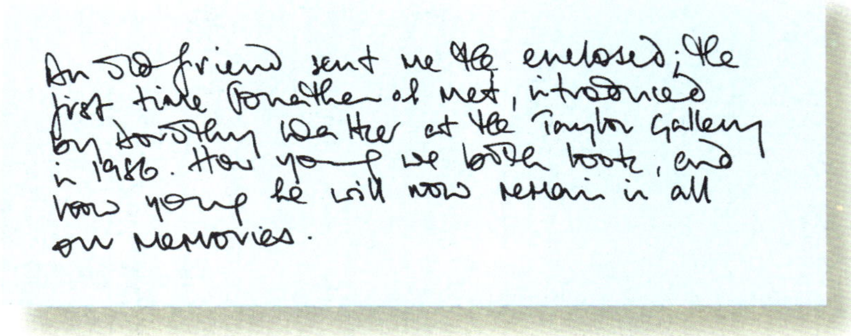

An old friend sent me the enclosed; the first time Jonathan & I met, introduced by Dorothy Walker at the Taylor Gallery in 1986. How young we both look, and how young he will now remain in all our memories.

Since he died, his exceptional abilities as a father have been much commented on. He could be attentive to others, too, especially to women, who were more likely to become his close friends than men. Women loved Jonathan because he so obviously loved them. He responded enthusiastically to their company and was wonderfully sympathetic to them when he felt they wanted him to be.

Of course, not everyone felt the same way about him, and he often gave unintentional offence. Those less articulate than him – i.e. almost everyone – could feel affronted by his fearlessness. Social timidity appeared unknown to Jonathan.

After his death, mutual friends remembered how they had introduced him to the pop impresario Malcolm McLaren who had been reduced to silence by someone so much younger and even more talkative. Jonathan bore more than a passing resemblance to McLaren, in his torrents of language and ideas and in his wild frizz of hair which was as incapable of being contained as his language.

That language was probably used to best effect in the mid-1990s when, together with Margaret Callanan [and Scott Williams], he fronted a morning radio show on FM104. This programme was the perfect outlet for his talents, as over the course of a couple of hours each day he had to cover an enormous variety of topics, some serious, others silly, all equally fascinating to him. He was a natural broadcaster but better as a presenter than a guest because in the latter he would often be constrained by the part given him to play. On his morning show, in many respects he anticipated the style of presentation now employed on the radio by Eamonn Dunphy and Vincent Browne – confrontational, challenging, strongly personal. The pity was that the station's owners failed to appreciate his gifts and he eventually left.

Jonathan was a pundit, something of a rarity in this country, despite the reputation we enjoy abroad for love of opinionated conversation. Britain possesses more of a culture of punditry than here and had he moved to London, perhaps he would have been

Anne Harris with Aengus Fanning at funeral

able to settle into the kind of position occupied there by Ned Sherrin or Mark Lawson.

In Dublin, he was a brilliant but isolated figure, a member of many circles although none of them quite matching his own blend of qualities. Having begun his public career so very young, by the time of his death Jonathan had reached the position most journalists occupy in their mid-forties.

The Irish Times, 11 March 2000

ANNE HARRIS – who was the editor to whom he worked in the *Sunday Independent* – wrote an appreciation under the headline 'A Buddhist boulevardier who used words the way Mozart used notes'. The introduction read: 'Anne Harris remembers Jonathan Philbin Bowman, a latter-day Dr Johnson who was only just beginning to get into his journalistic stride'.

Sunday Independent, 12 March 2000

The teenager sat on the edge of his chair outside my door at *Image*. A Pontormo angel in a pinstriped shirt, he was prepared to wait for hours. He wanted a job and he wasn't going to leave without an audience with the editor. Photographic work was in his mind and he pontificated about the merits of black and white photography over colour.

He looked so young, I wasn't sure that there wasn't a labour law governing him. But he was sixteen, had already left school and talked up a fabulous future CV. And that was how, through sheer tenacity, he got a job

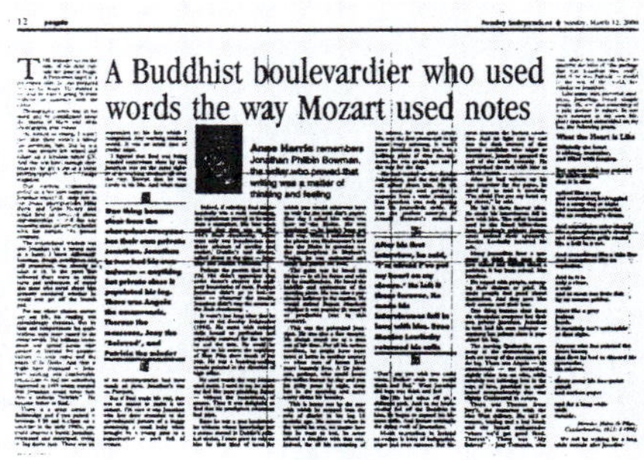

A Buddhist boulevardier who used words the way Mozart used notes

Anne Harris remembers Jonathan Philbin Bowman, the teller who proved that writing was a matter of thinking and feeling

His family commemorated Jonathan with a bookmark. His sister Emma drew scenes from his life: his earliest 'career' as a magician; his Teddy Bear; his joy in Saul and fatherhood; and the romantic friendships and spiritual quests of his later life.

as a social photographer for *Image* magazine. Our working relationship ended on a less than happy note. Jonathan wanted the same rate as top *Image* photographers Mike Bunn and Colm Henry and would hear no nonsense about apprenticeships still less any moaning about an editor's battles with her budget. We parted company.

The conventional wisdom was that Jonathan was a young man in a hurry. I knew differently. Jonathan, though prodigious and still precocious, was already an adult at sixteen. In the years that followed there were so many turns and arabesques of career that those who cared about him probably wondered whether he would ever get off the launch pad.

For one whose chosen university was life, his reading was astonishingly classical. But by taste and temperament his qualifications were more suited to the enfant terrible. His brilliant iconoclasm was spread across what passed in Ireland for counter-culture local radio and the pages of *In Dublin*. And thus it might have continued Jonathan settling into comfortable infantilism had not something happened in 1988 which ensured that Jonathan would never turn into a tedious 'terrible'. He became father to Saul.

There is a street corner in Ballsbridge and if you passed it between 5.30 and 6.15pm on a weekday in the early 1990s, you could observe a frantic Jonathan, briefcased and pinstriped, trying to flag down taxis. There was an expression on his face that I recognized. Any working mothers would. It was an acute case of crèche angst. I figured that Saul was being minded somewhere close by and Jonathan was on the same tightrope as working mothers all over the city. Except that he was barely in his twenties. And when most of his contemporaries had their minds on pints, Jonathan's was on Pampers.

But if Saul made life real, that was no reason to make it too earnest. I'm sure it was Jonathan who first drew attention to the aphrodisiacal powers of a buggy containing a small baby when brought by a young man to a supermarket or park full of women.

Indeed, if minding Saul single-handedly was a rude awakening, the experience proved to be more than a metaphor. His best work around that time was on FM104's *The Rude Awakening*. There were only two broadcasters that those arbiters of quality and cachet, Dublin's taxi drivers, talked about at the time: Jonathan and Marian Finucane. Perhaps the powers that be at FM104 didn't appreciate that satire doesn't observe the ordinary boundaries of taste. Perhaps Jonathan didn't go to bed on time; whatever the reason, Jonathan didn't stay the course at *The Rude Awakening*.

It wasn't too long after that he came to the *Sunday Independent*

(1994). He came with satirical skills honed to perfection and especially reserved for the terrorist and the trite. He could be savage in his satire: the sophistry of Sinn Féin drew much of his pith. He was a humbug-seeking missile pointed in the direction of high office. He used words the way Mozart used notes. I used to say he made me feel like poor plodding Salieri without the resentment, of course. Thus it was delightful to find that his prodigious education had gaps.

Since he was a true boulevardier without whose knowledge not a mouse moved in Dublin's political circles, I soon grew to rely on him for that kind of news for which you would otherwise have to wait for the next day's papers. One day I asked him what was new on the Rialto. He was perplexed he hadn't been out that way. When I explained that the phrase was Shakespeare's and that the Rialto in question was the marketplace in Shylock's Venice, he was enchanted and made the phrase his own.

The point was he loved the Rialto in all its forms and with all its ramifications. He loved the hubbub and excitement of the meeting place. He was also a passionate believer in the market. He would defend Rupert Murdoch whether it was popular (it wasn't) or profitable (not in this country).

This was the polemical Jonathan. He was also a fine essayist. He always struck me as a man out of his time. For all his techno nerdism, he might have been more at home in another century when men of letters lived more leisurely lives. A Dr Johnson, perhaps, who could haunt the coffee-houses by day and pen his pithy prose by night, sleep late in the morning and never worry about his laundry.

This is borne out by the ease with which he stepped into the role of diarist in his log eighteen months ago. No matter where in the world he was, no matter how late he went to bed, he never missed a deadline with that one. Indeed, for all his scattering of his talents, he was quite canny. His was the first phone-call to my house every morning. It wasn't mere devotion on his part. In a brilliant piece of time management, he was getting me out of the way for the day.

He had settled at the *Sunday Independent*, and the taxi drivers still talked about him. His wit was reaching and getting a response from a wider audience. But Jonathan was only getting into his journalistic stride. He was the perfect example of Arnold Bennett's stricture, 'Don't say you wish you could write. Rather wish you could think and feel.' What Jonathan did best was think and feel.

His life had taken off on a different path. And as the boulevardier fed off the Buddhist in him, he began to expand his

The bookmark also included the text of 'Daymakers', one of Jonathan's contributions to *A Living Word*. This was not broadcast.

DAYMAKERS

I WAS FEELING kind of miserable some time last January and I got two e-mails the same day, one from a friend in New York and one from a friend in Dublin. And they were both very nice, and fun and complimentary and they made my day. And I sent back an e-mail saying: 'You've just made my day. In fact I have a whole new word for you people. You're daymakers'. I thought about this and decided to write a book called 'A Handbook for Daymakers'. Or 'A Daymakers Manual'. I haven't decided yet; it's not published. So, if you have any ideas at all about how to make someone's day, send them out to me and I'll put them in the book... with your name. In the meantime go out there and make someone's day.

From *A Living Word* recorded for RTE by Jonathan on 29 February 2000

JONATHAN PHILBIN BOWMAN
1969 • 2000

features skills. And feature writing is the dying craft of journalism. Much journalism in Ireland nowadays is born of indignation, anger and even rancour. But features concern the human condition. And no light can be cast into the dark corners of that human condition with anger or resentment. Jonathan grasped the tool of the trade instantly. He approached the task with love as well as reason.

After he had written up his first interview for the paper, he asked me to read it carefully. 'I'm afraid I've put my heart on my sleeve,' he said. He left it there forever after. He made his interviewees fall in love with him. The office became used to the faxed *billet-doux* from Jonathan's subjects (sometimes indeed their spouses). Monica Lewinsky returned his calls.

Many journalists have a tendency to think that once they have visited and written about a problem, it has been solved. Not Jonathan. He stayed with people, assuaging their distress or grief. He made people feel good about themselves. And they gave him their secrets and their best.

Like many with powerful intellects, Jonathan loved simple people. He was also something of a pain diviner in others. In one such moment in my own life, there appeared unheralded on my fax, the following poem.

WHAT THE HEART IS LIKE

Officially the heart is oblong, muscular,
and filled with longing.
But anyone who has painted the heart knows
that it is also spiked like a star
and sometimes bedraggled
like a stray dog at night
and sometimes powerful
like an archangel's drum.
And sometimes cube-shaped
like a draughtsman's dream
and sometimes gaily round
like a ball in a net.
And sometimes like a thin line
And sometimes like an explosion.
And in it is only a river,
a weir
and at most one little fish
by no means golden.
More like a grey jealous leech.
It certainly isn't noticeable

at first sight.
Anyone who has painted the heart knows
that first he had to discard his spectacles,
his mirror,
throw away his fine-point pencil
and carbon paper
and for a long while walk outside.

MIROSLAV HOLUB (*b* Pilsen, Czechoslovakia, 1923; *d* 1999)

We will be walking for a long while outside after Jonathan.

Afterword

by ABIE PHILBIN BOWMAN

Since Jonathan's death I have lost almost all perspective on him. I now understand the truth of the saying, 'when someone dies, everybody mourns a different individual'. Amidst the grief at home, I have often found it difficult to find time to mourn the loss of 'my Jonathan'. Immediately following his death, I was overwhelmed, as were the whole family, by the level of public affection displayed for him. As time went on, I felt myself increasingly playing the 'bad guy' at home, reminding my parents of Jonathan's failings when I felt they were being overly romantic about him. In addition, I have voiced serious reservations about the usefulness of this book. I have been particularly worried that contributors writing to my father about his deceased son will be too generous in their praise and not honest enough in their criticism. Were I in their position, I know I would be guilty of these failings. Ultimately the reader can best judge the validity of my fears. I have not wanted to read this book at the pace necessary for editing purposes and so I will not comment on it further. All I will try to offer is an honest and faithful account of 'my Jonathan' – Donny.

From the first, Donny was a doting elder brother. My position in the family – born twelve years after Donny, eleven after Emma, and seven before Saul and then Daniel – ensured that I had the least complicated relationship with Jonathan. I was old enough to be an audience and young enough not to be a competitor. In some ways he and Emma were like second parents to me. Donny taught me the alphabet, accompanied me on my first day of school, and used me as an unsuspecting model during his early photography days.

After he left home – when I was seven – I saw considerably less of him. Naturally, with fatherhood came a new younger being to dote on, and his relationship with Saul remains the most loving and reciprocated - if not always practical - father-son relationship I have ever witnessed. That is not to say that Donny neglected his younger brother. Throughout his life he continued to supply me with unexpected and extravagant Christmas and birthday presents, often months late, but always worth waiting for.

Our relationship changed from a narrative into a random collection of encounters. It was difficult to make progress with him. On the few occasions when I encountered him down or depressed, I would do my best to comfort him, only to find that the next time I met him that all this had been swept away by another emotional flourish. He craved praise and hated criticism.

That said, when I did see him we generally got on very well, sharing, in particular, a love of comedy: black with no sugar. The one frequent point of contention between us was the cavalier attitude he expressed about women and sexuality. I still don't know if the attitudes he expressed were intended to provoke me, convert me, hasten my 'sexual liberation' or simply rile my parents. Having absorbed my mother's feminism, I would frequently object to these views, and he loved outwitting me and turning my arguments upside-down. His oratorical skills were frustrating: the more difficult a position, the more he revelled in defending it and he never admitted being wrong. I often felt that his wit enticed him into prizing cleverness above wisdom, which I considered unfortunate.

Growing up as Donny's sibling wasn't easy. I know that Emma, being only a year younger, bore the brunt of it. Twelve years down the line, I still had to endure insults, abusive comments and ridiculous presumptions. Most bizarre of all was the frequent expectation that I would agree wholeheartedly with total strangers' misinformed opinions about my brother. I have never understood this. Nor the second major assumption – one I still face upon first meeting people – that I am a carbon copy of Jonathan in every way. It never seems to dawn on some people how different they are from their own siblings.

I cannot possibly represent here the totality of my relationship with Donny. The more I think over and re-play that relationship, the more I distort what it was. All I can offer are a few of the stories that I remember him by.

In 1999, I spent the summer in France, staying for the first few weeks in the Pyrenees with six female members from three generations of the same French family. Naturally such a set-up was something of a culture shock, and I distinctly remember my delirious relief when we attended a reggae concert, at which I expended two weeks of testosterone in three hours of dancing. During the course of my stay I received a birthday package from home, containing – among other things – an article by Donny entitled: 'Stop all the talking – it's time to take the ballot box out of politics'.* It was an examination of the Northern Ireland peace process turned on its head, in which loyalists expressed difficulty in believing that the IRA was still genuinely committed to violence. The IRA maintained it was devoted to a ruthless strategy of bloodshed, though speculation that some of its members occupied senior positions in Sinn Fein was rife. The IRA would not 'condemn' the political activities of these fellow-travellers, stating 'obviously we cannot control what our members do in their spare time'. My hostesses were afraid to enter the room, such was the ferocity of my laughter.

While he was living in Fitzgerald Street there was a period when Donny was really broke. The gas had been disconnected, the heating wasn't working and there was no food in the house. On the nights when Saul was home – he has always been a popular lodger in at least three residences at any given time – his exceptional babysitter fed him on baked beans, bought in bulk on Henry Street. One night, Jonathan was going to dinner with some television executives to discuss work. Short of cash, he asked the babysitter if she could lend him any, and she gave him her ATM card and PIN, there being £120 in her account. She told him not to take it all out but she knew he would. And he did. He arrived home at 4am, blind drunk, wielding a £90 Alessi gas lighter that he'd bought in some chic design shop, saying, 'Isn't this really cool?'** This story still fills me with outrage and disbelief at Jonathan's capacity for blind insensitivity and self-centredness.

Of all the Sunday dinner tables he dominated, one in particular, stands out. It culminated with Jonathan improvising a parody of my father's archival radio programme *Bowman: Saturday: Eight-thirty* – which typically examines the careers of important figures or marks the anniversary of major events. *Philbin Bowman: Sunday: Ten-Thirty* opened 'This week sees the forty-fifth anniversary of the arrival of the light bulb in County Mayo. Bridget O'Flanagan, then six, remembers how she reacted on seeing her very first light bulb…'. He kept this up for a good five minutes, improvising an eclectic bunch of interviewees in quick succession. Most of all, he captured the gravitas my father brings to the programme (we have a long-running gag that he only knows five jokes).

* *Sunday Independent*, 18 July 1999

** This was Sinead Impey, see 137-40 above

Then Saul made a bid for the limelight by reciting a 'humorous' television ad. Having all seen it many times, none of us laughed. My father tried to explain to Saul why his joke had failed. (Saul's view of my father is on record as: 'John, I find interesting – in a Discovery Channel sort of way'.) 'It's funny the first time you hear it, Saul, but to be a really good ad, it has to still be funny the fifth or sixth time you hear it.' To which Donny added, 'Unlike a John Bowman joke, which has to be funny the ninety-ninth time you hear it.'

Two years before he died, Donny walked out during the family Christmas dinner. All I will say is that it was an emotionally charged gathering, and while he was no doubt partly responsible, the charge did not dissipate when he left. His account of the day, a week later, in his *Sunday Independent* journal was predictably unfair and one-sided. That January, when the rest of the family were away, I was just drifting off to sleep one night around midnight, when I heard the phone ring. Groggy, I answered it, and found Jonathan on the other end, wondering if he could drop by.

Half an hour later we were in the kitchen, discussing the Christmas debacle. The vehemence of the fallout had been such that I was pushed into the highly unusual role of mediator. So I found myself – most out of character – defending my parents. I can't have seemed very sympathetic: I recall ordering Donny to smoke in the garden while I continued our conversation from the doorway. High on my agenda was the unfairness of his article, though I also found time to object to his repeated use of the phrase 'God bless him' which offended my atheist sensibilities. For once I was determined to counter his wit with unyielding emotional rhetoric. Eventually we reached a compromise.

A week later, I read in his *Sunday Independent* diary about an argument he'd had with his younger brother: 'He's an adolescent, for god's sake'. It was the one time I stopped talking to him. My mother, who felt that Jonathan depended on me as an ally within the family, encouraged me to forgive him, for which I am grateful. Of course, there was no formal reconciliation, he just forgot it had ever happened or mattered to anyone, and carried on as before. I accepted this, and was soon very glad that I had done so.

Donny was exceptional. He was witty, insensitive, generous, selfish, flamboyant, depressive, enthusiastic and lonely, an entertaining and overbearing conversationalist, a talented and demanding son, an exciting and infuriating elder brother and a devoted and loving father. I miss him.

Jim Cogan the caricaturist for the *Sunday Independent* worked closely with Jonathan every week when preparing a drawing based on his diary. On 12 March, 2000 he published this drawing in his memory.

who else but jonathan?

by CONOR FERGUSON

I will conclude with CONOR FERGUSON, who, when he lived in Dublin was a friend of Jonathan. He entitled this poem 'who else but jonathan?' and it is dated Prague, 11 March 2000. He wrote that the poem was written 'because the words came and they wouldn't go away until I wrote them down. I must pass much of the credit to Jonathan for making me write it.' I have retained the use of lower case even on proper names such as Jonathan; only God gets a capital.

who else but jonathan?
there was no way round it:
we would all miss him:

the demon cherub with his forked tongue
weaving corkscrews under skywardly spiral locks
always crossing town at high speed

cutting a happy dash
and his victims down to size
deft in the black art of disparagement

he doubled them up as he cleft them in two
(and made them thank him into the bargain)
not a soul who knew him could fail to picture

the demon cherub now:
charging the gates of heaven
("and dinner for all my new friends!")

no need to foreclose then
on all the sweet words and kindnesses owed
or listen keenly to the munching of humble pie

but he'll get by – he'll manage
as down here we still look up to him
up there with his feet on God's desk

Index of Contributors

This index is not comprehensive. It is not based on the text's content, being merely an index of contributors.

Adams, Patch, 194-95, 201-202
Allen, Darina, 11
Allen, Harry, 142-43
Allen, Myrtle, 10
Allen, Timmy, 12
Arnold, Mavis, 85

Balfe, Brendan, 202-203
Barry, J.J., 57-58
Bates, Ray, 160
Begg, David, 181-182
Binchy, Maeve, 147-48
Binchy, Sarah, 179-81
Binchy, William, 181
Bland, Rick, 169-70
Bloxham, Hilary, 102-103
Boland, Eavan, 4-8
Bolger, Kathleen, 209-10
Bonnar, John, 85
Bowman, John, removal, 224-26; funeral, 229-36
Bradley, Fr Bruce, SJ 105-106
Brady, Charles, 160-1, 212
Brennan, Frances, 188-89
Brophy, Eanna, 80
Browne, Ivor, 200-201
Browne, Vincent, 89-90, 213-14
Burke, Helen Lucy, 88
Burke, M., 190
Byrne, Gay, 31-33, 54-56, 133-36, 215-16
Byrne, Joanne, 176

Callanan, Frank, 58-59, 114-15
Carroll, Joe, 83
Carroll, Sarah, 14
Carson, Noelle, 15
Casey, Sarah, 7
Clancy, Paddy, 216-17
Clark, Bruce, 41
Classon, Michael, 48
Cogan, Jim, 171
Collins, Greg, 33-35, 162-63
Collins, Liam, 238-39
Comerford, Patrick, 41
Conaty, Tom, poem, 210
Corcoran, Farrell, 158-59
Corcoran, Jacqui, 204-206
Couglan, Frank, 112-14
Crosbie, Alan, 75
Crowley, Jeananne, 91-95, 217-18
Cullen, Michael, 220

Daily Telegraph, obituary, 243-44
Daly, Emile, 35-36
Darcy, John, 57
Deevy, Patricia, 175-76
Donovan, Carol, 117
Doorly, Tom, 59, 129-31
Dorgan, Theo, 111-12
Douglas, Angela, 221-22
Dowds, Robert, 15-17, 18-19
Downes, Alexander, 184-85
Doyle, John S., 60-63
'Drapier', *Irish Times* columnist, 244-45
Duffy, Joe, 190, 196-97, 222-23
Duffy, Robert, 148-49
Duignan, Sean, 124-25
Dungan, Myles, 51-52, 221-22
Dunne, Simon, 67-68
Durcan, Paul, 119-20
Dwyer, Ciara, 217
Dyson, James, 203-204

Early, Ciaran, 208
East, Louise, 77-78
Edwards, Owen Dudley, 108-110
Eley, Rod, 40

Fanning, Aengus, 146-47
Feely, Eleanor, 85
Feely, Frank, 155-56
Fehily, Rachel, 21-24
Ferguson, Conor, 66-67, poem, 265
Finucane, Marian, 215-16
Finn, Mary, 208-209
Foot, Sarah, 140-41
Fox, Colm, 57
Freedman, Derek, 69-70, 199-200
Furney English, Caroline, 176

Gallagher, Djinn, 149-53
Geldof, Lyn, 144
Geoghegan-Quinn, Maire, 118
Gilfillan, Kathy, 90-91
Gill, Michael, 11, 143-44
Glacken, Triona, 156-57
Gleeson, Deirdre, 176
Gleeson, Mairead, 82-83
Gormley, John, 163-64
Gregg, Gerry, 40
Guerin, Bernadette, 159

Hall, Pauline, 1-2
Halligan, Ursula, 176
Hamilton-Tarleton, Yvonne, 76
Hand, Eithne, 178-79
Hanrahan, Dermot, 124
Harney, Mary, 158
Harris, Anne, 255-59
Harris, Constance, 218-19

Harris, Eoghan, 222-23, 240-42
Harris, John, 38
Haughton, Helen, 46-47
Healy, Alyna, 2
Healy, Shay, 182-83
Holt, Eddie, 245
Horgan, John, 147
Hourican, Emily, 145-46
Hourihane, Ann Marie, 100-101

Impey, Sinead, 137, 139-40
Ingram, Catherine, 239
Irish Times, obituary, ix-x

James, Dermot, 19-20
Jordan, Barbara, 132-33

Keane, Michael, 79-80
Keating, Justin, 117
Keatinge, Sue, 141-42
Kehoe, Paddy, 63
Kennedy, Kieran, 101
Kennelly, Brendan, 103-105
Kenny, Ethna, 42-43
Kenny, Mary, 172-73
Kenny, Pat, 191, 219-20
Kerr, Robert, 20-21
Kiely, Ben, 118-19
King, Adele 'Twink', 27-29

Lacey, Jill Bell, 37-38
Lambert, Eugene, 9
Lawson, Nigella, 248
Lowe, John, 121, 138-39
Lumley, Ian, 106-108
Lysaght, Charles, 97-98

McCafferty, Nell, 245-47
McDonagh, Fr Enda, 229, 249
McEldowney, Eugene, 186-88
MacGonigal, Ciaran, 116
McGrath, Sr Mary Loreto, 85
McGuinness, Frank, 63-64
McKeon, Barbara, 126
McLaughlin, Brighid, 173-75
McLynn, Pauline, 185-86
Madden, Lucy, 74-75
Magennis, Angela, xvi
Martin, Deborah, 176-77, 197-98
Mathews, Arthur, 166
Mathews, Tom, 156
Maxwell, Sr Elizabeth, 57
Mays, Laura, 43-44
Metcalfe, Owen, 41-42
Millea, Theresa, 83
Miller, Greg, 45
Minihan, John, 157-58
Moloney, Elizabeth, 2-4
Montague, Helene, 110-11
Montague, John, 198-99
Morgan, Don, 166-67
Morgan, Pat, 52-53
Mosse, Paul, 11-12
Mullen, Ronan, 177-78
Murphy, Gerry, 189
Murphy, Mike, 26-27
Murphy, Patrick J., 45

Nelson, Margaret, 203
Norris, David, 145

Oakley, Richard, 53-56
O'Briain, Colm, 8-9
O'Brien, Breda, 164-65
O'Byrne, Robert, 252-55
Ó Cathain, Eamonn, 213-14
O'Connell, Mark, 76-77, 148
O'Connor, David, 159-60
O'Connor, Eddie, 198
O'Connor, Kevin, 234
O'Connor, Sinead, 251-52
Ó Cuiv, Eamon, 182
O'Doherty, Iseult, 153-55
O'Donnell, Al, 26
O'Donnell, Anne, 50-51
O'Donnell, Liz, 171-2, 197
O'Donnell, Ruan, 17-18
O'Flaherty, Catherine, 201
O'Halloran, Beth, 12-14
O'Herlihy, Bill, 199
O'Higgins, Eleanor, 95
O'Leary, Pat, 250-51
O'Reilly, Gavin, 237
O'Rourke, Frances, 80-81
O'Sullivan, Mary, 126-28

Pearce, Stephen, 96
Philbin Bowman, Abie, 167-68, 228, 260-63
Philbin Bowman, Eimer, introduction, xi-xvii; journal/diary, 2n, 9n, 30-31, 36, 40, 48-50, 85-88, 206-207
Philbin Bowman, Emma, 226-27
Philbin Bowman, Jonathan, *A Living Word* broadcasts, 247-50
Pohlhammer, John, 168-69
Prone, Terry, 106
Purcell, Deirdre, 69

Quinn, Fergal, 143
Quinn, Frank, 68-69

Reynolds, Albert, 125
Reynolds, Andrea, 125-26
Reynolds, Kathleen, 125
Reynolds, Martin, 98-99
Ruane, Andy, 155
Rowan, Anna, 36
Ryan, Gerry, 217-18
Ryan, James, 37, 38-39, 45-46

Savage, Tom, 106
Scally, Seamus, 164
Scott, Patrick, 50
Sheehan, Philie, 136-37
Shelswell-White, Egerton, 160
Sherrin, Ned, 165-66
Shiels, Sally, 24-25, 30
Smith, Anthony, 90
Soualhi, Djamel, 170-71
Spring, Maria, 121-24
Stephenson, John, 96-97
Stephenson, Sam, 115-16
Smyth, Sam, 236-38

Timmermans, Glen, 95
Towers, Susan, 72-74
Townsend, Sue, 186
'Twink', *see* King, Adele

Wainwright III, Louden, 64-66
Walker, Dorothy, 50
Walsh, Caroline, 101-102
Walsh, Derek, 14
Waters, John, 70-72
Watson, Maeve, 40-41
West, Derek, 47-48
Whelehan, Tom, 99-100
White, Trevor, 75-76

Acknowledgements

All authors and editors are nuisances to very many people. And the more complicated the book the greater the nuisance. So it is with pleasure that I record my thanks here for the many kindnesses which have been shown to me throughout the preparation of this book. Our greatest debt is to the contributors: those whose journalism and broadcasting was first published when Jonathan died; those whose letters of condolence at that time revealed many different aspects of his character; and those who responded to subsequent requests to help fill out this biographical portrait

I wish to acknowledge permission from Independent Newspapers, RTE, *The Irish Times, Sunday Times, Sunday Tribune, Hot Press, Farmers Journal* and *Irish Catholic* to include material originally published by them. I wish to thank Derek Mahon for permission to quote his translation of Horace (Odes I, ii): 'How to Live' from *Collected Poems,* 1999, by permission of The Gallery Press; and to thank Peter Fallon for his courtesy. Thanks are also due to the many artists, cartoonists and caricaturists whose work has helped to illustrate this book: Scratch, Littleman, Wendy Shea and Beth O'Halloran; and Aongus Collins for the *In Dublin* cartoon, 'A literary night by JPB aged fourteen-and-a-half'; and Brian Lawlor for his etching of Henrietta Street. I wish to record my special indebtedness to Jim Cogan of the *Sunday Independent.* Already in these pages he has described his working relationship with Jonathan. The book concludes with his farewell caricature, first published in the *Sunday Independent,* and includes as a frontispiece, a cartoon based on an idea which might well have been Jonathan's riposte if he could have read this book.

I also wish to thank the photographer Conor Horgan for his considerable generosity: few boys have such a photographic record of their relationship with their father as has Saul. Thanks also to Maria Spring for help with photographs of Saul's years at St Clare's School, to Tom Godson for access to his photographic archive of the school and to Paddy Kiernan for helping me find the needle in the haystack. We would like to thank Tony Maxwell for his portrait photograph of Jonathan aged twenty-five.

Thanks are due to Jonathan's teachers: to Elizabeth Moloney and Alyna Healy at the Sunnyside playgroup; to Sally Shiels and Robert Dowds, both formerly of Sandford National School; to Greg Collins and Michael Whelan of Sandford Park School and to Philip Fitzpatrick for archival help; and to Derek West, Michael Classon, John Harris, Owen Metcalfe and the other teachers at Newpark Comprehensive School who had to accommodate the precocious Jonathan in his adolescent years. Special thanks to the novelist James Ryan, also a teacher at Newpark, for his contributions to this book and for archival help.

I wish to thank all those editors, publishers and producers who encouraged Jonathan and gave him the opportunity to develop his talents. I am indebted to John Waters and Tom Mathews for help with his *In Dublin* years; and especially to John S.Doyle for his help with back issues of the magazine and for his tribute, reproduced in these pages, when Jonathan died. Frank Quinn in *Computerscope* offered help on Jonathan's writing on information technology. I must also thank Michael Keane, Eanna Brophy and Frances O'Rourke for accounts of his time with the *Sunday Press* and Vincent Browne for recruiting him to *Magill* and the *Sunday Tribune*. Terry Prone, Tom Savage and their colleagues at Carr Communications should be thanked; as should Frank Coughlan and Michael Denieffe of the *Evening Herald*. Dermot Hanrahan of FM104 had the courage to back a very young Jonathan on the controversial and risqué *Rude Awakening*. Andy Ruane of Like It Love It productions selected Jonathan as quiz-master on *Dodge the Question*. We wish to thank Gay Byrne for many kindnesses. Bob Collins, Ronan Collins, Joe Duffy, Clare Duignan, Brian Farrell, Cathal Goan, Eithne Hand, Shay Healy, Kintilla Heussaff, Pat Kenny, Aiden Maguire, Tom Manning, Derek Mooney, Ed Mulhall, Ann Marie O'Callaghan, Pauline O'Donnell, Bernadette O'Sullivan, Myles Neylin, Kathleen O'Connor, Tim O'Connor, Miriam O'Callaghan, Noel Roberts, Helen Shaw, Stephen Wallace, Marty Whelan and Mick Wright are among those in RTE to whom we are indebted. We wish to record our special thanks to Jacqui Corcoran for inviting Jonathan to present *A Living Word*; to Betty Purcell for friendship, advice and support; and to Noelle O'Reilly for her programme on Jonathan broadcast on the Saturday morning after his death.

Mary Leland reckoned that the *Sunday Independent* enabled Jonathan to progress 'from brilliant dilettante to reflective analyst' and recognized – as do I – his indebtedness to the paper. Anne Harris, Liam Collins, Willie Kealy and the editor, Aengus Fanning, deserve thanks as do the rest of the staff, including Gavin O'Reilly and Michael Roche in management. I must also thank Brian Farrell, art editor at the paper, for invaluable assistance; and the library staff and especially Paddy Farrell. Nor should Harry Allen of the credit union be omitted from this list: in Jonathan's case he proved to be one of the most important people in Independent House.

Others who should be thanked include: Edwin Allen; Myrtle and her late husband, Ivan Allen and their family; Paul Allen; Chloe Blake; Sarah and Mary Carroll; Gerard Colleran; Susan Crosbie, librarian of the *Irish Examiner*; Jeananne Crowley; Michael Cullen; Rachel Fehily; Conor Ferguson; Kathy Gilfillan; Eoghan Harris; Emily Hourican; Maire Hughes; Sinead Impey who identified a number of important graphics and provided others; Dermot James; Geraldine Kearney of the Gaiety Theatre; Noel Kelliher; Robert Kerr; Eugene and Ronan Lambert; Deborah Martin; CaraIosa and Ogie Mehigan; Ciara Moore; Sinead O'Connor; Austin Tichenor,

Claire Walker and everybody who works for the Reduced Shakespeare Company; Maeve Watson and Stephen Wynne. Other debts to be recorded include Avril Lynch and Pat Deane who maintained order and sanity amidst the chaos.

I gladly record my indebtedness to my colleagues in all branches of RTE's reference libraries: print, radio and television. No individual has a more encyclopaedic knowledge of RTE's television archive than Barbara Durack. She not only sourced all of the recordings I sought but searched further – and well beyond the call of duty – to discover other long-forgotten broadcasts by Jonathan. Marion Osborne in graphics was also generous with advice and practical help; as were Robert Canning, Willie Finnie, Amy Kerr, Ian Lee, Dolores Meaney, Malachy Moran, Joan Murphy and Margaret Mary O'Mahony.

Among the first to encourage the book was the designer, the late Jarlath Hayes. He was one of those rare colleagues with whom one strikes up an immediate rapport. His judgement on all matters of book design I found impeccable. His was the initial design for this book, working in collaboration with his daughter, Susan Waine of Ashfield Press. Jarlath died in May 2001 and since then I have worked with Susan who has proved indefatigable and tolerant of my trespasses on her busy schedule. My agent Jonathan Williams read many drafts closely and sceptically and made valuable suggestions – most of them acted on. I am indebted to Ray Lynn of Betaprint, Tony Harris and Dave Field of Printcraft Imaging and Michael Gill and Paul Neilan of Gill and Macmillan for their encouragement and support. I owe a very special debt of gratitude to Niamh Moore for working with me at the initial research stage and for her invariably generous response to very many subsequent requests for help. I am all too aware that this list of acknowledgements is incomplete. The conditions under which the book was undertaken were complicated; and if I have failed to acknowledge a debt or, if guilty of some other sin of omission, I beg that those trespassed against will be forgiving.

Eimer worked with me on the final drafts of the manuscript as is evident throughout these pages and the text owes much to her judgement and indispensable contributions. Daniel helped with copy-editing chores; Abie's sustained scepticism had the merit of keeping us on course; and Emma's considered reading of an early draft resulted in many improvements. Saul, with the advantage of having been a witness to many of the episodes and escapades of Jonathan's later years, also provided invaluable help.

One voice was audible to me throughout – that of Jonathan. Occasionally when making an editorial judgement that I found difficult I consulted him. I asked how he might have called it. For this and for his thirty-one years we record our final thanks to him.